P O S T **HUMAN**

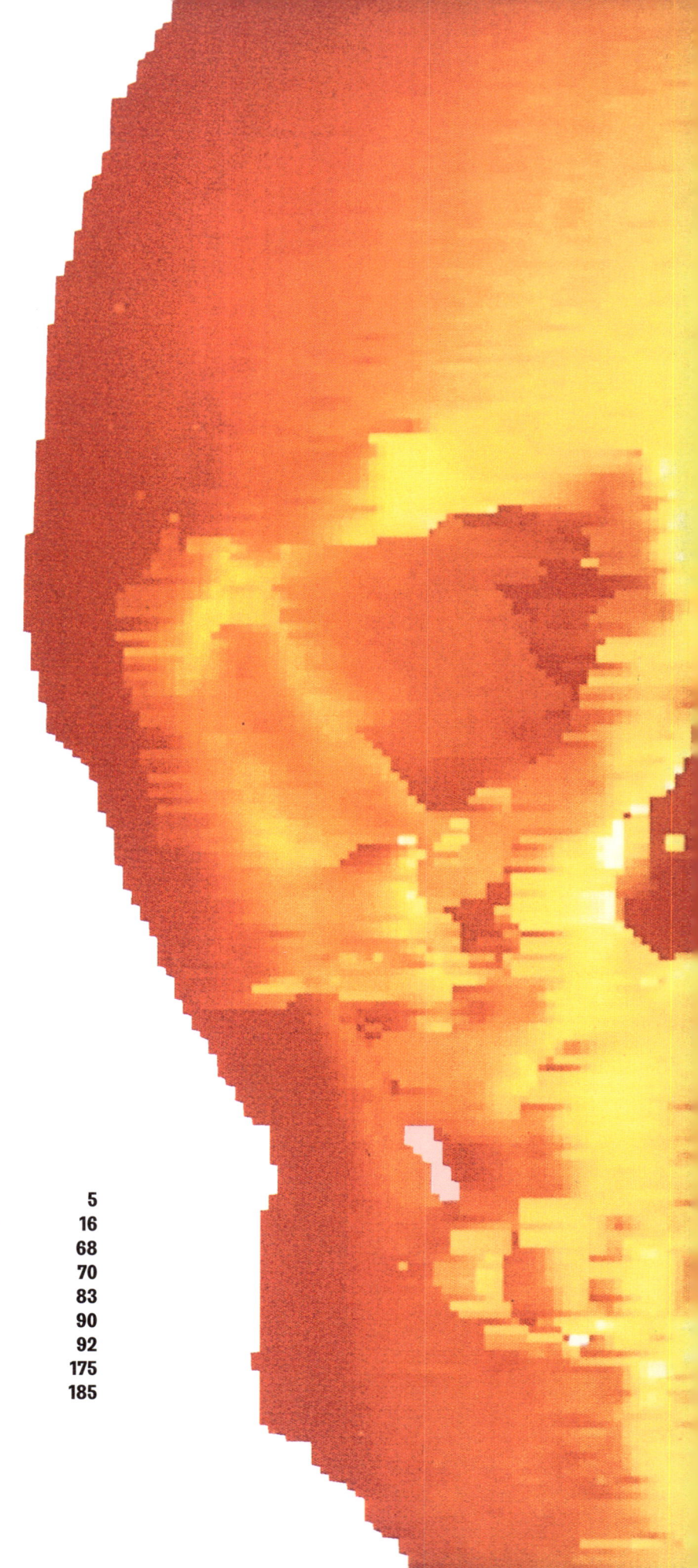

POST HUMAN (2024–25)

Jeffrey Deitch
Los Angeles
September 12, 2024–January 18, 2025

POST HUMAN (1992–93)

FAE Musée d'Art Contemporain
Pully/Lausanne
June 14–September 13, 1992

Castello di Rivoli
Museo d'Arte Contemporanea
Rivoli (Torino)
October 1–November 22, 1992

Deste Foundation for Contemporary Art
Athens
December 3, 1992–February 14, 1993

Deichtorhallen Hamburg
Hamburg
March 12–May 9, 1993

Israel Museum
Jerusalem
June 23–October 10, 1993

CONTENTS

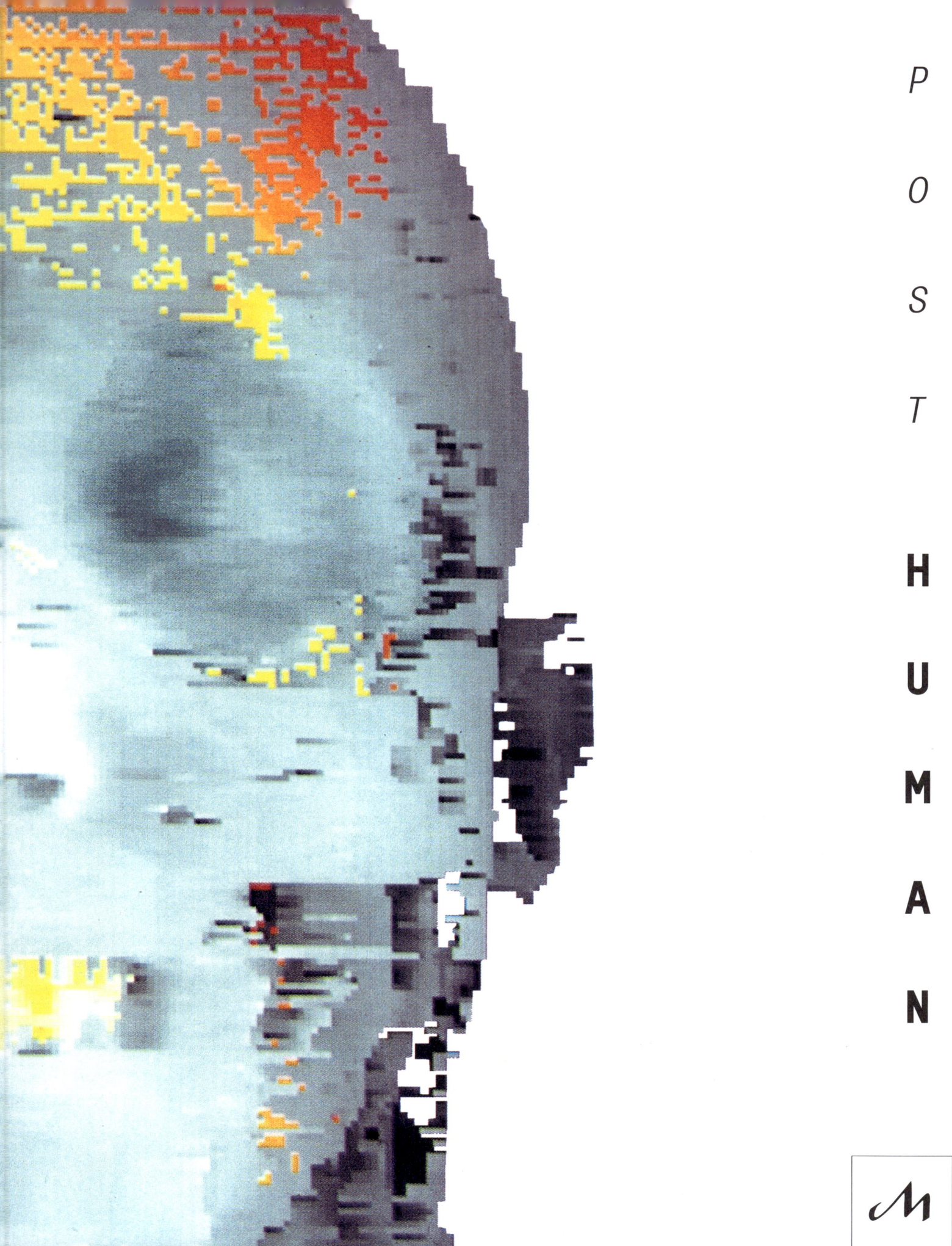

P
O
S
T

**H
U
M
A
N**

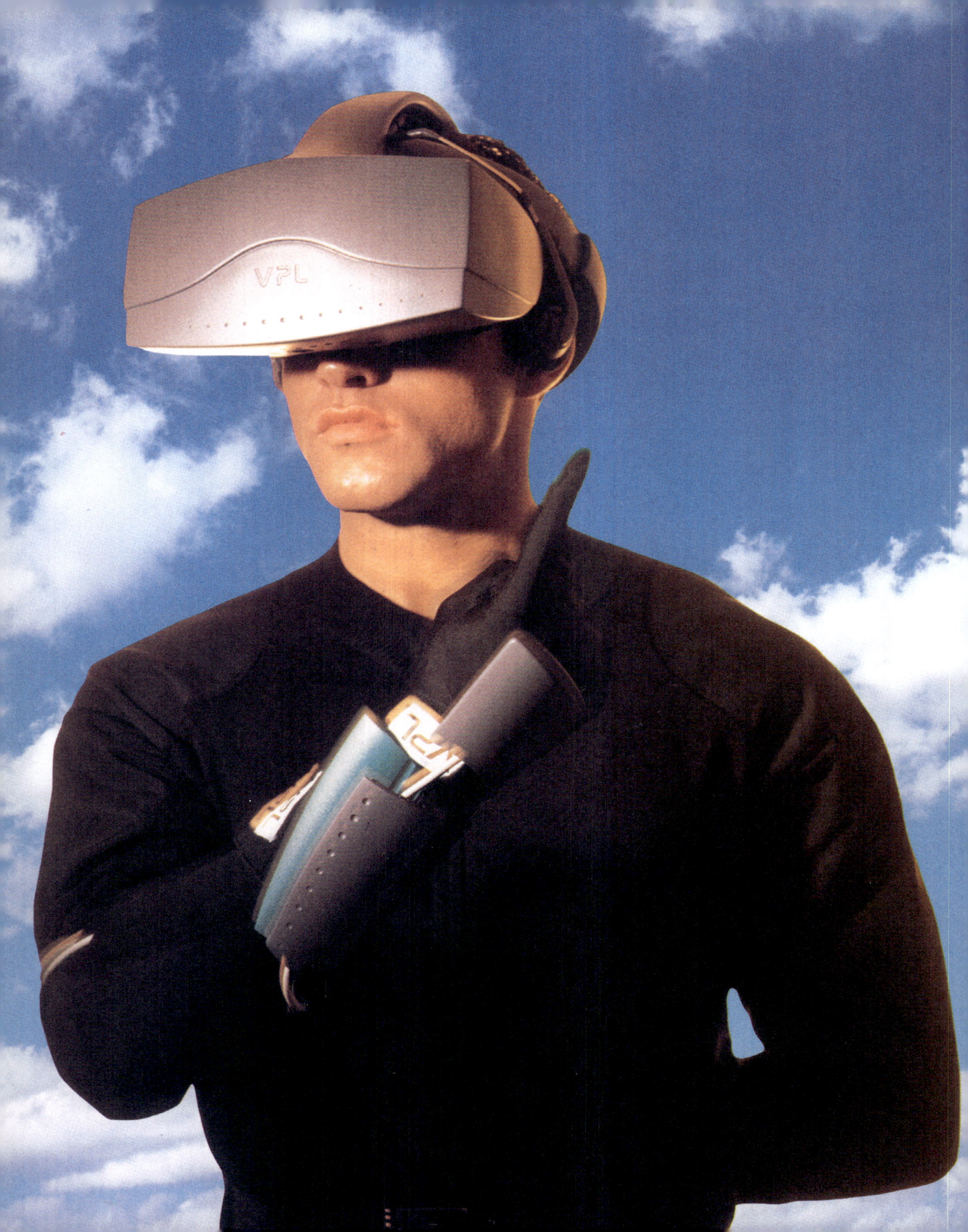

When *Post Human* opened in June 1992 at a private foundation in Lausanne, Switzerland, I would not have anticipated that its title would enter the language. The exhibition plan did not begin with the term *Post Human*. The original working title of the show was *The Conceptual Figure*. The objective was to present the work of a new generation of artists who were reinventing figuration from a performative and conceptual direction. Thinking about the exhibition plan on my daily run around New York's Central Park, I had a jolt of inspiration: *Post Human* was the title that would describe the project in a much more arresting way.

Many elements converged to help make *Post Human* one of the curatorial projects that set the artistic agenda for the 1990s and which would continue to resonate into the present. The show provided a platform for a remarkable generation of artists from Asia, Europe, and the Americas who were creating a new approach to figurative art. The timing of the project was fortuitous. A number of the artists in the show, who would go on to influence contemporary art history, were just beginning to achieve wide recognition. *Post Human* traveled from Lausanne to four additional venues in Torino, Hamburg, Athens, and Jerusalem. Thousands of visitors experienced the show in its two-year run, but more than the exhibitions, it was the accompanying book that disseminated the concepts behind the project.

Unlike a conventional art exhibition catalog, the *Post Human* book was like an artwork itself. Working with the brilliant graphic designer Dan Friedman, we created a visual essay with provocative images overlayed with text. No exhibition catalog had ever looked like this before. People who did not read English could understand the meaning of *Post Human* through the visuals alone.

Thirty-two years after the opening of *Post Human*, it was time to revisit the project. Many of the then outlandish predictions in the text and visual essay have become reality. *Post Human* is no longer science fiction: it is arguably already here. A new generation of artists is extending the concept of *Post Human* in unexpected ways. For this new version of the book which documents the updated exhibition presented in my Los Angeles gallery from September 2024 to January 2025, we are honored to include texts by the remarkable young writer Philippa Snow and by the dean of posthuman studies, Professor Rosi Braidotti.

Viola Angiolini edited the book and coordinated the Los Angeles exhibition. Wesley Chou and his colleagues at Folder Studio have incorporated the original design by Dan Friedman to create this updated version of *Post Human*. It is daunting to think about what a new version of Post Human will look like thirty-two years from today.

Jeffrey Deitch (2025)

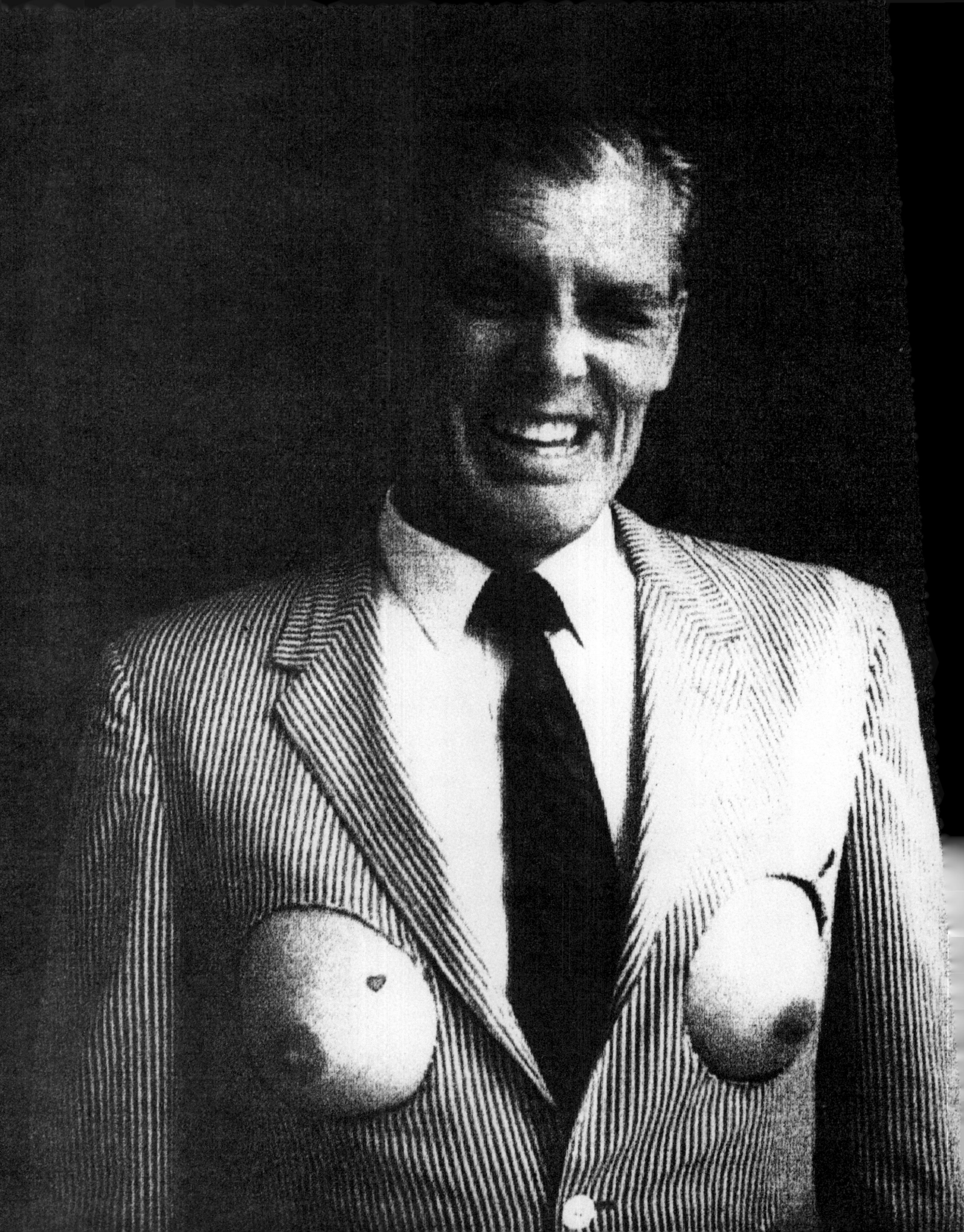

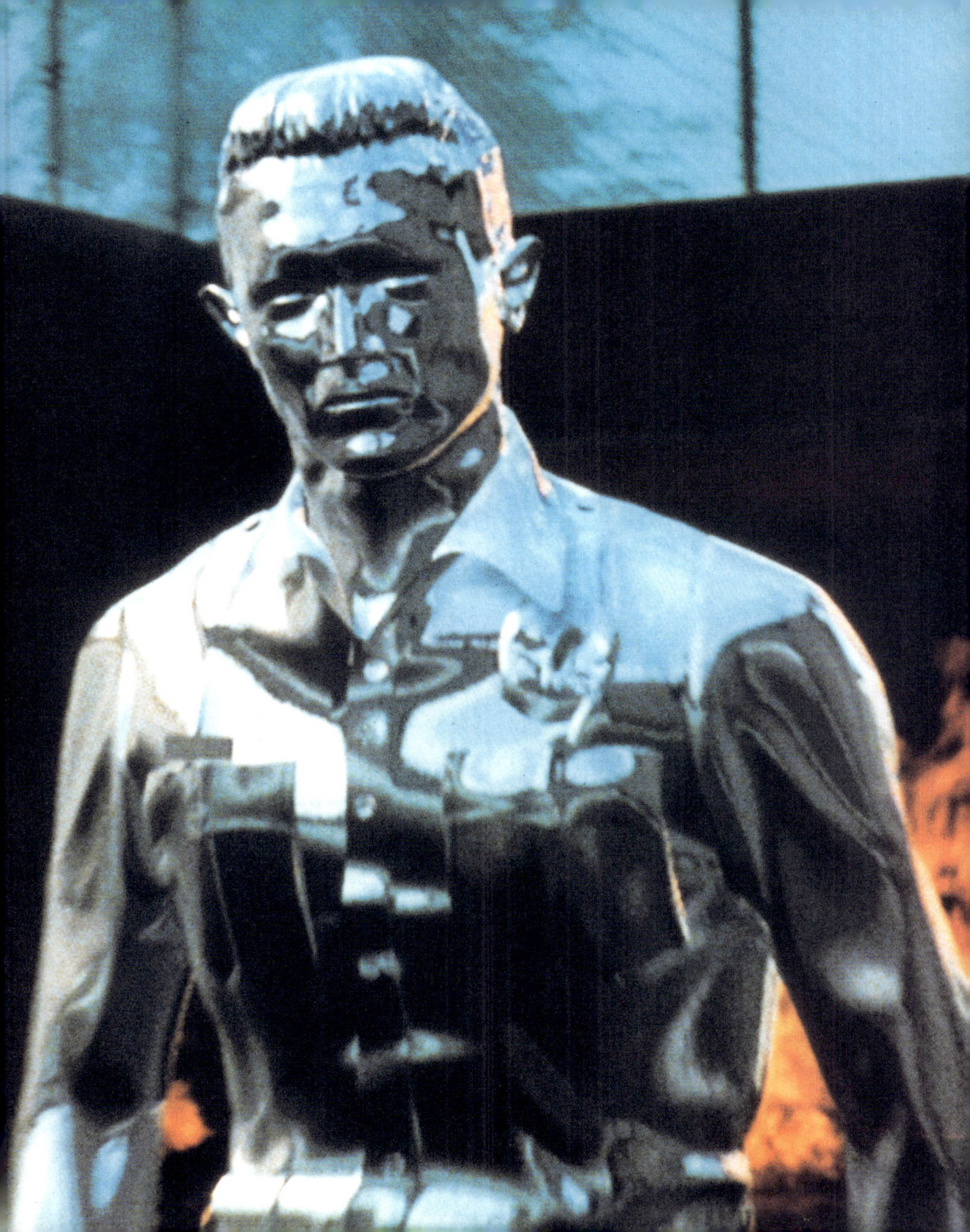

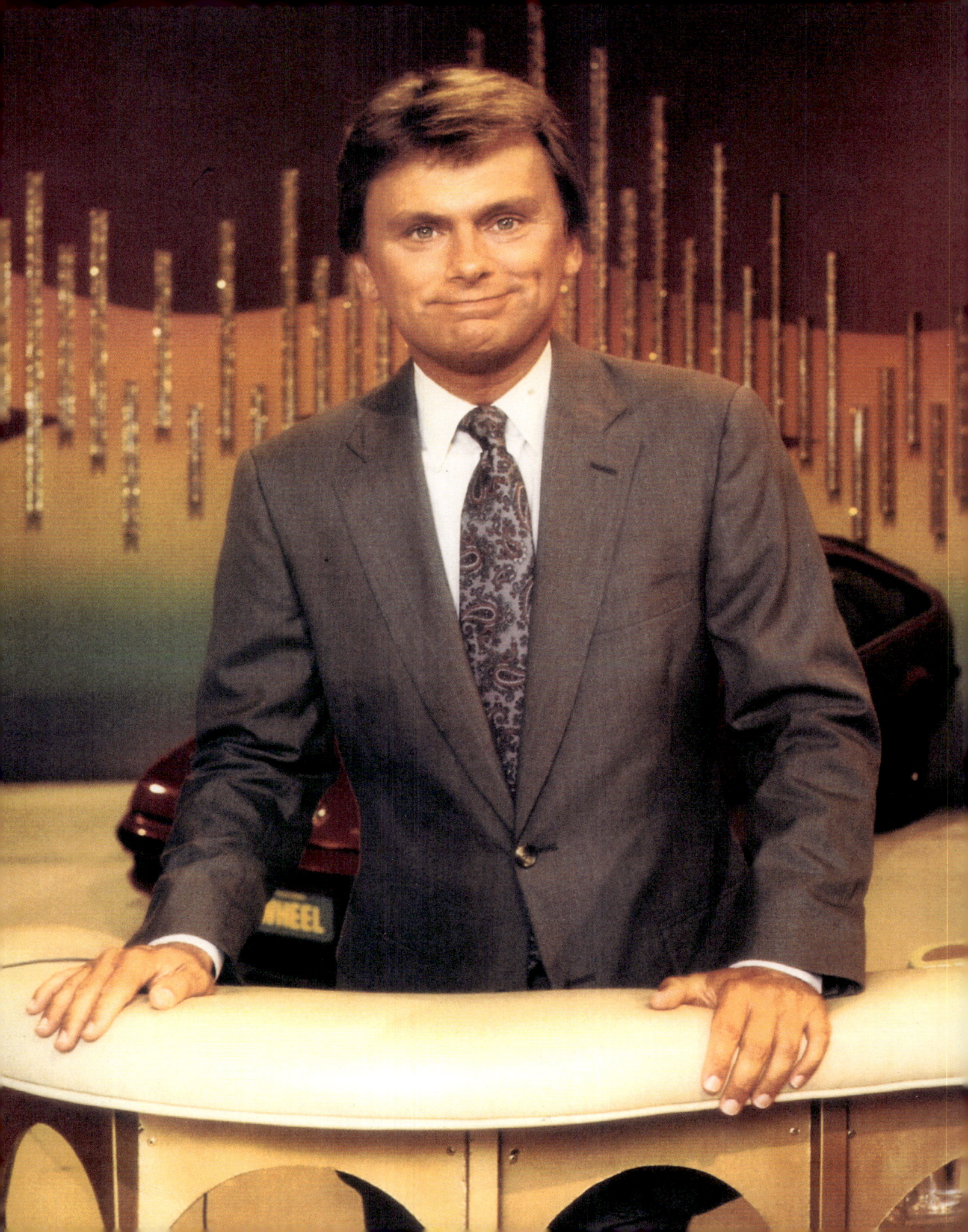

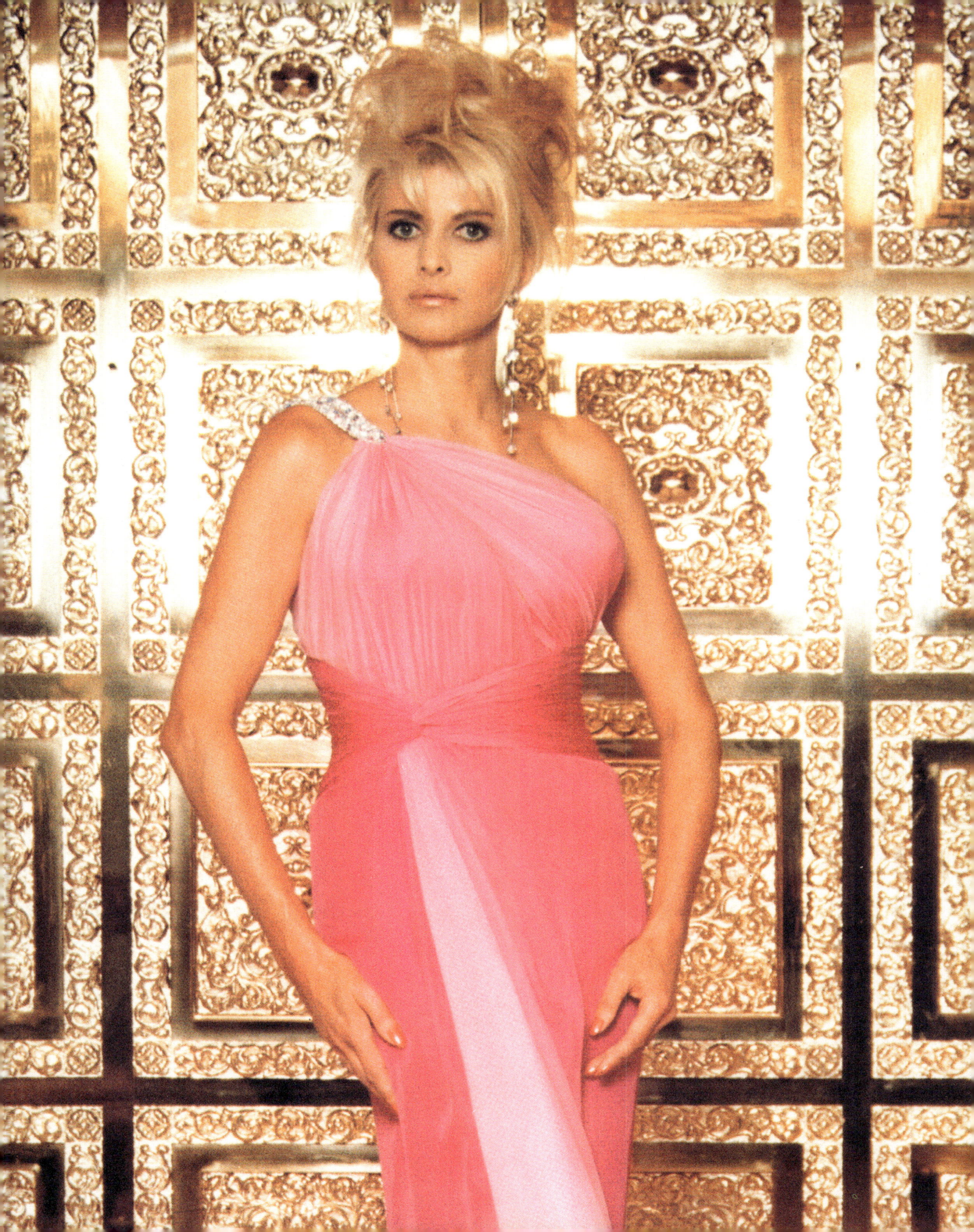

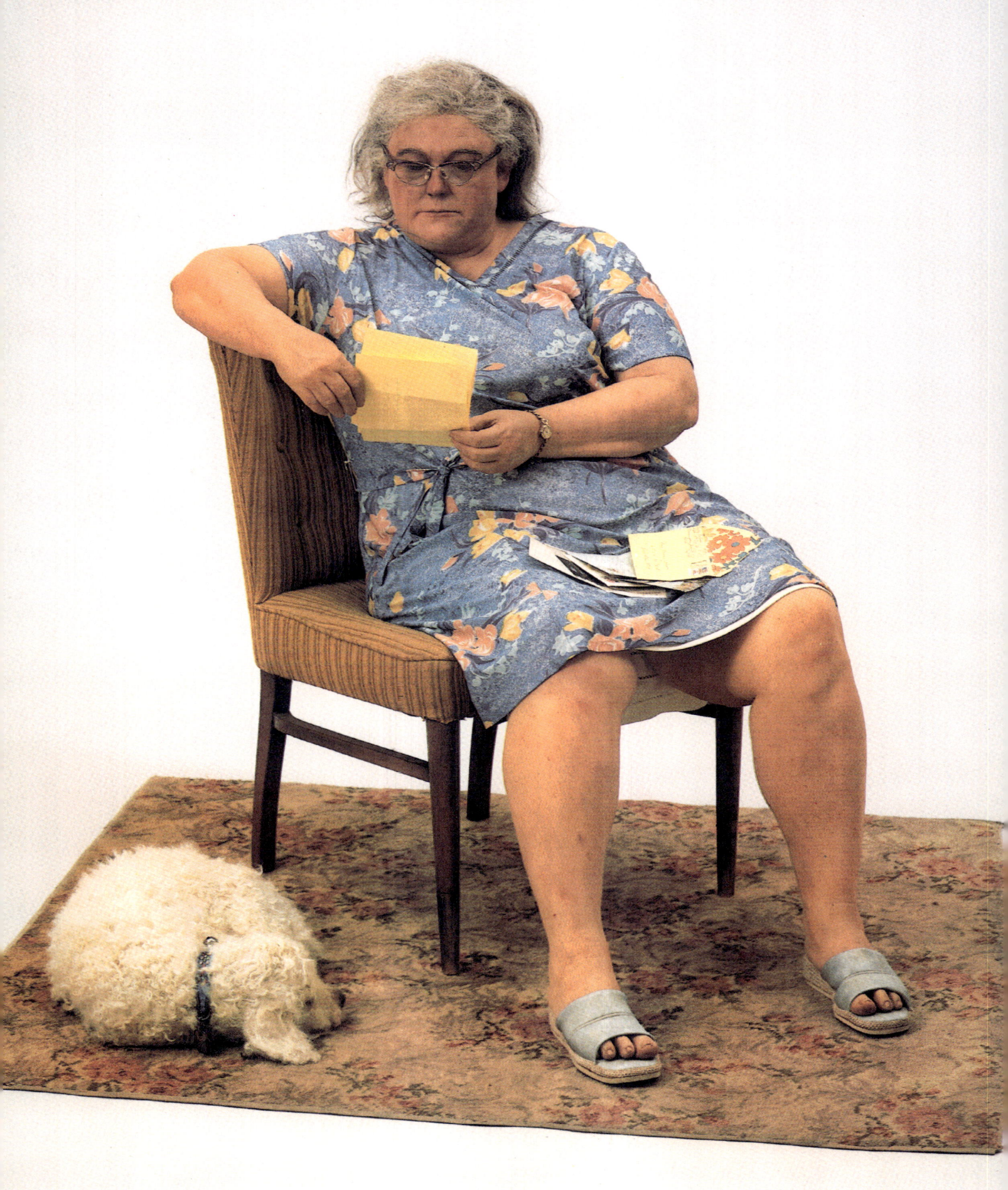

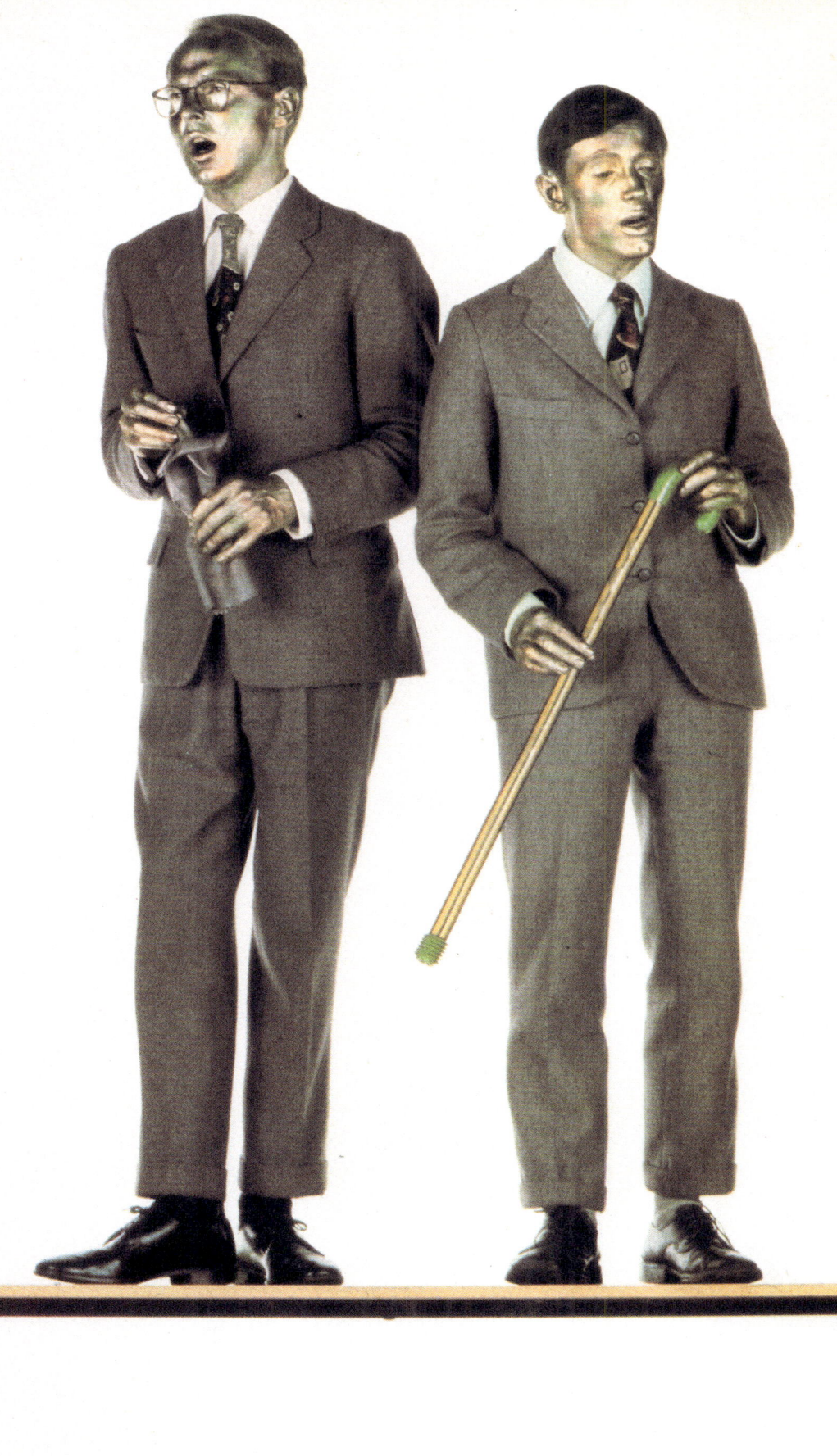

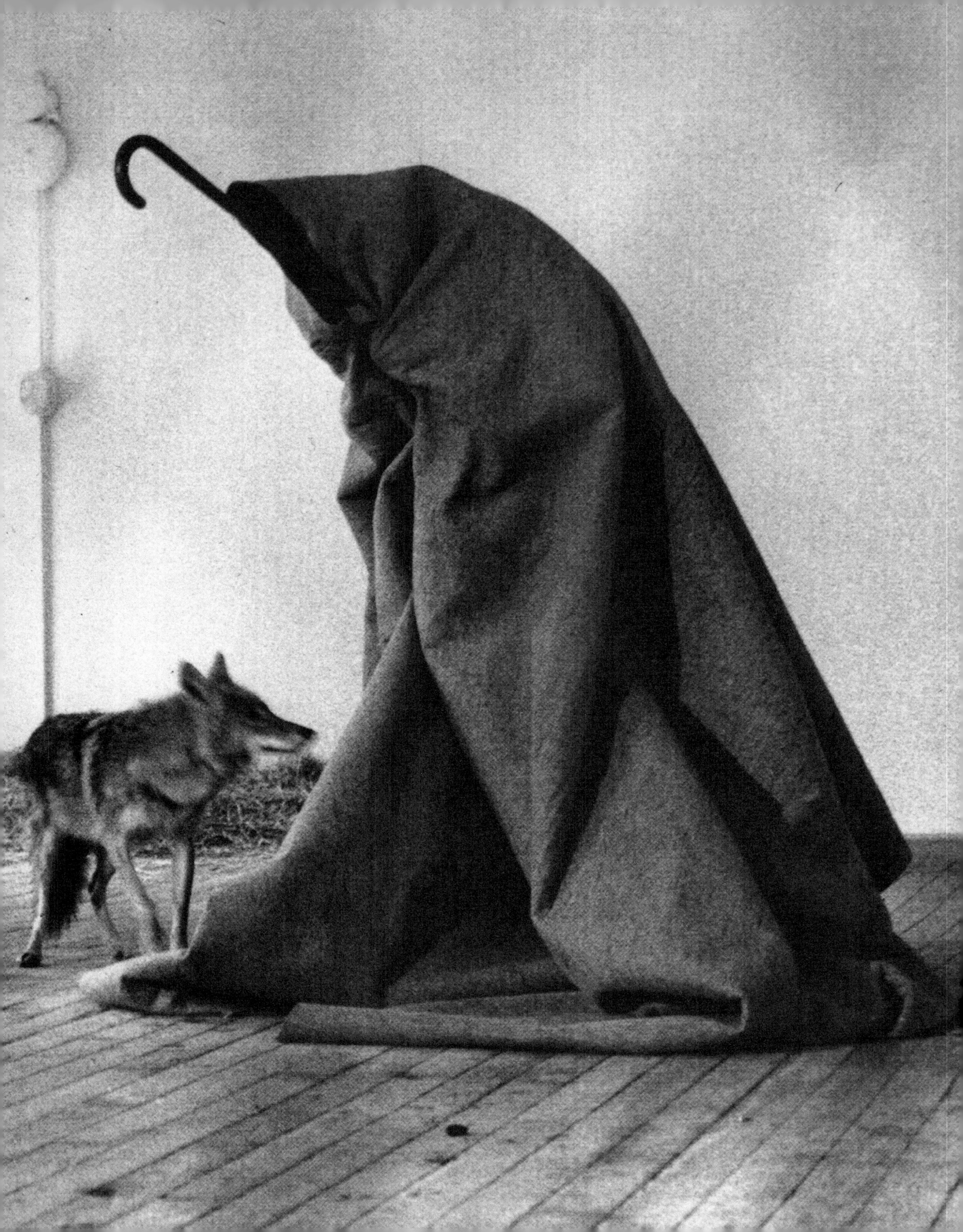

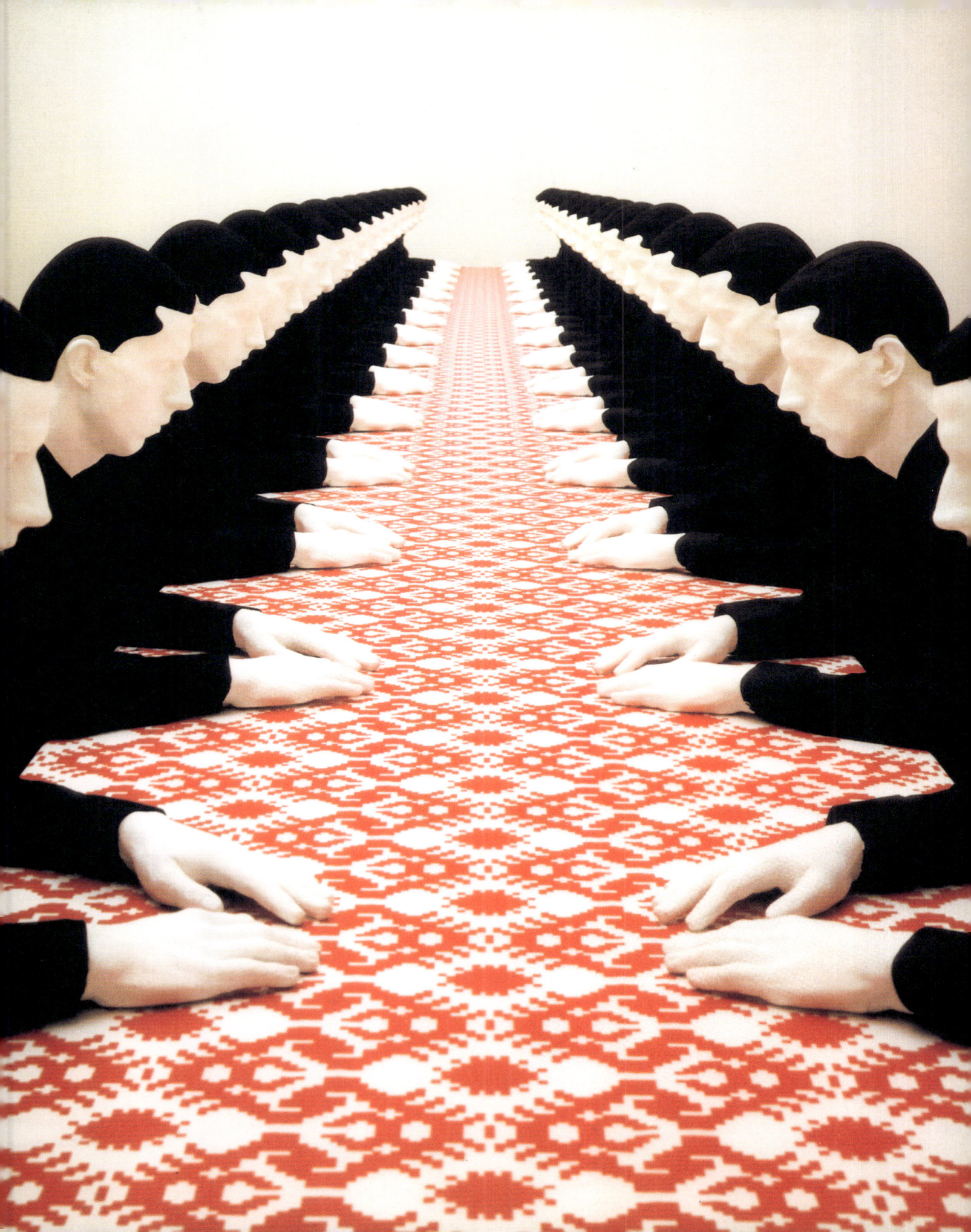

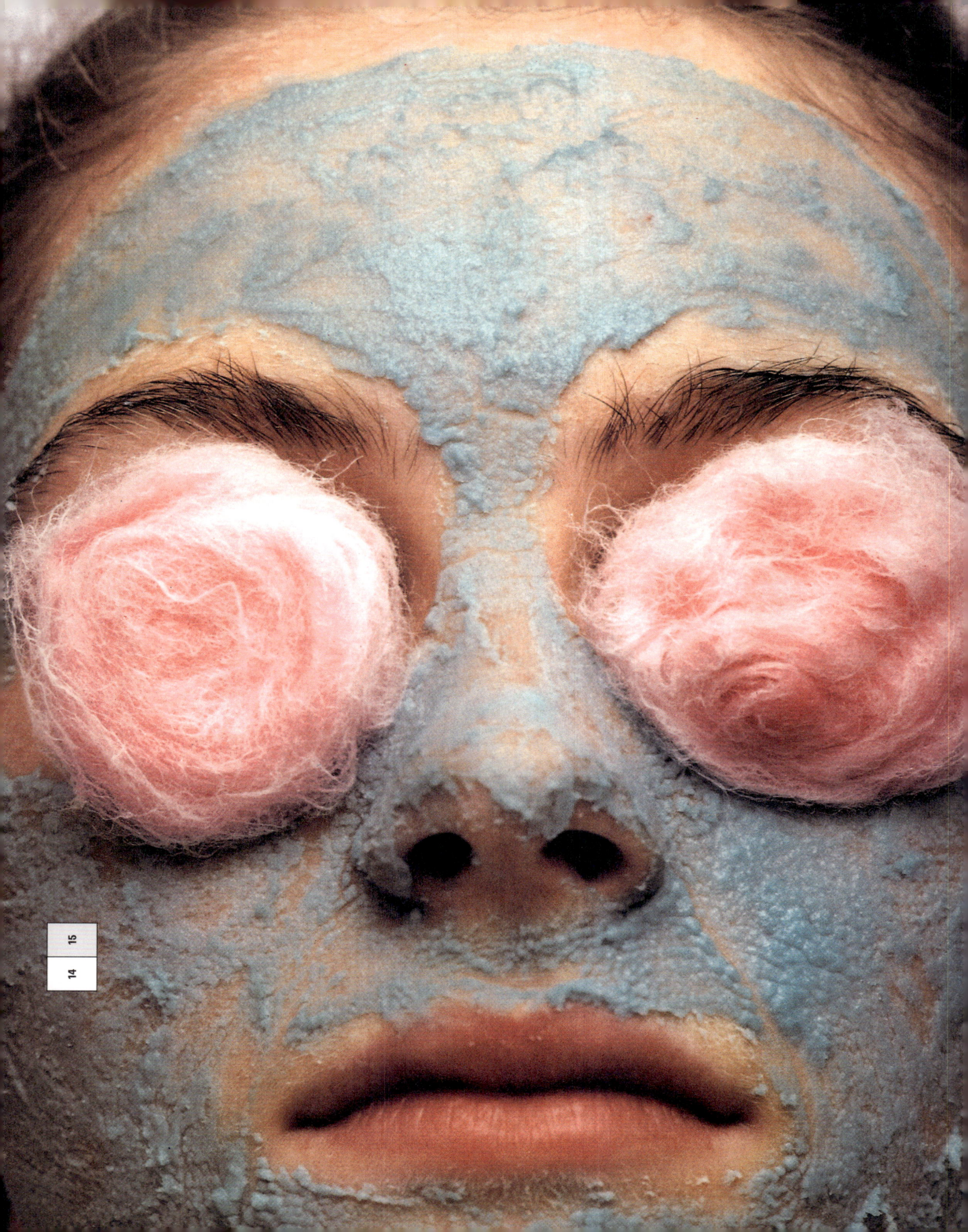

There is probably nothing more fascinating to people than other people, and almost every generation produces interesting figurative art. The generation of artists who are presented in this book and exhibition are not just producing interesting figurative art, however, they are virtually reinventing it. Their new concept of figuration reflects the new conception of self that is developing in the society at large. The advances in bio-technology and computer science and the accompanying changes in social behavior are challenging the boundaries of where the old human ends and the Post Human begins.

The emerging world of easy plastic surgery, genetic reconstruction, and computer-chip brain implants may soon be adding a new stage to Darwinian human evolution. These technological innovations will also begin to radically alter the structure of so-cial interaction. The dawn of this post-human world cannot be portrayed in the same way as the world of Picasso, or even the world of Andy Warhol. Its portrayal demands a new conception of figurative art that takes as much from television talk shows as it does from art history.

Does the art presented in this book and the exhibition warn of a world from which humanity has been drained? Or, on the contrary, does it celebrate a world where one will have unprecedented freedom to reinvent oneself? It is quite unclear whether the post-human future will be better, or worse, or whether it will even be post human at all. In any case, it is hoped that the art and the ideas that are explored through this project will stimulate one's thinking about how the future of art and the future of the human species will intersect.

Jeffrey Deitch (1992)

JANUARY 27, 1992 $1.99

People
weekly

OOH! LA LA... ...OR OOPS?

PLASTIC SURGERY OF THE STARS

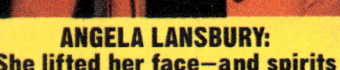

ANGELA LANSBURY:
She lifted her face—and spirits

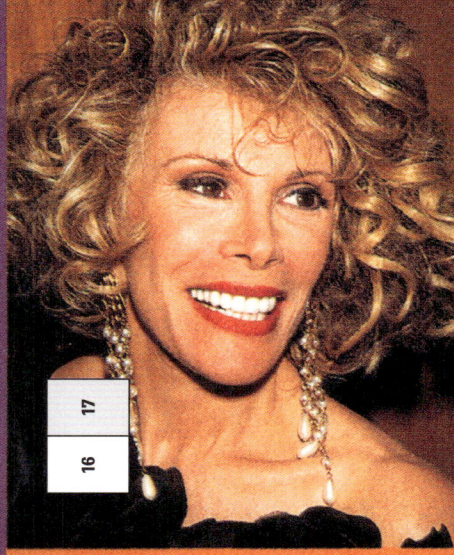

JOAN RIVERS:
Putting on a pretty new look

CHER:
"My breast operations were a nightmare!"

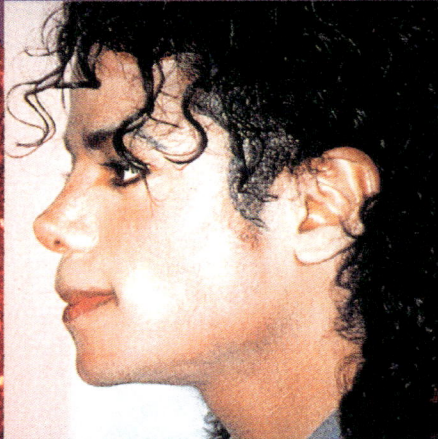

MICHAEL JACKSON:
A major work in progress

Do they or don't they? Here's an inside report on the miracles, mishaps and real risks of looking forever young.

16 17

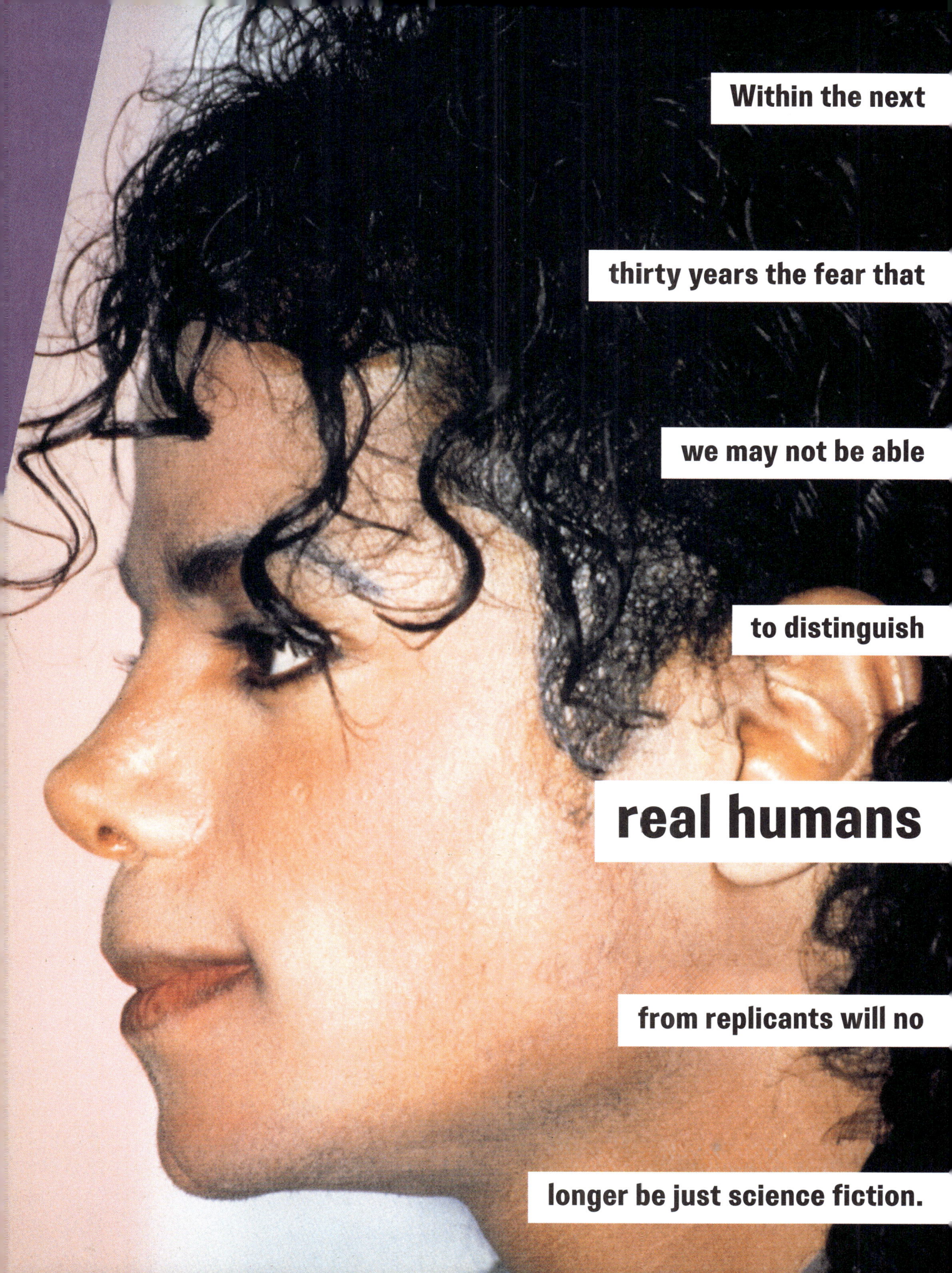

Within the next thirty years the fear that we may not be able to distinguish **real humans** from replicants will no longer be just science fiction.

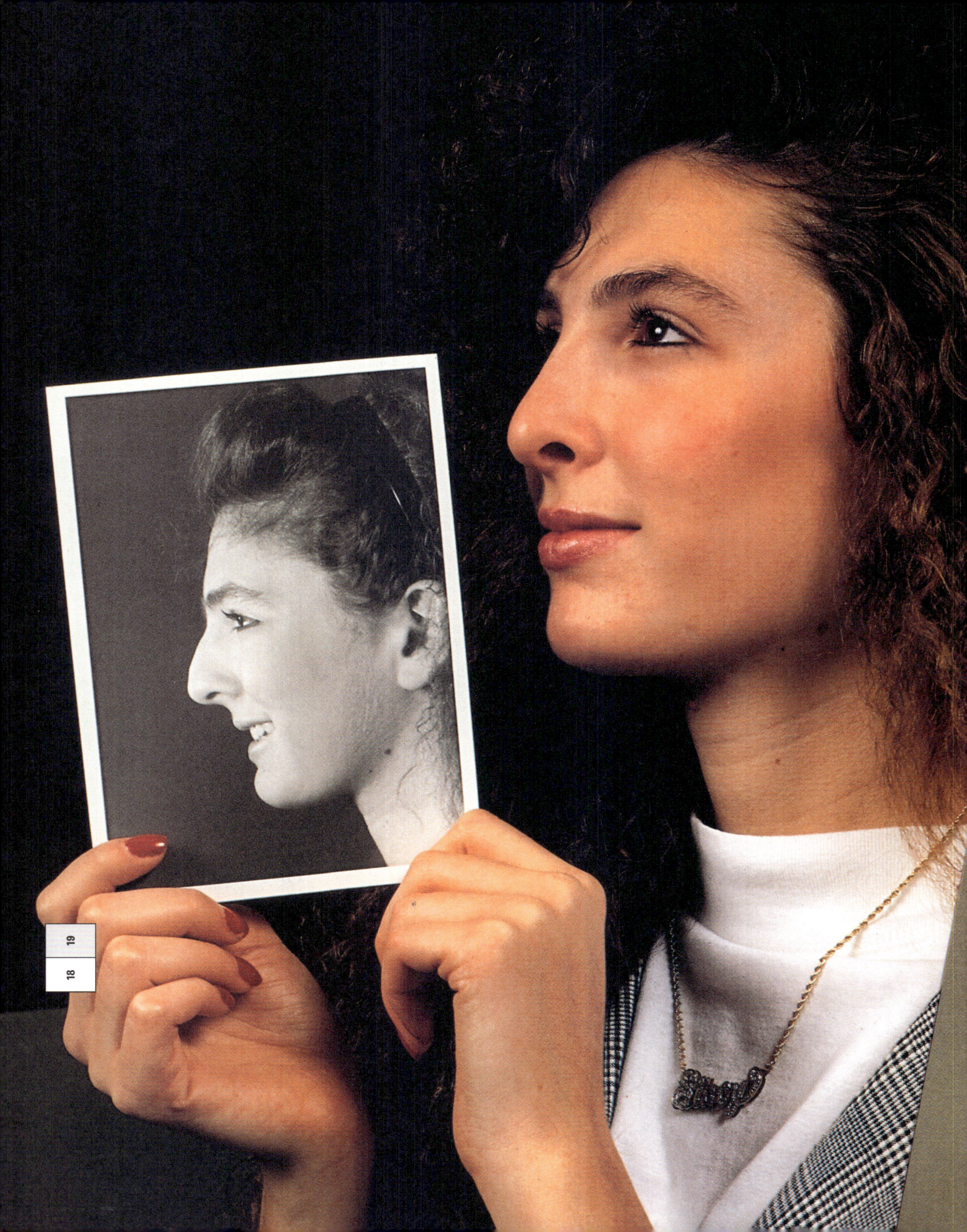

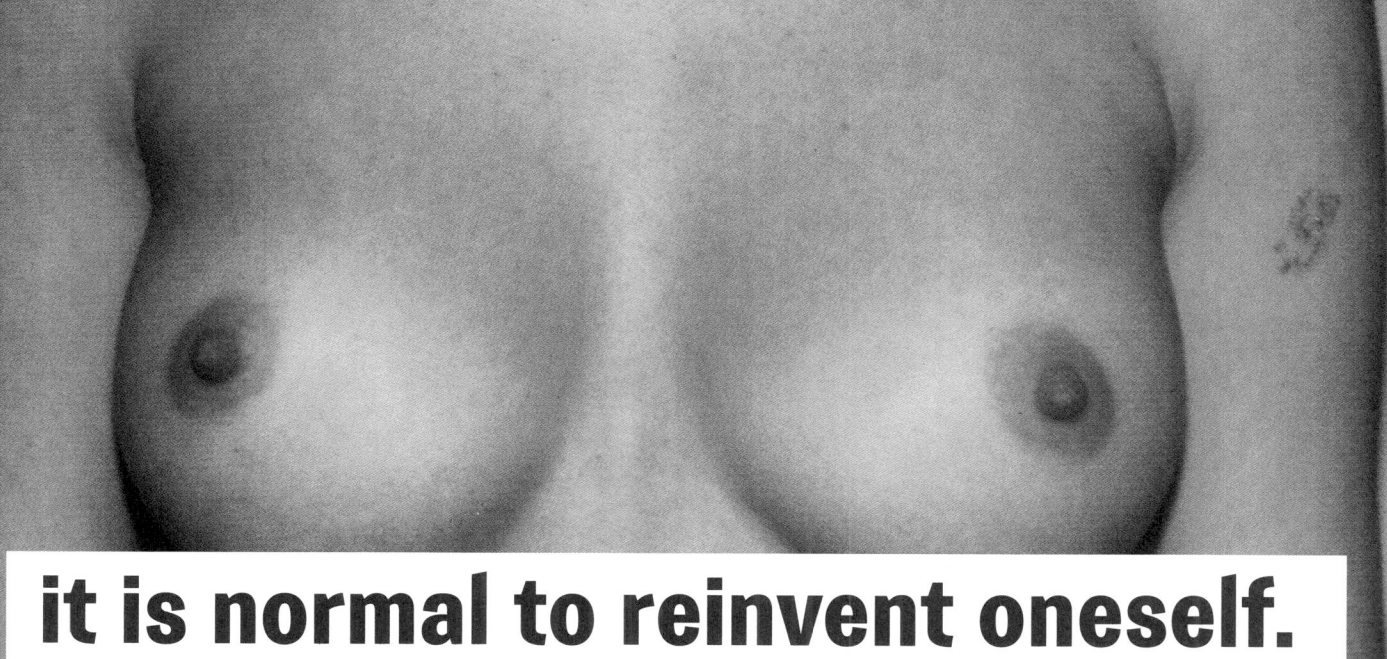

The matter-of-fact acceptance of one's "natural" looks and

one's "natural" personality is being replaced by a growing sense that

it is normal to reinvent oneself.

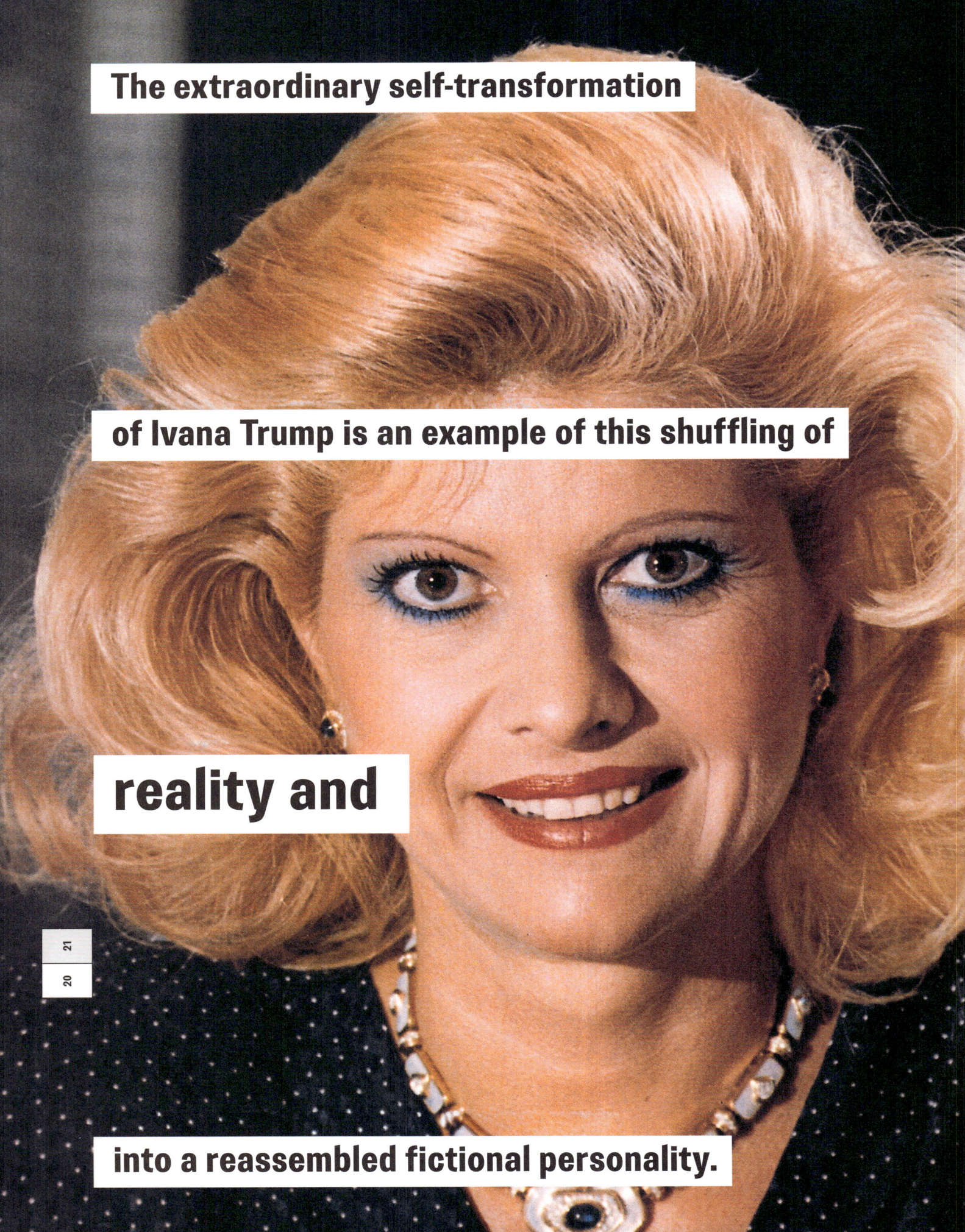

The extraordinary self-transformation

of Ivana Trump is an example of this shuffling of

reality and

into a reassembled fictional personality.

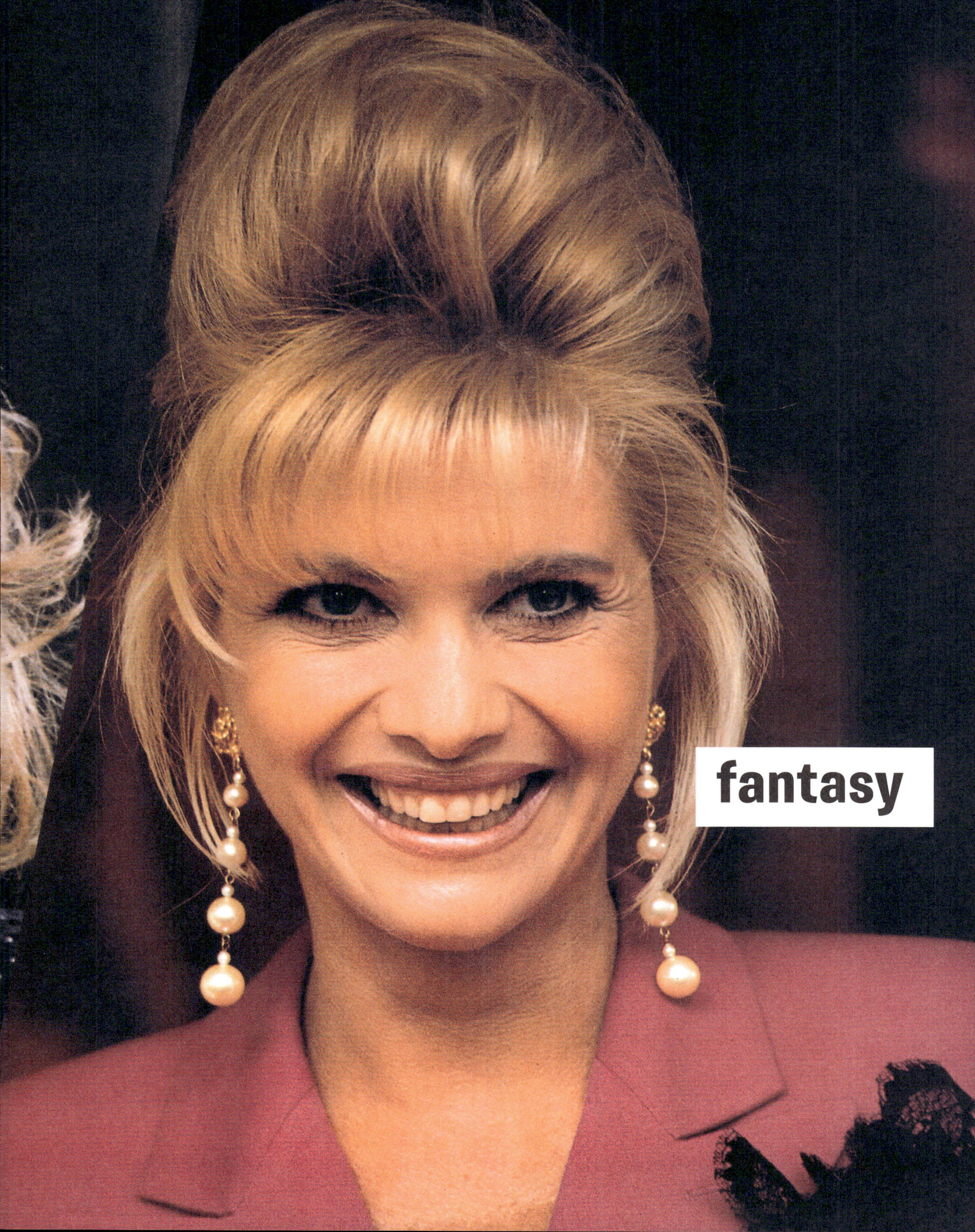

fantasy

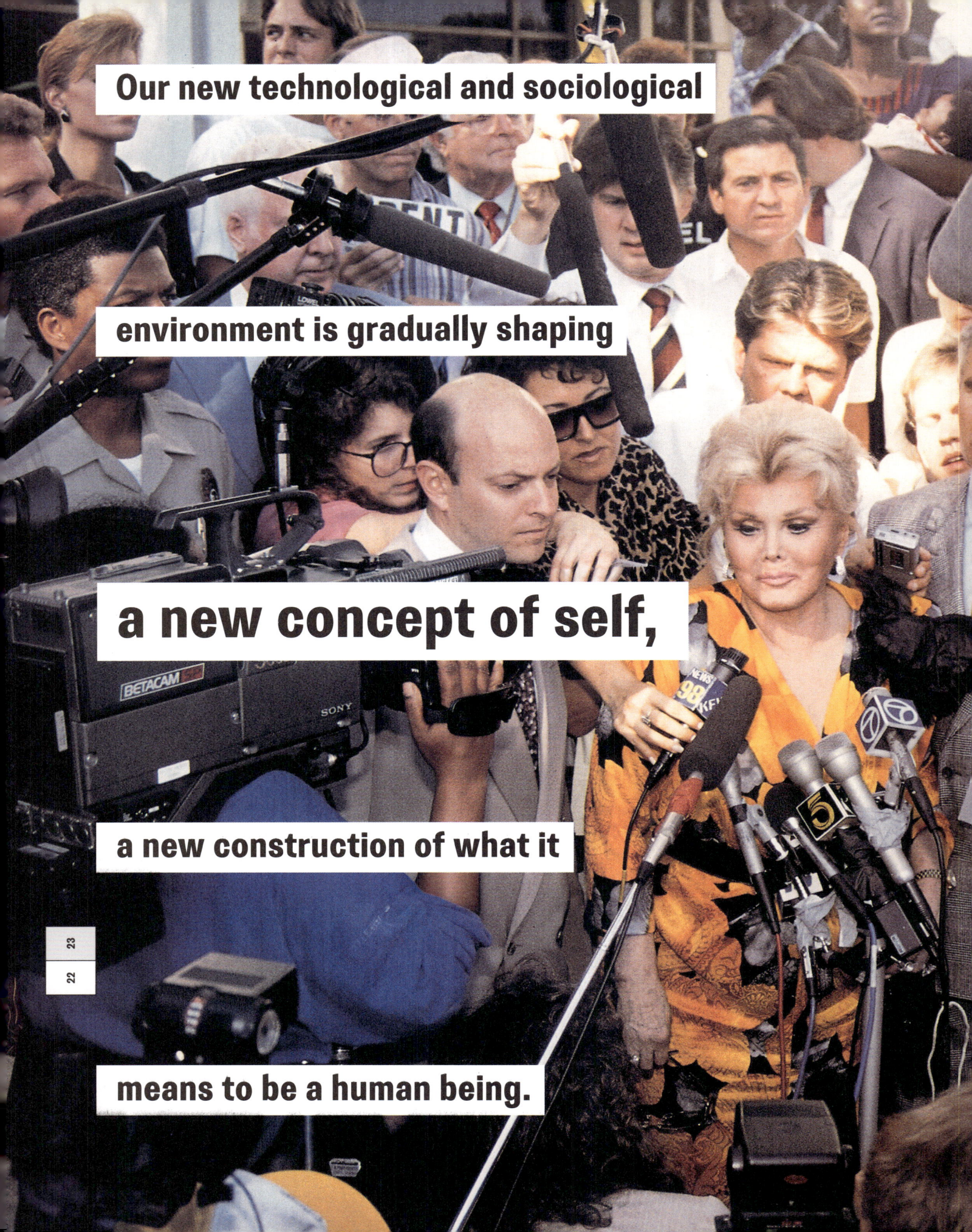

Our new technological and sociological

environment is gradually shaping

a new concept of self,

a new construction of what it

means to be a human being.

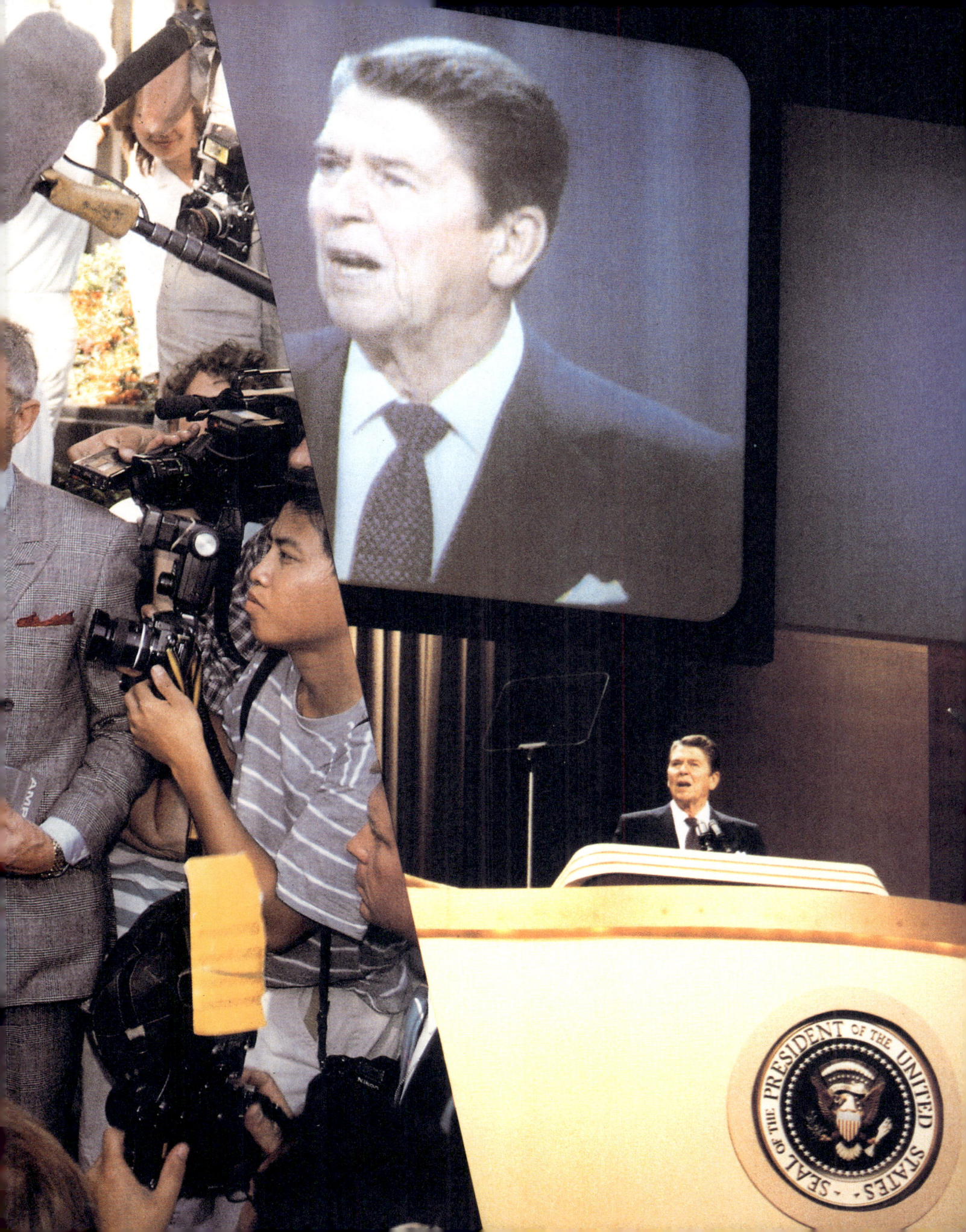

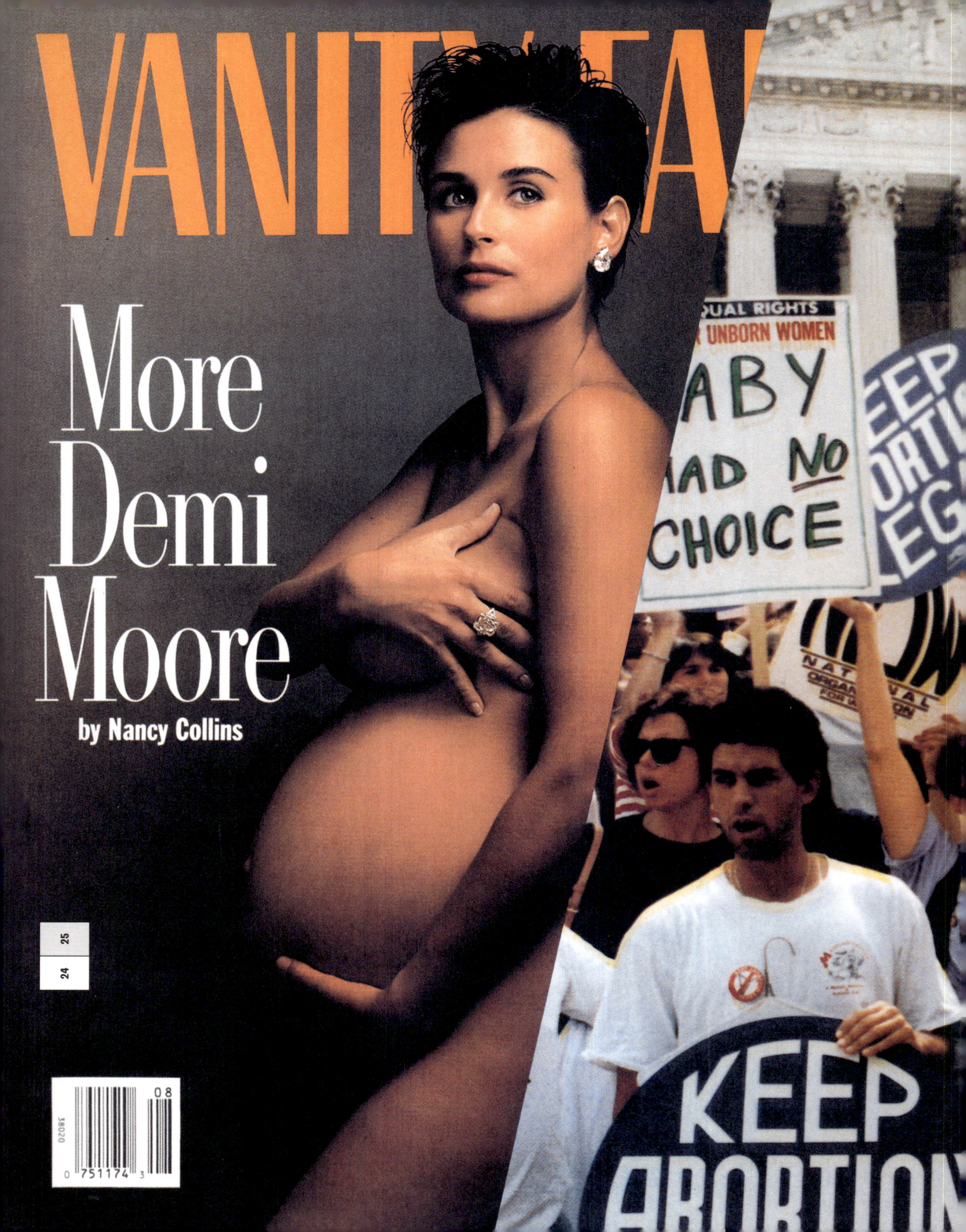

VANITY FAIR

More Demi Moore

by Nancy Collins

EQUAL RIGHTS

UNBORN WOMEN

BABY HAD NO CHOICE

EEP ORTIS EGA

NATIONAL ORGANIZATION

KEEP ABORTION

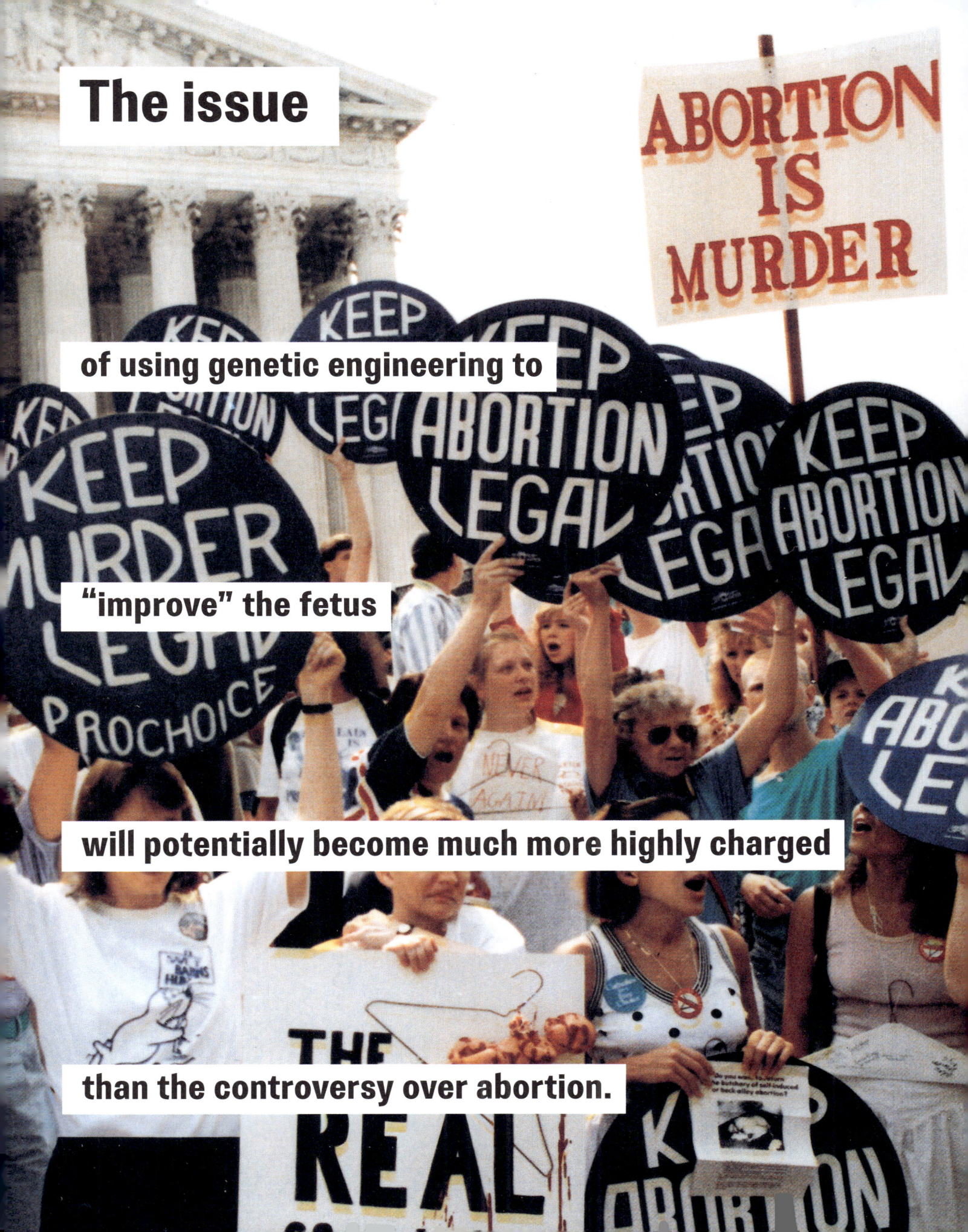

The issue

of using genetic engineering to

"improve" the fetus

will potentially become much more highly charged

than the controversy over abortion.

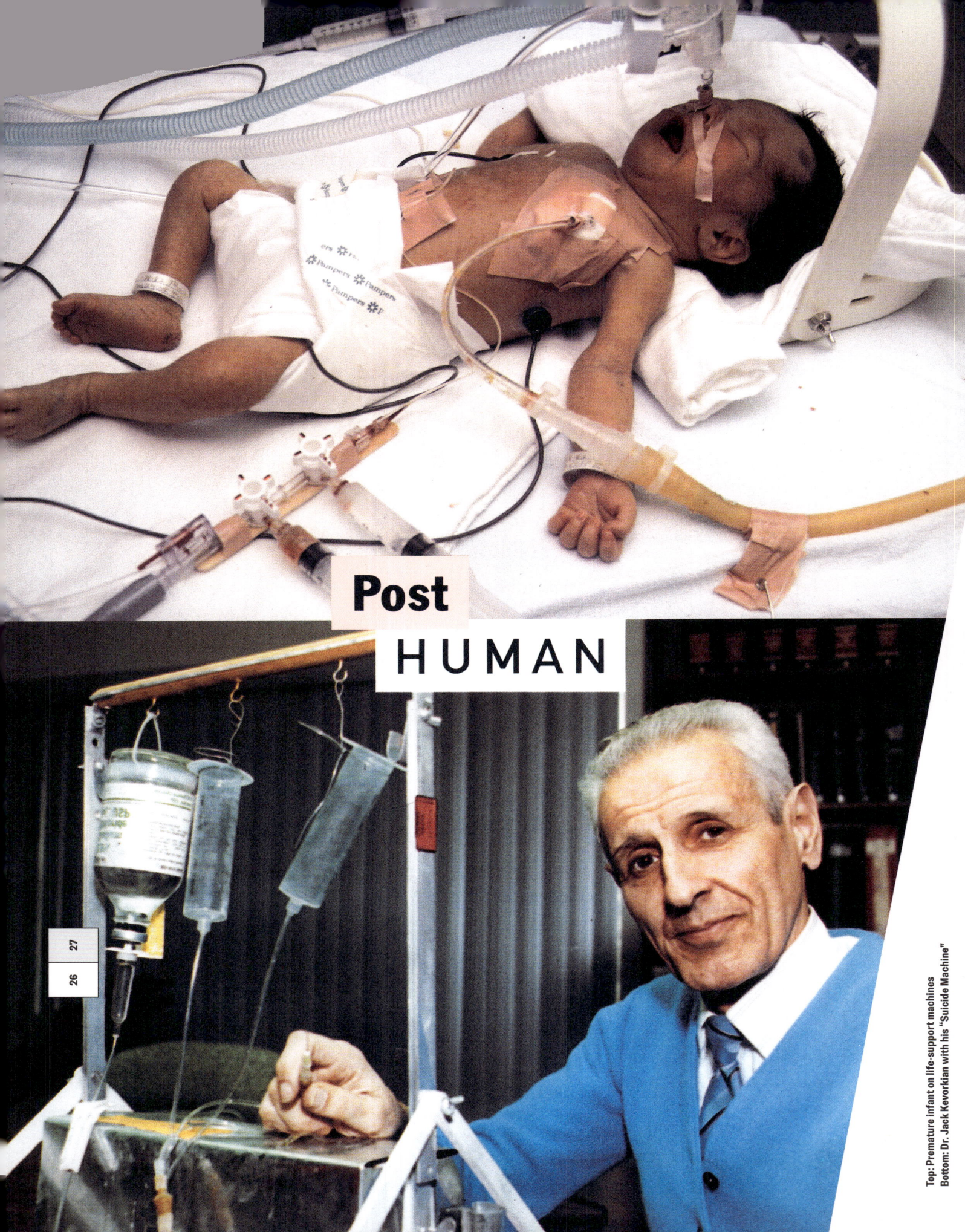

Post
HUMAN

Top: Premature infant on life-support machines
Bottom: Dr. Jack Kevorkian with his "Suicide Machine"

On most people's beauty scale, Stacey Stetler would be a 10. A blond, blue-eyed, 5-foot-11 New York model, she has confidently sashayed down the runway for Yves Saint Laurent in Paris and has graced the covers of fashion magazines. But until recently, when Ms. Stetler looked in the mirror she saw less perfection and more flaws. "I was flat-chested," Ms. Stetler said. "You couldn't tell if I was coming or going. My back protruded almost as much as my front."…Ms. Stetler enhanced her boyish figure by having breast implants. She is not alone.

—*The New York Times*, February 6, 1992, front page

Stories about breast implants, crash diets, and mood drugs have moved from the health and beauty page to the front page. The public has been galvanized by explosive testimony about sexual harassment and by the sensational rape trials of public figures. Questions about the new boundaries of appropriate inter personal behavior are attracting unprecedented interest. There is a growing sense that we should take control over our bodies and our social circumstances rather than just accepting what we inherited.

Social and scientific trends are converging to shape a new conception of the self, a new construction of what it means to be a human being. The matter-of-fact acceptance of one's "natural" looks and one's "natural" personality is being replaced by a growing sense that it is normal to reinvent oneself. The Freudian model of the "psychological person" is dissolving into a new model that encourages individuals to dispense with the anguished analysis of how subconscious childhood experiences molded their behavior. There is a new sense that one can simply construct the new self that one wants, freed from the constraints of one's past and one's inherited genetic code.

Human evolution may be entering a new phase that Charles Darwin never would have envisioned. The potential of genetic reconstitution may be quickly propelling us beyond Darwinian natural evolution and into a bold realm of artificial evolution. Our society will soon have access to the biotechnology

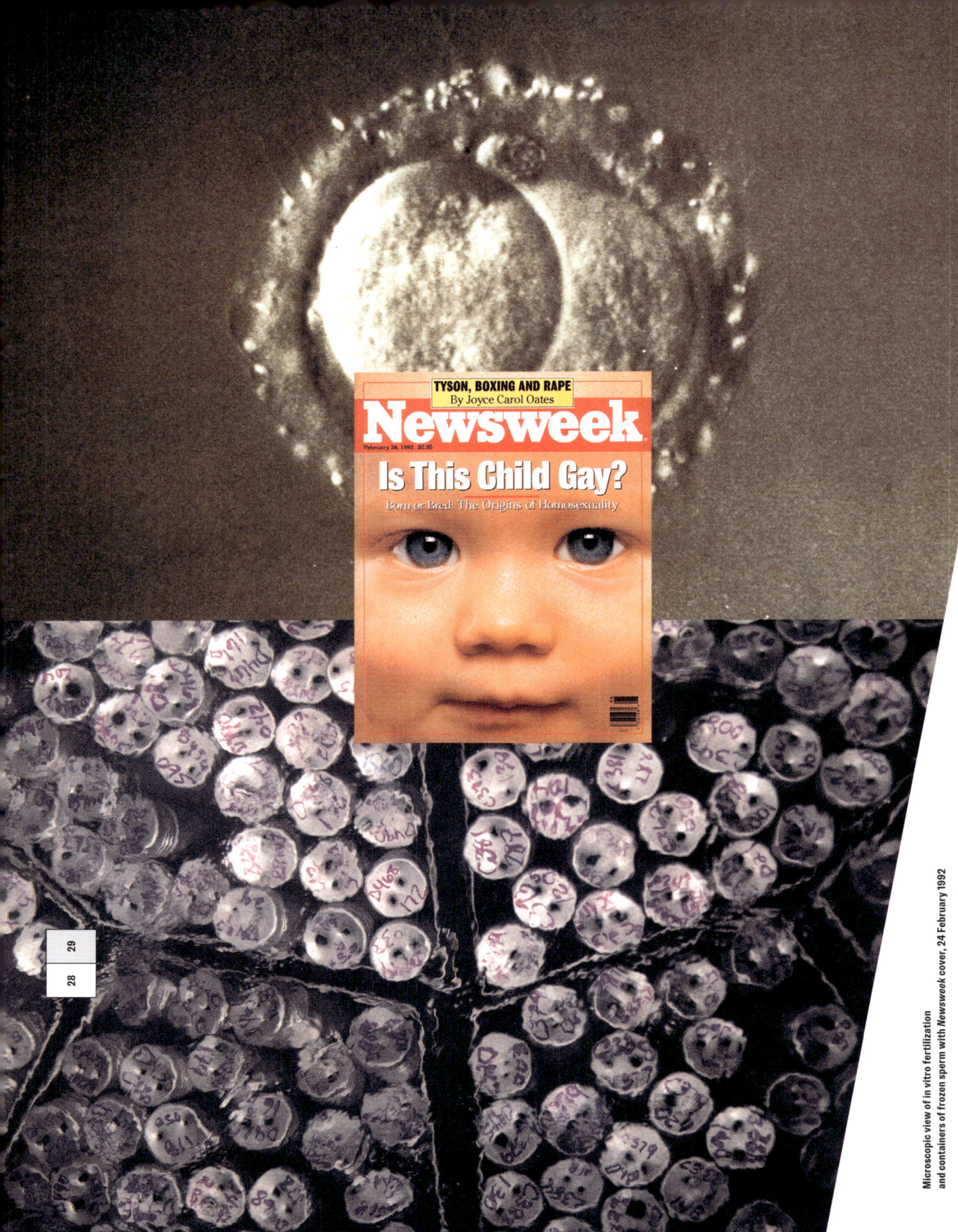

Microscopic view of in vitro fertilization
and containers of frozen sperm with *Newsweek* cover, 24 February 1992

TYSON, BOXING AND RAPE
By Joyce Carol Oates

Newsweek

February 24, 1992 $2.95

Is This Child Gay?

Born or Bred: The Origins of Homosexuality

that will allow us to make direct choices about how we want our species to further evolve. This new techno-evolutionary phase will bring us far beyond eugenics. Our children's generation could very well be the last generation of "pure" humans.

This new sense of one's power to control and, if desired, reconstruct one's body has quickly developed a broad acceptance, but there is still a significant segment of society that is deeply disturbed by its implications. The bitter debate over abortion rights is an example of how explosive the controversy over the limits of "natural" life will become. The battle over the abortion issue and the outcry over euthanasia and the right to choose suicide may be just the beginning of an enormous social conflict over one's freedom to use the new biotechnology to take greater control over one's body and to enhance the course of one's life.

The issue of using genetic engineering to "improve" the fetus will potentially become much more highly charged than the controversy over abortion. It may not be an exaggeration to say that it will become the most difficult moral and social issue that the human species has ever faced. Genetic engineering is not just another life-enhancing technology like aviation or telecommunications. Its continued development and application may force us to redefine the parameters of life.

Our consciousness of the self will have to undergo a profound change as we continue to embrace the transforming advances in biological and communications technologies. A new construction of the self will inevitably take hold as ever more powerful body-altering techniques become commonplace. As radical plastic surgery, computer-chip brain implants, and gene-splicing become routine, the former structure of self will no longer correspond to the new structure of the body. A new post-human organization of personality will develop that reflects people's adaptation to this new technology and its socioeconomic effects.

New approaches to self-realization are generally paralleled by new approaches to art. With each successive transformation of the social environment, great artists have both reflected and helped to define the new personality models that have developed out of society's absorption of technological, political, and social change. Looking back through the history of art, we can see how artists have portrayed the changes in models of self-realization that have accompanied profound changes in the social environment.

Starting with the Renaissance as an example, we can see how an artist such as Hans Holbein the Younger captured the ethos of Humanism in his famous portrait of Erasmus. This new concept of portraiture portrayed a new human attitude that characterized the enhanced sense of self shared by Holbein and his friends. Holbein's portraits also helped to define and communicate this new organization of personality to a broadening audience. The new conception of self that developed with the Enlightenment in the late eighteenth century is captured and communicated by Jean-Antoine Houdon in his portrait of Denis Diderot. Théodore Géricault reveals an increasingly complex concept of the individual in his famous portrait of the kleptomaniac. The deepening sense of individuality that characterized the modernist attitude is portrayed and communicated by a succession of great nineteenth century artists from Ingres to Manet.

The modern model of the self goes through numerous phases as the concepts of individual freedom and individual expression become more sharply focused. A more profound model of self that reflects the late-nineteenth-century's progressively deeper exploration of the inner mind is manifested in the art of Edvard Munch. The adaptation of personality to the increased velocity of the early-twentieth-century's new urban industrial society is reflected by the Cubist portraits of Picasso. The profound contribution of the Freudian psychological model of the self is communicated through the expressionistic portraiture of Kokoschka. After assimilating the Dada phase, the existential phase, and the celebrity-as-an-art-form Pop phase, the history of the modern self reaches its culmination with the free-for-all, "let it all hang out" ethos of the late 1960s counterculture. The attitude reflected by the body art of Vito Acconci represents both the ultimate fulfillment of modernist unrestrained individualism as well as the undermining of the utopian modern dream. It is both the final phase of the progression of modern models of self-construction and the beginning of a search for a new postmodern construction of personality.

The year 1968 was a watershed, when the culture of Modernism reached both its culmination and its collapse. The sexual, ethnic, and political liberation movements that we associate with 1968 were the logical fulfillment of the modern dream of unrestrained personal freedom, but also represented the shattering of the utopian modern search for absolute truth. The events of 1968 and their repercussions demonstrated a new sense that there were numerous ways to look at the world and numerous equally valid standards of behavior. The long-accepted male-dominated, Eurocentric world view of the Western political, economic, and intellectual power structure began to be punctured.

Although attitudes seem to have regressed since the youth-culture euphoria of the late '60s and early '70s, many of the liberating impulses of 1968 have led to significant changes in the way our society defines itself. There is now a much greater consciousness of the world's multiculturalism and an understanding that not every country aspires to the same modern model of progress that the West once believed to be an unquestioned absolute. Feminism, in particular, has spurred tremendous changes in the structure of society during the past twenty-five years, creating perhaps the most significant revolution in human behavior since the Renaissance. Even the drug culture of the years around 1968 has had its effect on how people perceive the world today. Can corporate executives who experienced the alternative realities of mind-altering drugs while they were college students have as absolute a sense of reality as their parents' generation?

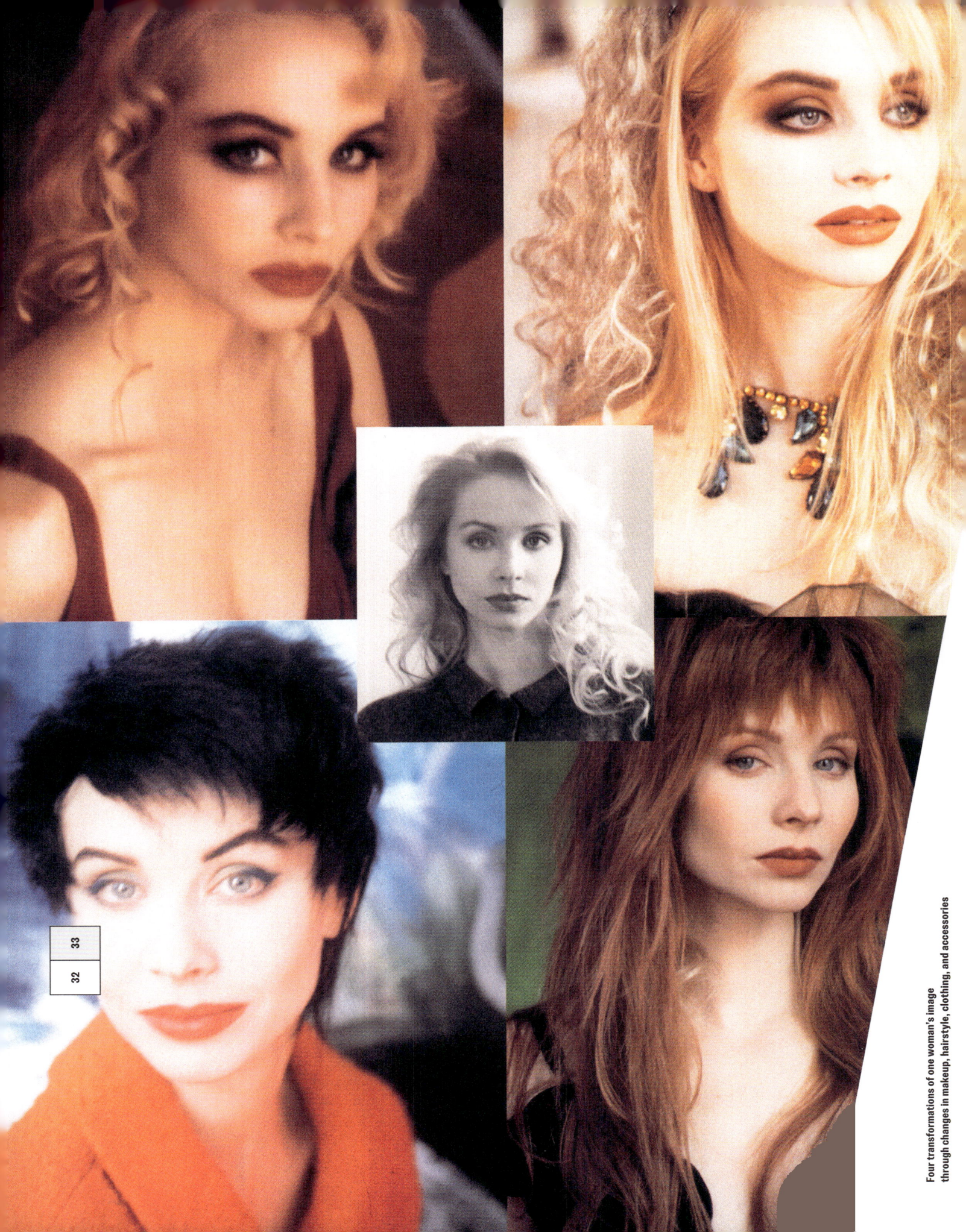

Four transformations of one woman's image
through changes in makeup, hairstyle, clothing, and accessories

The post-1968 period has been a time of transition, when the radical impulses of the counterculture have slowly penetrated the more traditional segments of society. Along the way, of course, many of the more radical features of counterculture consciousness have been muted, but many of its most significant innovations, such as feminism, have begun to take hold. A distinct new model of behavior and a new organization of personality that is distinct from the modern model is still in the process of developing. The tentative term of "Post Modern is probably the appropriate one to describe this intermediate state of consciousness that constitutes the transition between the modern model and the new model of reality that we are building.

The obsession with self-awareness and self-improvement in the 1970s (the "Me" decade), and with self-image and self-indulgence in the 1980s. demonstrated the intense interest in redefining and perhaps reformulating society's definition of the self. The new broader understanding of the multiplicity of possible realities has inspired a widespread desire to break with older constraining models of personality. It is becoming routine for people to try to alter their appearance, their behavior, and their consciousness beyond what was once thought possible. The modern era might be characterized as a period of the discovery of self. Our current post-modern era can be characterized as a transitional period of the disintegration of self. Perhaps the coming "post-human" period will be characterized by the reconstruction of self.

The new construction of self is conceptual rather than natural. A key element of the emerging consciousness of personality is that an individual need not be tied to his or her "natural" looks, "natural" abilities, or the ghosts of his or her family history. People used to live not just their own lives but their parents' lives and their children's lives as well. The sense of self was tied to the structure of the family. People had a strong sense of their obligation to the traditions and attitudes of their parents and to their obligation to pass these attitudes on to their children. Now the changing social patterns of our

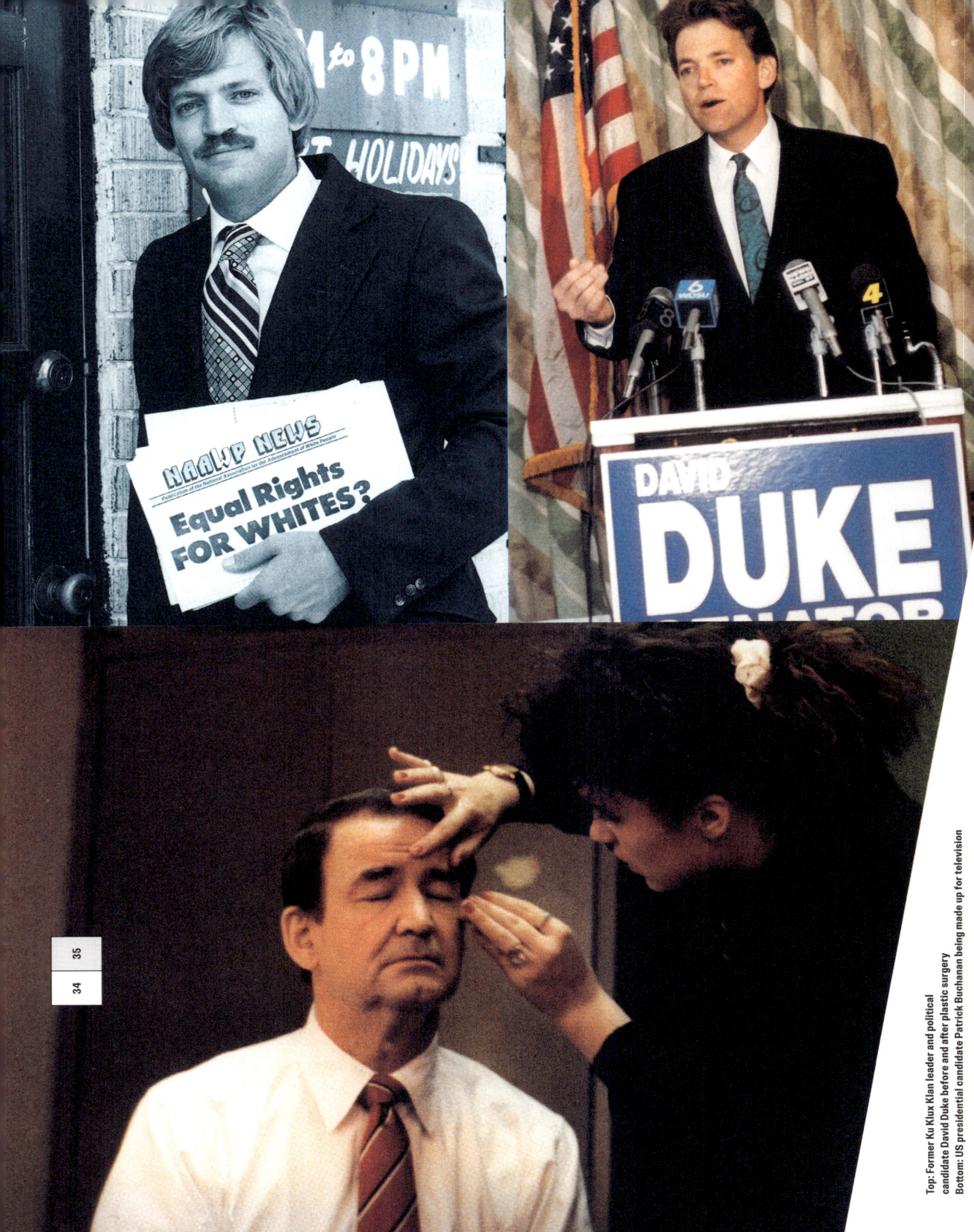

Top: Former Ku Klux Klan leader and political candidate David Duke before and after plastic surgery
Bottom: US presidential candidate Patrick Buchanan being made up for television

society have led to a sense that people's lives are their own to invent and their own to lead. With the deepening penetration of the electronic media, models of self-construction will increasingly be as likely to be taken from celebrities and other media role models as they will be from parents and grandparents.

The decentered television reality that we experience, with its fragmentation, multiplicity, and simultaneity, is helping to deepen the sense that there is no absolutely "correct" or "true" model of the self. Increasingly people may come to feel that it is no longer relevant to try to "cure" a personality disorder. Instead it may seem more appropriate to try to alter, rather than cure, the self. We are likely to be witnessing the dissolution of the Freudian psychological model with its emphasis on childhood experiences and family background. The latest statistics show that in American inner cities, more than half of the school-age children come from one-parent homes and as many as 10 percent from "no parent" homes. The process of self-construction has to be radically different from the way it was in turn-of-the-century Vienna. Many contemporary people have little sense of past and little sense of future, only a sense of the present. Disconnected from traditional family history, people are more prone to start their self-identity with the present There is less need to psychologically interpret or "discover" oneself and more of a feeling that the self can be altered and reinvented. Self-identity is becoming much more dependent on how one is perceived by others, as opposed to a deeply rooted sense of inner direction. The world has become a mirror.

Reality, fantasy, and fiction are merging into the inspiration for a new model of personality organization. The interchangeable identities of Madonna and the extraordinary self-transformation of Ivana Trump are examples of this shuffling of reality and fantasy into a reassembled fictional personality that quickly becomes fact. The search for the absolute "true" self has been replaced by a constant scanning for new alternatives.

The contemporary collapse of absolutes applies not only to personality models, but to political and social models as well. The crumbling of Communism in the Soviet Union marked the dissolution of one of the most absolute of all belief systems. In the capitalist sphere, as well, the Japanese bubble economy has been punctured and the ideologies of Reaganism and Thatcherism have been tarnished. Corporate restructurings, with their plant closings and forced early retirements, have shattered the long-nurtured assumption that the modern corporation would make every effort to take care of its dedicated employees. The belief system at the foundation of modern corporatism has been seriously weakened, leading to new models of how individuals perceive their place in the free-market structure.

The public has even experienced an unprecedented collapse of the reputation of many of its most trusted and admired heroes. It turned out that Ben Johnson's astounding athletic prowess was the product of steroids and that Donald Trump's vast wealth was not real, only simulated. The recent deflation of all these "absolutes" in our cultural, socioeconomic, and political environment has set the stage for a new kind of belief structure based on multiple realities and multiple perceptions.

In addition to the way social and economic forces are shaping a new method of seeing and experiencing the world, two extraordinary new technologies will soon be challenging definitions and perceptions of reality in a way that is beyond anything previously imagined. Computer science with its ever closer realization of virtual reality and biotechnology with the amazing potential of genetic engineering are on the verge of creating a new environment where most of our assumptions about what is reality and even what is life will have to be reexamined. The combination of these two sets of technologies will create not only new life forms and new communications channels, but will shape new perceptions of time and space and even lead to new structures of thinking.

We are already experiencing a new kind of electronic space and a new kind of simultaneous television time. The former sense of the vast distances that separated, for example, a metals trader in New York from his customer in Tokyo has already been collapsed by twenty-four-hour online trading. Economic space once encompassed a sense of the long journeys involved to move goods and information from one city to another. Now, with computer networks, videoconferencing, and DHL overnight service, company offices on different continents can function as if they were next door to each other. The new sense of time experienced through CNN's live broadcasts of the Gulf War and the August 1991 Soviet coup has changed forever the way world affairs will function. There will no longer be the cushion of time between an event and its interpretation in the newspaper. The electronic media has networked the world into a new kind of simultaneous real-time structure, speeding up the course of social interchange. The current communications revolution is likely to be just a prelude, however, to the advent of cyberspace, a vast computer universe that will further restructure our understanding of time and space.

The new electronic time and space also seem to be shaping a new kind of thinking, oriented toward images and sound bites. The former emphasis on deductive rational structures and lengthy narrative has been eclipsed by the electronic media's compressed sense of time. The television audience is being trained to take in complex issues through quick successions of images and compact, packaged commentary. As previous generations learned structures of complex thinking through essays and novels, today's advanced television generation learns how to think through news anchorpeople and talk-show hosts.

The structure of thinking is changing, and it appears that the quality of thinking is changing as well. Patterns of thinking are becoming less rational. With the collapse of many of the modern era's hierarchical belief systems, and their replacement by multifaceted alternatives, people are moving away

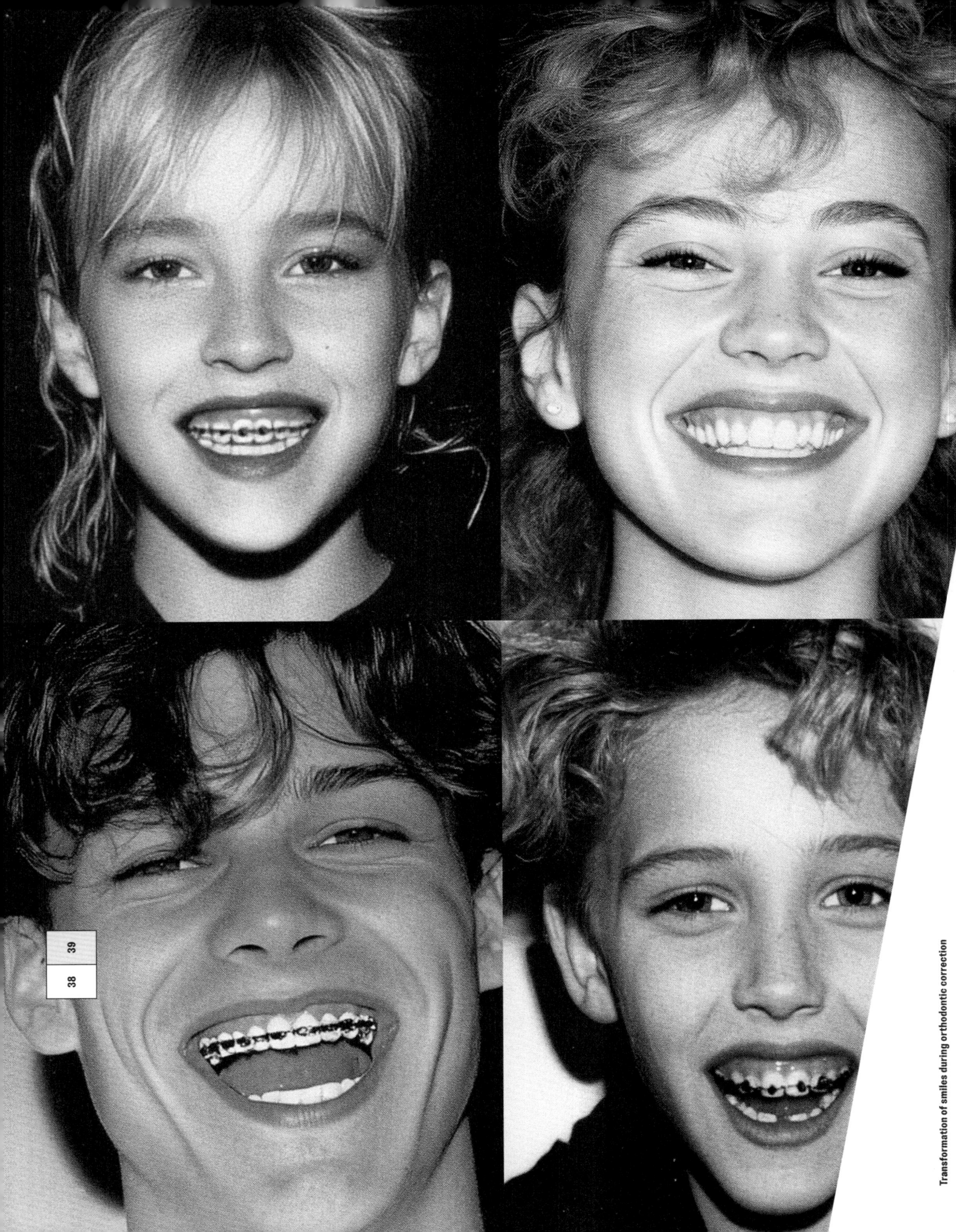

Transformation of smiles during orthodontic correction

from hierarchically structured rational thinking to a more perceptual, less structured outlook and a more irrational mode of thought. An irrational outlook in fact might be a more appropriate approach to a world that seems to have outgrown its modern utopian faith in rational solutions.

This feeling of irrationality is furthered by the sense that the explosive new technologies may also be unleashing some explosive new pathologies. We are experiencing a surge of seemingly untamable viruses: biological, social, environmental, and computer viruses as well. There is a sense that we are advancing but not progressing, mired in a swirl of unexpected side effects that have undermined our belief in a rational order and moved us closer to embracing an irrational model of the world.

Our transition to the post-human world of cyberspace and genetic engineering is occurring gradually. Many of the new attitudes toward the body and the new modes of social behavior do not seem particularly significant in isolation, but viewed together they demonstrate a decided trend toward a radically new model of the self and of social behavior. They constitute a kind of prelude that is likely to make society attitudinally more ready than one would have expected for the truly radical technologies that are soon to come.

It is assumed that the average person can and should alter his or her body through rigorous diet and exercise. The virtues of mind exercise and even of mind-altering drugs have also achieved wide acceptance. Plastic surgery is not only accepted and encouraged by many of our social role models but is enthusiastically shown off. For the generation that has watched and perhaps tried to imitate the self-transformation of Jane Fonda, there is already a strong sense of one's freedom to control and alter one's body. As more powerful technology becomes accessible, the next logical step might be for members of the post–Jane Fonda generation to want to create a genetically improved child who would already incorporate the enhanced physical endowments that years of exercise, liposuction, and implant surgery had

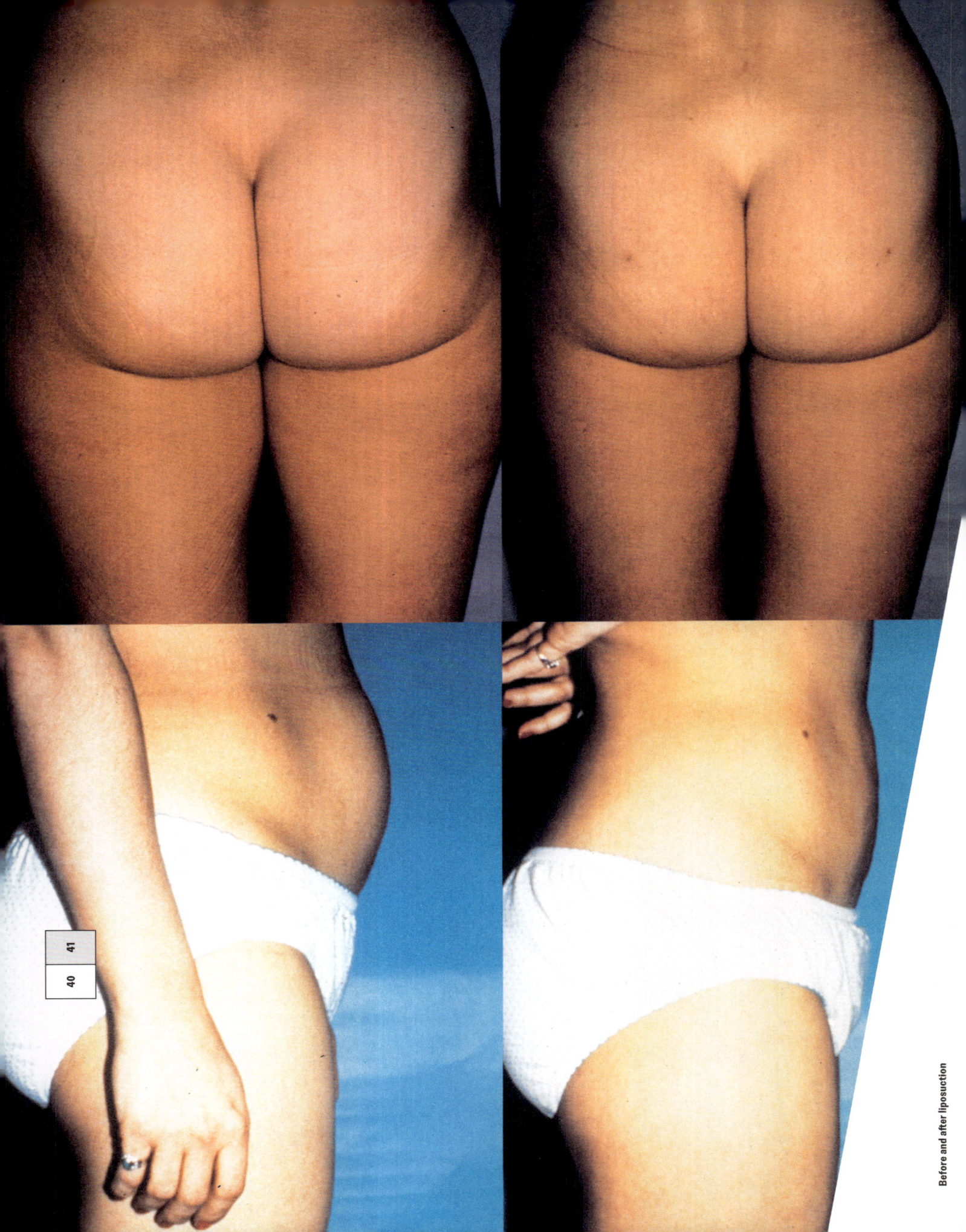

41

Before and after liposuction

accomplished. How large a jump would it be for someone with an elaborate home-computer system to install a chip in his or her brain that stored the entire Encyclopedia Britannica and images of every important painting in art history? The attitudes that may make us ready to embrace the post-human person may already be here.

We are also already well on our way to assimilating a new set of nearly post-human social structures. These new types of social behaviors first seemed to assert themselves in the realm of mating rituals. The social dislocations that began to isolate young people from their traditional family and community networks led to numerous artificial structures to facilitate introductions. First there were personal ads and singles clubs, then singles bars and an organized singles industry. Now, with the threat of AIDS and perhaps a growing sense of human alienation, phone sex has become especially popular. People can conduct fantasy relationships without the mess that often goes along with real human contact. From phone sex it is only a small step to virtual sex, the multisensual sexual experience that people will soon be able to have in three dimensions with their home computer. A virtual-sex program featuring every simulated sound and sensation is not only likely to be better in many ways than the real thing, for future generations it may *become* the real thing.

In Japan, which, as in other areas, is in the vanguard of post-human behavior, there has emerged a new personality type known as otaku. Otaku people are defined more by their possessions than by their inherent character. They can be described as a concept of person-as-information. Travelers to Tokyo are often amazed by the proliferation of vending machines for all sorts of goods and services, even for matchmaking. Survey research has shown that much of the popularity of these vending machines is due to the preference of young Japanese for interacting with machines instead of with real people.

These emerging social and technological trends that are redefining our concepts of the self and of social behavior have begun to exert tremendous influence on artists. There is an enormous new artistic interest in the body and in the presentation of the self. Much of today's most innovative new artistic practice involves new concepts of the figure and new approaches to the figure. This new interest in the figure is, however, not to be found where it would traditionally be expected, in painting and in conventional sculpture. The new interest in figuration, in keeping with the social and technological trends that are inspiring it, is conceptual rather than formal. The new figurative art is emerging through the channel of the conceptual, body, and performance art of the late '60s and '70s rather than through the figurative painting tradition.

Many of the most interesting younger artists are dealing with the new conceptions of the body and the new definitions of self that the vanguard of our society is also dealing with. They are exploring through their art the same questioning of traditional notions of gender, sexuality, and self-identity that is taking place in the world at large. Much of the new figurative art is reactive to and descriptive of the "real" world, but it cannot in fact be called realistic in the conventional sense. That is because so much of the "real" world that they are reacting to has in fact become artificial. With the concept of the real disintegrating through an acceptance of the multiplicity of reality models and through the embrace of artificiality, Realism as we used to know it may no longer be possible. This new figurative art may actually mark the end of Realism rather than its revival.

The redefinition of the figure is being approached by a number of artists through its breakup and reassembly. Robert Gober shockingly isolates segments of the body from the whole, creating an eerie new reality of free-floating limbs and disconnected emotions. Body parts are disassembled and reassembled in the sculpture of George Lappas, who also mixes time frames from the past and the present. This shuffling of historical, present, and future time is also characteristic of the approaches of Wim Delvoye and Yasumasa Morimura. The figures in their works function in historical, present, and future time simultaneously, giving a picture of the kind of time mix that is likely to be more and more characteristic of the way we will experience the world.

Time is not the only element that is shuffled. Humans and animals are conflated in the work of Mike Kelley, humans and mannequins in the work of Charles Ray, and humans and machines in the work of Paul McCarthy. These artists present a shocking reformulation of humanity that gives a disquieting glimpse of the coming post-human situation. In Kelley's world, the ever more intense underflow of violence and perversity bubbles over into an uneasy confusion of artificiality, innocence, and bestiality. In Ray's sculpture, frighteningly out of scale mannequins represent intensified visions of posthuman evolution, drained of all emotion and affect. McCarthy's *Garden* depicts an alien post-human future in which the figure becomes a robotic shell seized by an uncontrollable sexual obsession from which all "human" passion is absent.

Future genetic manipulation may spawn a race of post humans who are outwardly perfect but whose inner neuroses and instincts may not be so easily controlled. Artists are sensitive to this murky underside of displaced urges that may not be quite as easy to re-mold as a pair of flabby thighs. Janine Antoni's cube of gnawed chocolate reveals the neurotic and desperate behavior sometimes hidden beneath the sleek facade of a woman's image perfected through cosmetics. Kiki Smith's flayed bodies, dripping with excretions, bear witness to the emotional wreckage that festers below the plastic surface. Artists are giving us a frightful warning of the irrational reservoir of dislocated emotions that may overwhelm the advances of technology.

The emphasis on appearance versus essence, a central feature of the new construction of self-identity, is explored by Clegg & Guttmann through their seemingly normal images of corporate-type personalities, which subtly reveal something empty and abnormal underneath. The new way in which

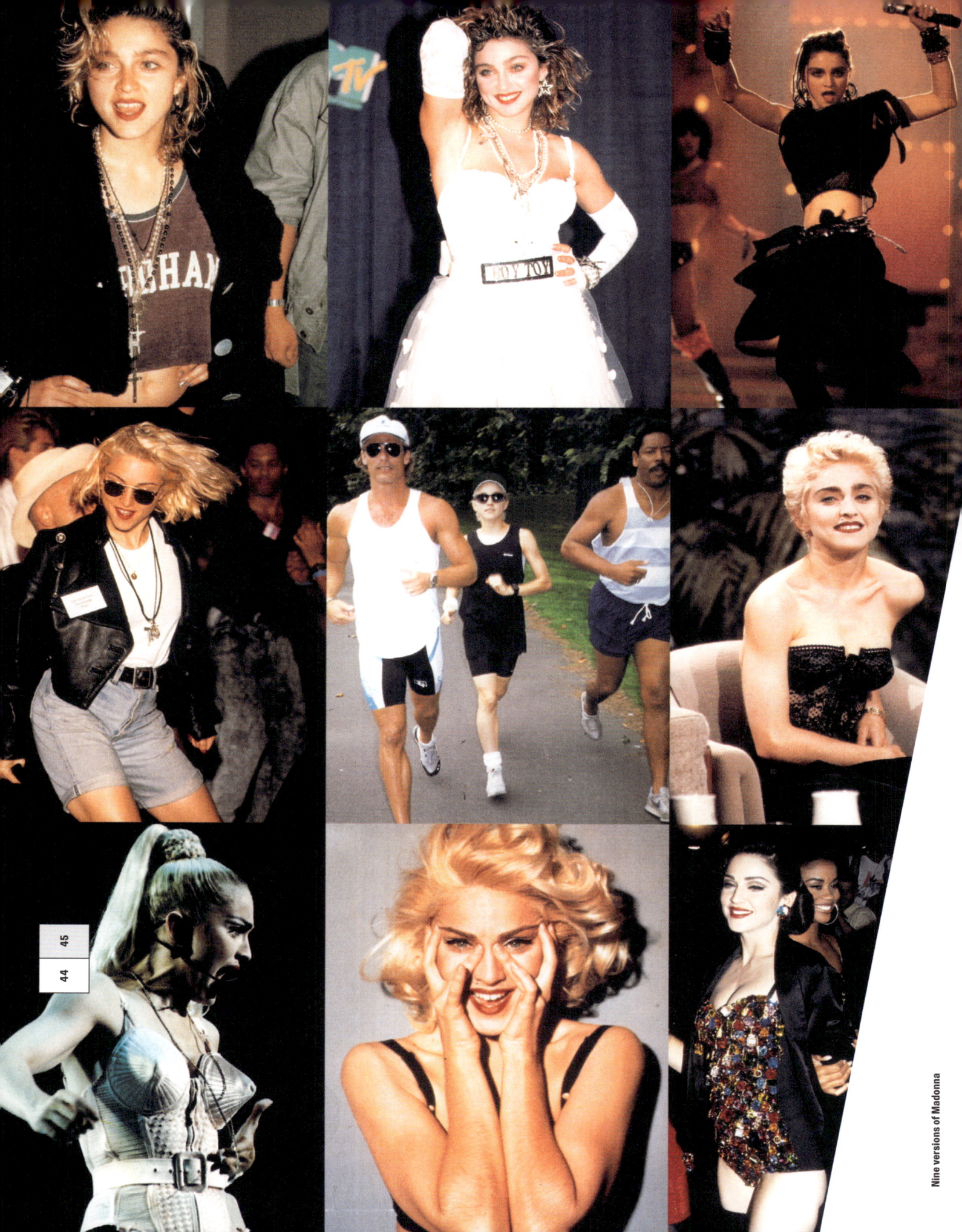

Nine versions of Madonna

personal identity is being constructed is examined through the mind-flow drawings of Karen Kilimnik, which enter into the interplay between models of celebrity and models of self. The fascinating collapse of the border between public and private lives is also explored though Kilimnik's work. As evidenced by the new approaches to the private versus public, in everything from the scrutiny of the personal lives of political candidates to the behind-the-scenes revelations of Madonna's *Truth or Dare*, our entire understanding of the meaning of private life is in the process of being redefined.

The re-creation of self through an embrace of fantasy and fiction is embodied in the life and work of Jeff Koons. In the course of a two-year period, Koons transformed his body and his life through his courtship and marriage with Cicciolina. The biological and material sculpture resulting from their union dissolves the dividing line between artificial and real, creating art that can truly be described as post human.

As the organic, naturally evolving model of human life is replaced by the artificial evolution into the Post Human, art is likely to assume a much more central role. Art may have to fuse with science as computerization and biotechnology create further "improvements" on the human form. Many of the decisions that will accompany the applications of computerized virtual reality and of genetic engineering will be related to aesthetics. Technology will make it possible to remodel our bodies and supercharge our minds, but art will have to help provide the inspiration for what our bodies should look like and what our minds should be doing.

Will the onset of the Post Human mean unprecedented freedom for the individual and for the artist? Will we soon have almost unlimited ability to recreate ourselves and break through the constraints of genetic history? Will we have the opportunity to express ourselves in any way we want through physical appearance? Will we be able to create art that is also biology?

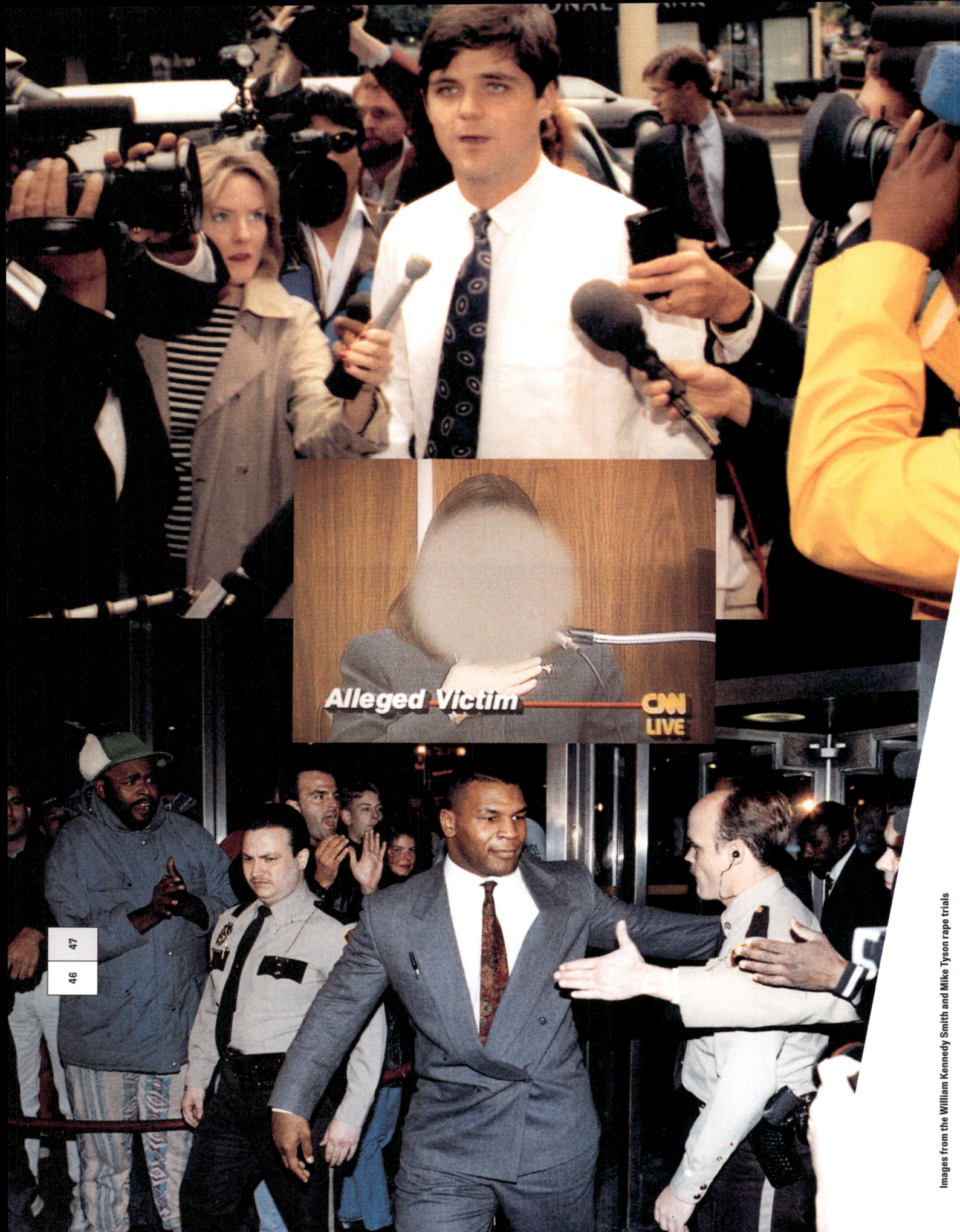

Alleged Victim

CNN LIVE

Images from the William Kennedy Smith and Mike Tyson rape trials

Or will it happen that all these extraordinary new possibilities will result in increased social repression and a push toward conformity? Will the persuasive skills of the advertising industry convince us all to buy the same two or three genetic-improvement programs? Will governments assert their control over the powerful new biotechnology and restrict its use? Or will they take a more aggressive stance, exploiting the new technology to create genetically improved populations for economic and military superiority? Could the world evolve into a nightmarish situation with new, improved Post Humans in the wealthy countries ruling over the "old humans" in countries where the new technologies cannot be readily afforded? All these scenarios remain unclear.

What we do know is that we will soon be forced by technological advances to develop a new morality. We will need to build a new moral structure that will give people a framework of how to deal with the enormous choices they will have to make in terms of genetic alteration and computerized brain enhancement. We will have to face decisions not only about what looks good, but what *is* good or is bad about the restructuring of the mind and body. The limits of life will no longer be something that can be taken for granted. We will have to create a new moral vision to cope with them. In the future, artists may no longer be involved in just redefining art. In the posthuman future artists may also be involved in redefining life.

Jeffrey Deitch (1992)

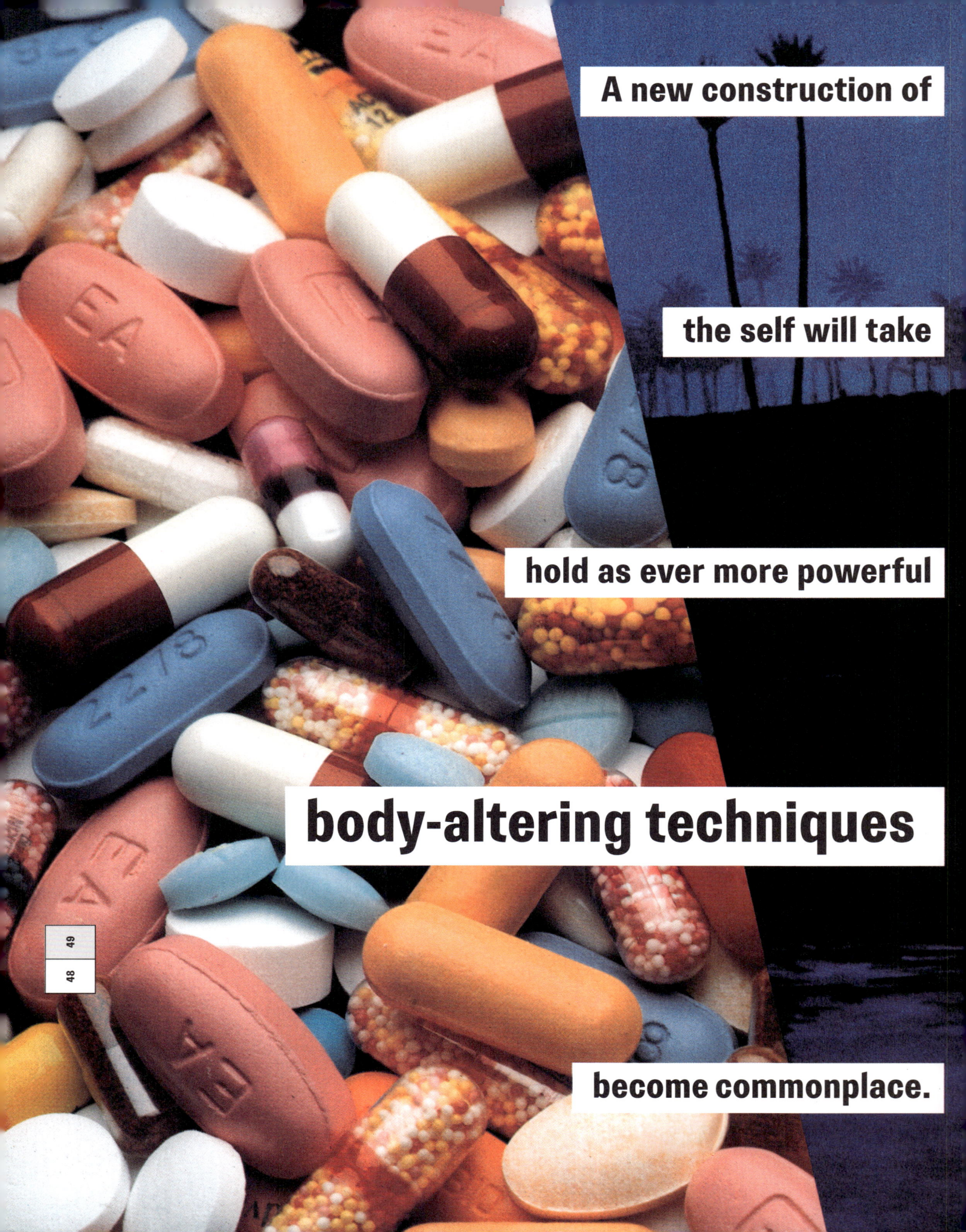

A new construction of

the self will take

hold as ever more powerful

body-altering techniques

become commonplace.

49
48

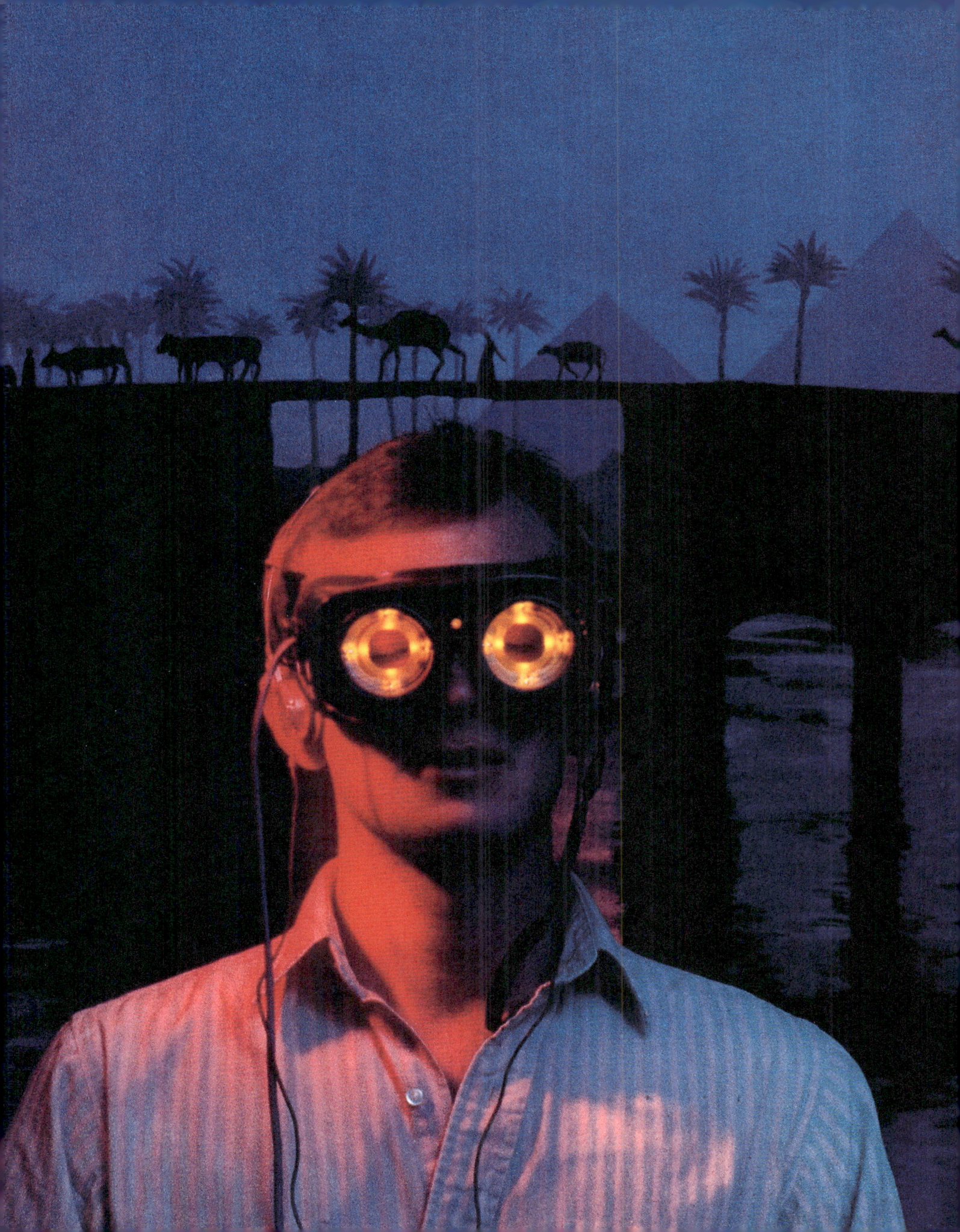

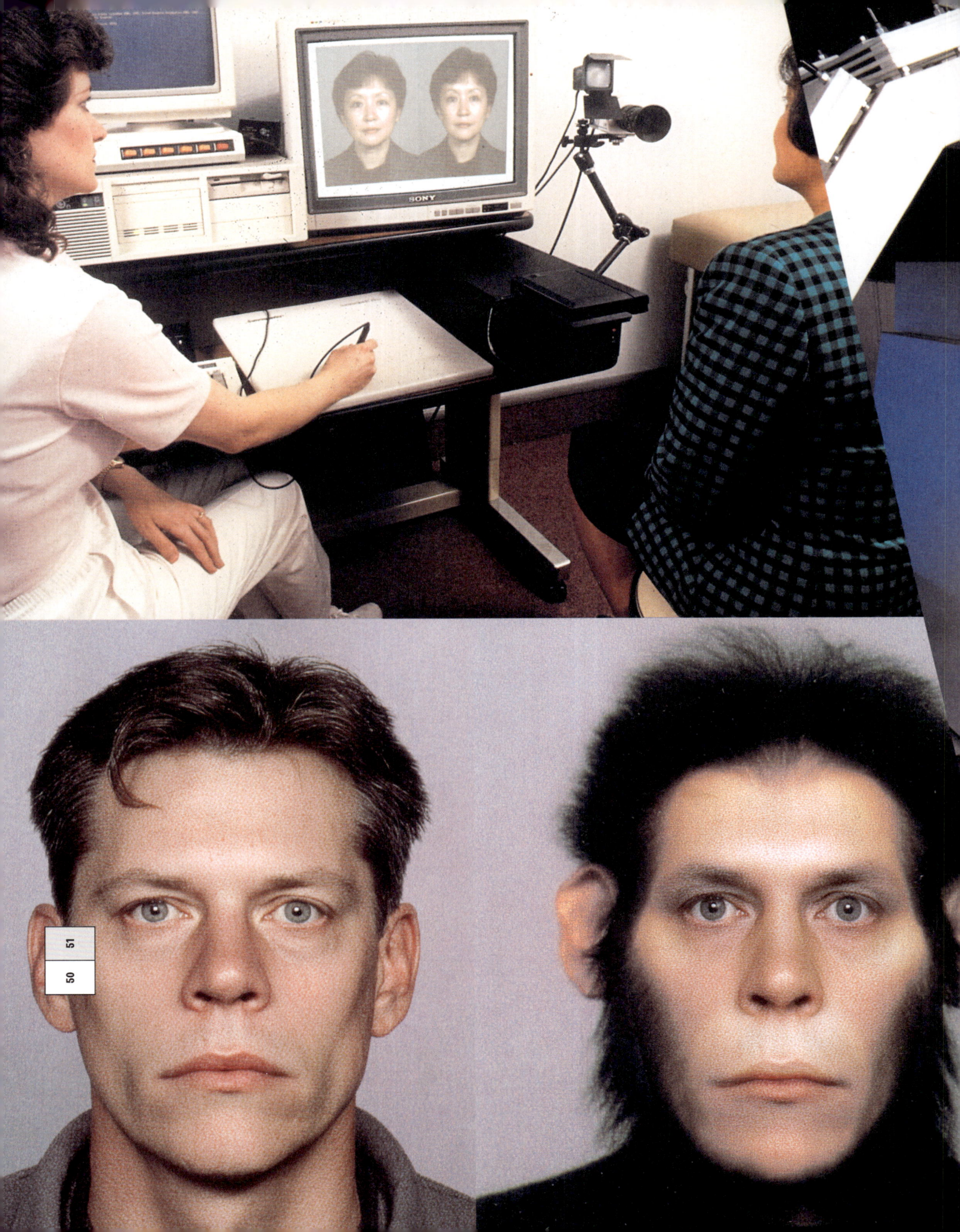

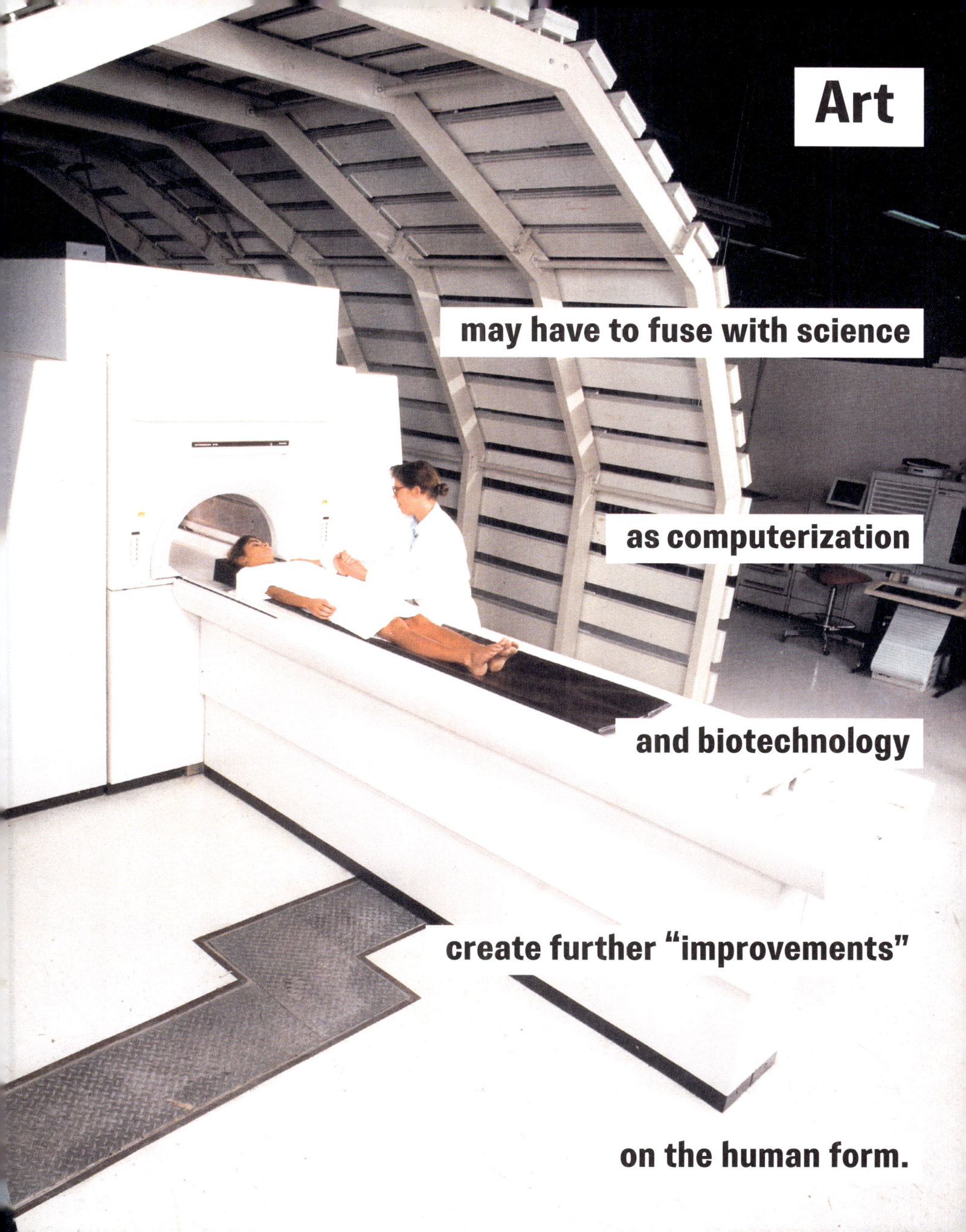

Art

may have to fuse with science

as computerization

and biotechnology

create further "improvements"

on the human form.

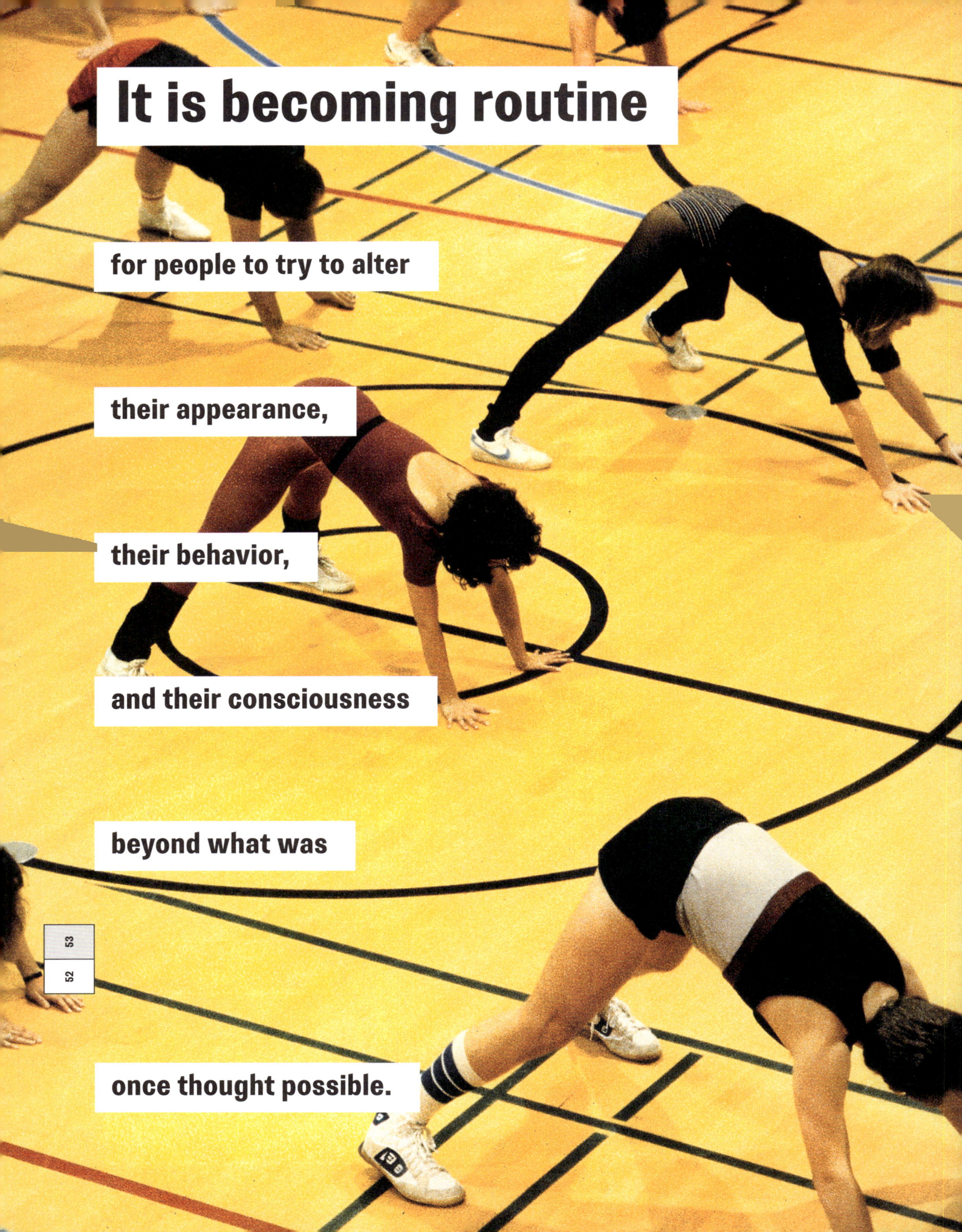

It is becoming routine

for people to try to alter

their appearance,

their behavior,

and their consciousness

beyond what was

once thought possible.

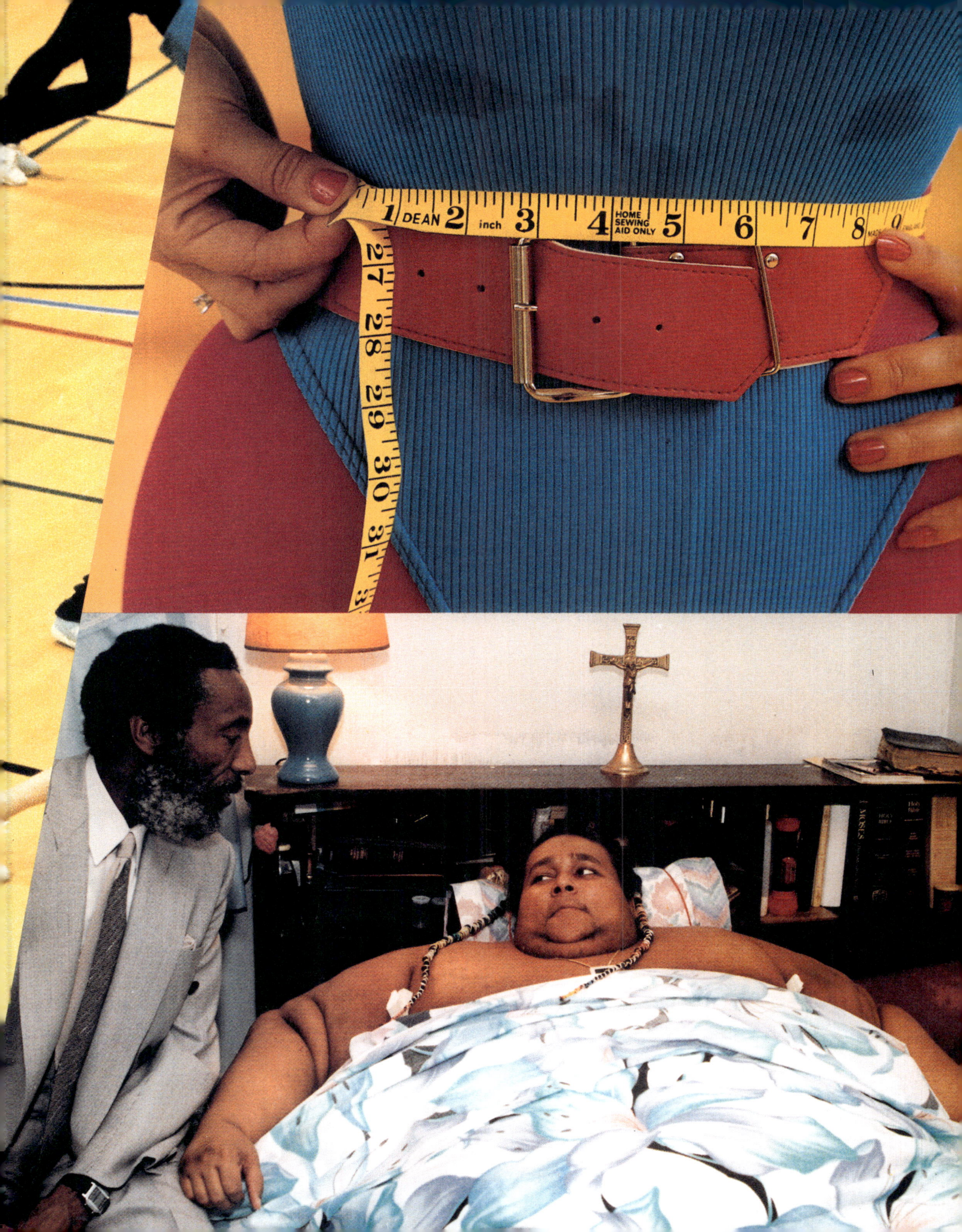

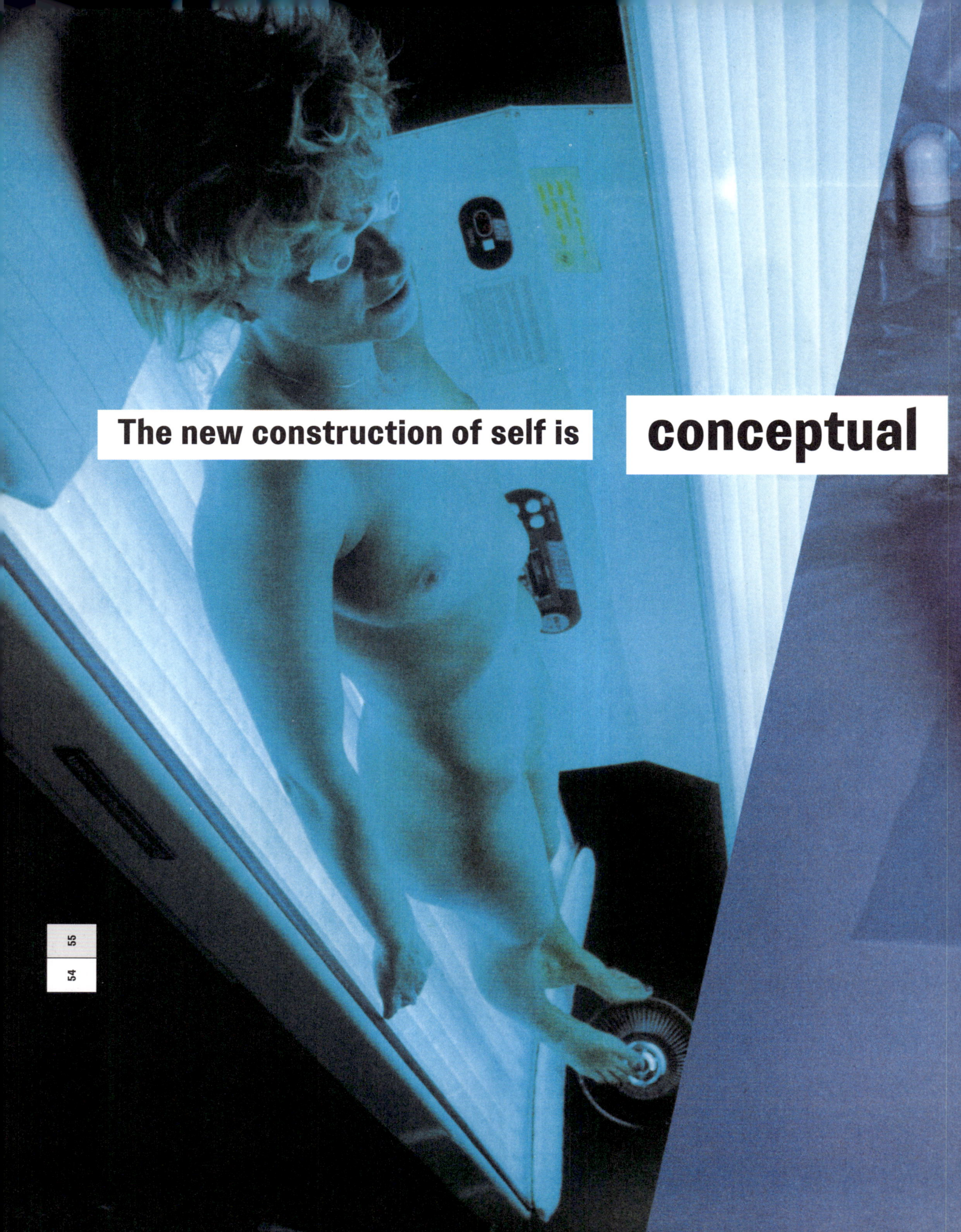

The new construction of self is **conceptual**

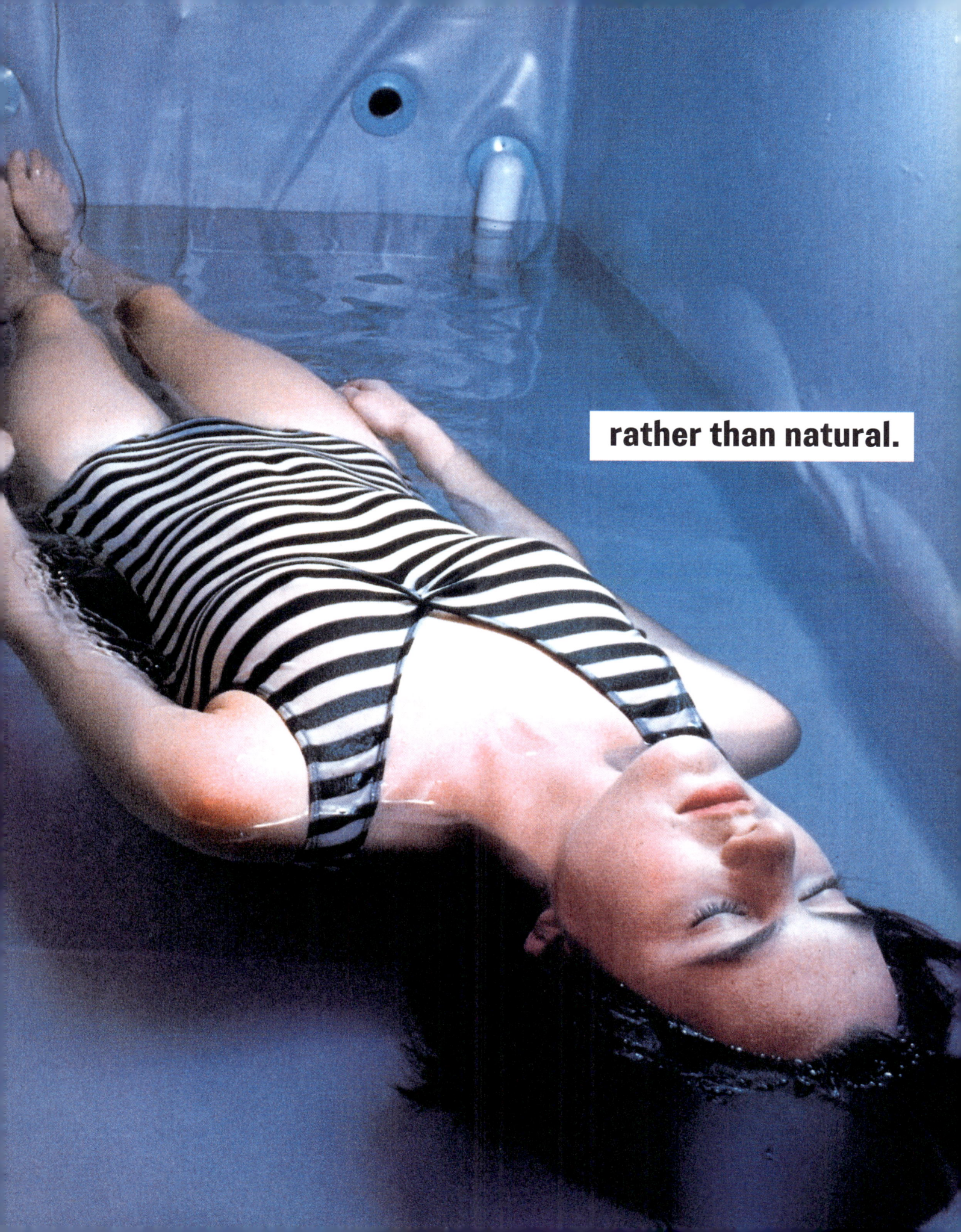

rather than natural.

With the embrace of

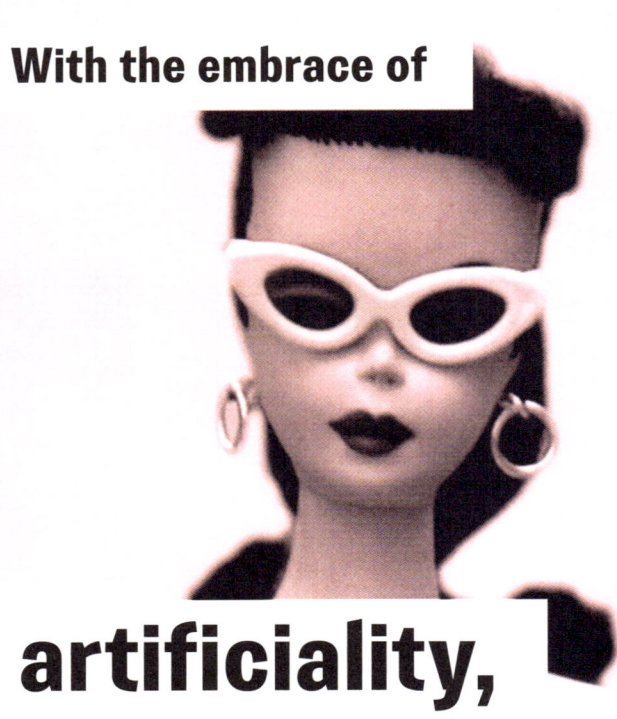

artificiality,

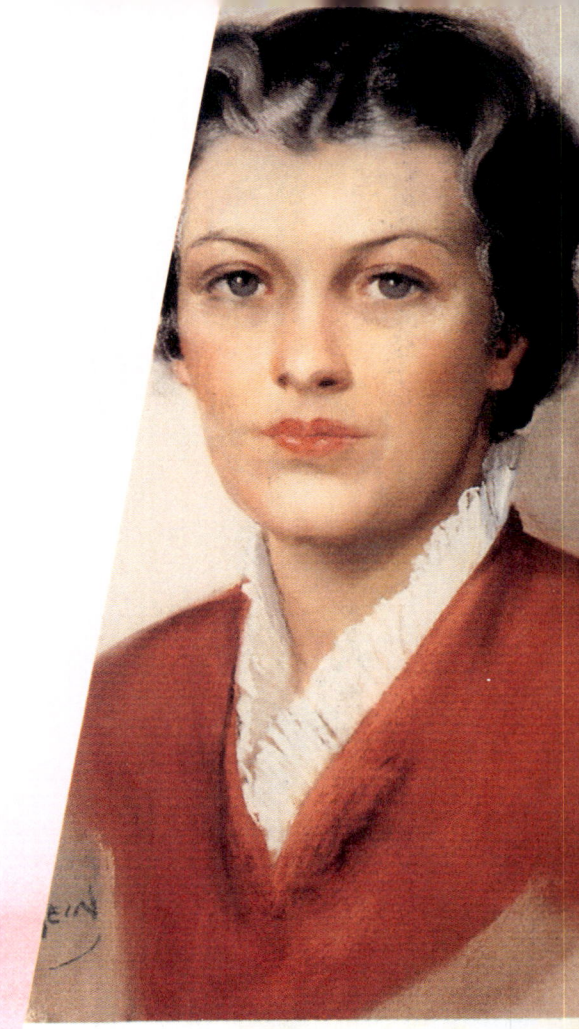

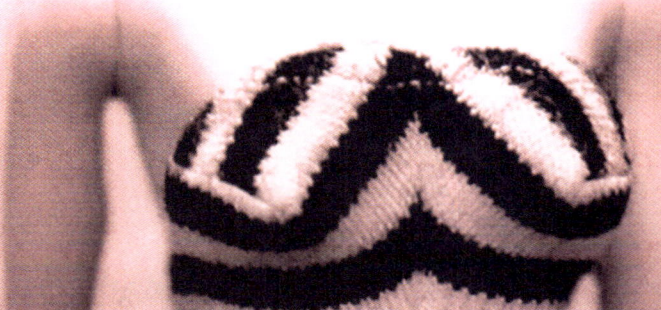

realism as we used to know it

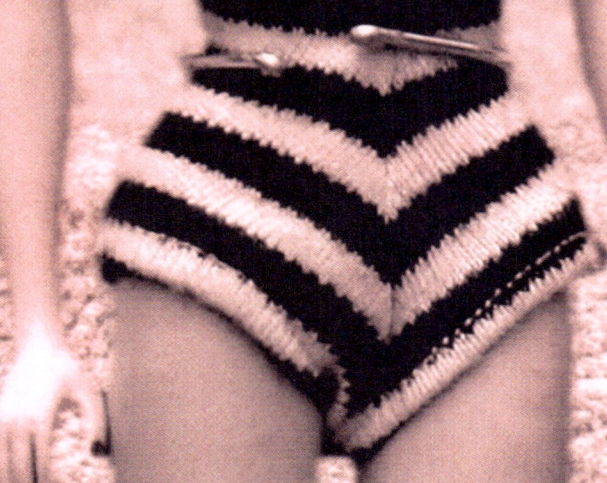

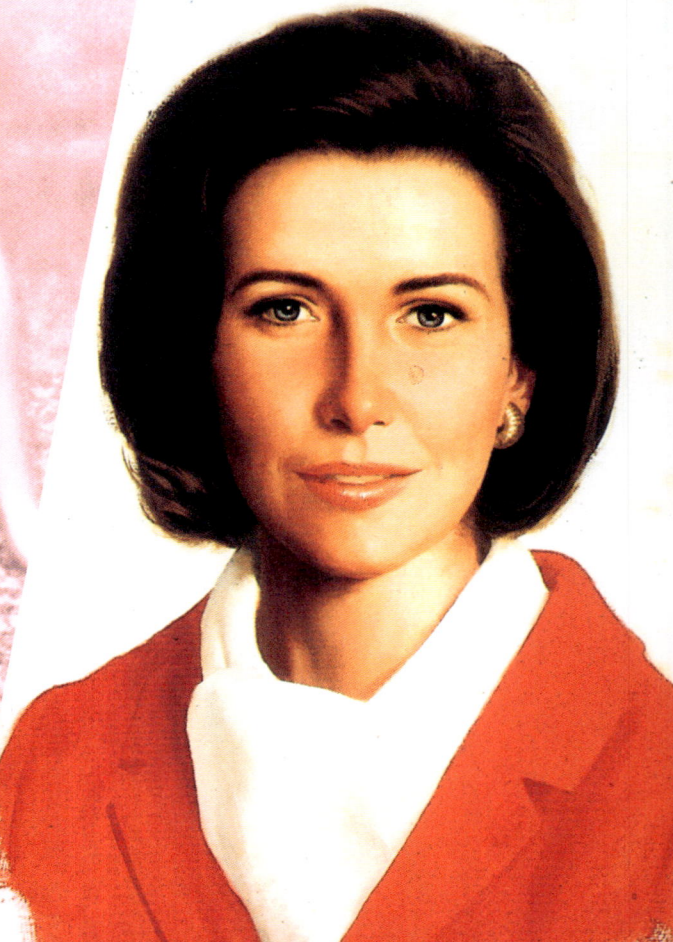

may no longer be possible.

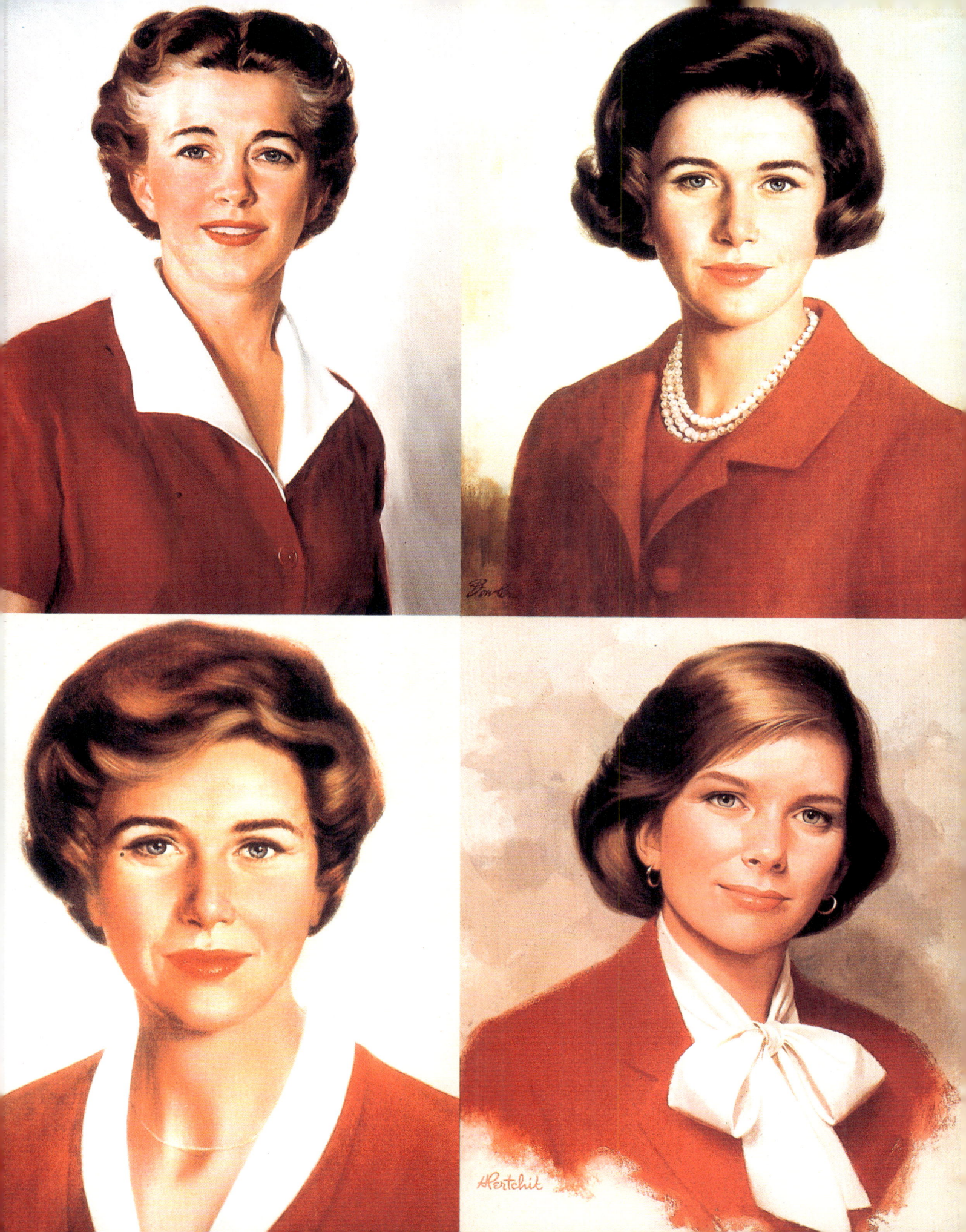

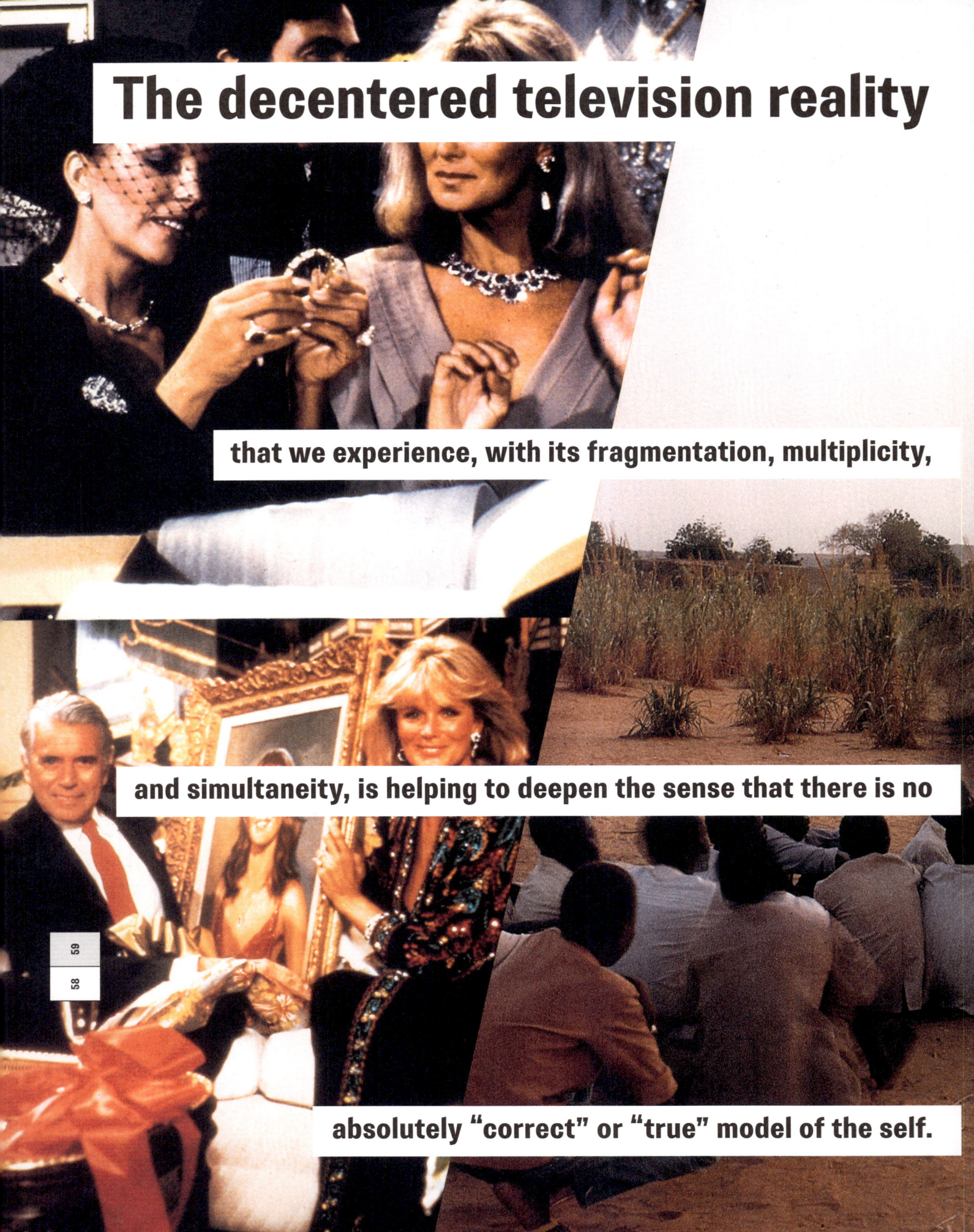

The decentered television reality

that we experience, with its fragmentation, multiplicity,

and simultaneity, is helping to deepen the sense that there is no

absolutely "correct" or "true" model of the self.

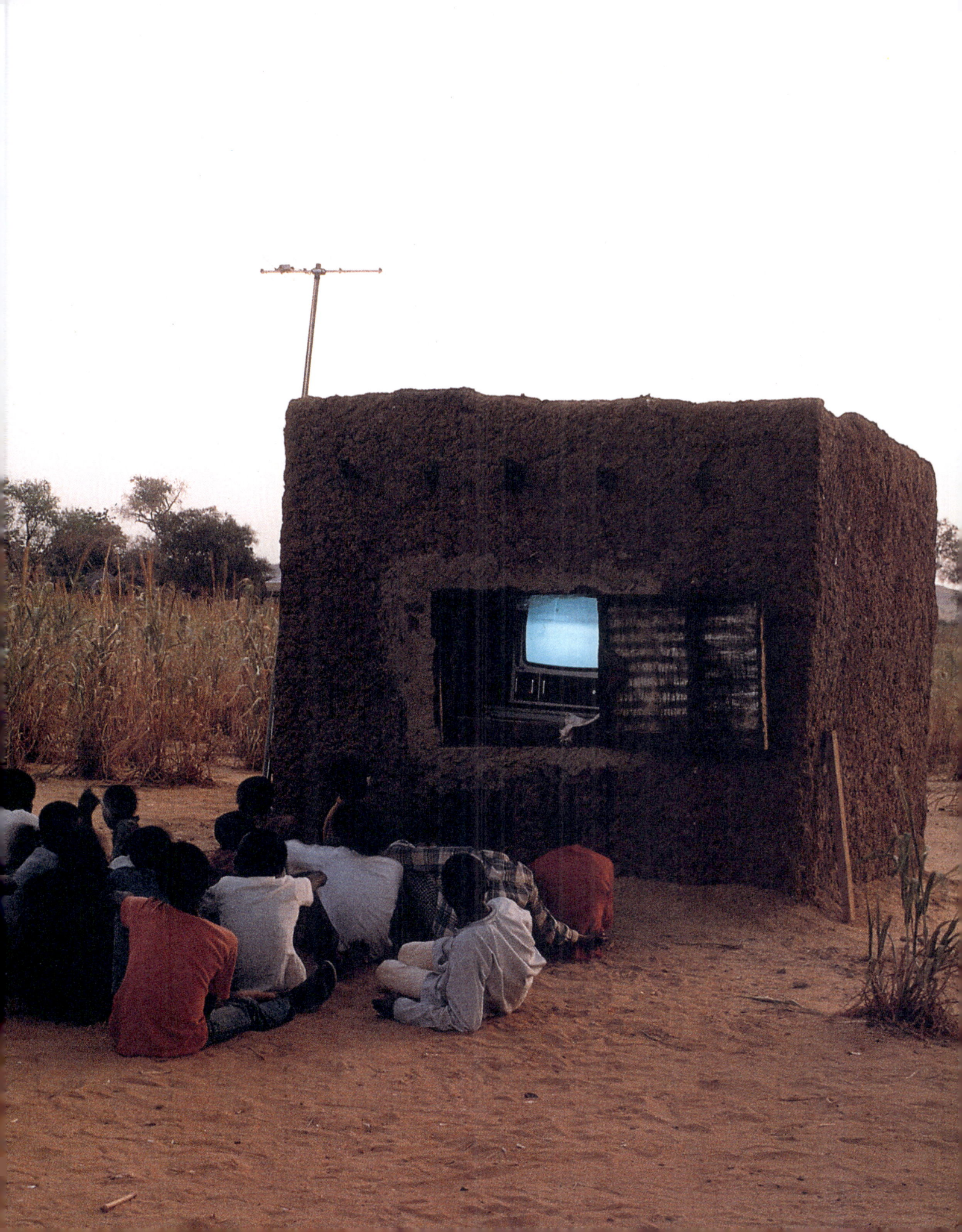

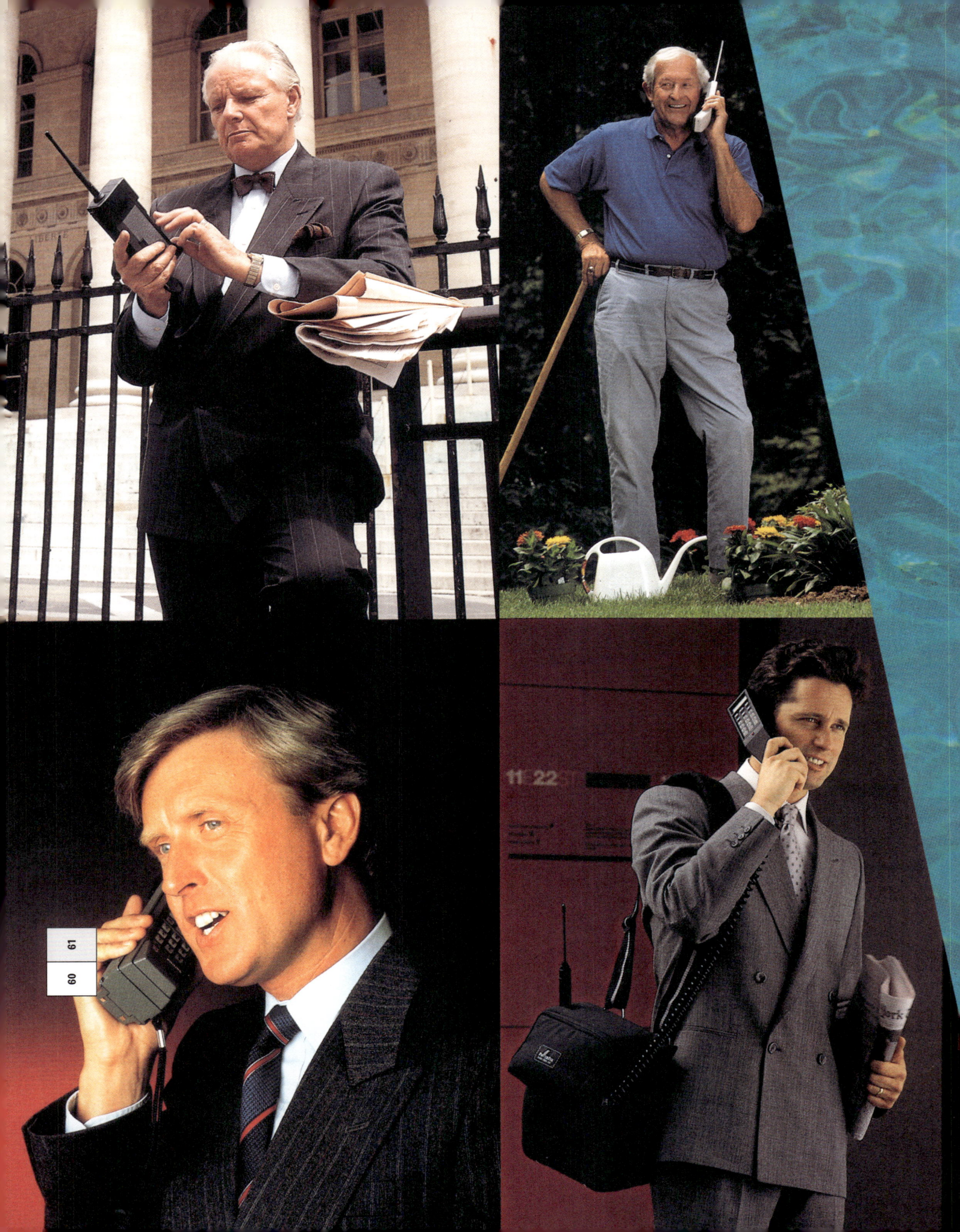

61
60

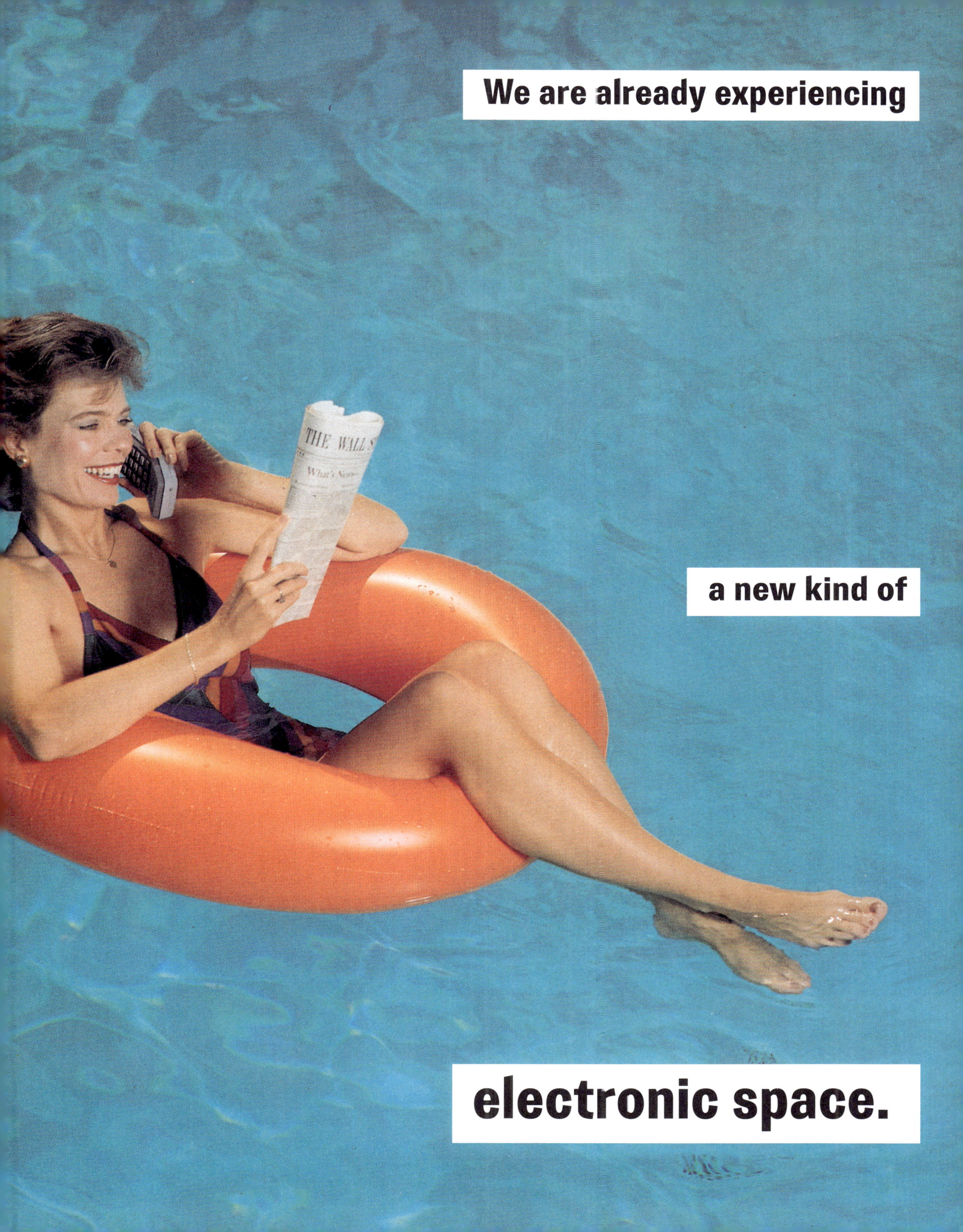

We are already experiencing

a new kind of

electronic space.

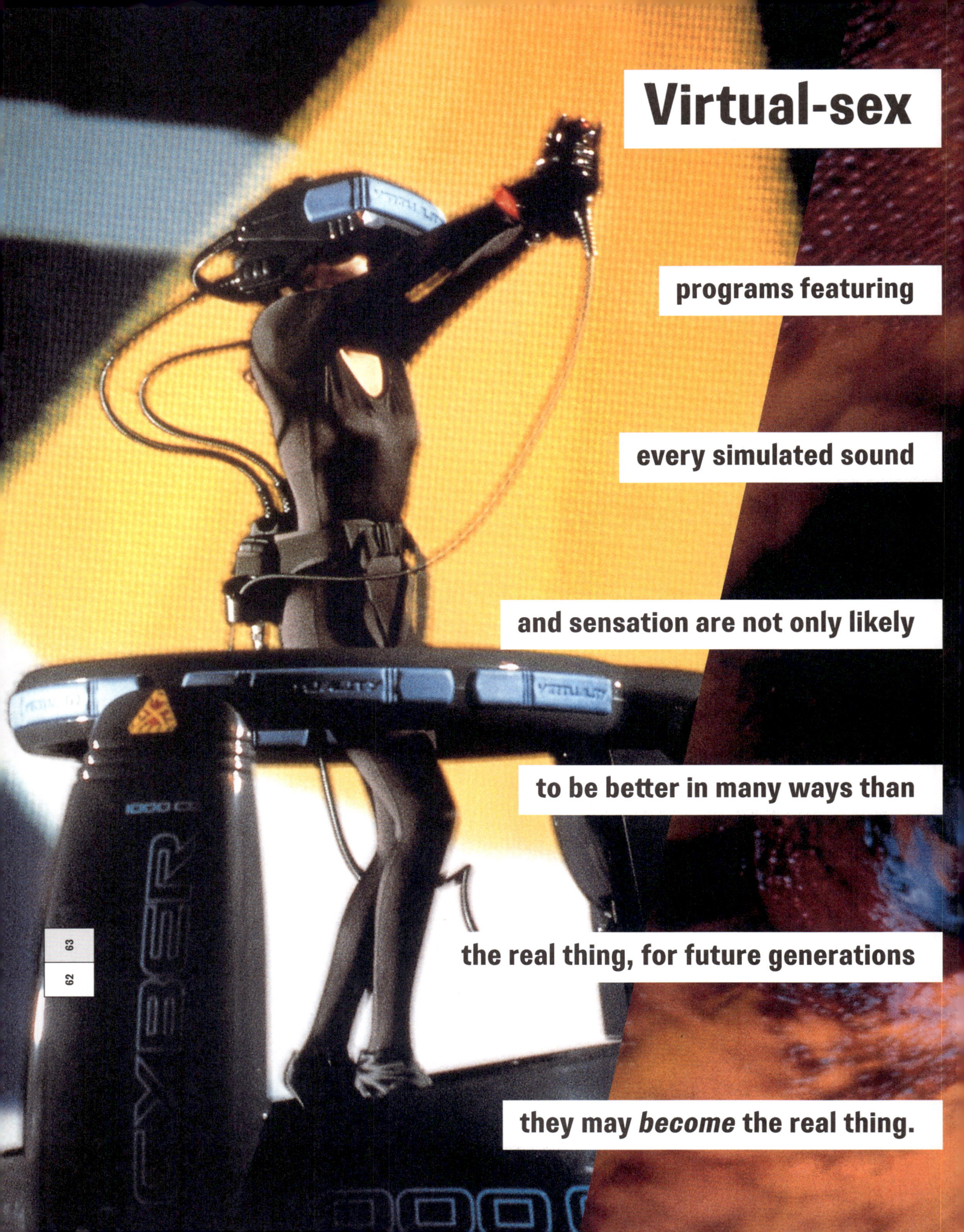

Virtual-sex

programs featuring

every simulated sound

and sensation are not only likely

to be better in many ways than

the real thing, for future generations

they may *become* the real thing.

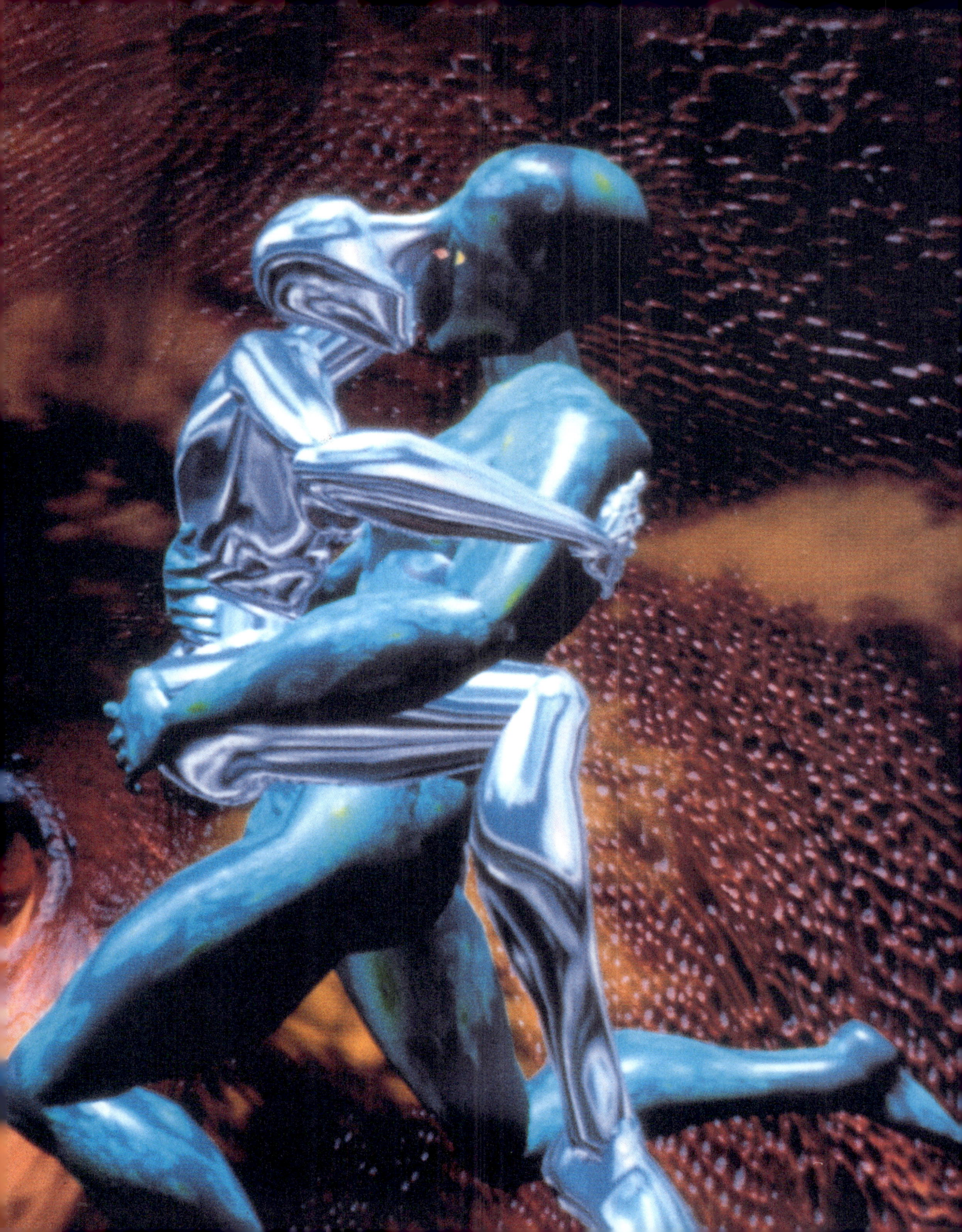

1. The Humanist

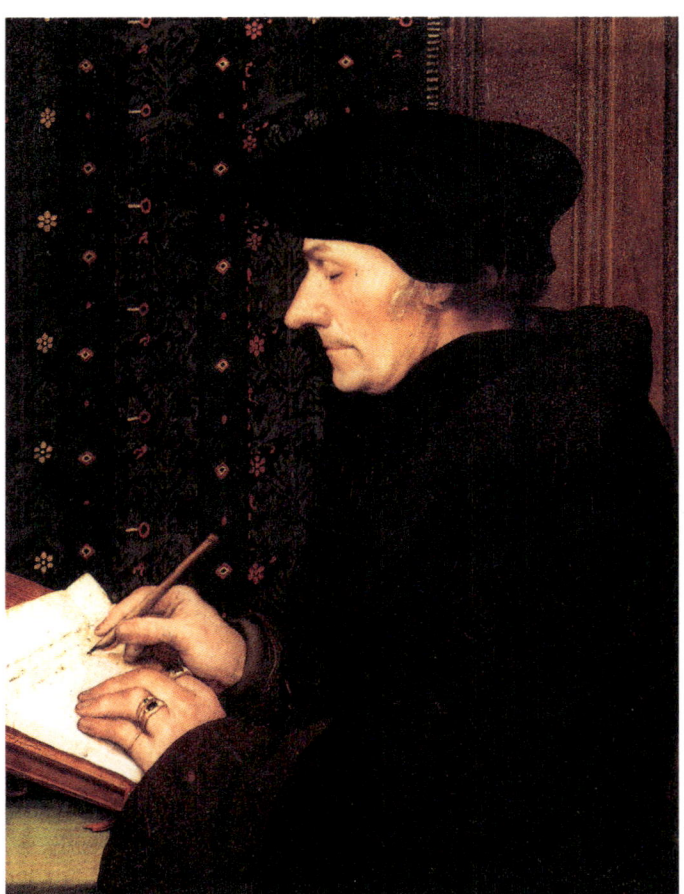

2. "I think therefore I am"

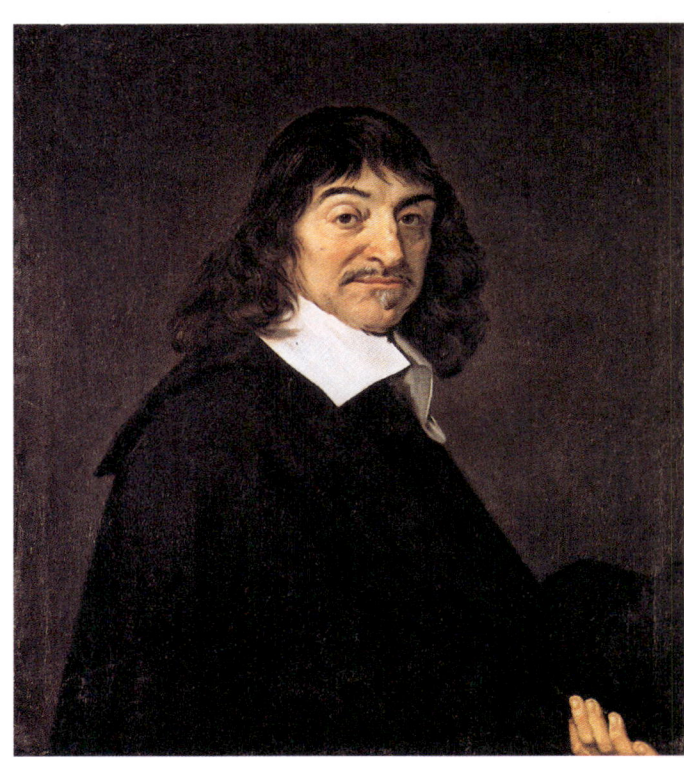

3. The Enlightenment Man

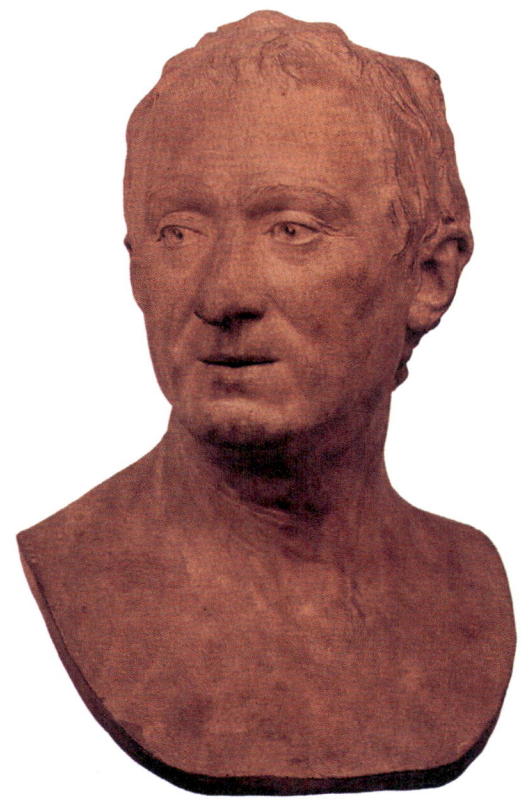

4. The Bourgeois

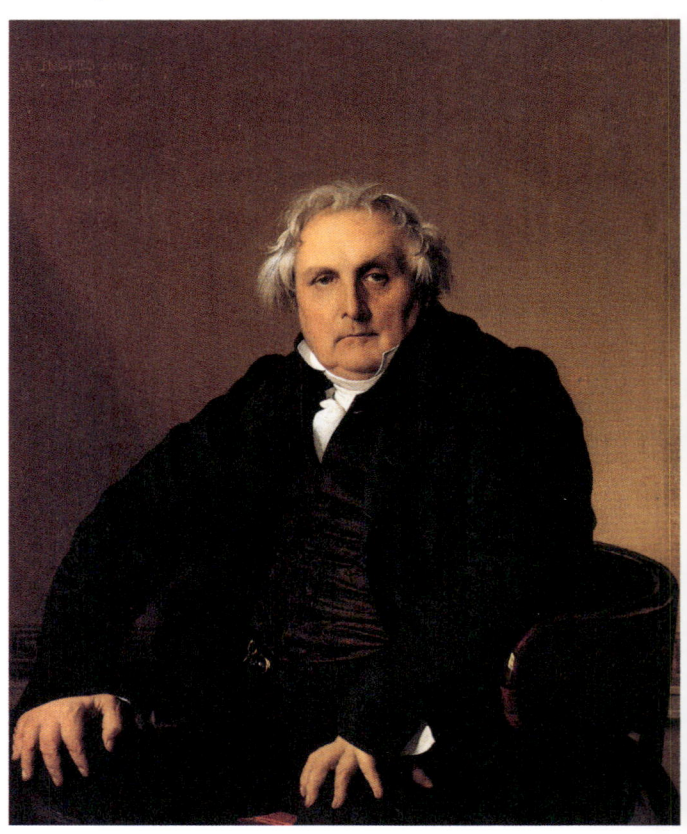

65

64

Art History Personality Timeline (1523-1970)

5. The Tortured Romantic

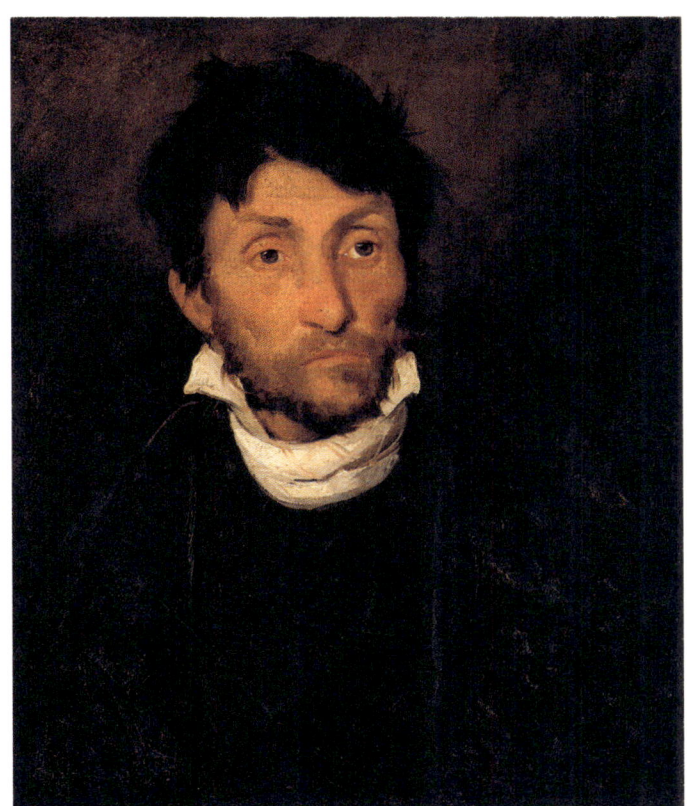

6. The Modern Woman

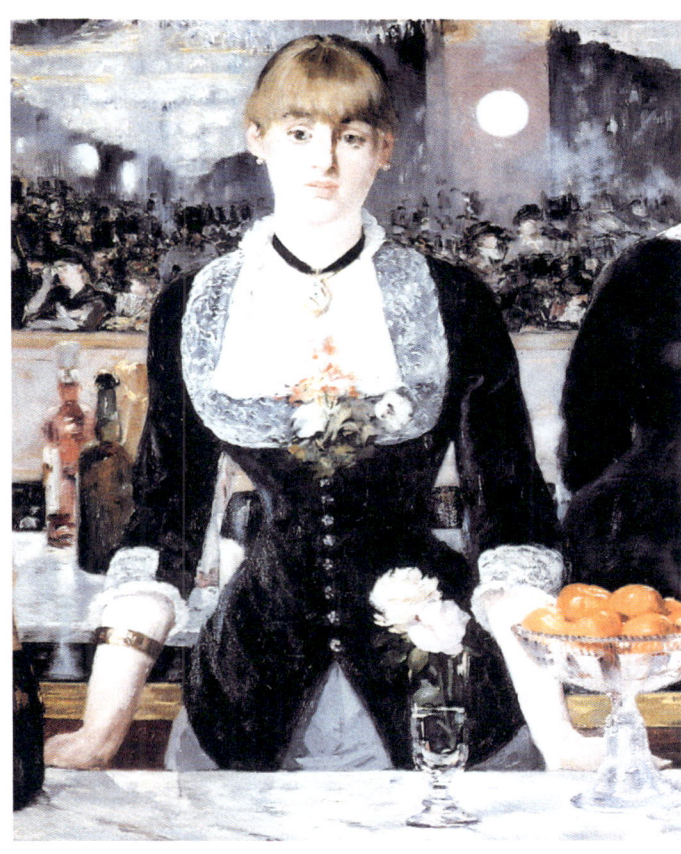

7. Angst

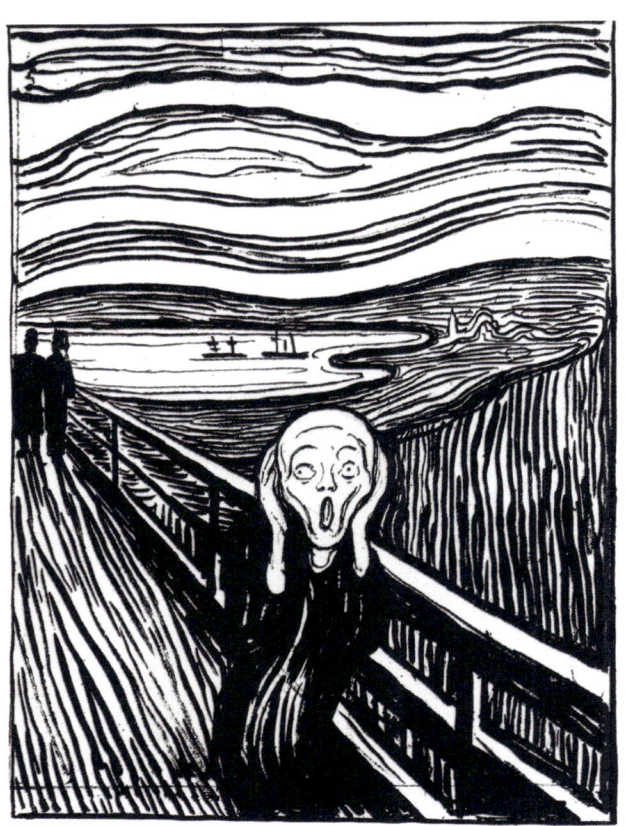

8. The Cubist Man

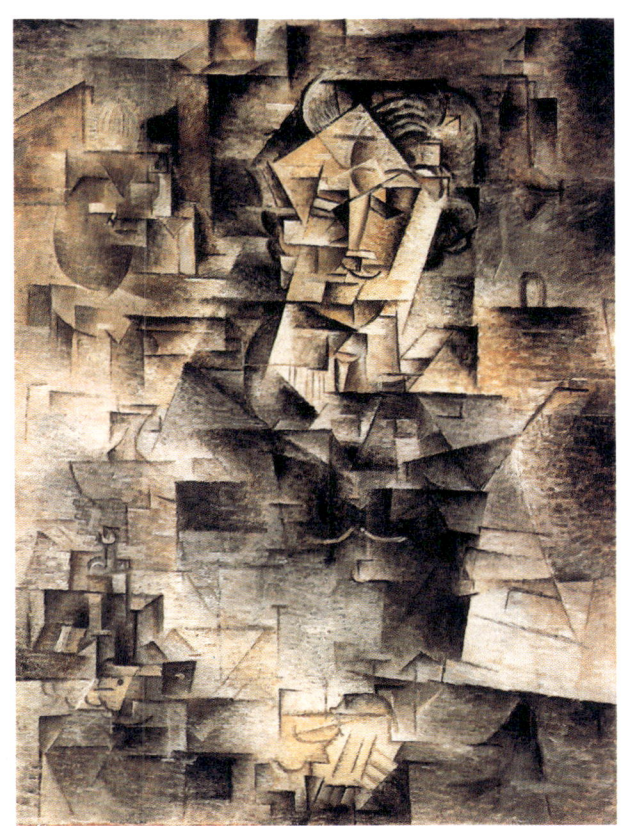

9. The Psychological Man

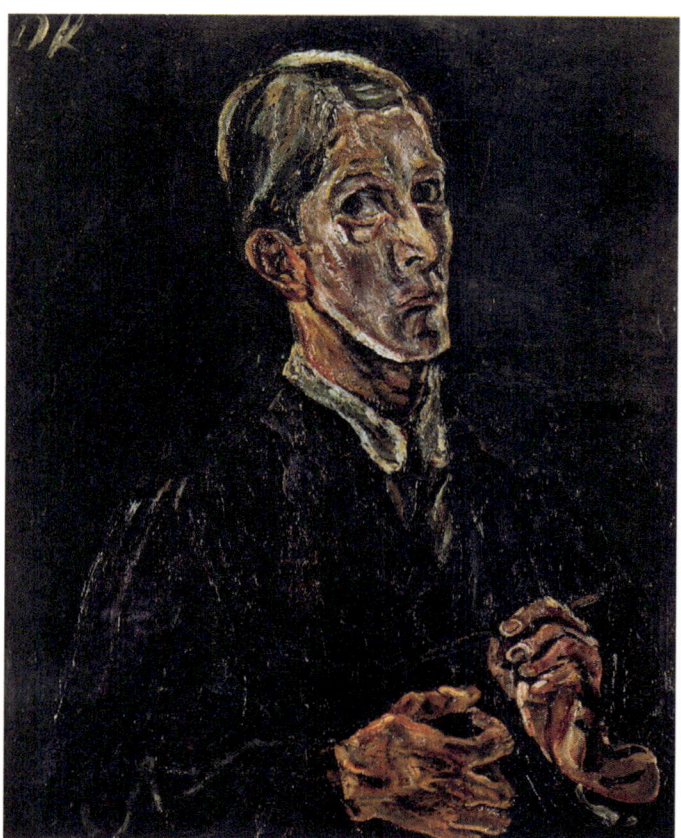

10. The Dadaist

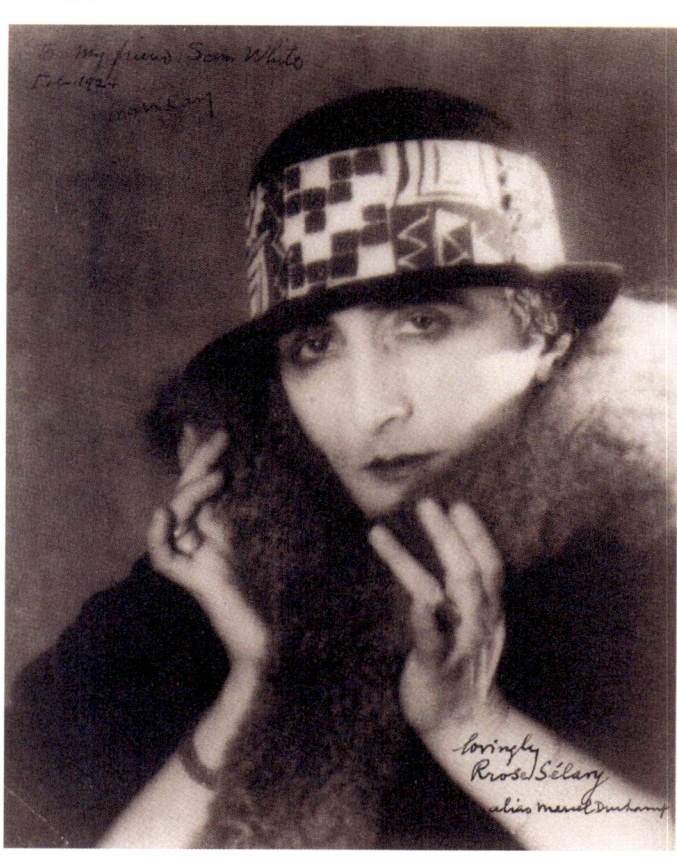

11. Her Own Woman

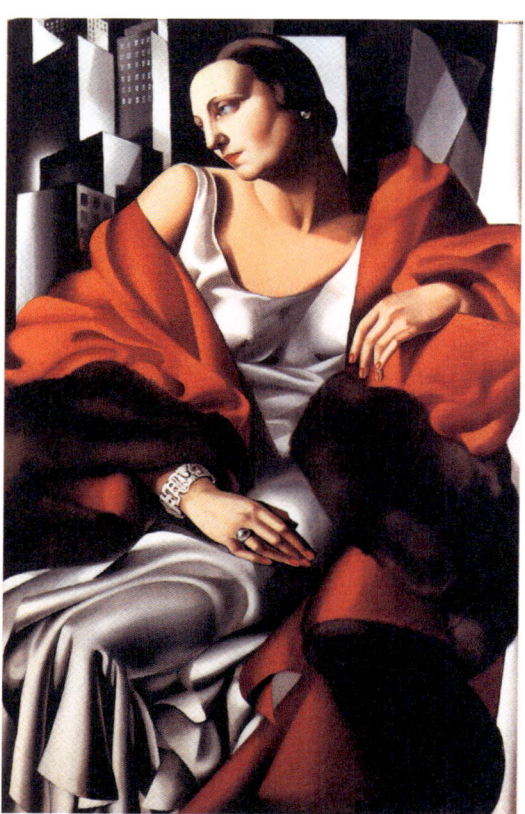

12. The Existentialist

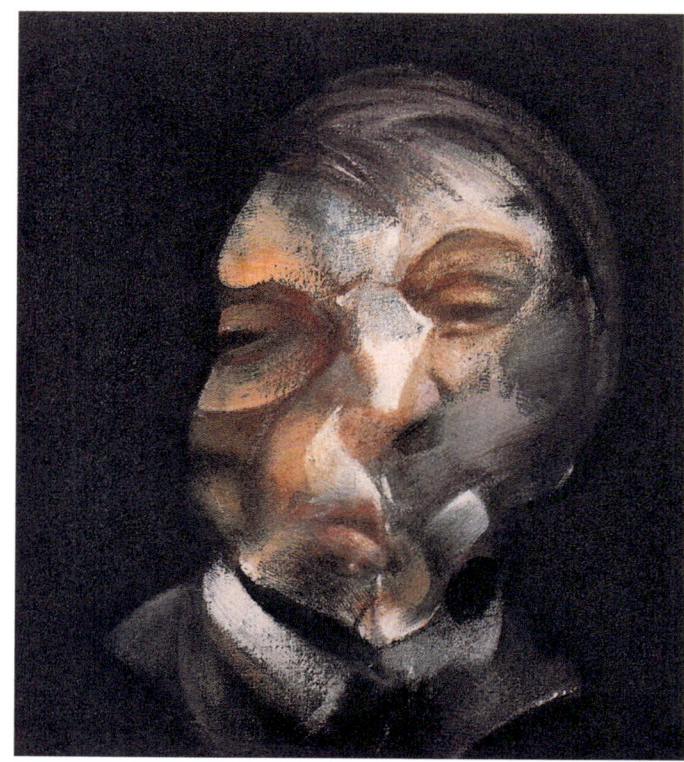

Art History Personality Timeline (1523-1970)

13. The "It" Person

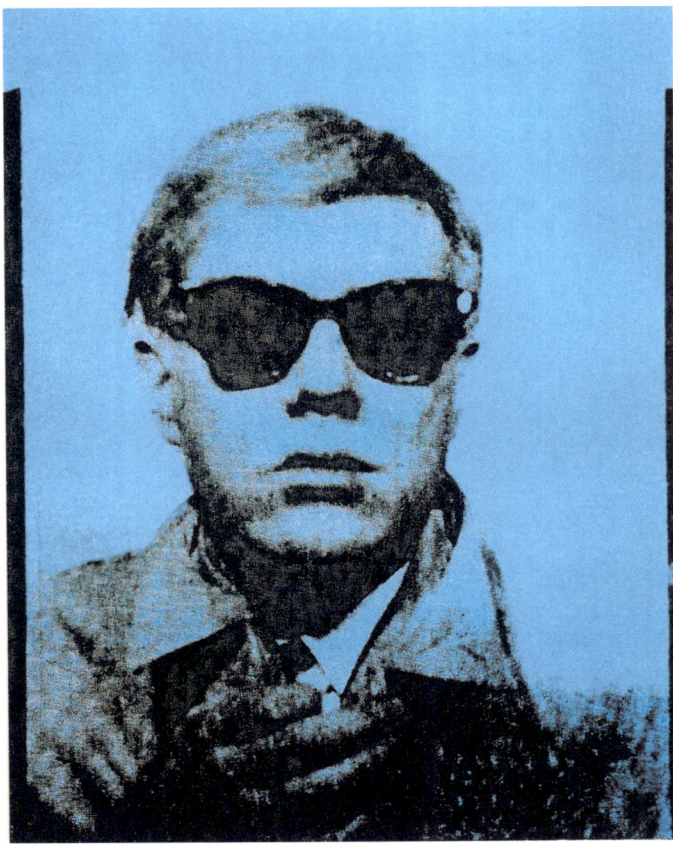

14. Radicality

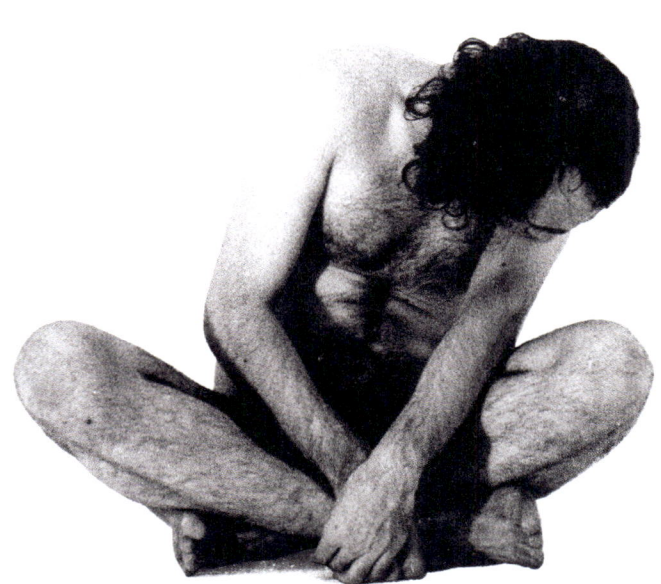

1.
Hans Holbein the Younger
Erasmus of Rotterdam writing
(1467–1536)
1528
Oil on wood
16.54 × 12.6 in. (42 × 32 cm)
Musée du Louvre/Paris/France
©RMN-Grand Palais/Art Resource, NY

2.
Frans Hals
Portrait of René Descartes (1596–1650)
c. 1625–1650
Oil on canvas
30.51 × 26.97 in. (77.5 × 68.5 cm)
Musée du Louvre/Paris/France
©RMN-Grand Palais/Art Resource, NY

3.
Jean-Antoine Houdon
Denis Diderot
1771
Terracotta on wood base
20.47 × 10.59 × 8.66 in.
(52 × 26.9 × 22 cm)
Musée du Louvre/Paris/France
©RMN-Grand Palais/Art Resource, NY

4.
Jean Auguste Dominique Ingres
Portrait of Louis-Francois de Bertin,
called Bertin the Elder (1780–1867)
1832
Oil on canvas
45.67 × 37.4 in. (116 × 95 cm)
Musée du Louvre/Paris/France
©RMN-Grand Palais/Art Resource, NY

5.
Théodore Géricault
Portrait of a Kleptomaniac
ca. 1820–24
Oil on canvas
24.09 × 20.12 in. (61.2 × 51.1 cm)
Museum of Fine Arts Ghent
The Friends of the Museum Ghent, 1908

6.
Édouard Manet
A Bar at the Folies-Bergère
1882
Oil on canvas
37.8 × 51.18 in. (96 × 130 cm)
The Courtauld, London (Samuel
Courtauld Trust)
Photo ©The Courtauld/Bridgeman Images

7.
Edvard Munch
The Scream
1895
Lithograph
Lithograph: 13.94 × 10 in.
(35.4 × 25.4 cm)
Sheet: 20.67 × 15.87 in. (52.5 × 40.3 cm)
©The Museum of Modern Art/Licensed by
SCALA/Art Resource, NY

8.
Pablo Picasso
Daniel-Henry Kahnweiler
1910
Oil on canvas
39.53 × 28.5 in. (100.4 × 72.4 cm)
©2025 Estate of Pablo Picasso/Artists
Rights Society (ARS), New York

9.
Oskar Kokoschka
Self-Portrait with Brush
1914
Oil on canvas
32.4 × 25.98 in. (82.3 × 66 cm)
©2025 Fondation Oskar Kokoschka/
Artists Rights Society (ARS), New York/
ProLitteris, Zürich

10.
Man Ray
Marcel Duchamp as Rrose Sélavy
ca. 1920–21
Gelatin silver print
Image and sheet: 8.50 × 6.81 in.
(21.6 × 17.3 cm)
The Philadelphia Museum of Art
©Man Ray 2015 Trust/Artists Rights
Society (ARS), NY/ADAGP, Paris 2025

11.
Tamara de Lempicka
Portrait of Madame Boucard
1931
Oil on canvas
53.15 × 29.53 in. (135 × 75 cm)
©2025 Tamara de Lempicka Estate, LLC/
ADAGP, Paris/Artists Rights Society
(ARS), NY

12.
Francis Bacon
Self Portrait
1971
Oil on canvas
13.19 × 12.01 in. (33.5 × 30.5 cm)
Centre Pompidou-Musée national d'art
moderne
©The Estate of Francis Bacon/DACS,
London/Artists Rights Society (ARS), NY

13.
Andy Warhol
Self-Portrait
1964
Synthetic polymer silkscreened on
canvas
20.08 × 16.14 in. (51 × 41 cm)
©2025 The Andy Warhol Foundation for
the Visual Arts, Inc./Licensed by Artists
Rights Society (ARS), New York

14.
Vito Acconci
Trademarks
1970
Performance photograph
New York
Courtesy of Barbara Gladstone Gallery,
New York
©Vito Acconci/Artists Rights Society
(ARS), New York, courtesy Maria Acconci

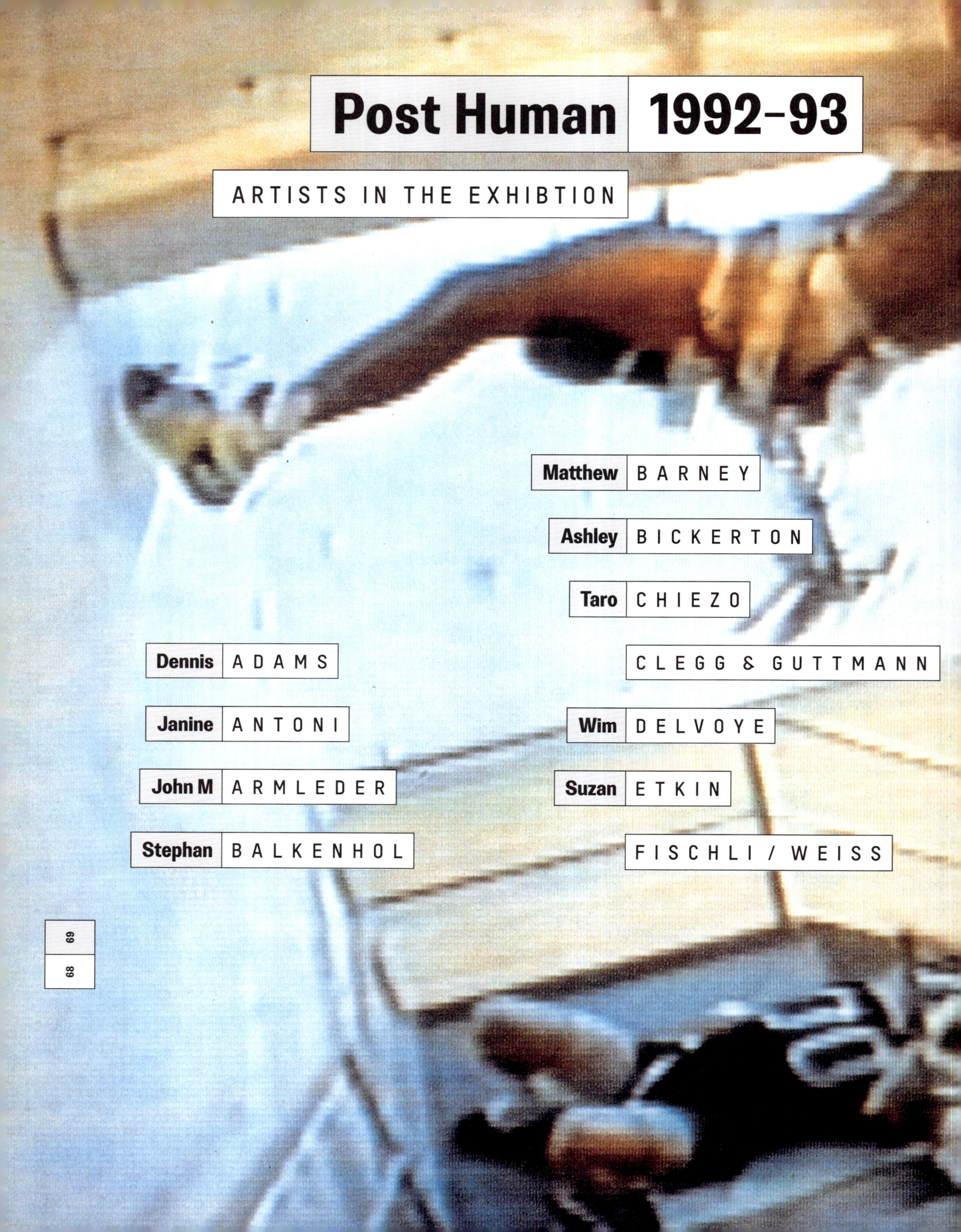

Post Human | 1992-93

ARTISTS IN THE EXHIBTION

Matthew B A R N E Y

Ashley B I C K E R T O N

Taro C H I E Z O

C L E G G & G U T T M A N N

Dennis A D A M S

Janine A N T O N I

Wim D E L V O Y E

John M A R M L E D E R

Suzan E T K I N

Stephan B A L K E N H O L

F I S C H L I / W E I S S

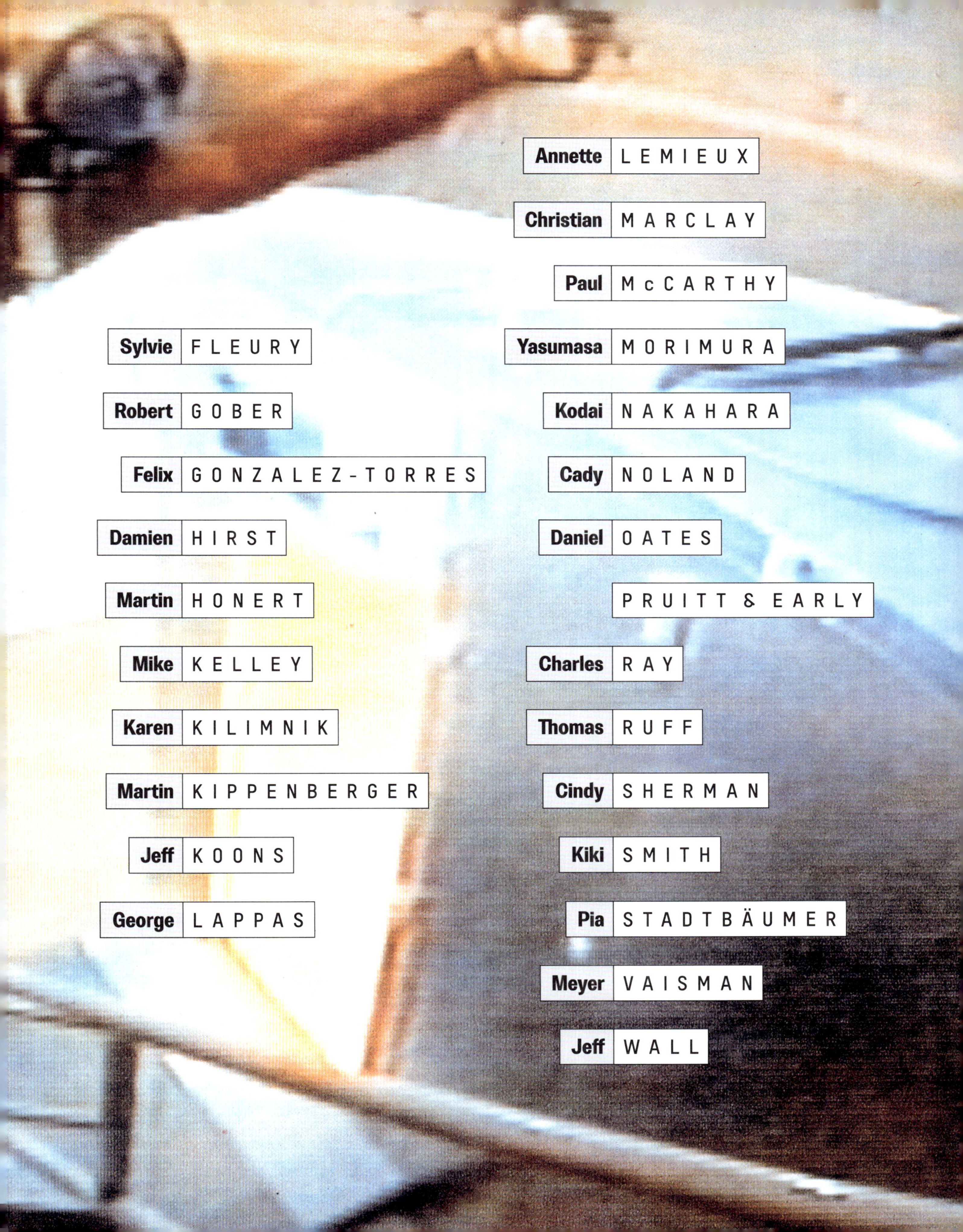

Annette L E M I E U X

Christian M A R C L A Y

Paul M c C A R T H Y

Sylvie F L E U R Y

Yasumasa M O R I M U R A

Robert G O B E R

Kodai N A K A H A R A

Felix G O N Z A L E Z - T O R R E S

Cady N O L A N D

Damien H I R S T

Daniel O A T E S

Martin H O N E R T

P R U I T T & E A R L Y

Mike K E L L E Y

Charles R A Y

Karen K I L I M N I K

Thomas R U F F

Martin K I P P E N B E R G E R

Cindy S H E R M A N

Jeff K O O N S

Kiki S M I T H

George L A P P A S

Pia S T A D T B Ä U M E R

Meyer V A I S M A N

Jeff W A L L

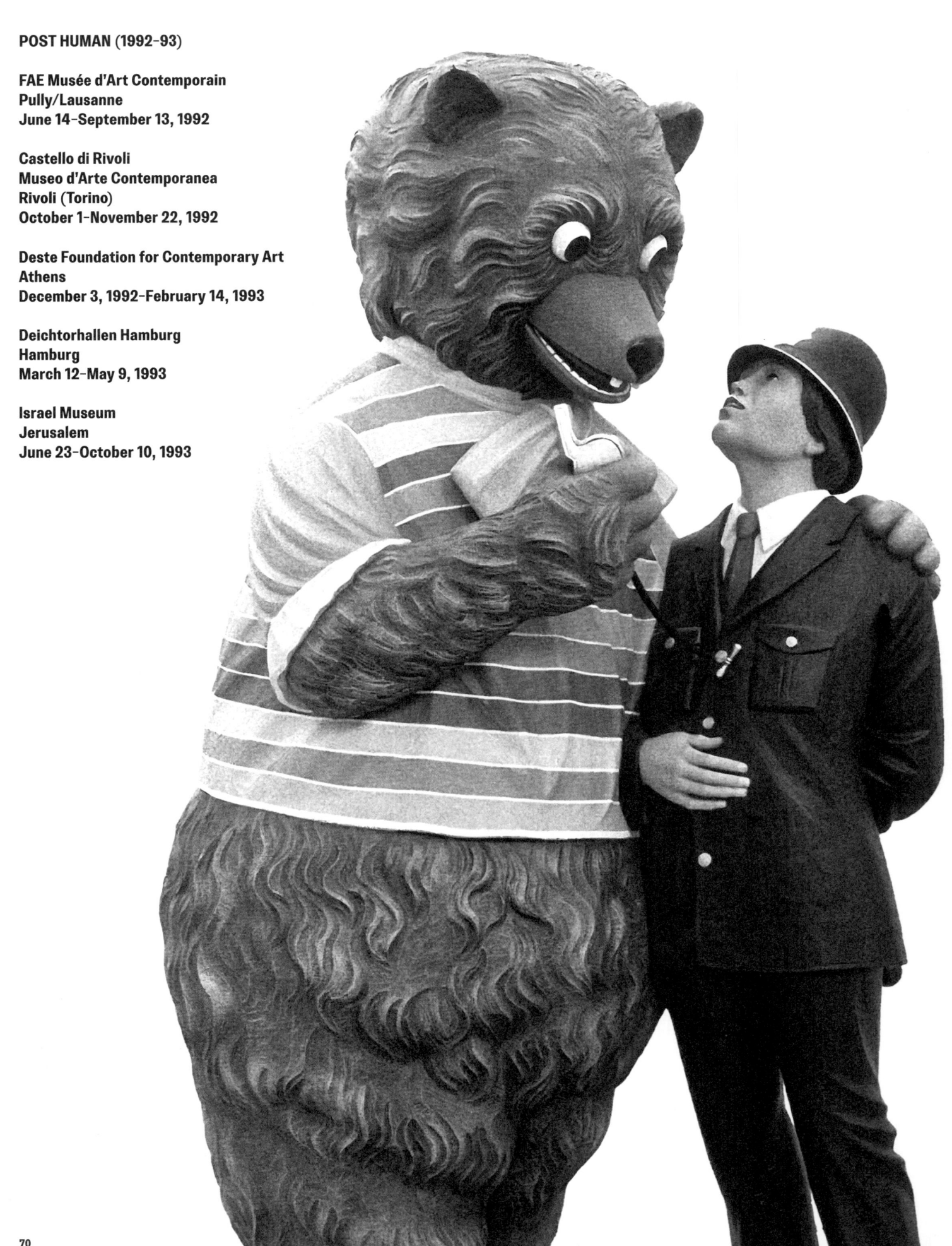

POST HUMAN (1992–93)

FAE Musée d'Art Contemporain
Pully/Lausanne
June 14–September 13, 1992

Castello di Rivoli
Museo d'Arte Contemporanea
Rivoli (Torino)
October 1–November 22, 1992

Deste Foundation for Contemporary Art
Athens
December 3, 1992–February 14, 1993

Deichtorhallen Hamburg
Hamburg
March 12–May 9, 1993

Israel Museum
Jerusalem
June 23–October 10, 1993

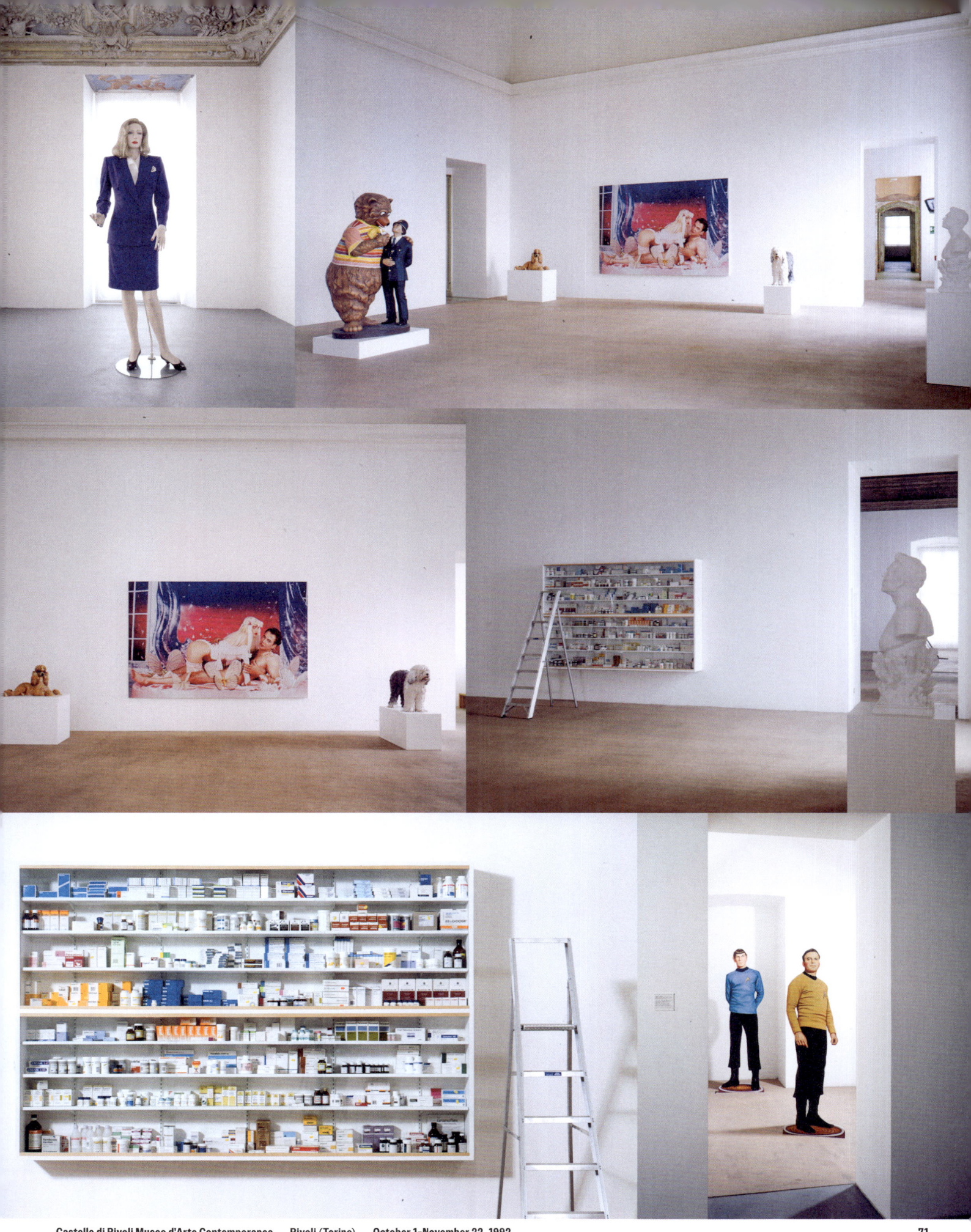

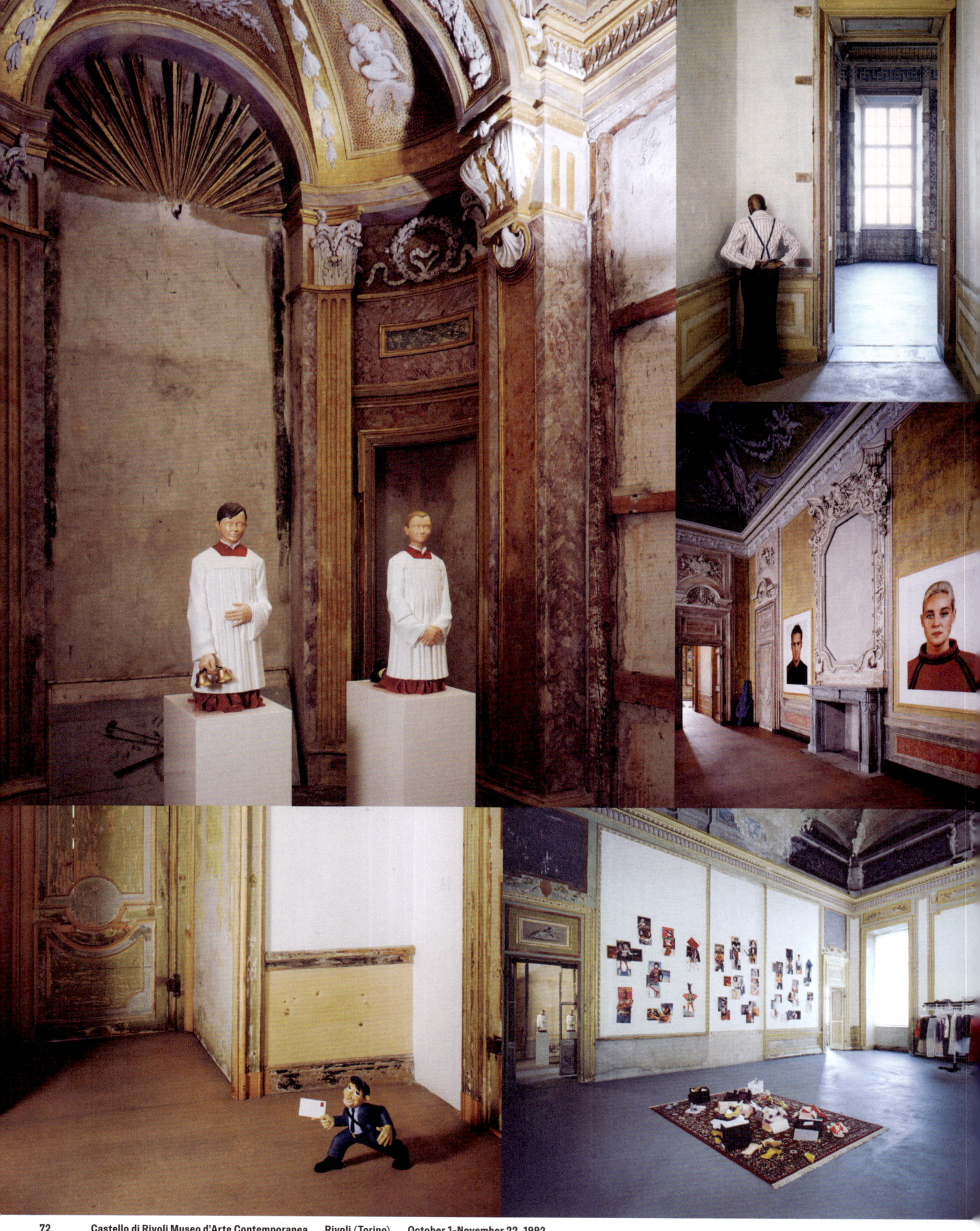

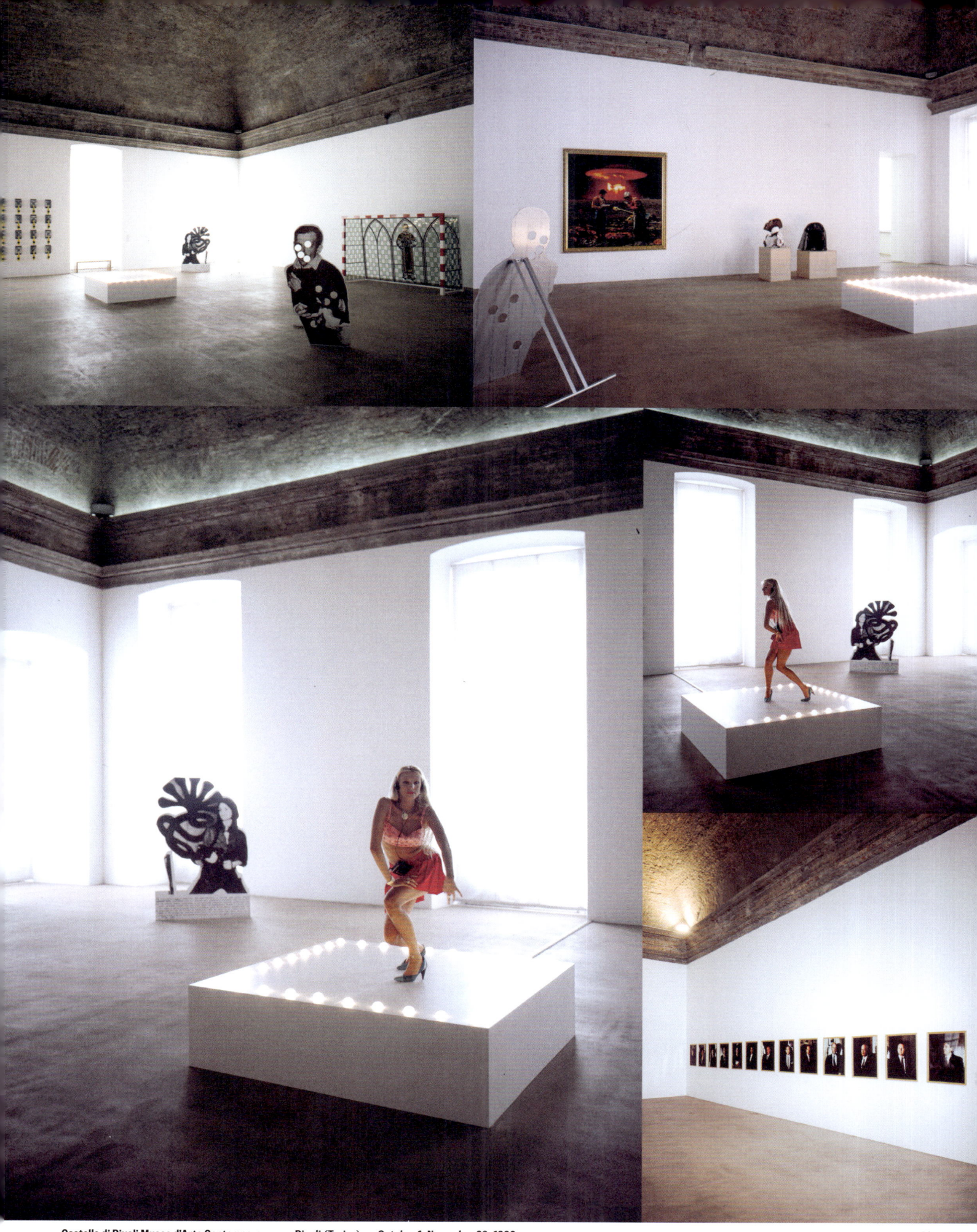

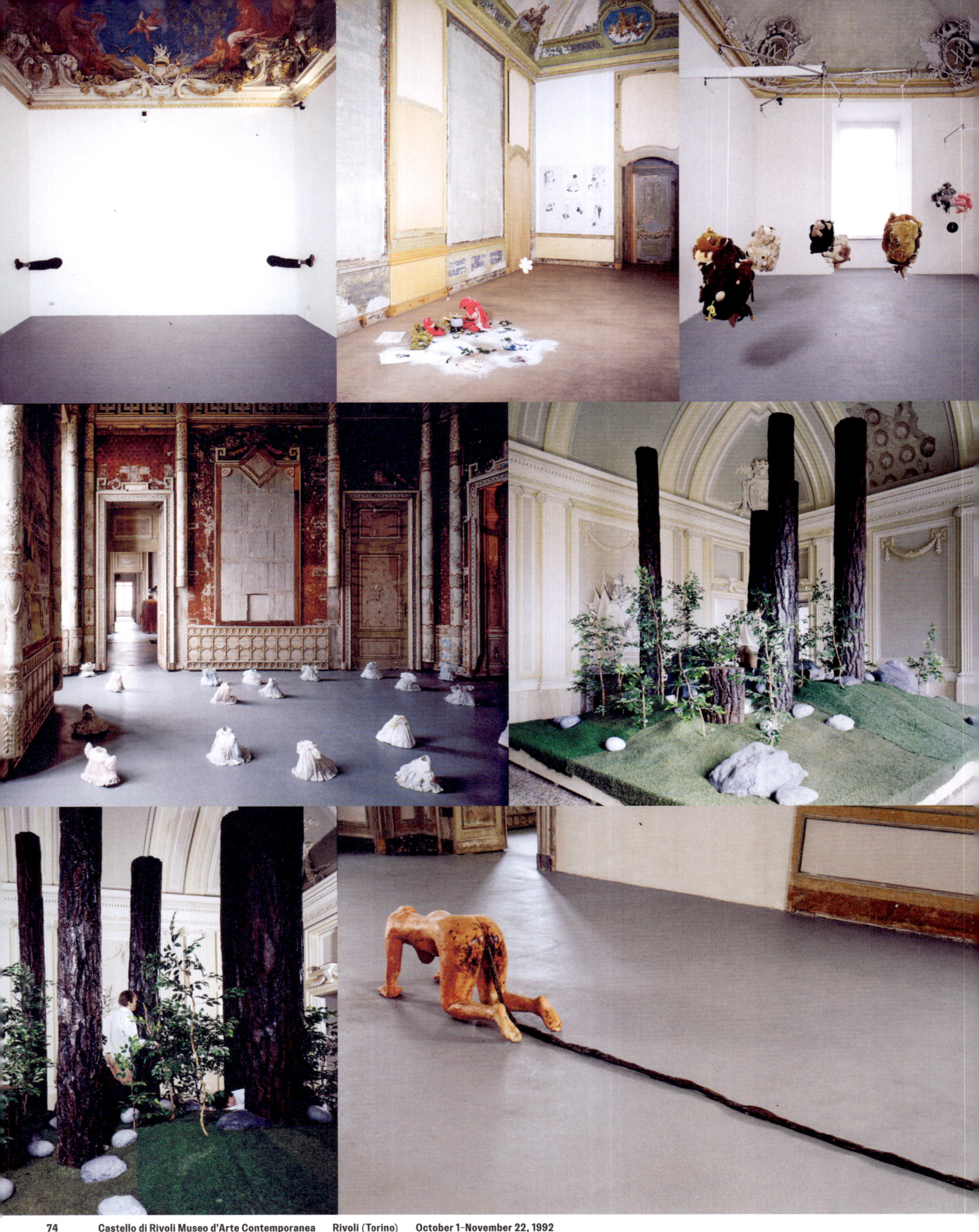

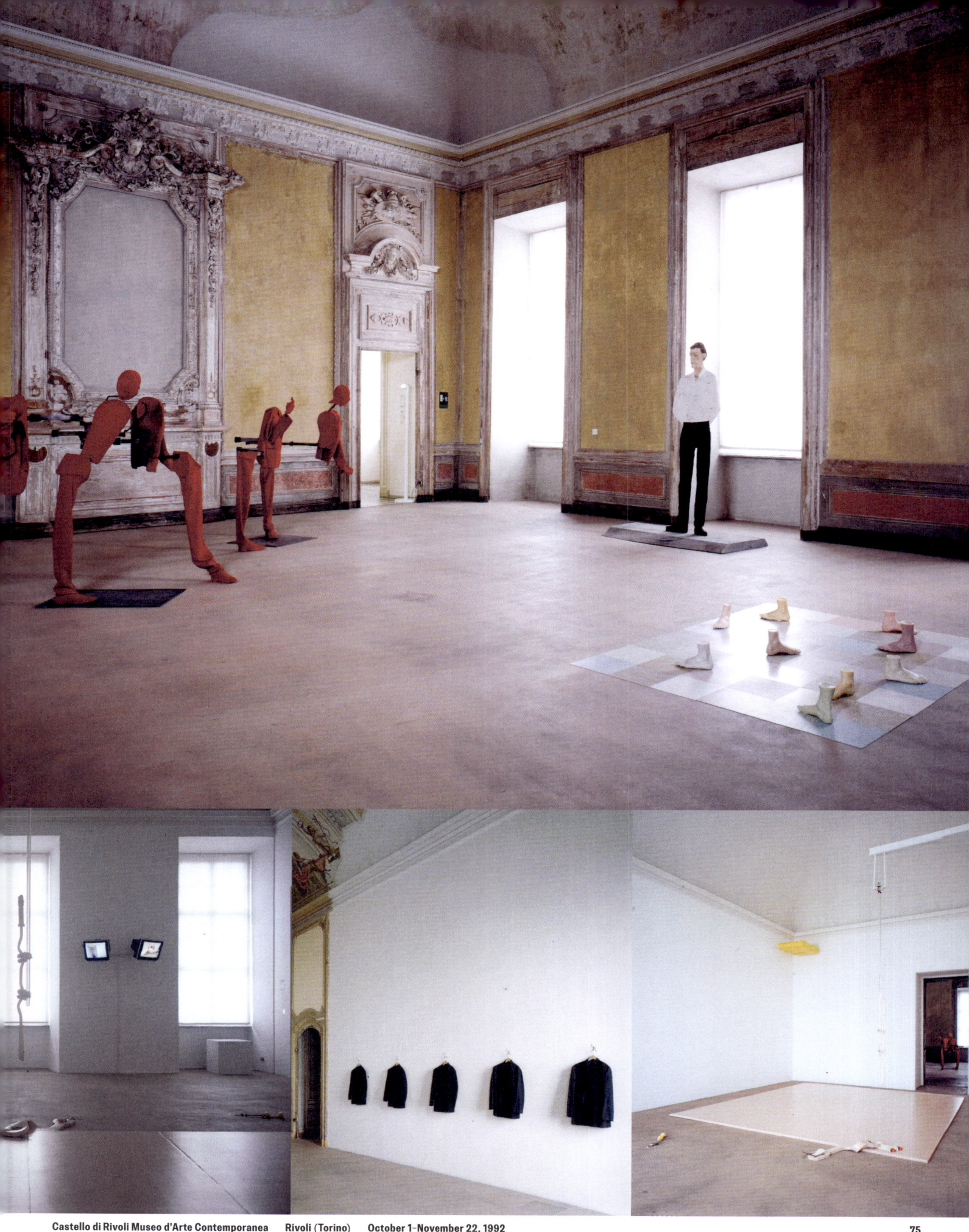

Castello di Rivoli Museo d'Arte Contemporanea   Rivoli (Torino)   October 1–November 22, 1992

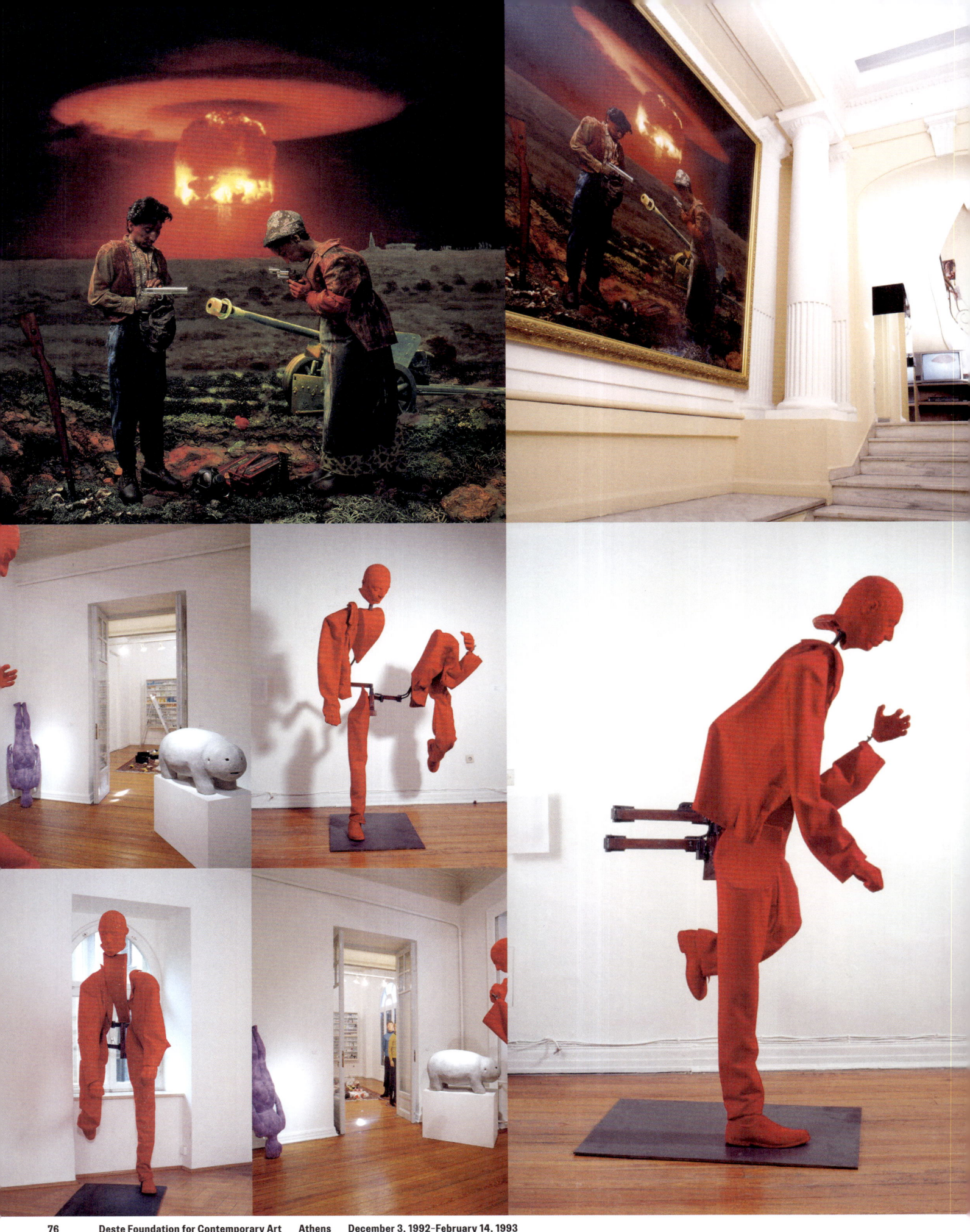

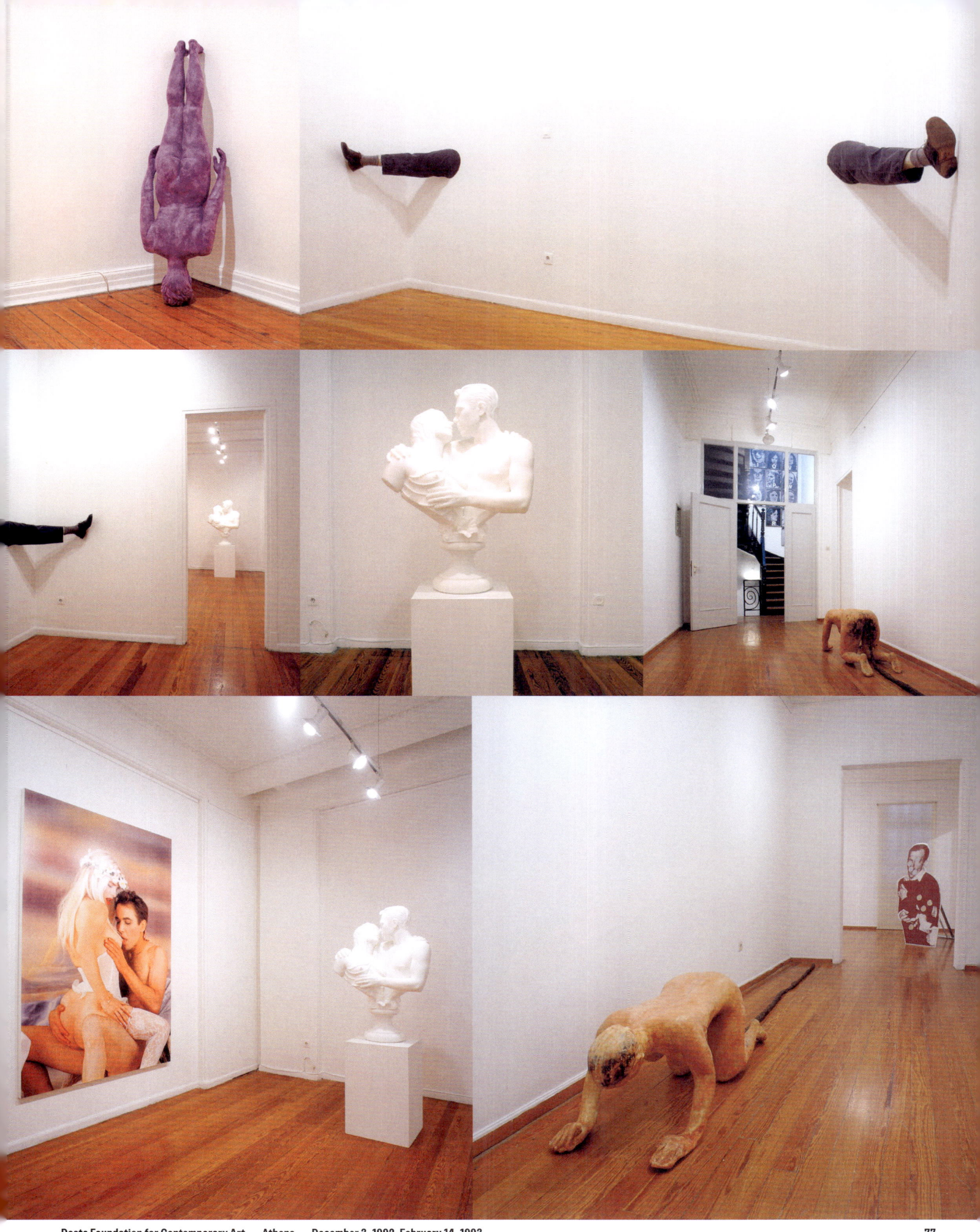

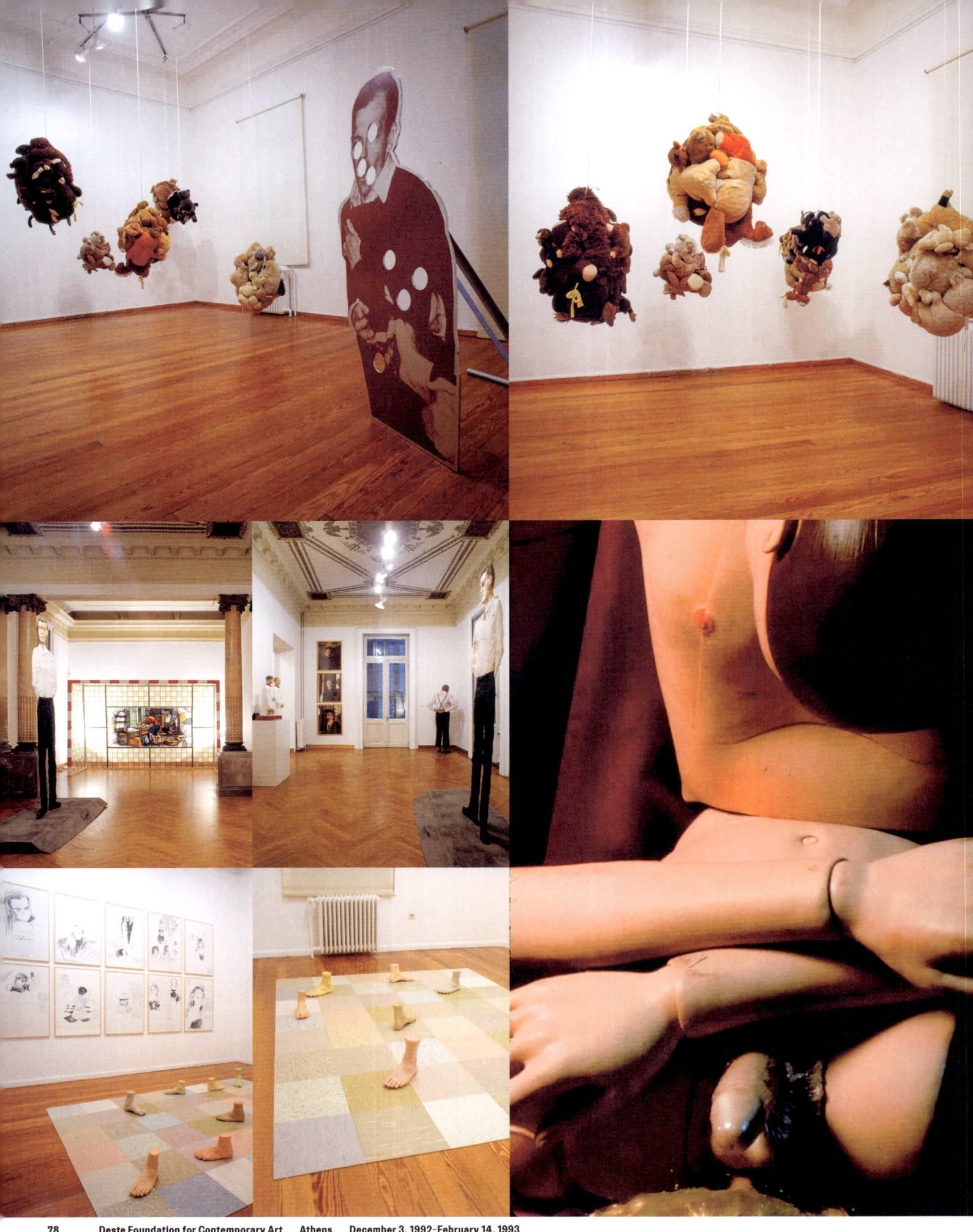

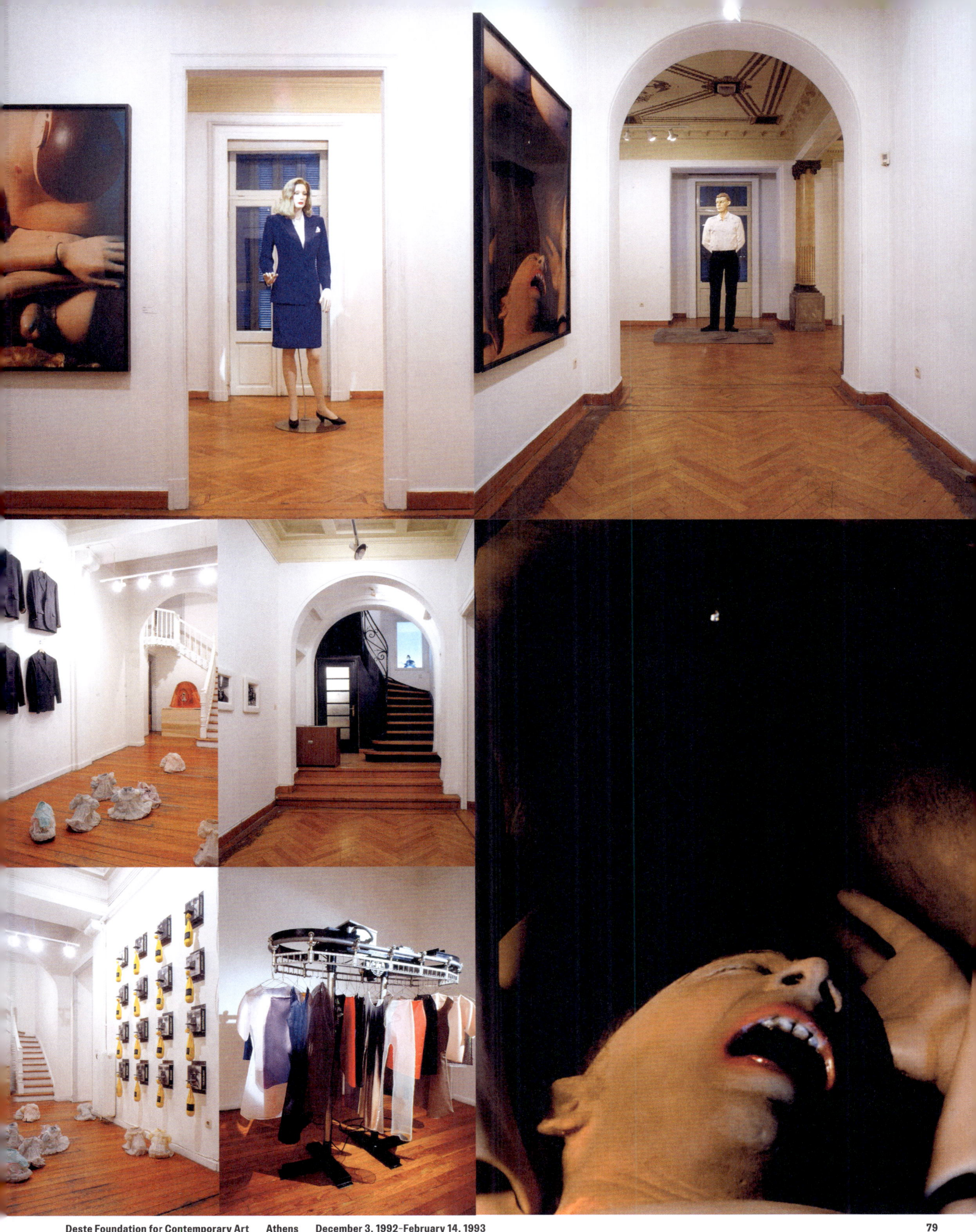

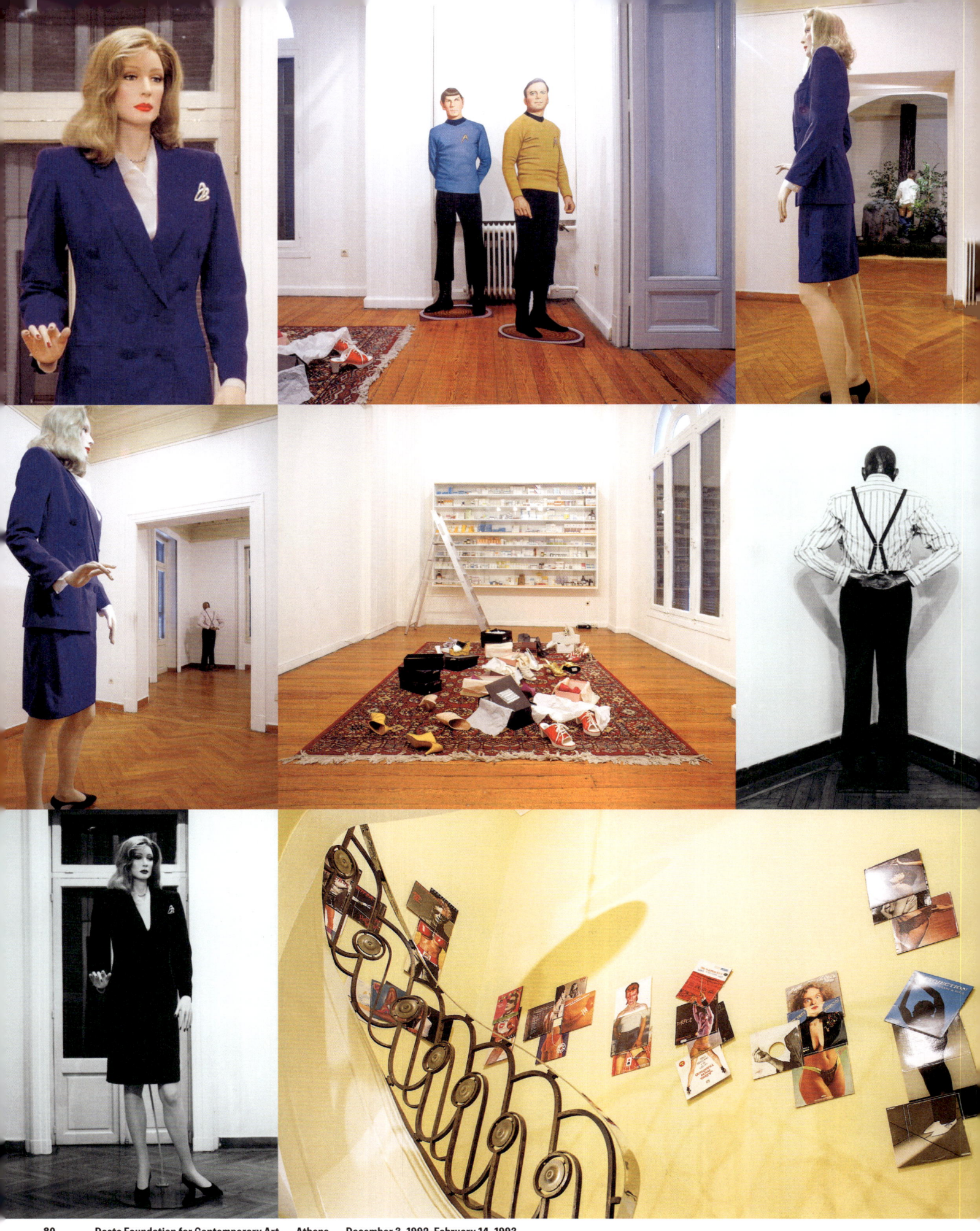

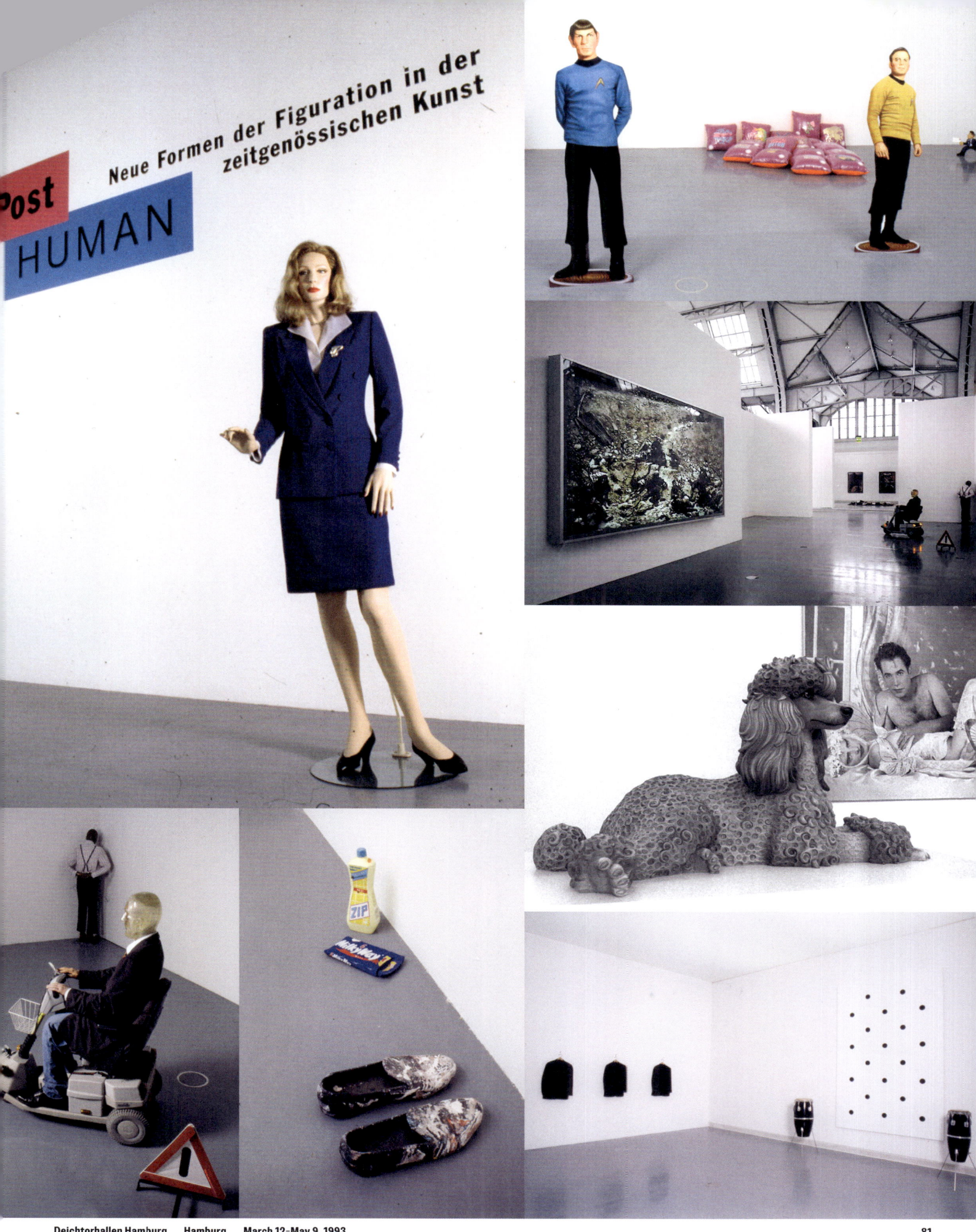

Post HUMAN

Neue Formen der Figuration in der zeitgenössischen Kunst

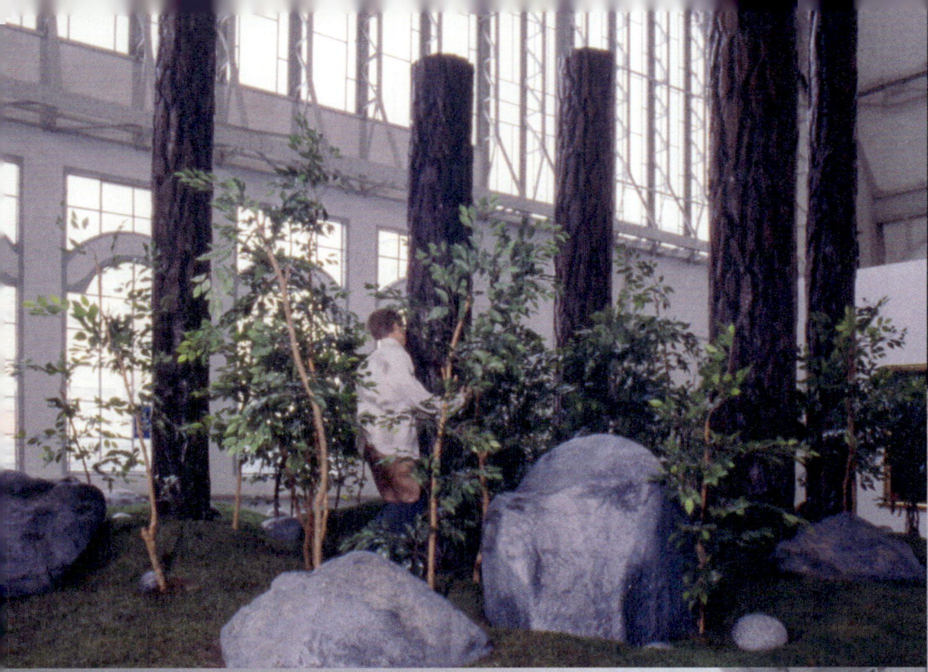

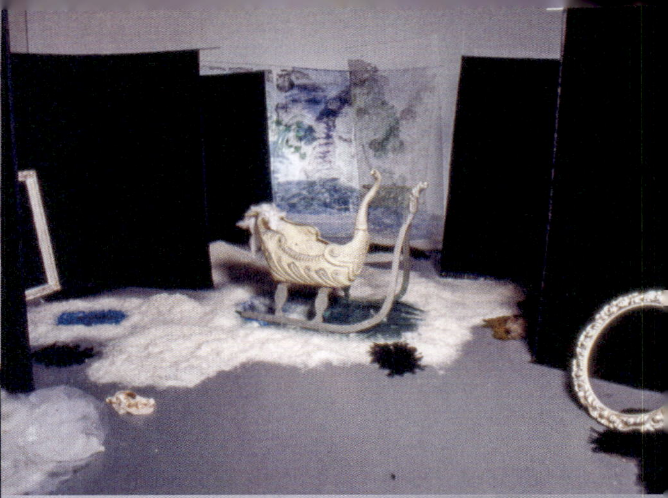

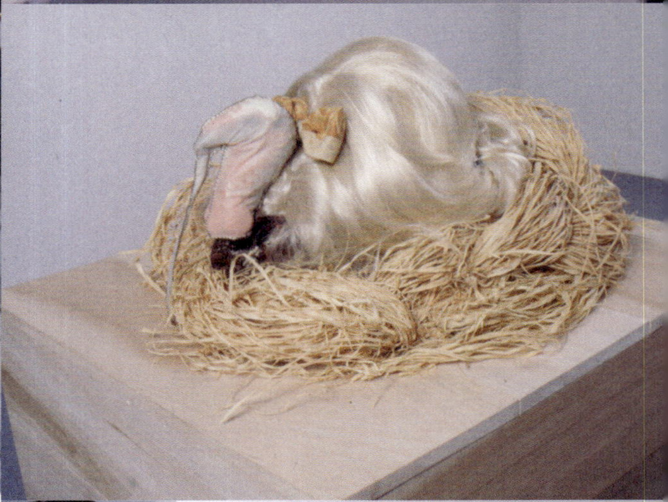

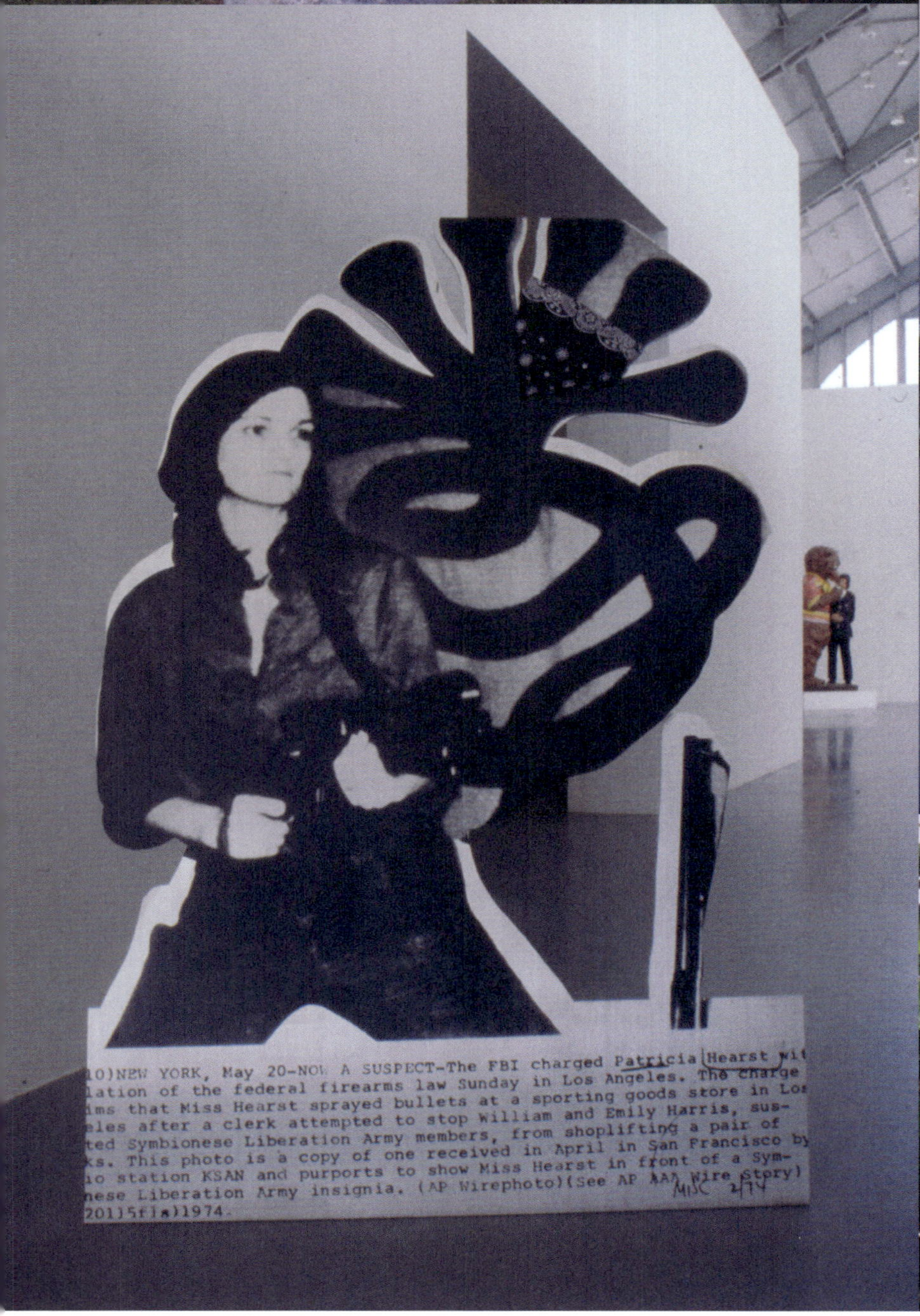
0)NEW YORK, May 20-NOW A SUSPECT-The FBI charged Patricia Hearst wi
lation of the federal firearms law Sunday in Los Angeles. The charge
ims that Miss Hearst sprayed bullets at a sporting goods store in Los
eles after a clerk attempted to stop William and Emily Harris, sus-
ted Symbionese Liberation Army members, from shoplifting a pair of
ks. This photo is a copy of one received in April in San Francisco by
io station KSAN and purports to show Miss Hearst in front of a Sym-
nese Liberation Army insignia. (AP Wirephoto)(See AP AAA Wire Story)
201)5fla)1974.
MISC 2/74

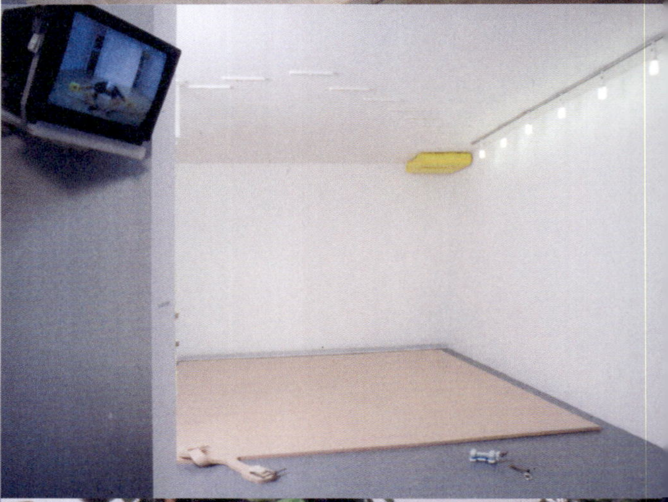

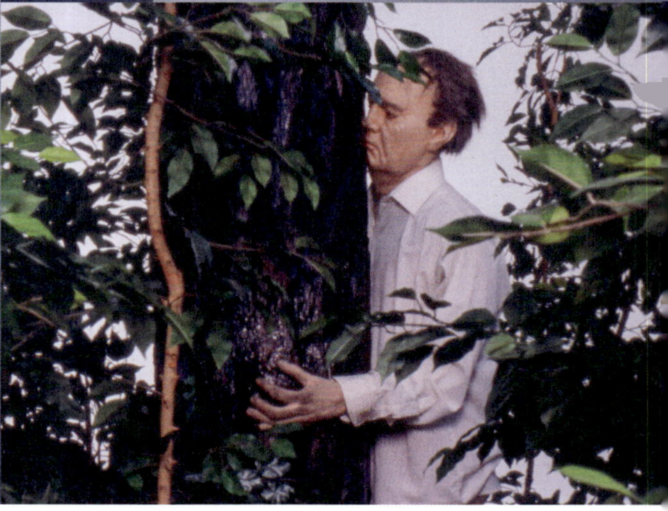

Posthuman Time Capsules   Rosi Braidotti

It is an honor to comment on this new edition of a text that has had a lasting impact on my own thinking. The watershed 1992 art exhibition *Post Human*, curated by Jeffrey Deitch, is a time capsule that captured perfectly the spirit of its moment, but also moved well beyond it, sensing a major transformation to come. That transformation is the posthuman convergence of the digital, environmental, and social factors which have radically altered our subjectivity, culture, and society. The focus on what kind of subjects we are in the process of becoming is what attracted me first to Deitch's work, because that angle is often missing even in cultural studies of technology, let alone in social theories of science and technology. What is at stake in his project is more than an avant-gardist fascination for the disruptions induced by the media and the new technologies, notably the way in which they blur the boundaries between subjects and objects, humans and nonhumans. What the exhibition brings into sharp focus is rather the effects of these disruptions on our embodied selves, namely the extent to which self-improvements and the embrace of artificiality are becoming normal. Plastic surgery, dieting, exercises, mind-altering drugs, and other technology-driven practices were already then starting to enhance humans beyond their natural state. And the contradictions surrounding the female body and becoming-woman were at the heart of it all. *Post Human* moreover showed that art and media were assuming a much more vital role as they merged with science, philosophy, computerization, and biotechnology in further reshaping the human form and perfecting it. That was a breakthrough moment.

The message is clear: the pleasures of the inorganic have become second nature, producing a deeper intimacy with technological artifacts. Although a flair for the artificial—simulacrum, hyperreal, impersonal, and pastiche—was the standard repertoire of the postmodern movement, that moment, according to Deitch, described the beginning of a process of transition which led directly into posthuman horizons. The posthuman—contrary to the postmodern—does not stand for cognitive and moral relativism, but points instead to a radical shift in the grounding of contemporary subjectivity—a new ontological phase. This is why it has become so stunningly relevant and pathbreaking today. Postmodernism was only an intermediate state.

The red thread between those two moments is the critique of dualism and the systematic erasure of the boundaries between the (Pythagorean) classical opposites such as male/female, dark or black/white or light, human/nonhuman, rest/motion, one/many, etc. The force that demolishes the partitions between them is the impact of technologies upon the human bodies and psyches, as the postmodern philosopher Jean-François Lyotard also argued. The interrelation between carnal reality—"proud to be flesh"—and virtual or automated reality—"the desire to be wired"—became one of the critical issues at stake in the early 1990s discussions about our highly mediated world. A new vision of the self—as a heterogeneous, in process, nomadic subject—emerged from these conceptual shifts. Whereas the flair for the artificial in postmodernism was a critical and even polemical gesture aimed at undoing the universal claims of classical humanistic standards of truth, beauty, and moral goodness, in the posthuman convergence it became a praxis.

The healthy disregard for the distinction between high and low cultures, initiated by pop art in the 1960s and perfected by postmodernism, is another line of continuity. The postmodern critique of metaphysical foundationalism produced an aesthetic revolution and the rejection of the classical art culture of authenticity. The taste for the inauthentic replaced naturalistic aesthetics. But it also challenged the canons of classical beauty, just as fast-moving technologies collapsed the distinction between real/fake, born/manufactured, and procreated/biotech-engineered entities. The triumph of the hybrid, messy, heterogeneous, and capital-intensive aesthetics culminated in those two masterpieces of naturalized artifice: Dolly Parton and Dolly the sheep.

In the posthuman perspective, calling into question the myths of authenticity and purity and the chain of binary distinctions is just the starting point in processes of subjectivization which involve complex negotiations with social and symbolic systems. Foregrounding the intimate and all-encompassing impact of technology upon our self-understanding resulted moreover in a more impersonal and distributed posthuman sensibility. Deitch is quick in perceiving that such a sensibility is altering the relationship between art, media, and technology and, therefore, that artistic practice does indeed lead the way in experimenting with new forms of mediated subjectivities.

The sexuality of posthuman subjects is geared differently and functions otherwise. The pleasures of the inorganic and the intimacy with the technological world have brought on a reorganization of our sensorial structures and erotic landscapes. A post-psychoanalytic horizon encourages us to explore new unorganized and disorganized, feminist, queer, and trans desiring bodies which negotiate and cope with the challenges of their times. The material carnality of bodies plunges its genetic roots into ancestral animality and the nonhuman elements of our shared humanity. Interconnected informational codes—genetic, genealogical, unconscious—spin the web of the multiple ecologies of belonging which structure our patterns of becoming.

They converge on the ineluctable imperative that we all shall die, but the posthuman predicament, with its double displacement of anthropocentrism and humanism, suggests that even death may be delayed, if not replaced, by techniques of replication, simulation, and cloning. Similarly, reproduction has become technologically assisted to such a degree that the conservative opposition to reproductive and abortion rights will have to be expanded to turn against the libertarian uses of biotechnologies to reproduce in radically transgressive ways. A new evolutionary phase begins, socially, ecologically, and symbolically, which goes well beyond modernist biopower and brings on *zoe*—that is to say, the potency of nonhuman, interspecies, techno-mediated living systems.

In a media society which in the 1990s was still dominated by television, Andy Warhol's prediction that everyone would be famous for fifteen minutes came true. In our world, dominated by Instagram and other social media, everyone will be famous, but for about thirty seconds. What this means fundamentally is that we all live in the eyes of others: we exist on globally interactive screens. The posthuman world is a mirror of the simultaneous, but fragmented "timeless time" of 24/7 broadcasting—livestreaming. This constant flickering of images means that the distinction between being and appearing, reality and artificiality has collapsed: posthuman bodies exist as geo and techno–mediated entities. But what matters to Deitch is the next step of this argument: because of such overexposure, it has become imperative to look our best at all times. To do so, it is necessary to reinvent and reimage ourselves. The internet, artificial intelligence, mood-enhancement drugs, biotechnologies in general, and plastic surgery in particular have changed dramatically how we become human. Self-improvement and technologically supported human enhancement are the new normal. As more powerful technologies become accessible, the next logical step might be to want to create a genetically improved child who would already incorporate the enhanced physical endowments that years of exercise, liposuction, and implant surgery had accomplished. In this process of perfecting the artificial and renaturalizing it into the construction of posthuman bodies, art again is assuming a much more central role, particularly as it fuses with science, computerization, and biotechnology to further reshape the human form. But it is taking antinaturalistic and nonrealistic forms, and it has no inbuilt teleological structure; in fact, it may be going in any direction at once.

Featuring contemporary artists like Matthew Barney (then married to singer Björk), Jeff Koons (then married to porn star Cicciolina), Paul McCarthy, and Cindy Sherman, this agenda-setting exhibition was inspired by Hassan's 1977 posthumanist analyses of the post-natural world of technological mediation. Deitch does not hesitate to present it as an evolutionary step through technological enhancement at an almost everyday level and embraces it thoughtfully but also joyfully. Describing the posthuman era as an experimental period, marked by the loss of naturalistic certainties, the advances of technology, and the redefinition of the self, the *Post Human* exhibition defined the new identities to come as conceptual practices and collective endeavors.

In a further intuition, which he shares with postmodern feminism, Deitch rightly predicted that, considering the impact of media and the degree of digital mediation, the new role models of human liberation will most likely be taken from celebrities, popular culture, and other media icons. Thus, the interchangeable and fast-changing identities of pop singer Madonna and the commercially minded self-transformations of Ivana Trump—President Trump's first wife—can be taken as the emblem of real-life fictional entities, reassembled and improved or retouched by technologies.

The pioneer of this movement for systematic body sculpting and self-transformation as part of a larger emancipation project is Jane Fonda, who single-handedly started the fitness craze in 1979 when she opened a popular workout studio in LA and wrote a series of best-selling fitness books.

The new power relations and contradictions surrounding the female body remain central in the *Post Human* exhibition, which foregrounds the emergence of new stylizations of female figures and new feminine sexualities. The posthuman bodies undergo a massive process of becoming-woman, but in so doing, they also splinter femininity into a sequence of interlocking images which range from popular culture icons to the everyday liberated women. It is significant in this respect that a giant female figure of an Armani-clad businesswoman towered at the entrance of the exhibition and spectators had to walk in between her legs. More Hillary Clinton than Lady Gaga, the posthuman female is both a sign of the fast-changing times and a monument to neoliberal power formations in the making.

But at the same time posthuman feminism is already reorganizing itself: arguing "we will not play nature to your culture," feminist artist Barbara Kruger, along with Jenny Holzer and Cindy Sherman, explored multiple variations of the new ways of what I called the becoming-woman of technological culture. Together, they capture the zeitgeist when the postmodern posture mutates into a posthuman gesture. Building on the rich anarchic tradition of cyberfeminism, they explored the posthuman as an opportunity to develop alternative and subversive images of feminist subjectivities. It will take over a decade for large-scale feminist art exhibitions to redress the gender and feminist politics balance in public art and strike a distinctive note of their own.[1] And the struggle for diversity and decolonial perspectives is still ongoing, with the rich tradition of Afrofuturism leading the way to rethink posthuman futures.

By the mid-1990s, posthuman feminism was coming into its own theoretically as well. J. Halberstam's original work on media culture rejected the very separation of fleshy, embodied subjects from their mediated images and representations which have become their second nature. What defines posthuman bodies is the familiarity they have developed with unnatural, transgressive, and countercultural sexualities

1   Especially noteworthy is the LA-based 2007 feminist art retrospective *WACK! Art and the Feminist Revolution* (https://www.moca.org/exhibition/wack-art-and-the-feminist-revolution) and the Paris-based 2009–10 exhibition of women artists *Elles: Women Artists from the Centre Pompidou.*

and gender roles. Posthuman feminism radicalizes the technological apparatus into multiple practices for constructing alternative bodies. These bodies get dematerialized by technological interventions—be they biochemical, biotechnological, or media and digital platforms—but they also get regrounded and rematerialized in producing enhanced or alternative embodied subjects. I have argued that this double pull—toward de/rematerialization, toward the virtual and the actual—is a process that stylizes posthuman subjectivity in general and posthuman feminism in particular. This double pull is not a crisis, but an energizing practice which finds its ideal image today in popular culture icons like Lady Gaga. *Gaga feminism* is thus born as an affirmative approach to the posthuman predicament, aimed at the promotion of counter- and subcultural subjectivities. Posthuman feminism expresses a kind of queer anarchism reminiscent of cyberfeminism, resisting the pull of digital data culture, going off the grid, causing creative chaos, challenging gender binaries, and embracing a thousand little sexes, as Deleuze and Guattari put it.

Such passion for transformative encounters with mediated iconic figures is not confined to humans only: animals, earth others, and extraterrestrials are also in the posthuman picture. The symbol of posthuman celebrity is Dolly the sheep—the twentieth-century icon that defined the twenty-first-century public imaginary as a clone and triggered a popular phenomenon known as "Dollymania." Dolly is not an animal, but a transgenic entity, made of mixed bio-mediated matter—just like Haraway's cyborgs and oncomice. Delinked from reproduction and divorced from descent, orphan and generator of itself, this new entity is also beyond the gender dichotomies of the patriarchal kinship system. A copy made not from one but several originals, and hence not from one single matrix, structurally untimely because positioned across contradictory chronological axes, Dolly died of a nineteenth-century disease: rheumatism. It was subsequently embalmed and exhibited forever in a science museum. But, as a phenomenon, it pushed the logic of the postmodern simulacrum to the deep end, till it exploded into a posthuman supernova.

At the tail end of postmodernism, the posthuman turn promoted a further leap toward technological transformation and enhanced the role of nonhuman entities—be they animals, plants, algorithms, viruses, or genes—in coconstructing new human subjects. Driven by a profound ethical aspiration, the posthuman condition assumes a fluid interaction between all these entities, and it is less concerned with deconstructing old humanistic universal ideas than with reconstructing new, situated ethical values and practices which match the complexities of the times. The postmodern sought for just and fair representation of that which they—the dominant subjects—taught us to despise. The posthuman, on the other hand, labors toward the adequate expression of that which is not yet fully actualized, but already virtually active. The posthuman subject is materialist and vitalist, embodied and embedded. It is a multifaceted and relational subject, conceptualized within the vitality and elemental complexity that mark the contemporary understanding of living matter itself. The posthuman contains an active decolonial core, and it has critiqued humanistic Eurocentrism, shedding its false universalism, longing for what the xenofeminists called "a politics without the infection of purity." That reference to cultural purity is significant in the contemporary world, where racisms of all kind are proliferating. The inclusive flair for the hybrid, the anomalous, the damaged, and the left behind is far more central to posthuman aesthetics and its cultural politics than the glossy appeal of the postmodern inorganic. Posthuman thought is a critical philosophy for times of crisis, and it rises to the occasion by foregrounding ethical and political values of social justice, collaboration, and solidarity.

Jeffrey Deitch was very aware of the darker, more pernicious aspects of the posthuman turn and warned us against them: there is no knowing whether the posthuman future will be better or worse or whether it will even be posthuman at all. He is especially concerned about the rise of irrationality as a result of the collapse of modernist scientific culture with its focus on linear logic, rational thinking, and progress through the deployment of technology. The *Post Human* exhibition teaches us that progress may be inevitable, but it may not be an improvement all round: the collapse of political utopias and the end of ideology have cracked the social fabric. Each of the axes of the posthuman convergence—the technological, the environmental, and the social—carries its own explosive new social and individual pathologies. We are mutating, but are we really advancing? Will democracy survive the technological takeover of living matter?

The posthuman moment makes a robust case for a new ethics to redefine the emergent life-forms and the new heterogeneous subjects in sustainable social systems in an affirmative and collaborative manner. Deitch's work bears witness to this deep ethical bond and in this fundamental gesture reinscribes artistic practice as a pillar of collective justice, endurance, and care. Posthuman, all too human.

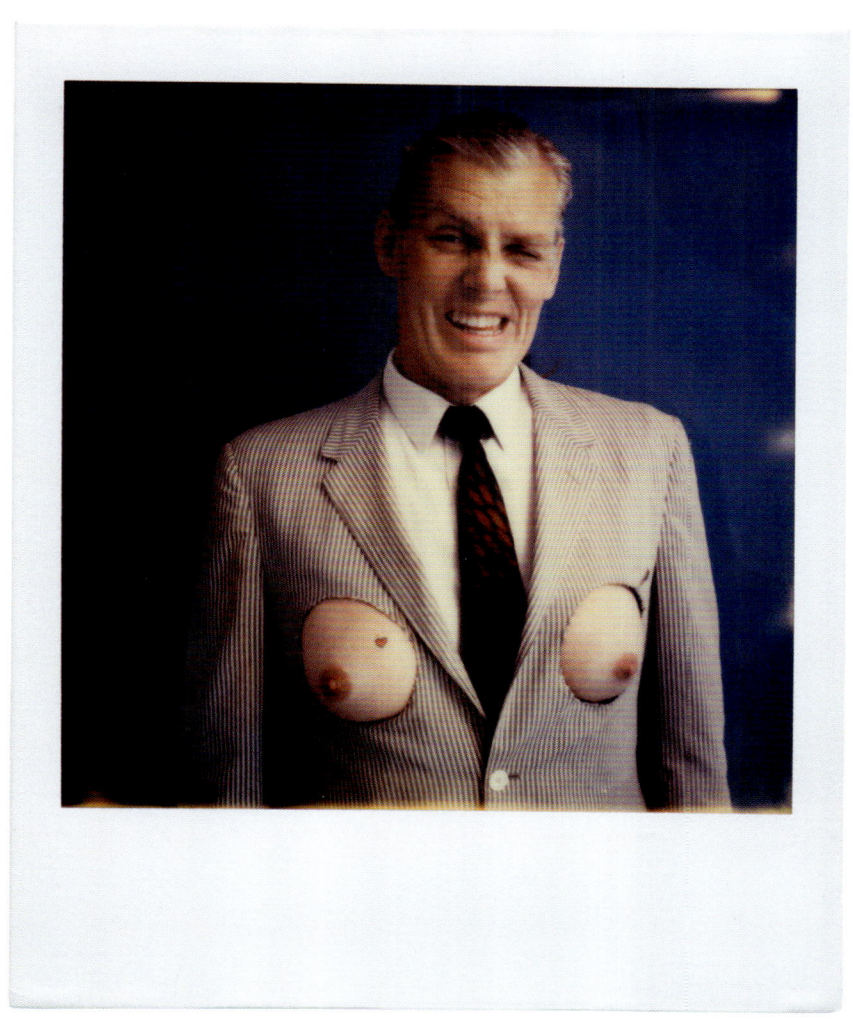

Pippa Garner, *Manette*, 1992. Polaroid photograph. 4.2 × 3.5 in. (10.7 × 8.9 cm)

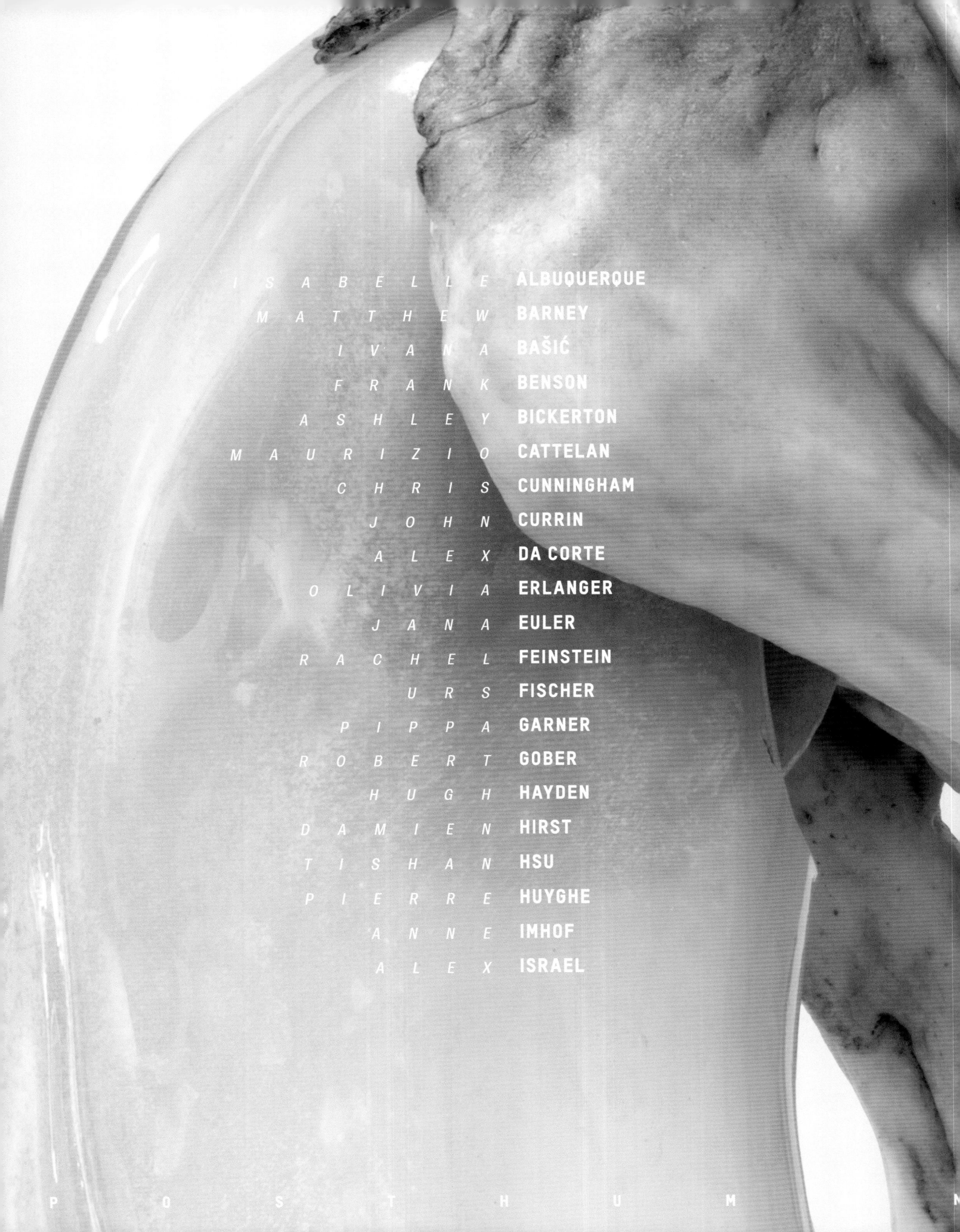

ISABELLE **ALBUQUERQUE**
MATTHEW **BARNEY**
IVANA **BAŠIĆ**
FRANK **BENSON**
ASHLEY **BICKERTON**
MAURIZIO **CATTELAN**
CHRIS **CUNNINGHAM**
JOHN **CURRIN**
ALEX **DA CORTE**
OLIVIA **ERLANGER**
JANA **EULER**
RACHEL **FEINSTEIN**
URS **FISCHER**
PIPPA **GARNER**
ROBERT **GOBER**
HUGH **HAYDEN**
DAMIEN **HIRST**
TISHAN **HSU**
PIERRE **HUYGHE**
ANNE **IMHOF**
ALEX **ISRAEL**

POSTHUM

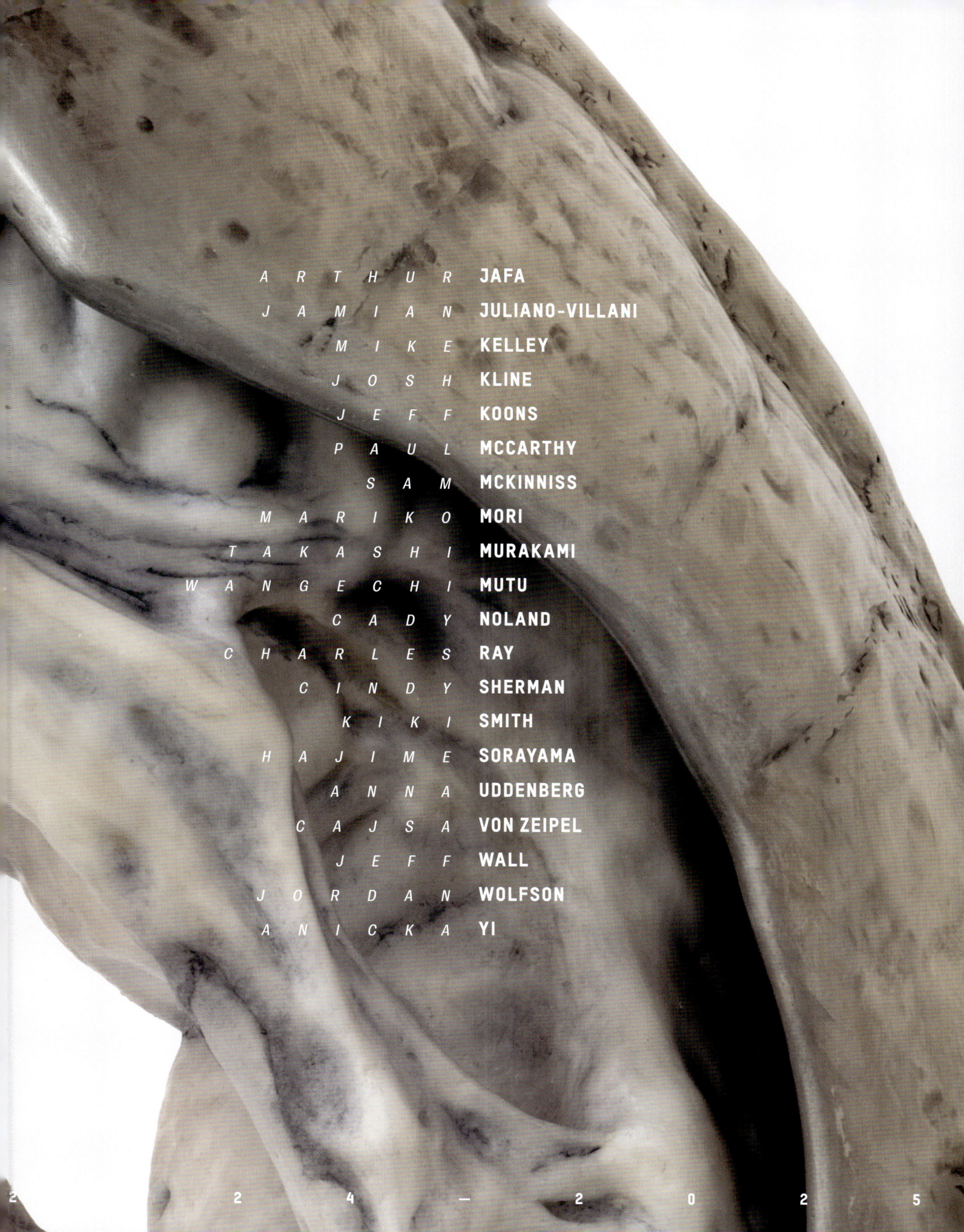

ARTHUR **JAFA**
JAMIAN **JULIANO-VILLANI**
MIKE **KELLEY**
JOSH **KLINE**
JEFF **KOONS**
PAUL **MCCARTHY**
SAM **MCKINNISS**
MARIKO **MORI**
TAKASHI **MURAKAMI**
WANGECHI **MUTU**
CADY **NOLAND**
CHARLES **RAY**
CINDY **SHERMAN**
KIKI **SMITH**
HAJIME **SORAYAMA**
ANNA **UDDENBERG**
CAJSA **VON ZEIPEL**
JEFF **WALL**
JORDAN **WOLFSON**
ANICKA **YI**

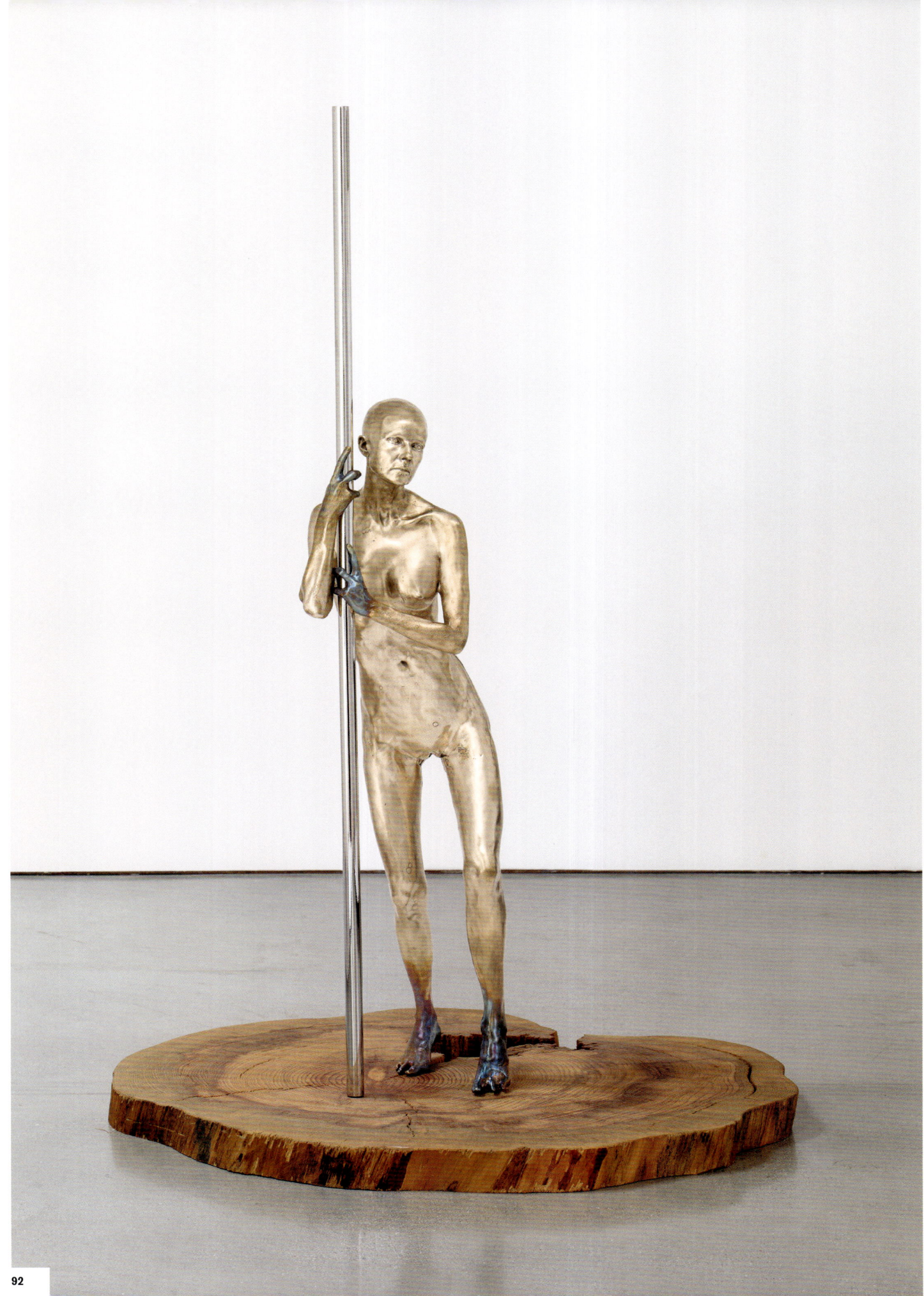

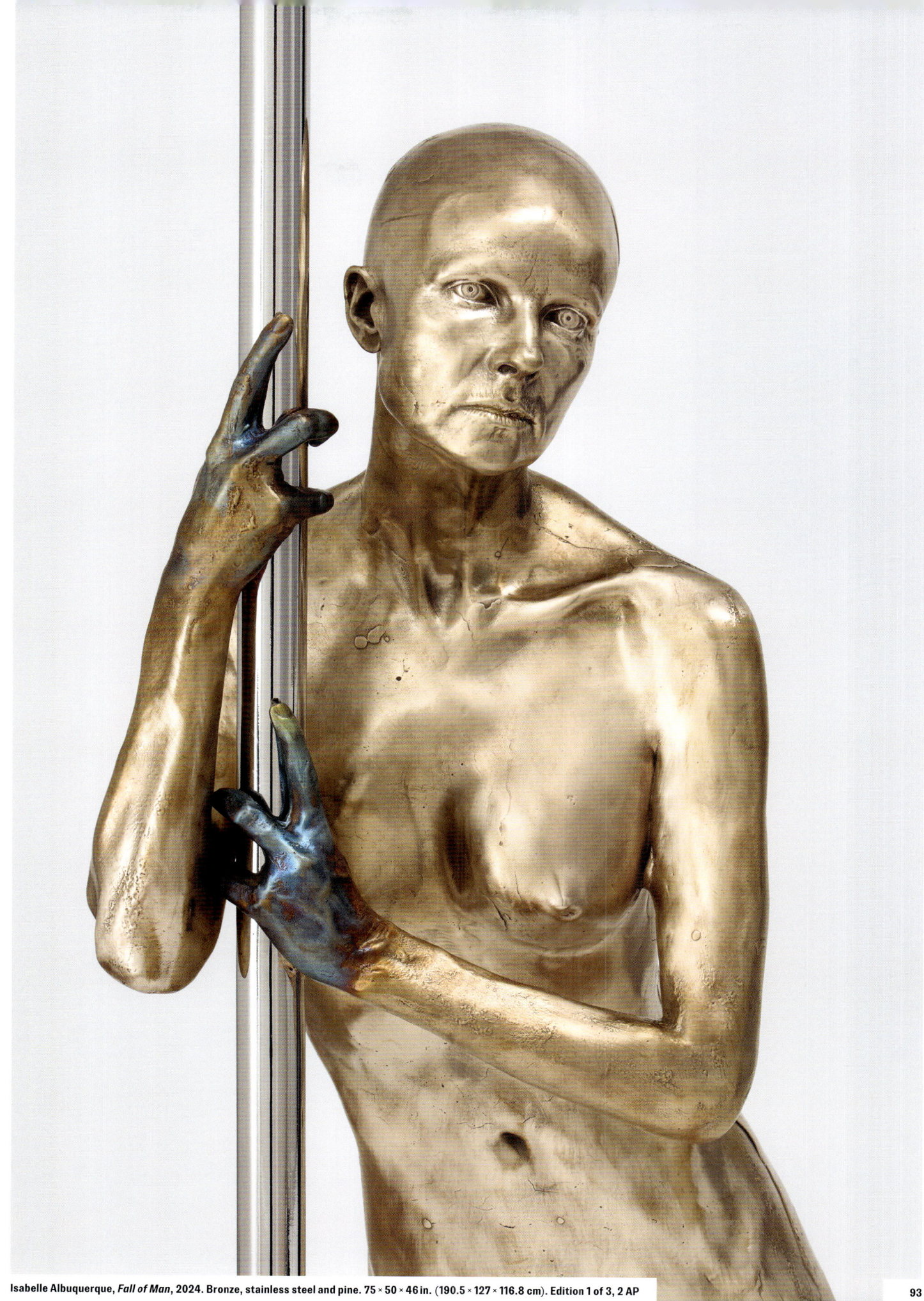

Isabelle Albuquerque, *Fall of Man*, 2024. Bronze, stainless steel and pine. 75 × 50 × 46 in. (190.5 × 127 × 116.8 cm). Edition 1 of 3, 2 AP

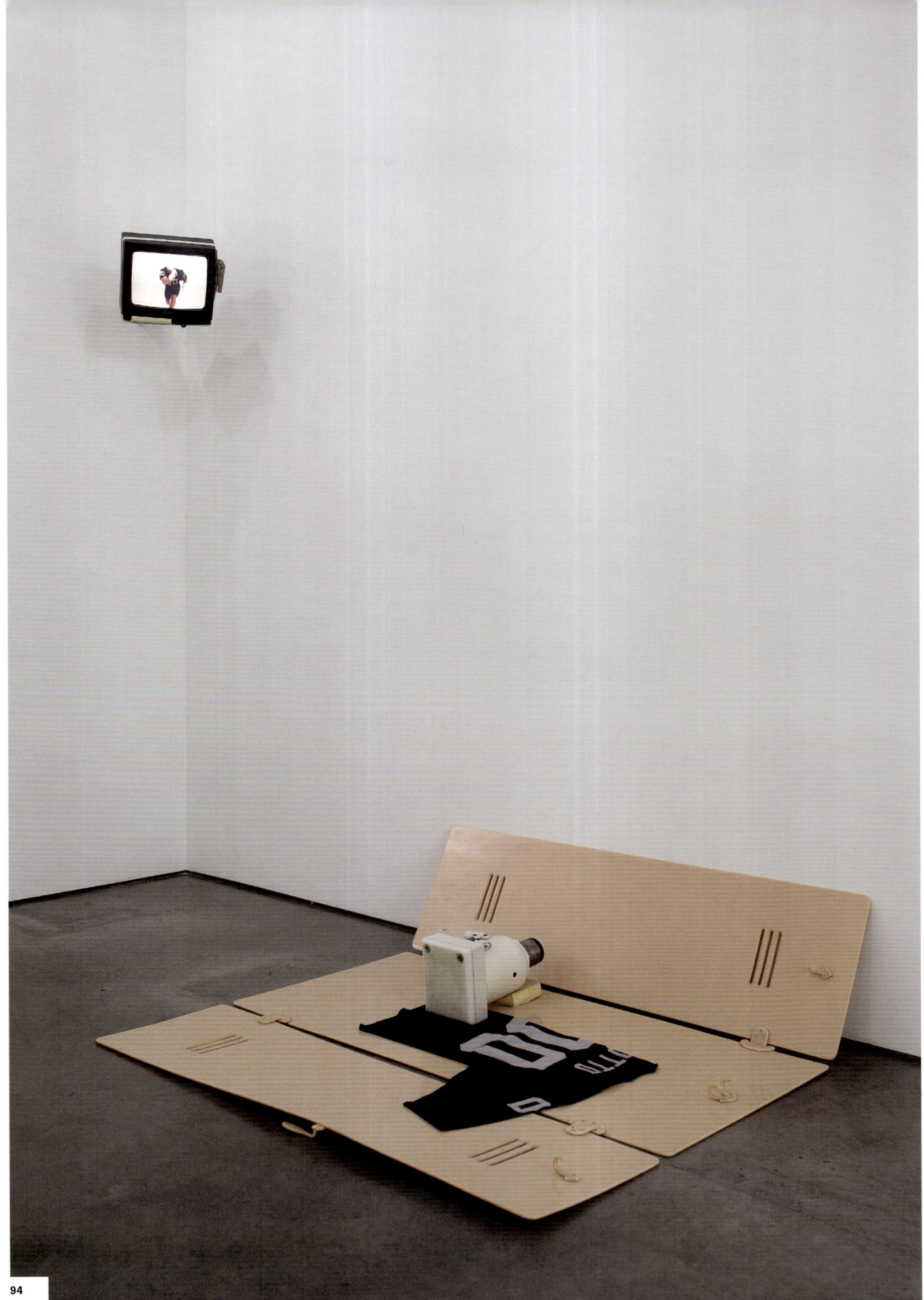

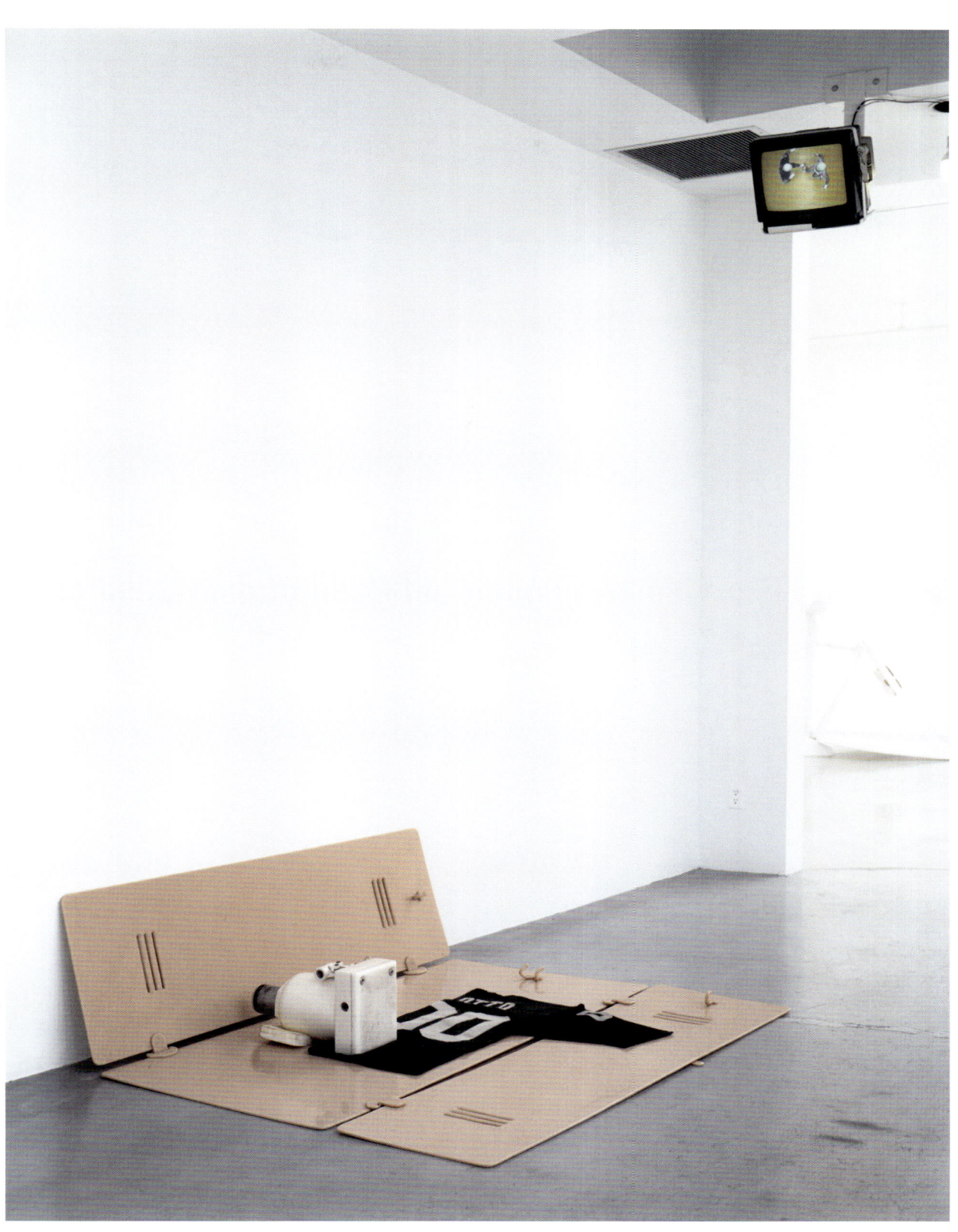

Matthew Barney, *The Jim Otto Suite*, 1991. Light-reflective vinyl, prosthetic plastic locker, NFL jersey, hydraulic jack with glucose syrup, petroleum jelly and video. **Dimensions variable**

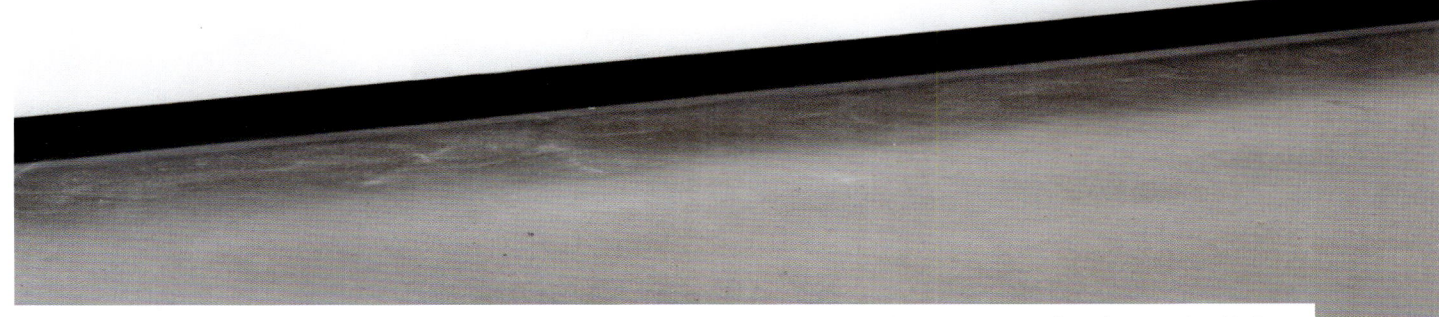

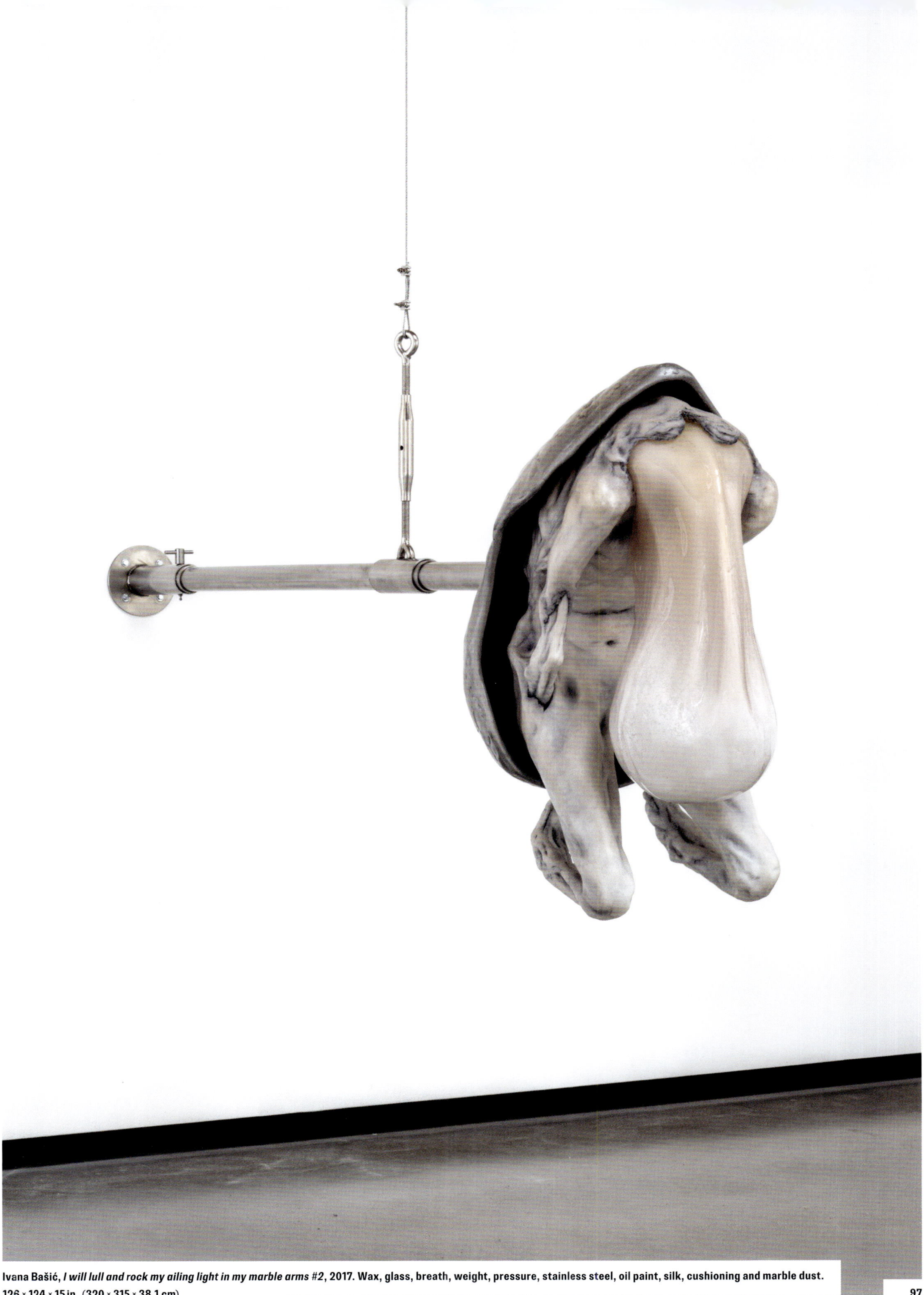

Ivana Bašić, *I will lull and rock my ailing light in my marble arms #2*, 2017. Wax, glass, breath, weight, pressure, stainless steel, oil paint, silk, cushioning and marble dust.
126 × 124 × 15 in. (320 × 315 × 38.1 cm)

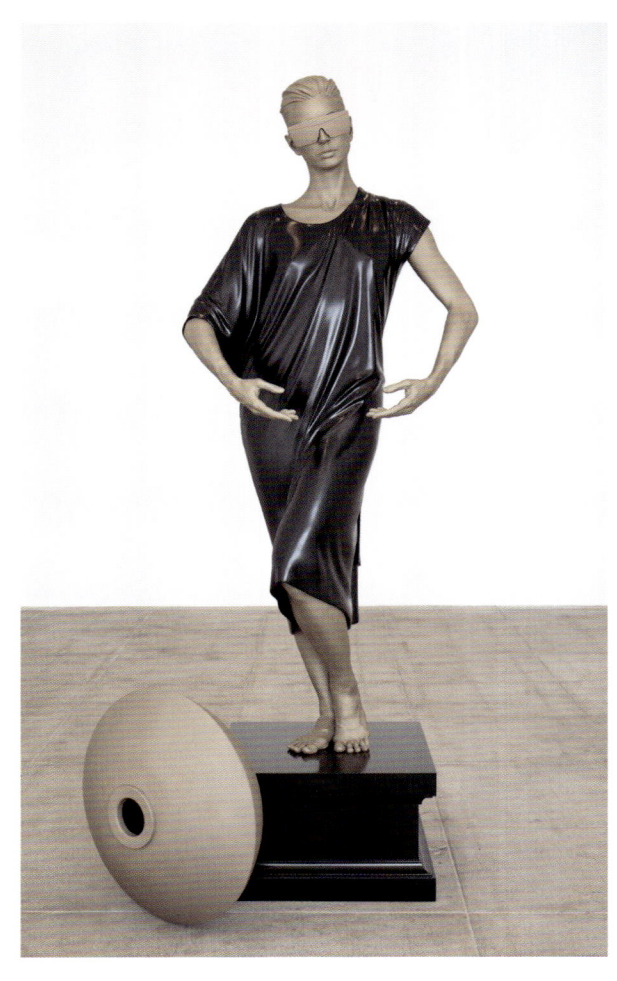
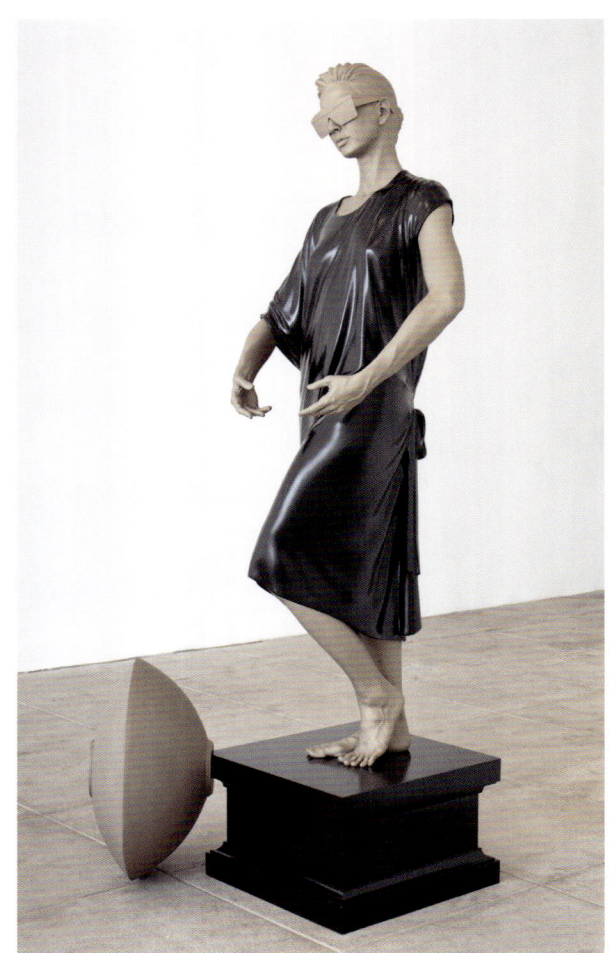
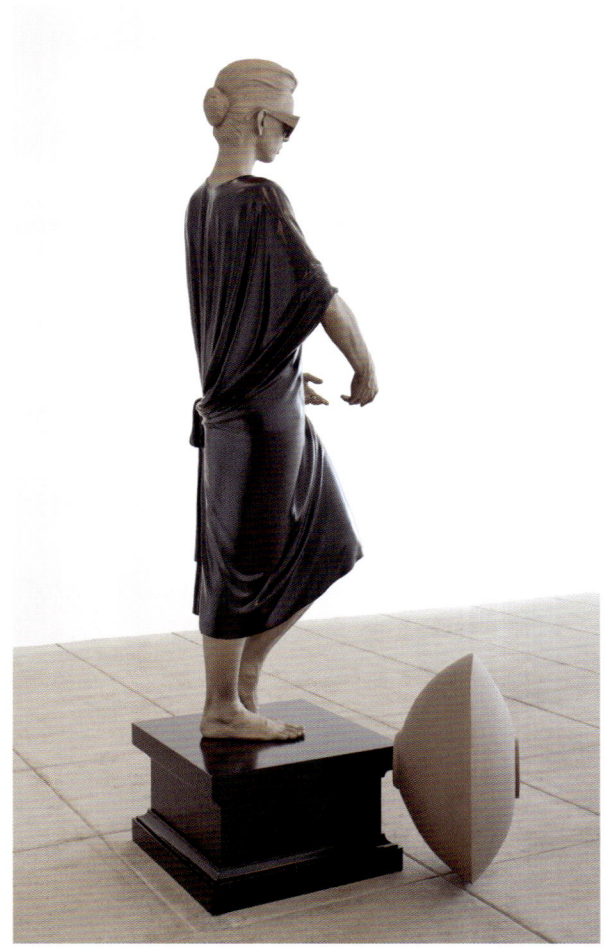
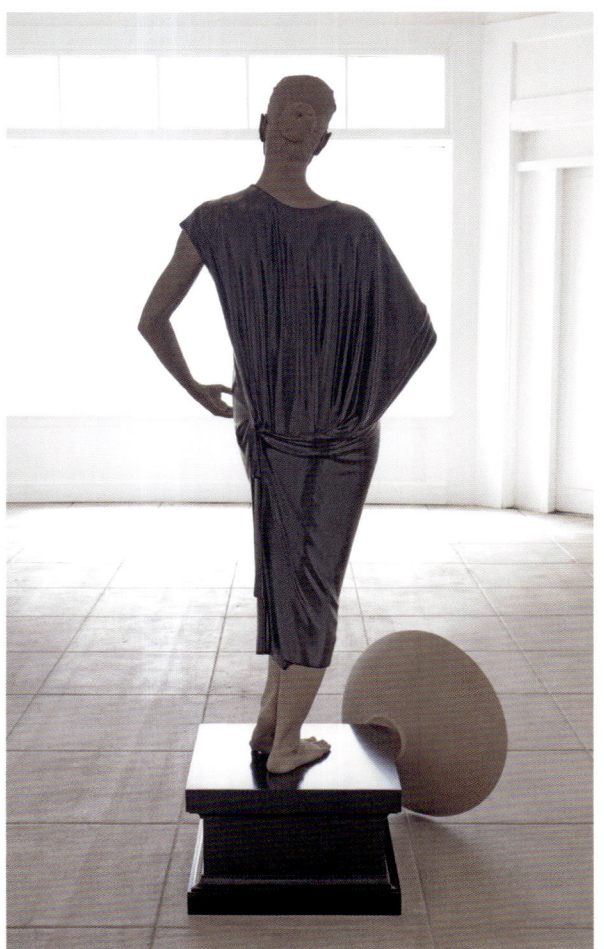

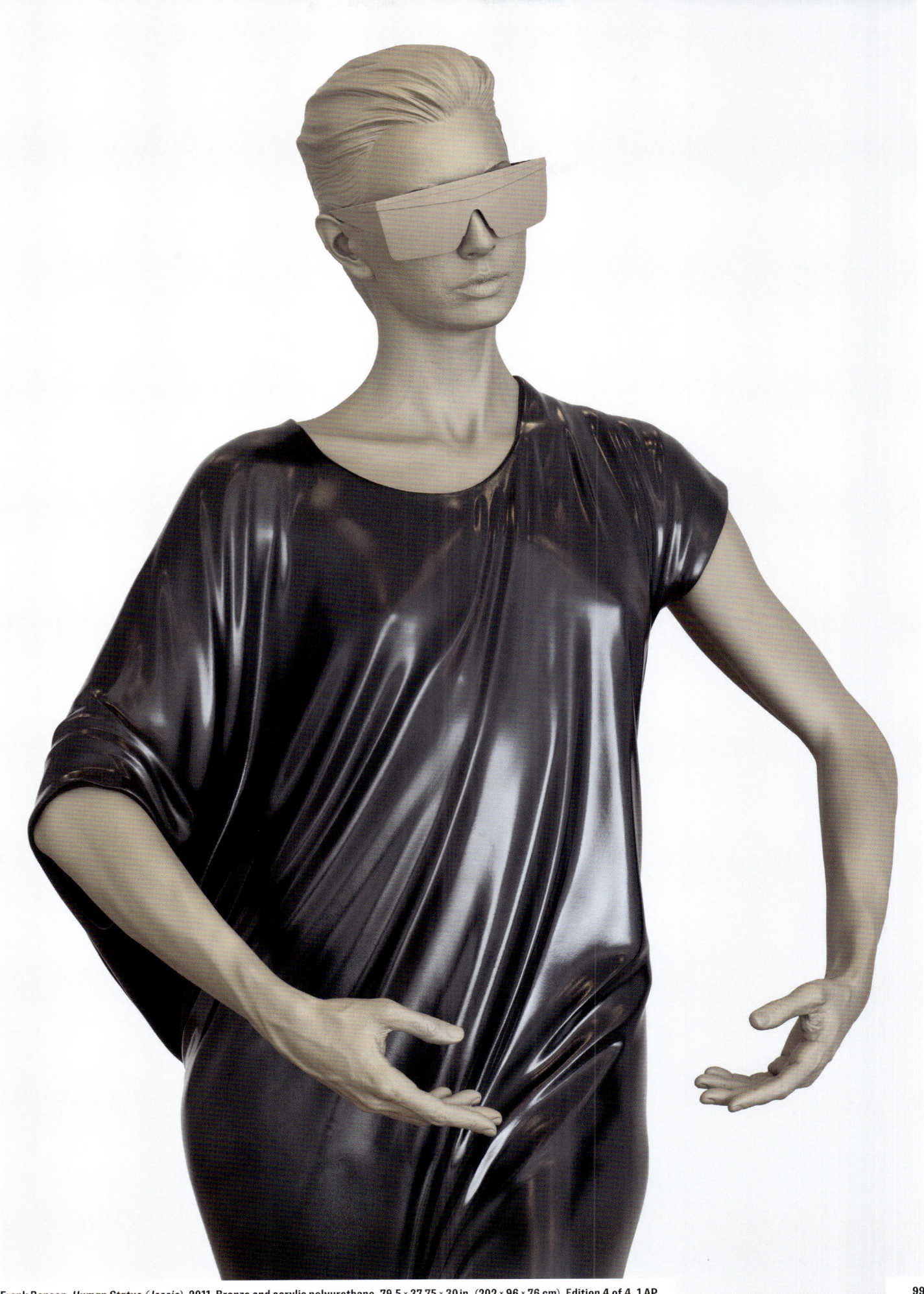

Frank Benson, *Human Statue* (*Jessie*), 2011. Bronze and acrylic polyurethane. 79.5 × 37.75 × 30 in. (202 × 96 × 76 cm). Edition 4 of 4, 1 AP

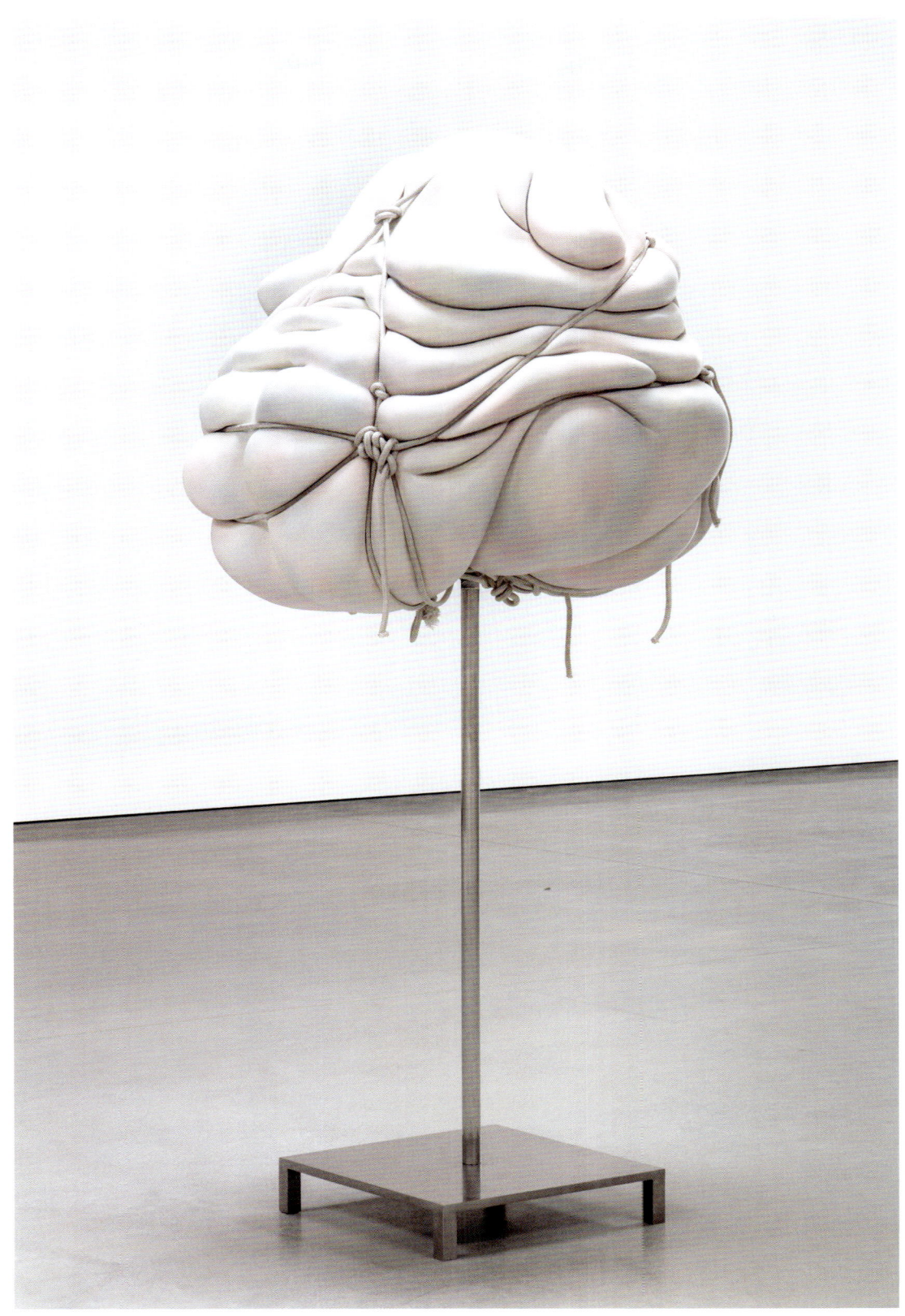

Ashley Bickerton, *F.O.B.: Tied (White)*, 1993/2018. Fiberglass, rope and steel. 75 × 40 × 33 in. (190.5 × 101.6 × 83.8 cm). 1 of 5 unique variations

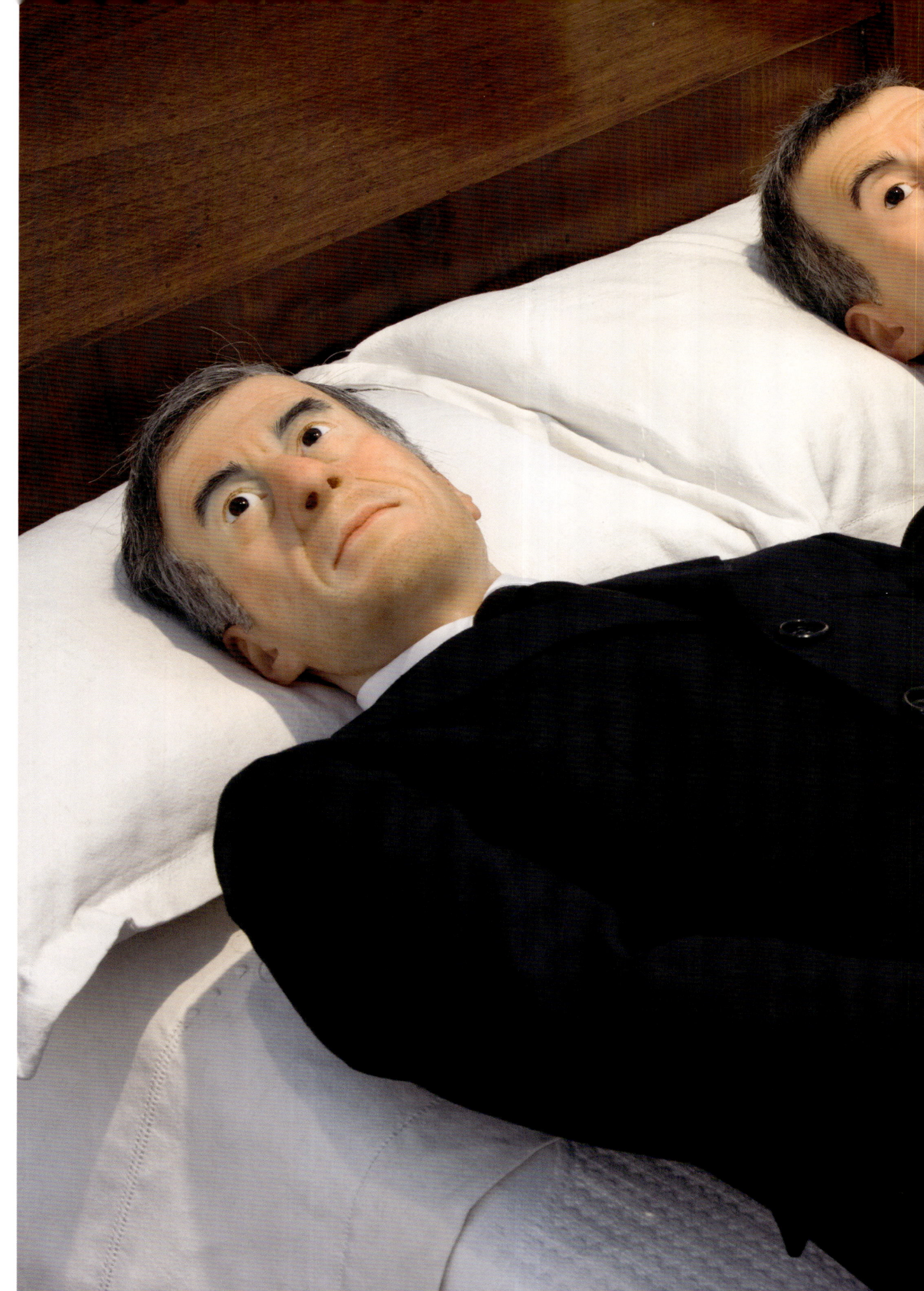

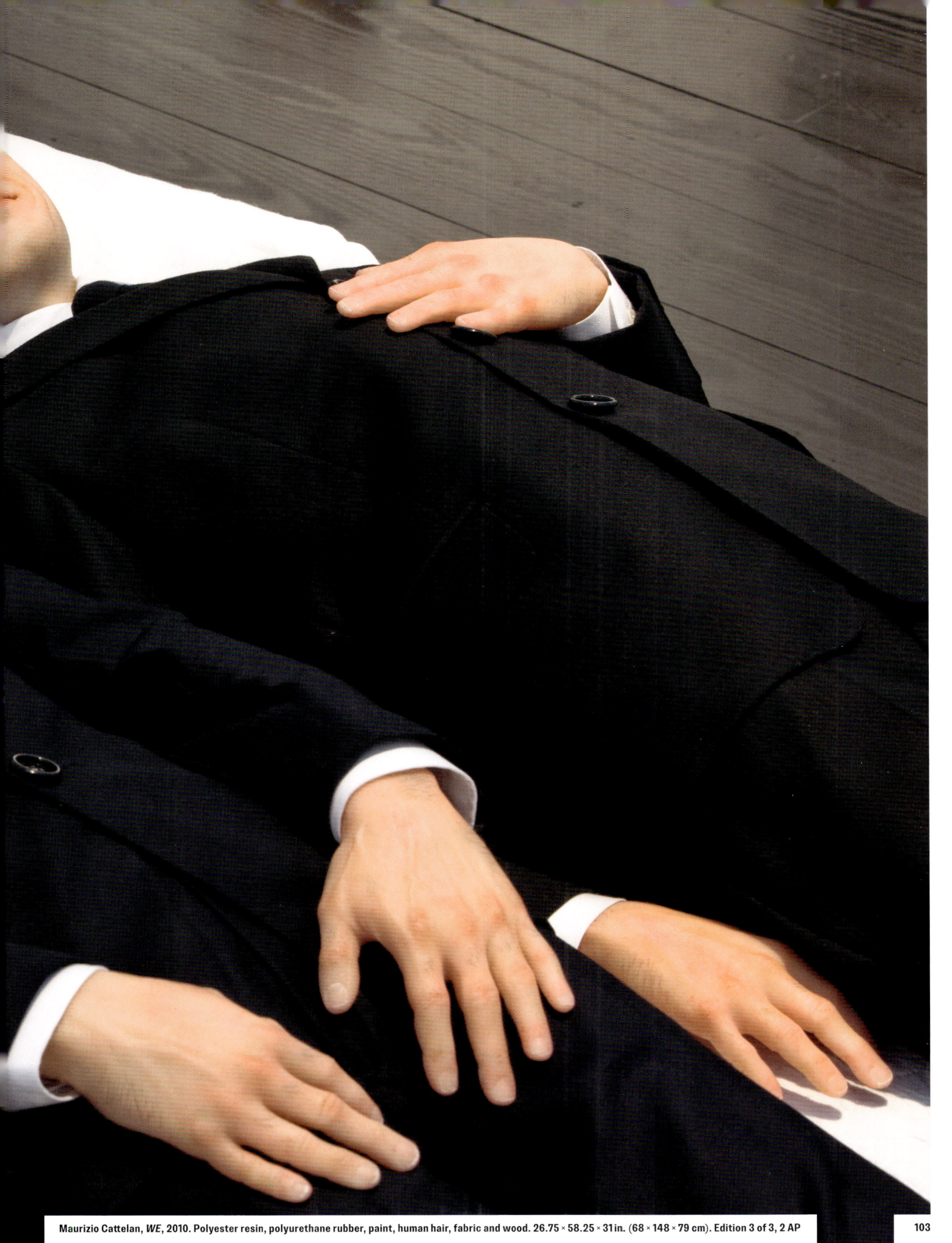

Maurizio Cattelan, *WE*, 2010. Polyester resin, polyurethane rubber, paint, human hair, fabric and wood. 26.75 × 58.25 × 31 in. (68 × 148 × 79 cm). Edition 3 of 3, 2 AP

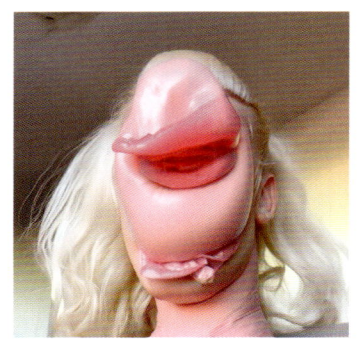 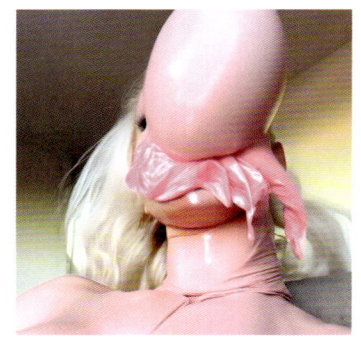 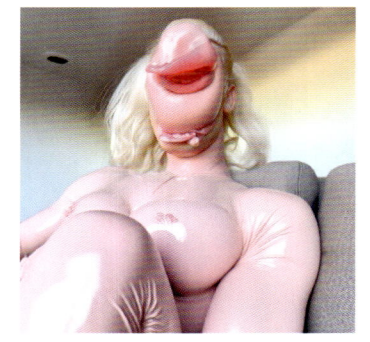 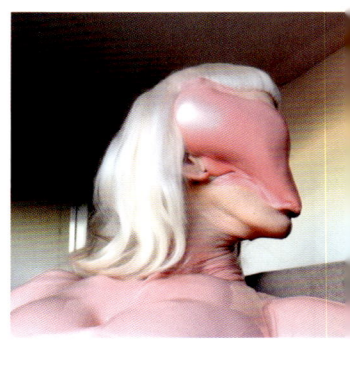

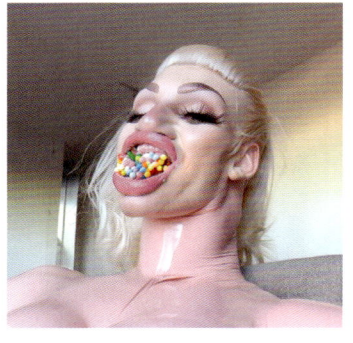 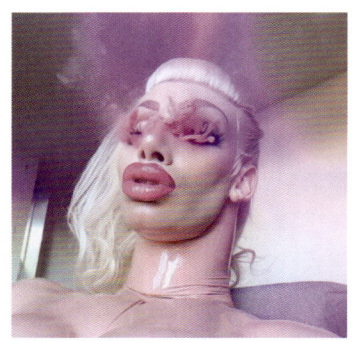 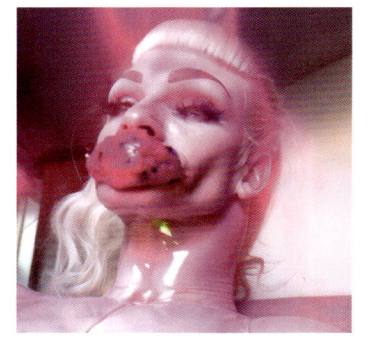 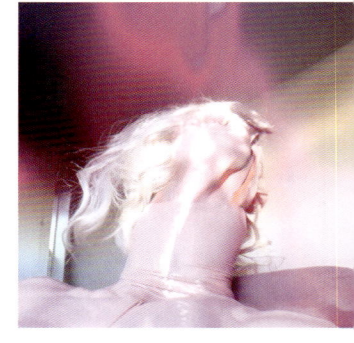

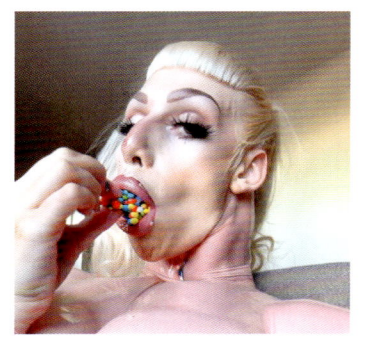 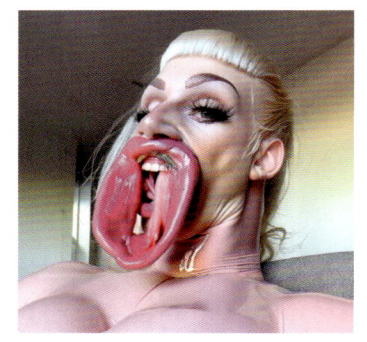 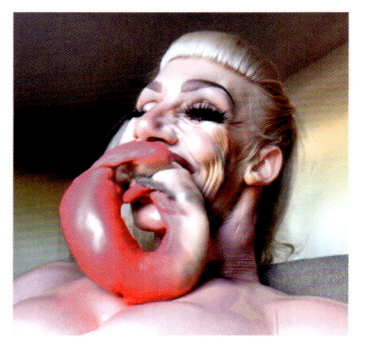 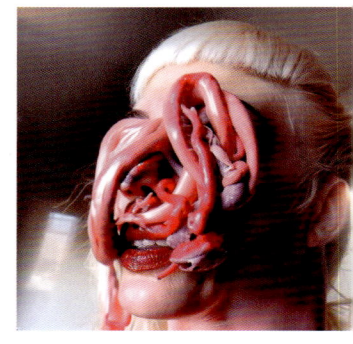

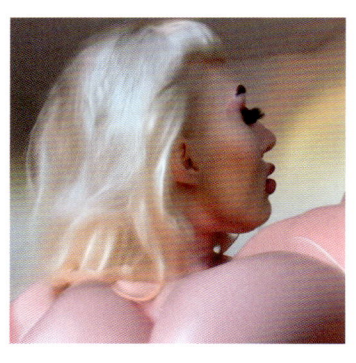 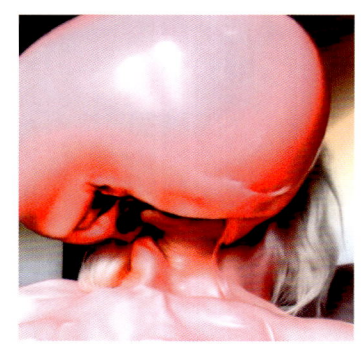 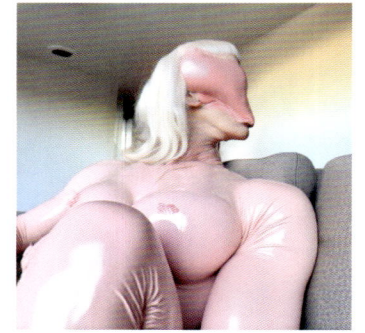 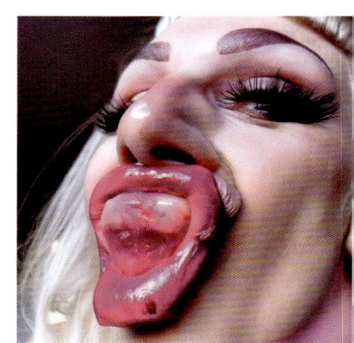

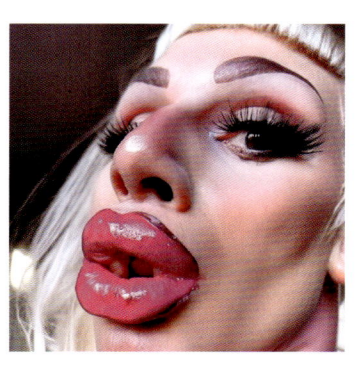 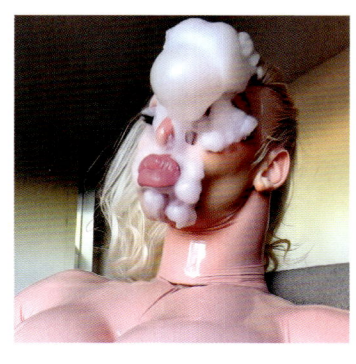 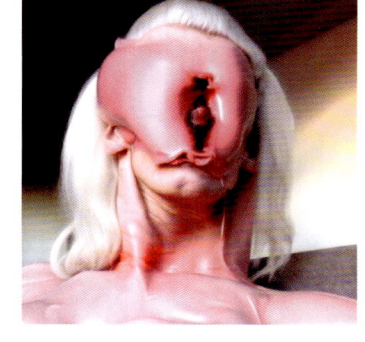 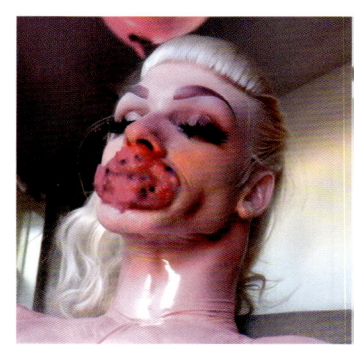

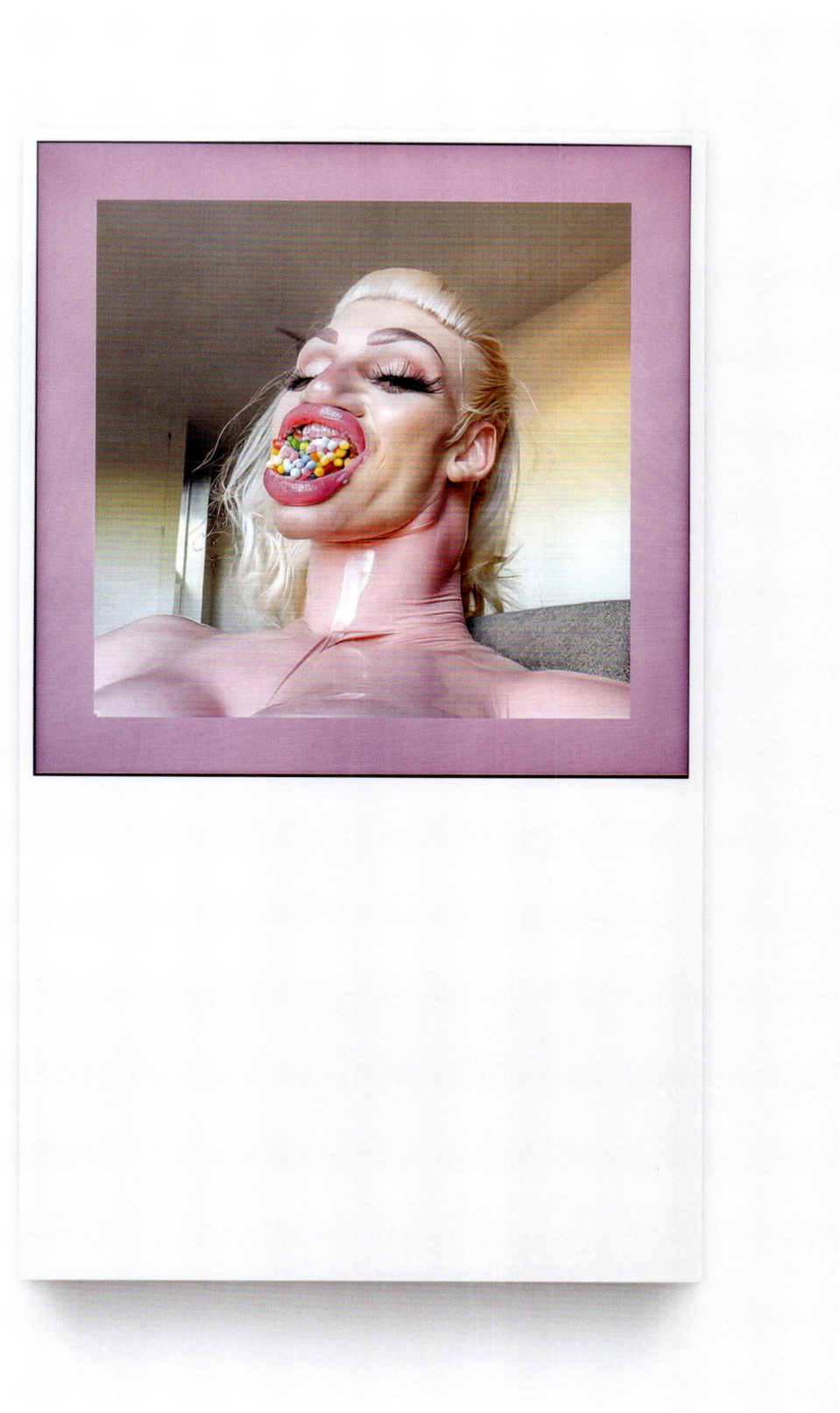

Chris Cunningham, *PolyCandy* **(Study), 2024. HD video, sound, color, 7:13 min. Video light-box display: acrylic, HD television, media player and SD card. 38.25 × 66.5 × 3 in. (97.2 × 168.9 × 7.6 cm)**

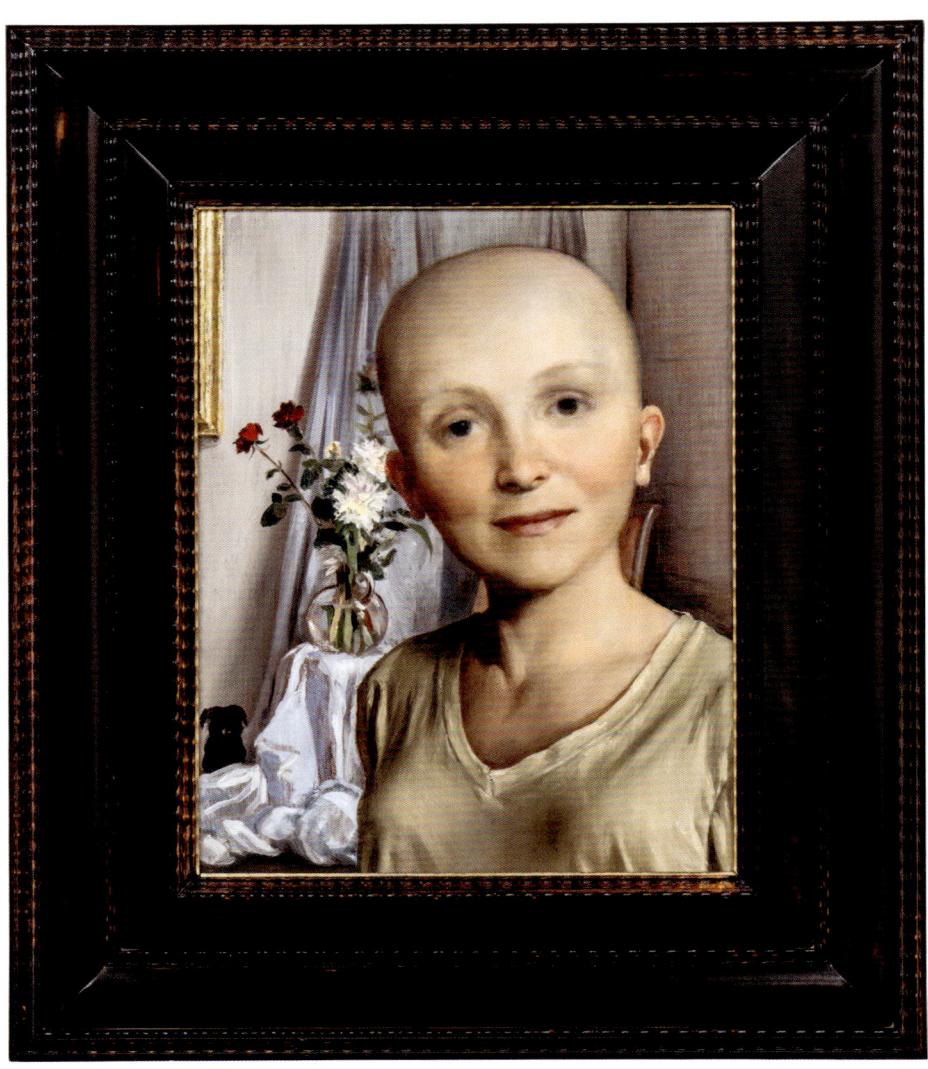

John Currin, *Portrait of Chewy*, 2001. Oil on canvas. Framed: 27.5 × 11 × 1 in. (69.8 × 27.9 × 2.5 cm)

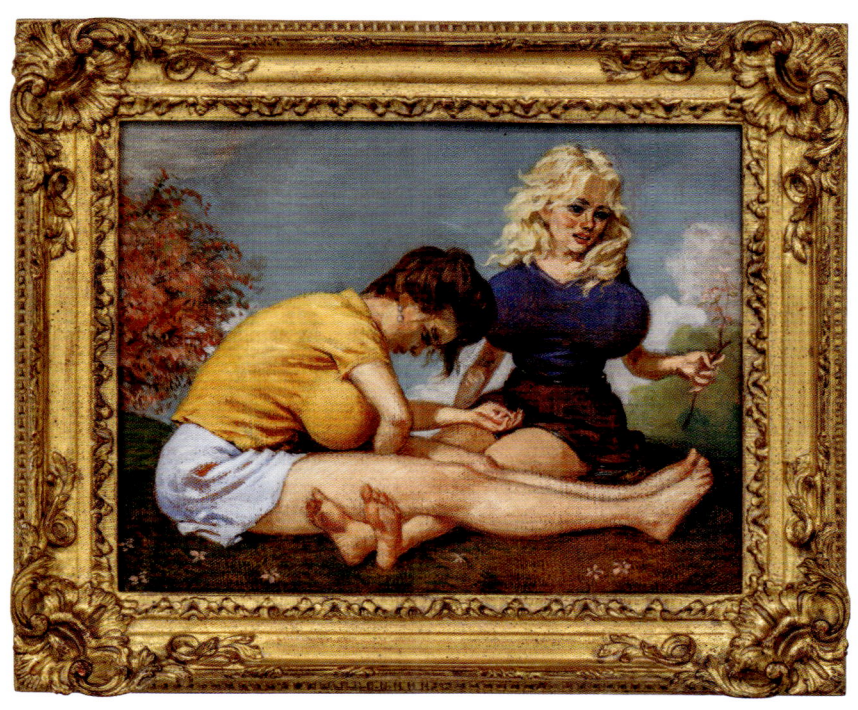

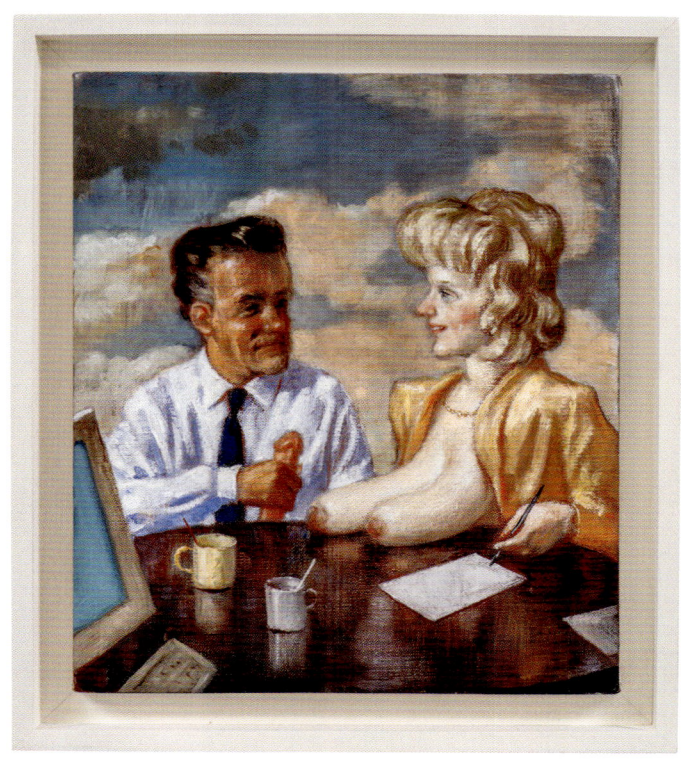

Top: John Currin, *Dogwood*, 1997. Oil on canvas. Framed: 15.25 × 18.25 × 2 in. (38.7 × 46.4 × 5.1 cm)

Bottom: John Currin, *Equality in the Workplace*, 2002. Oil on canvas. Framed: 16.5 × 14.5 × 2 in. (41.9 × 36.8 × 5.1 cm)

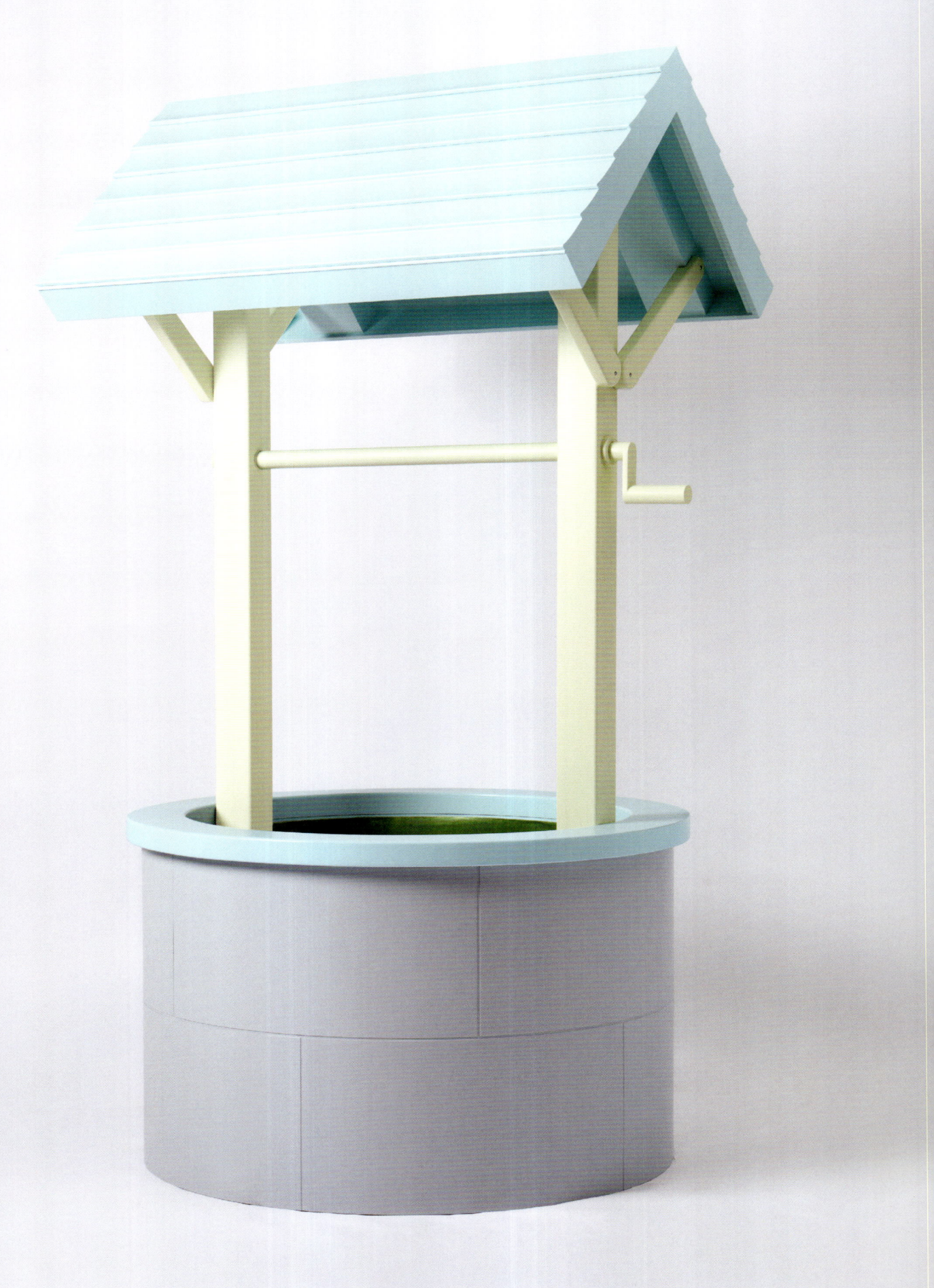

Alex Da Corte, *Well for Sensitive Boys*, **2022. Automotive paint, vinyl siding, two-part sculpting epoxy, lusterboard, wood, vinyl fenceposts, expanded PVC, PVC pipe, steel fencepost sleeves, aluminum tubing, foamboard, velvet, hardware and sound. 101.5 × 54.25 × 51 in. (257.8 × 137.8 × 129.5 cm)**

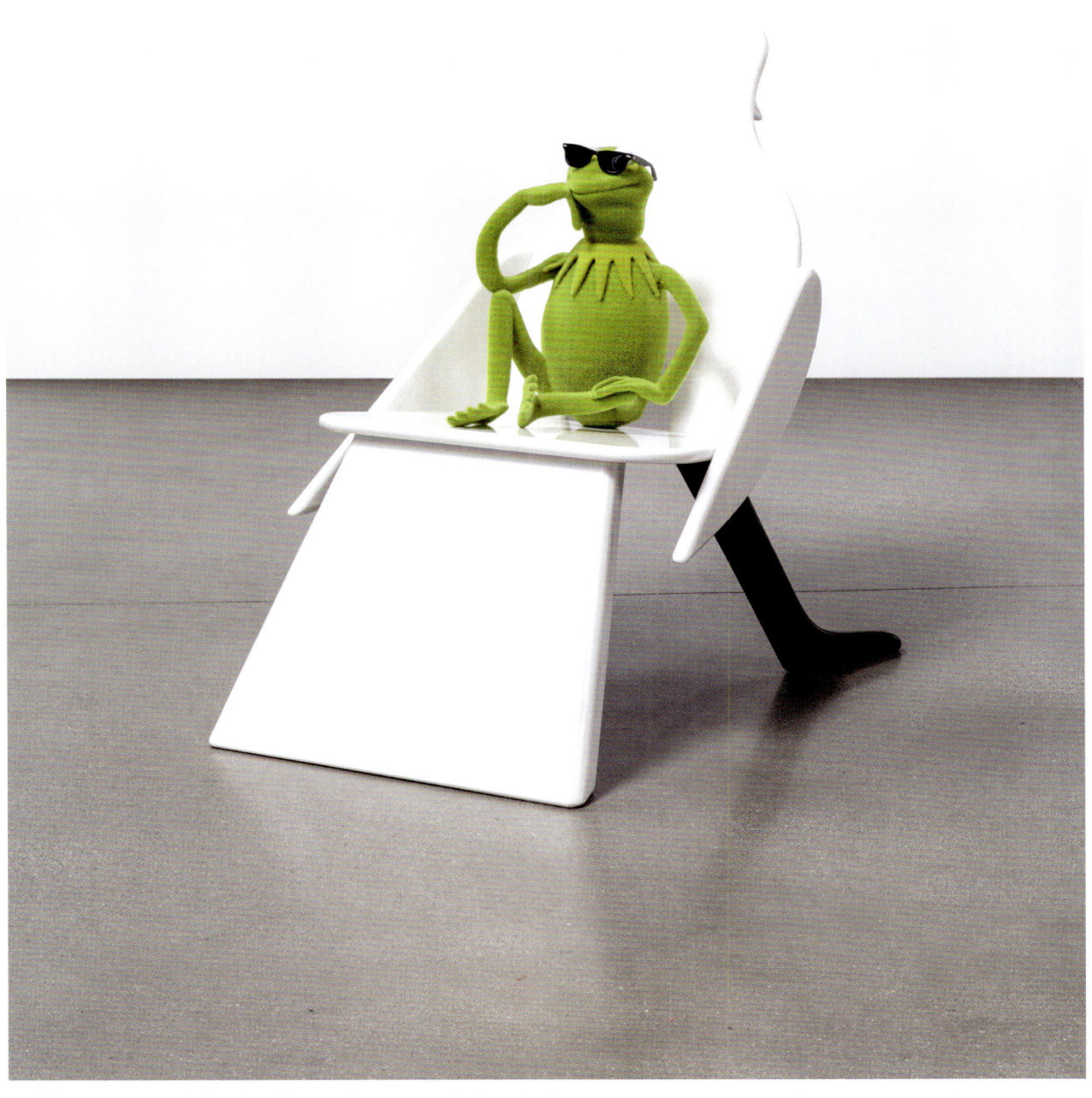

Alex Da Corte, *Cool Kermit*, 2024. Coloured Himacs, stainless steel, fibreglass, acrylic, nylon flocking fibres and white gold. 35.88 × 23.63 × 37.75 in. (91 × 60 × 96 cm).
Edition 1 of 2, 1 AP

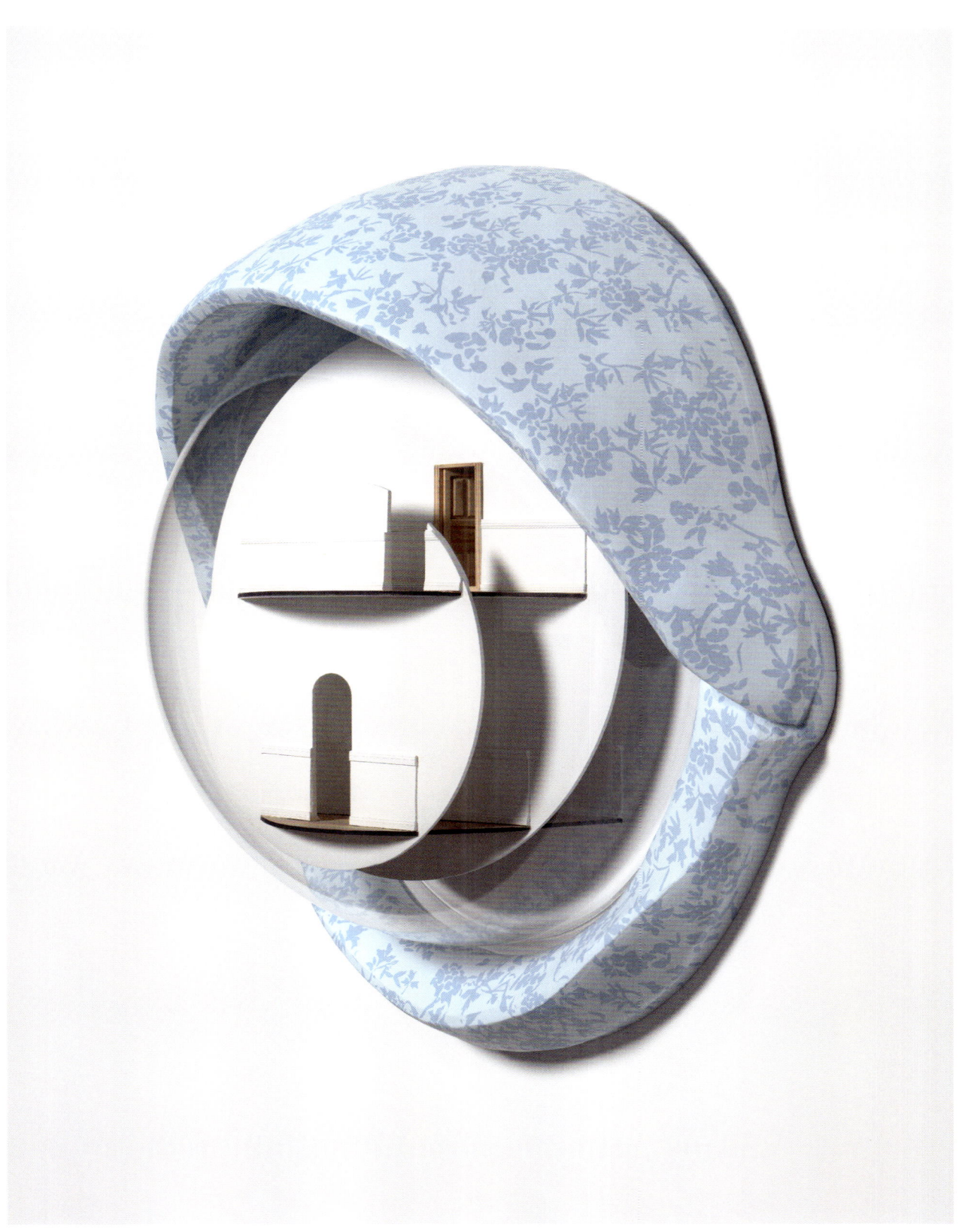

Olivia Erlanger, *Act V*, 2023. Basswood, plexiglass, MDF, aqua resin, wallpaper and paint. 53 × 49 × 20 in. (134.6 × 124.5 × 50.8 cm)

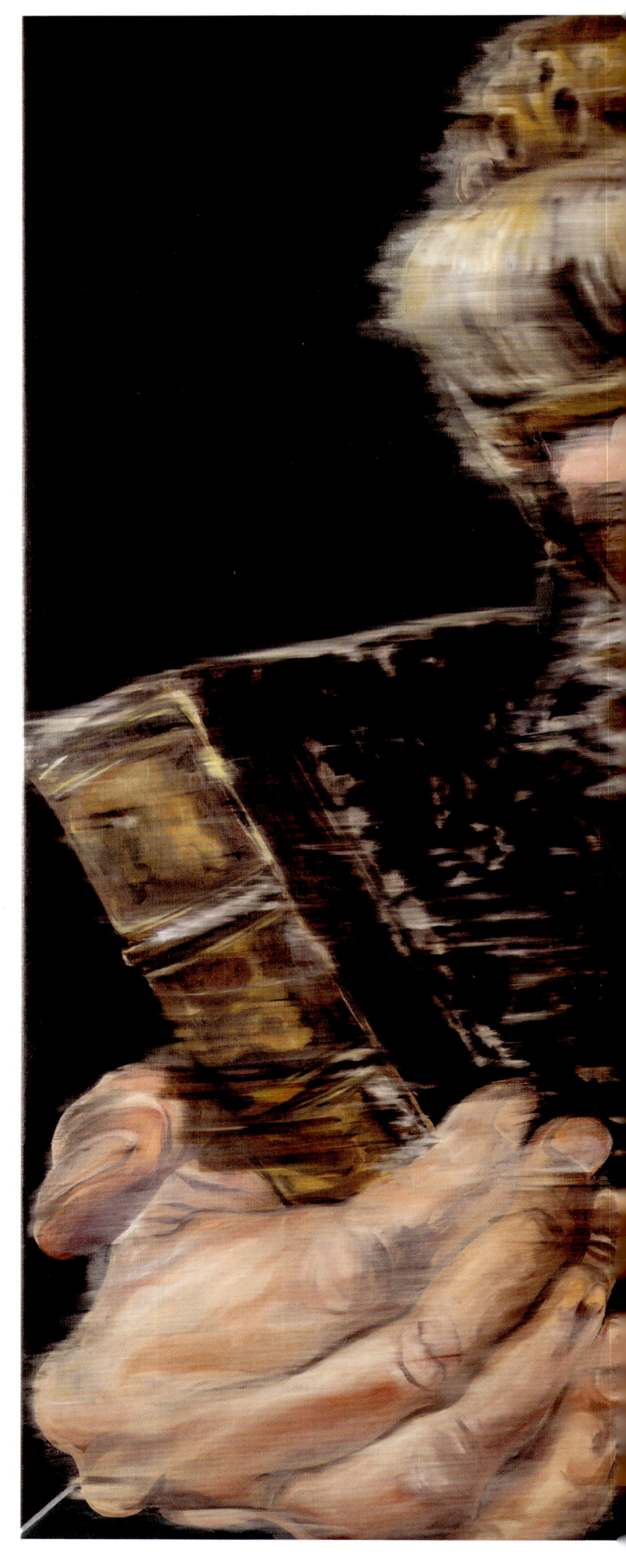

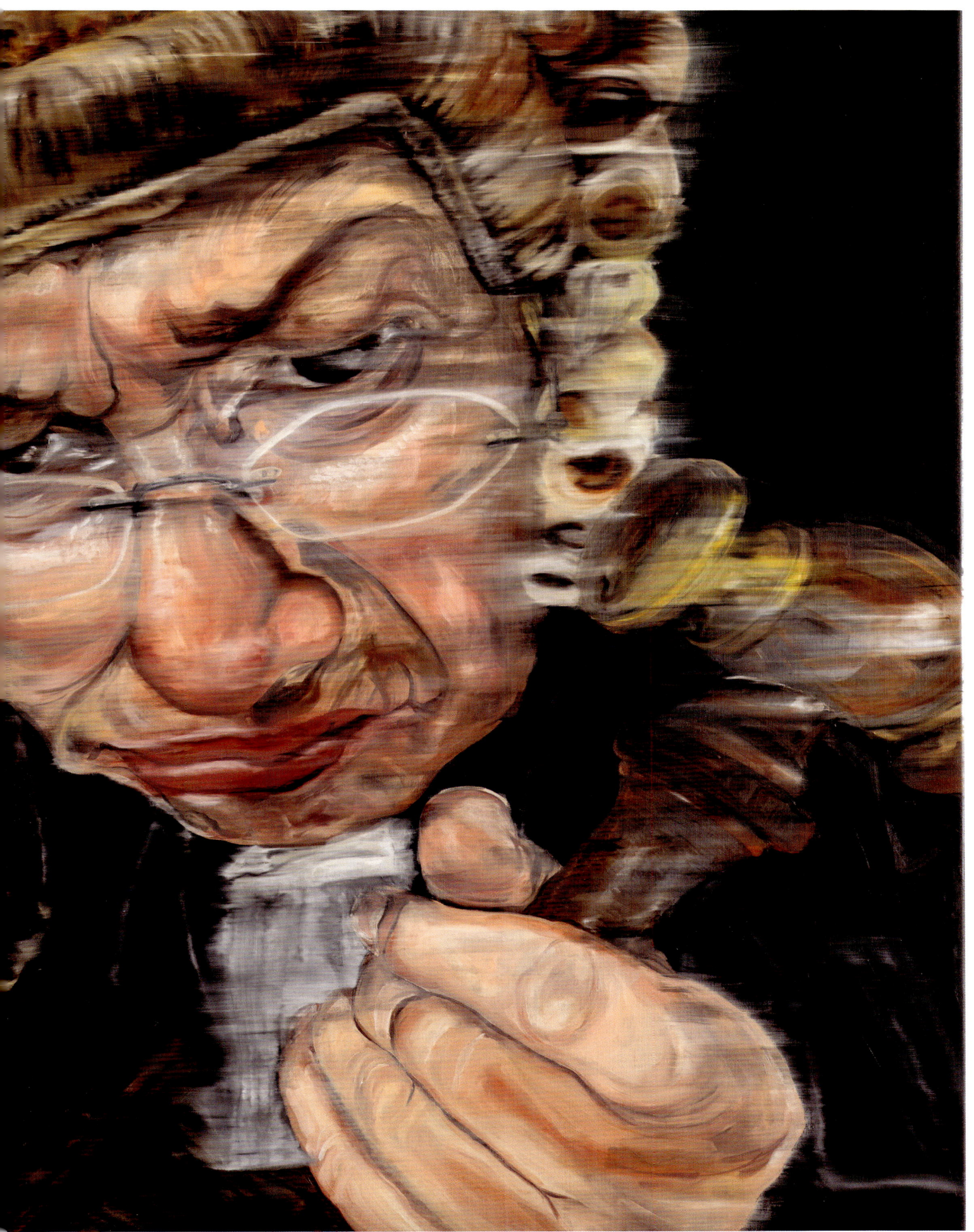

Jana Euler, *The Judge*, 2018. Oil on canvas. 78.74 × 94.49 in. (200 × 240 cm)

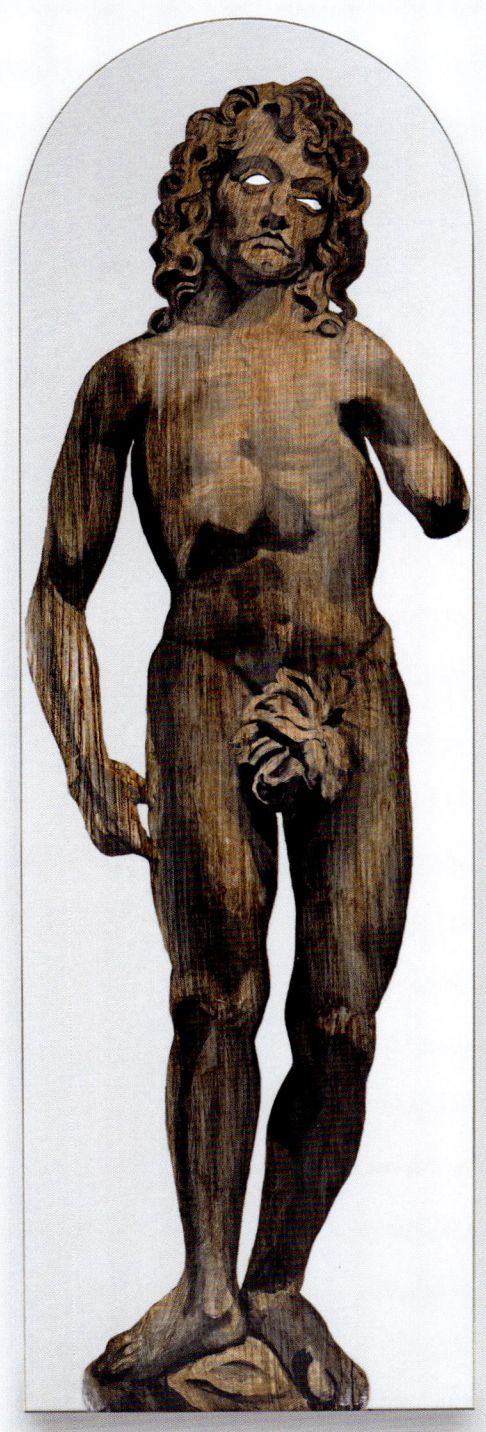
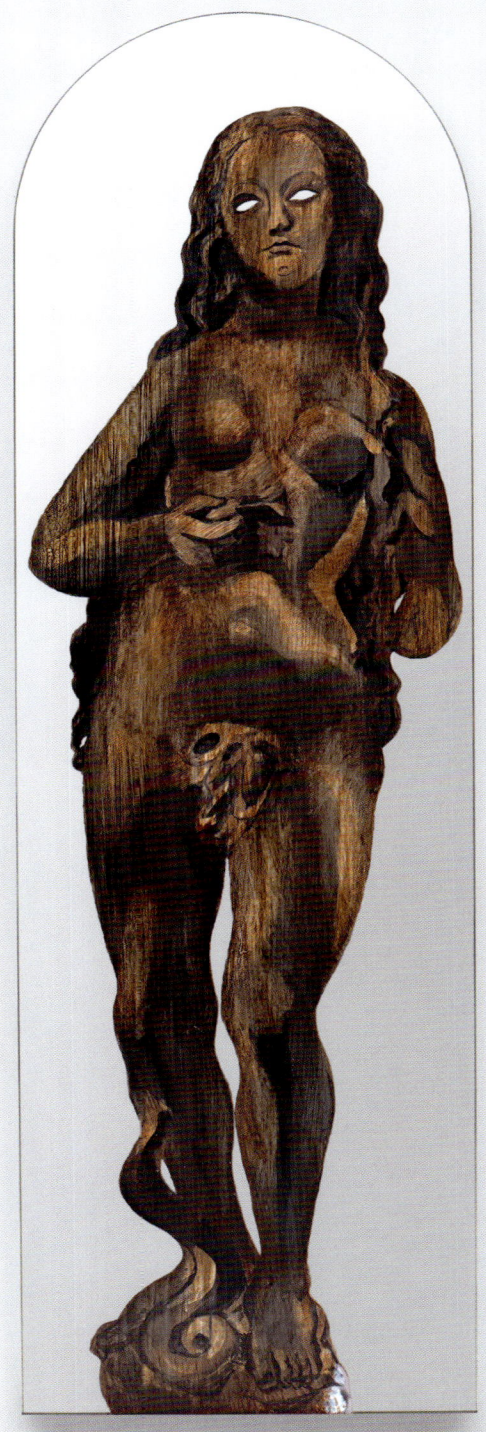

Rachel Feinstein, *Adam*, 2021, and *Eve*, 2021. Acrylic, acrylic urethane and charcoal on mirror. Each: 76 × 24 × 1.5 in. (193 × 61 × 3.8 cm)

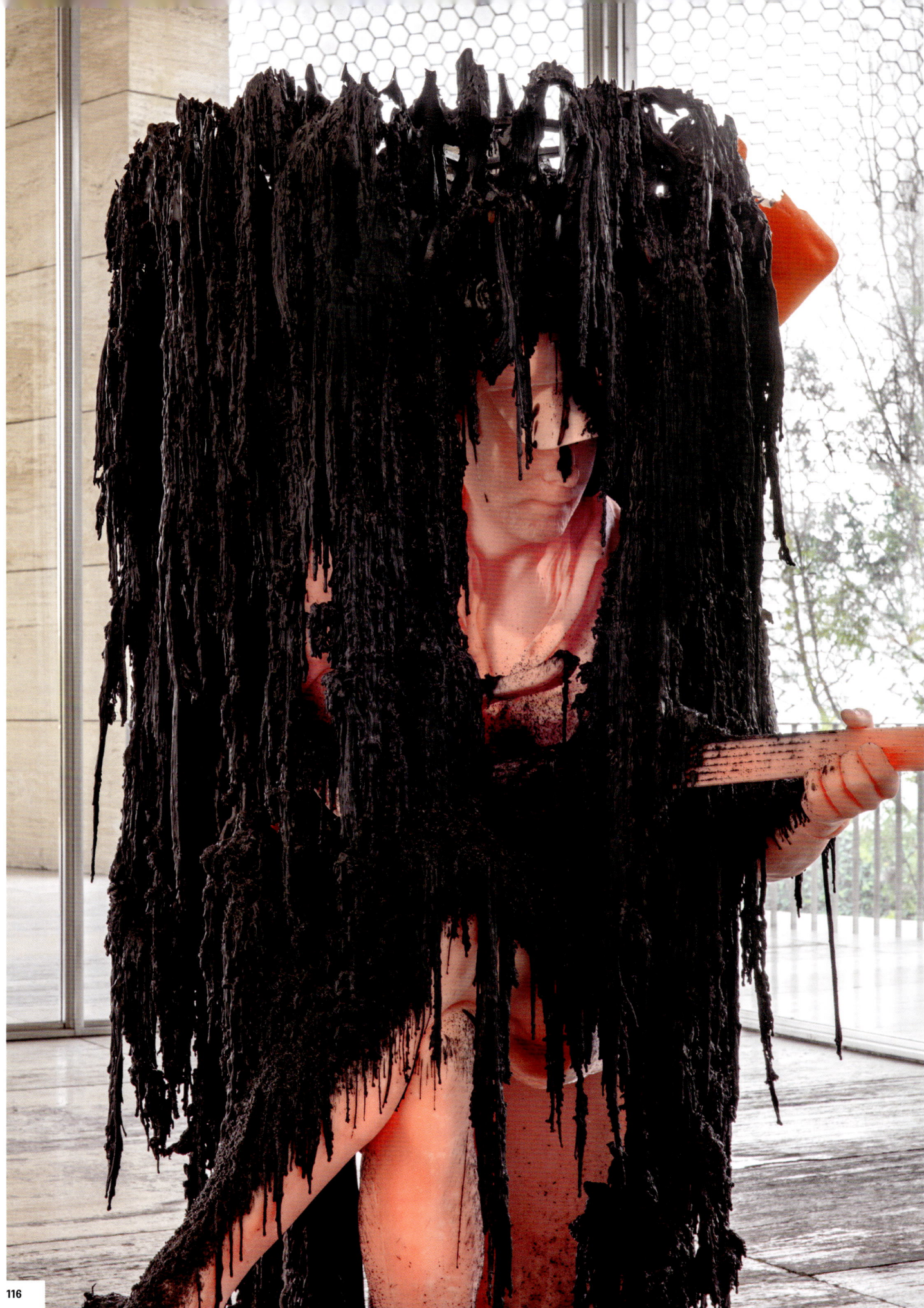

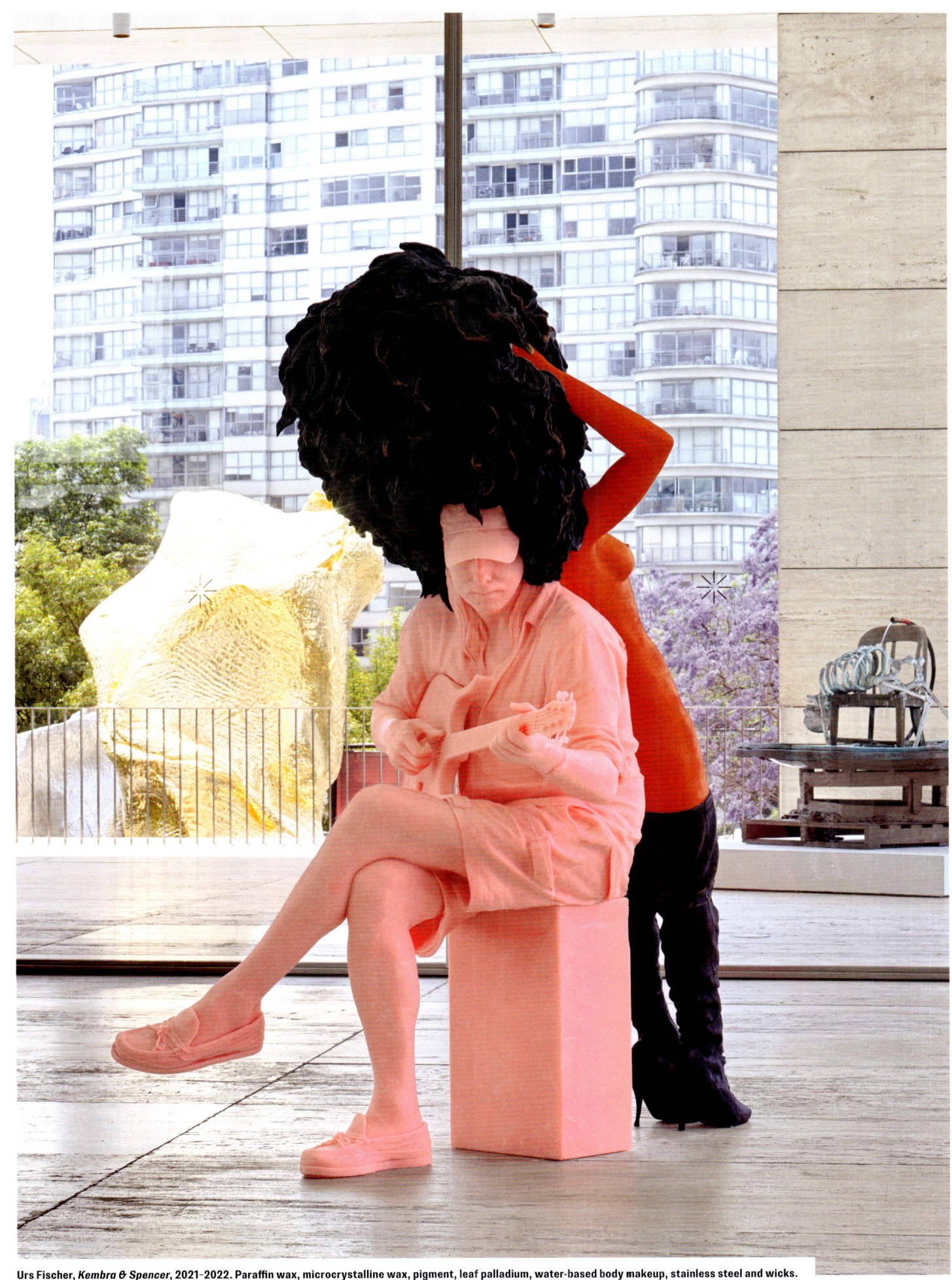

Urs Fischer, *Kembra & Spencer*, 2021–2022. Paraffin wax, microcrystalline wax, pigment, leaf palladium, water-based body makeup, stainless steel and wicks. 86.13 × 48.63 × 61.38 in. (218.8 × 123.5 × 156 cm). Edition 1 of 2, 1 AP

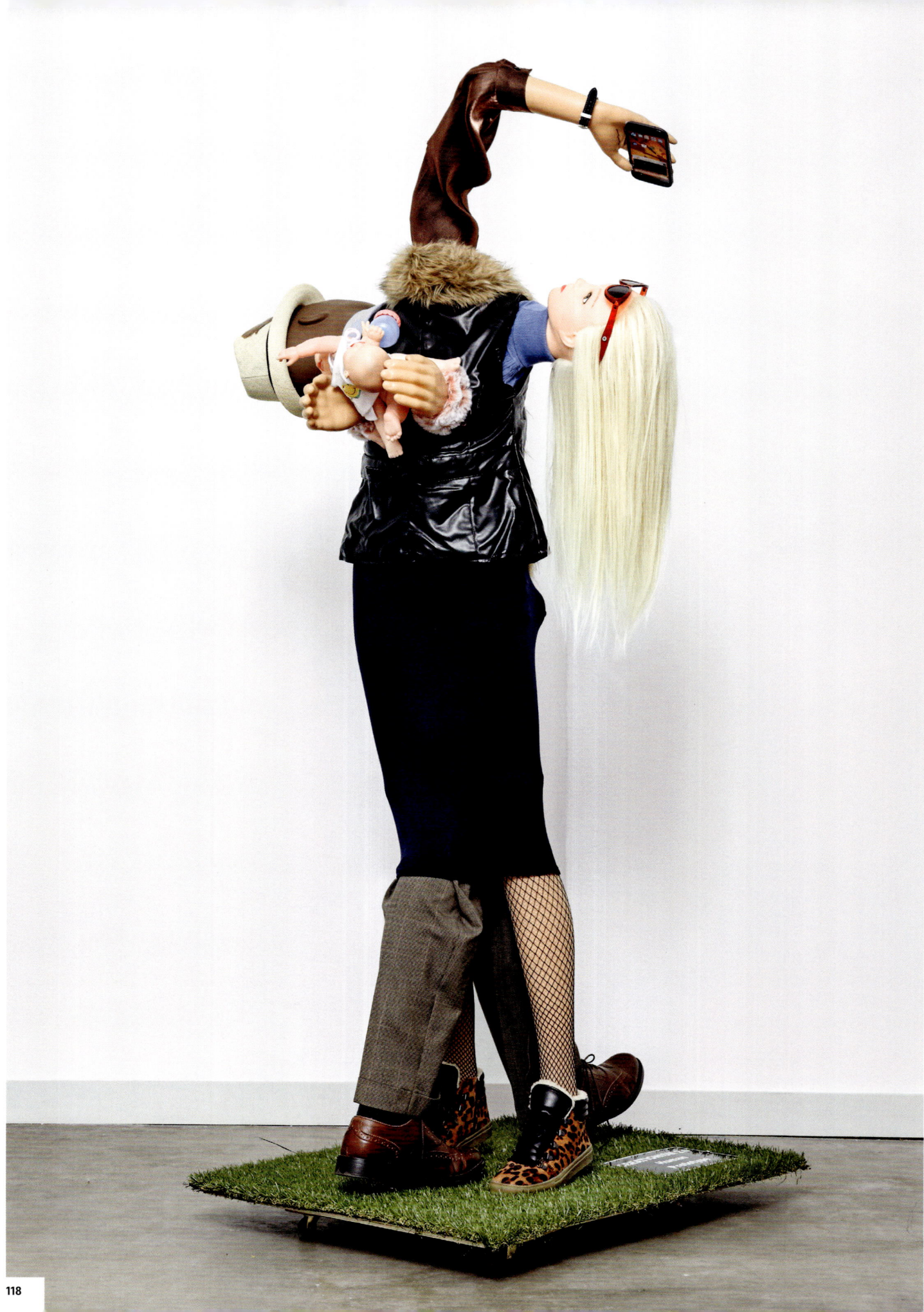

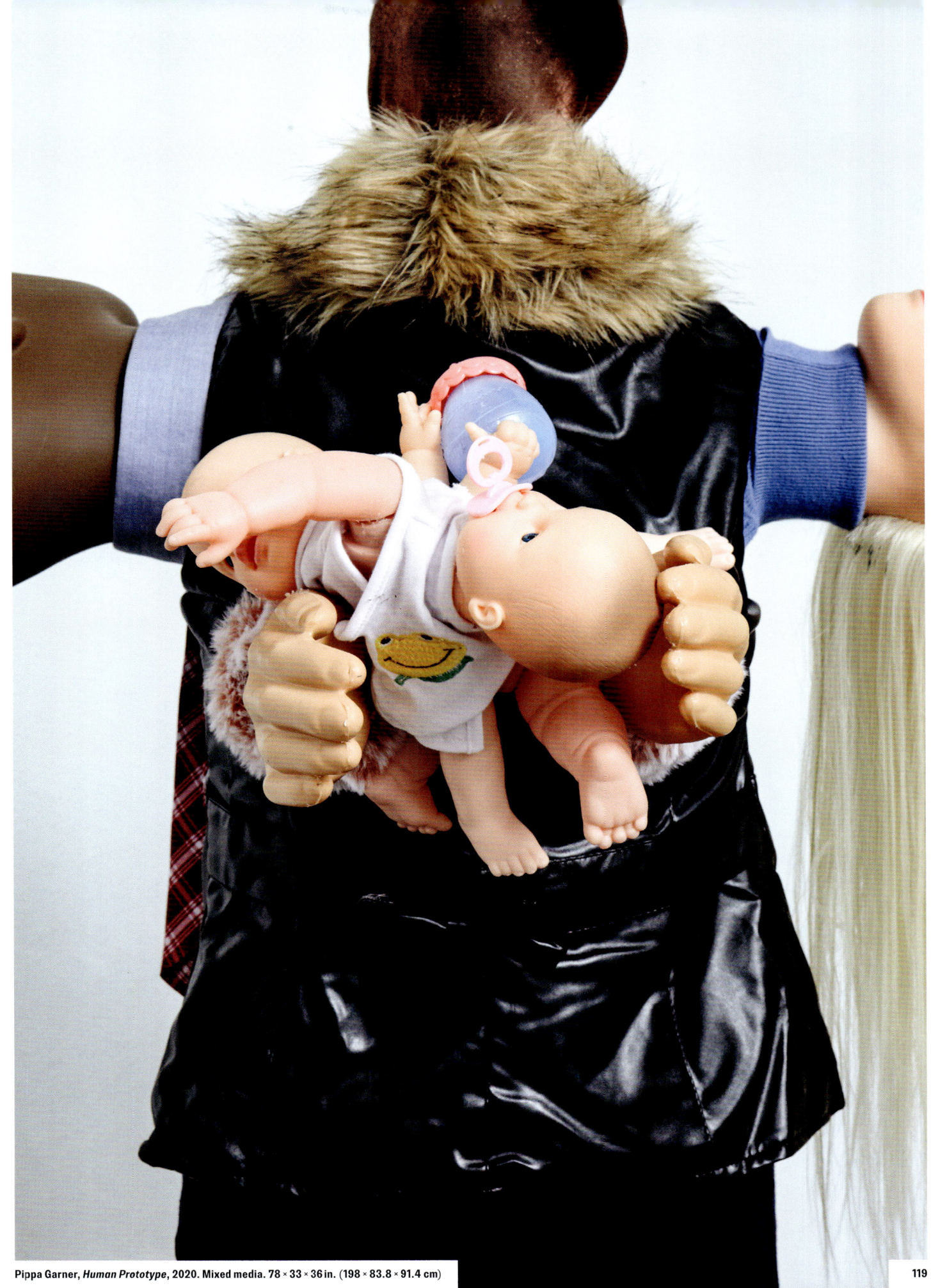

Pippa Garner, *Human Prototype*, 2020. Mixed media. 78 × 33 × 36 in. (198 × 83.8 × 91.4 cm)

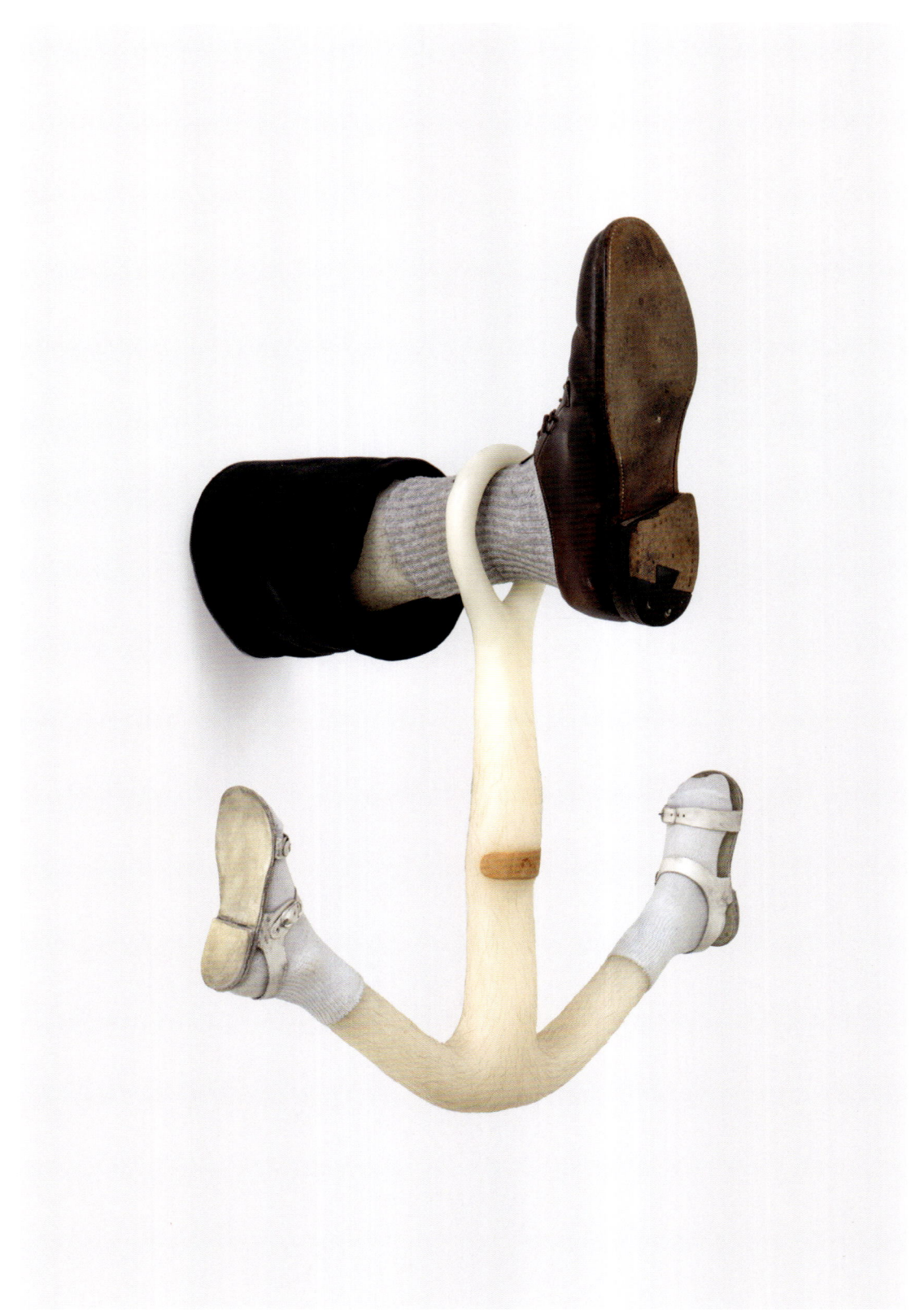

Robert Gober, *Untitled*, **2008–2009. Beeswax, cotton, leather, aluminum pull tabs, human hair and oil paint. 30.32 × 22.05 × 19.69 in. (77 × 56 × 50 cm)**

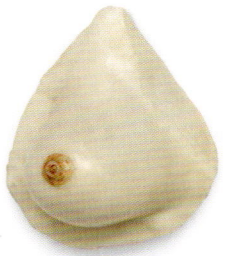

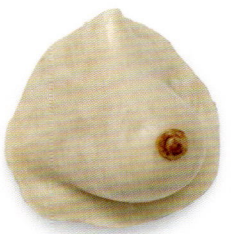

Robert Gober, *Two Breasts*, 1990. Beeswax and pigment. Left: 8.27 × 7 × 3.94 in. (21 × 17.8 × 10 cm). Right: 7.28 × 7 × 4.13 in. (18.5 × 17.8 × 10.5 cm)

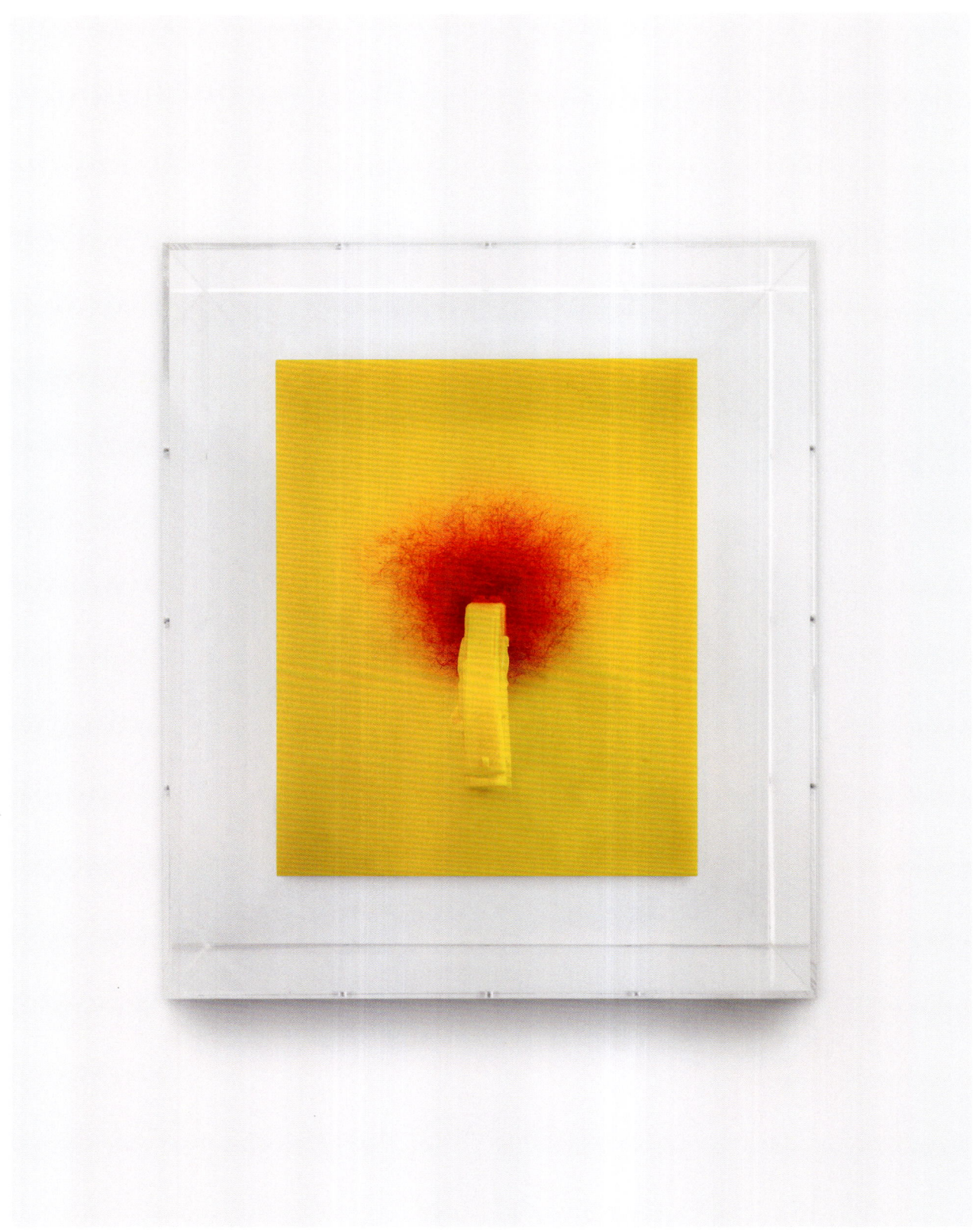

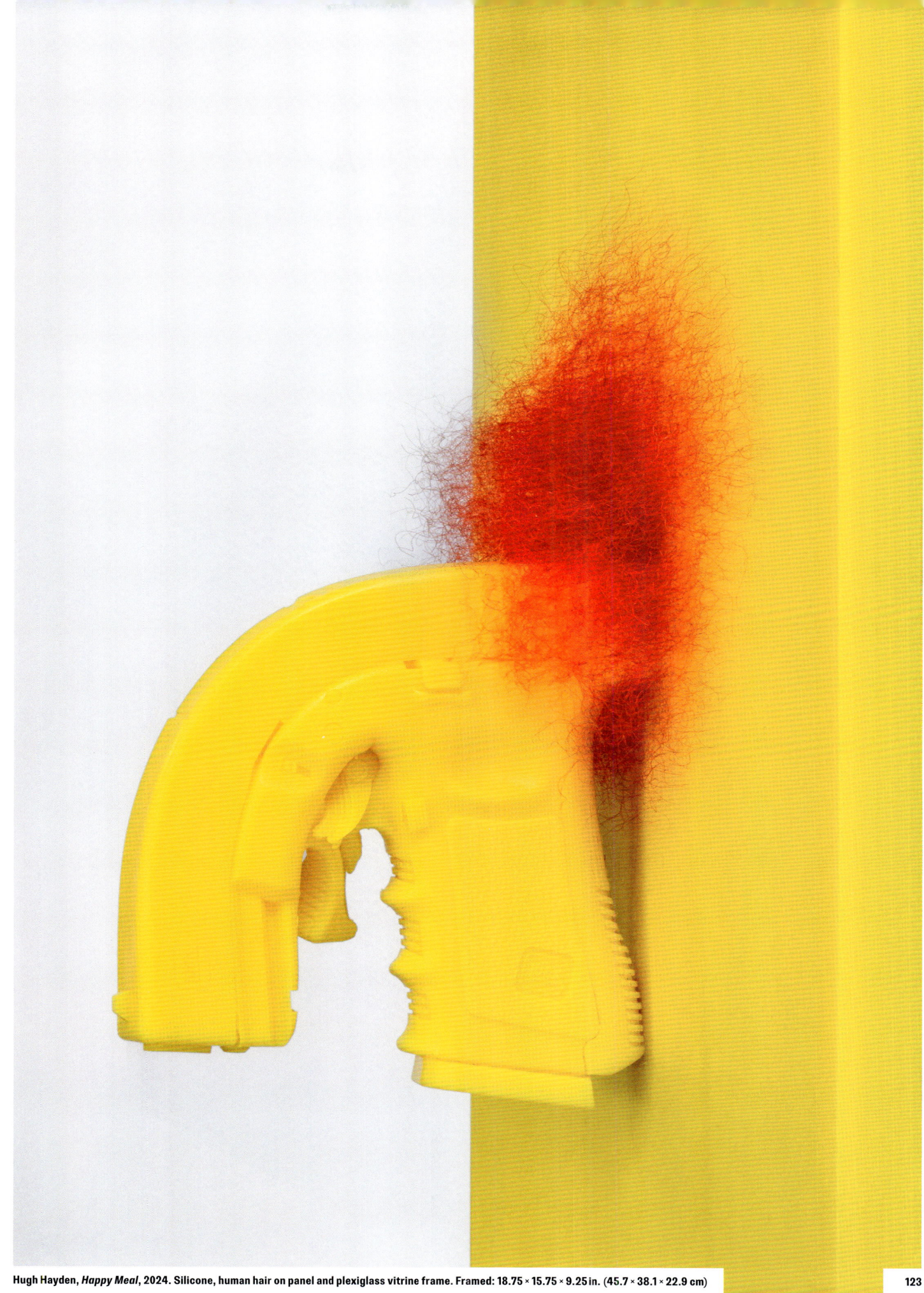

Hugh Hayden, *Happy Meal*, 2024. Silicone, human hair on panel and plexiglass vitrine frame. Framed: 18.75 × 15.75 × 9.25 in. (45.7 × 38.1 × 22.9 cm)

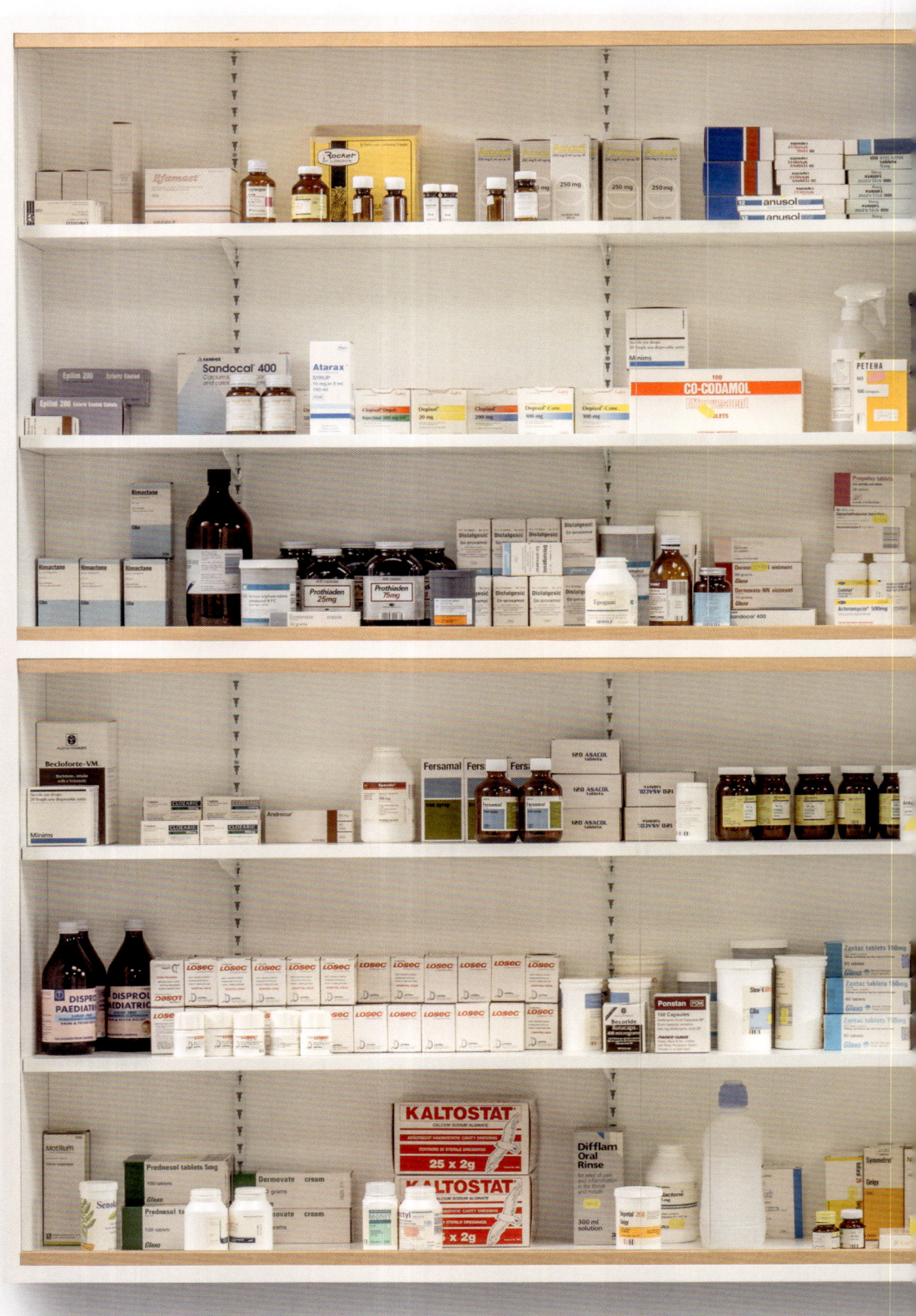

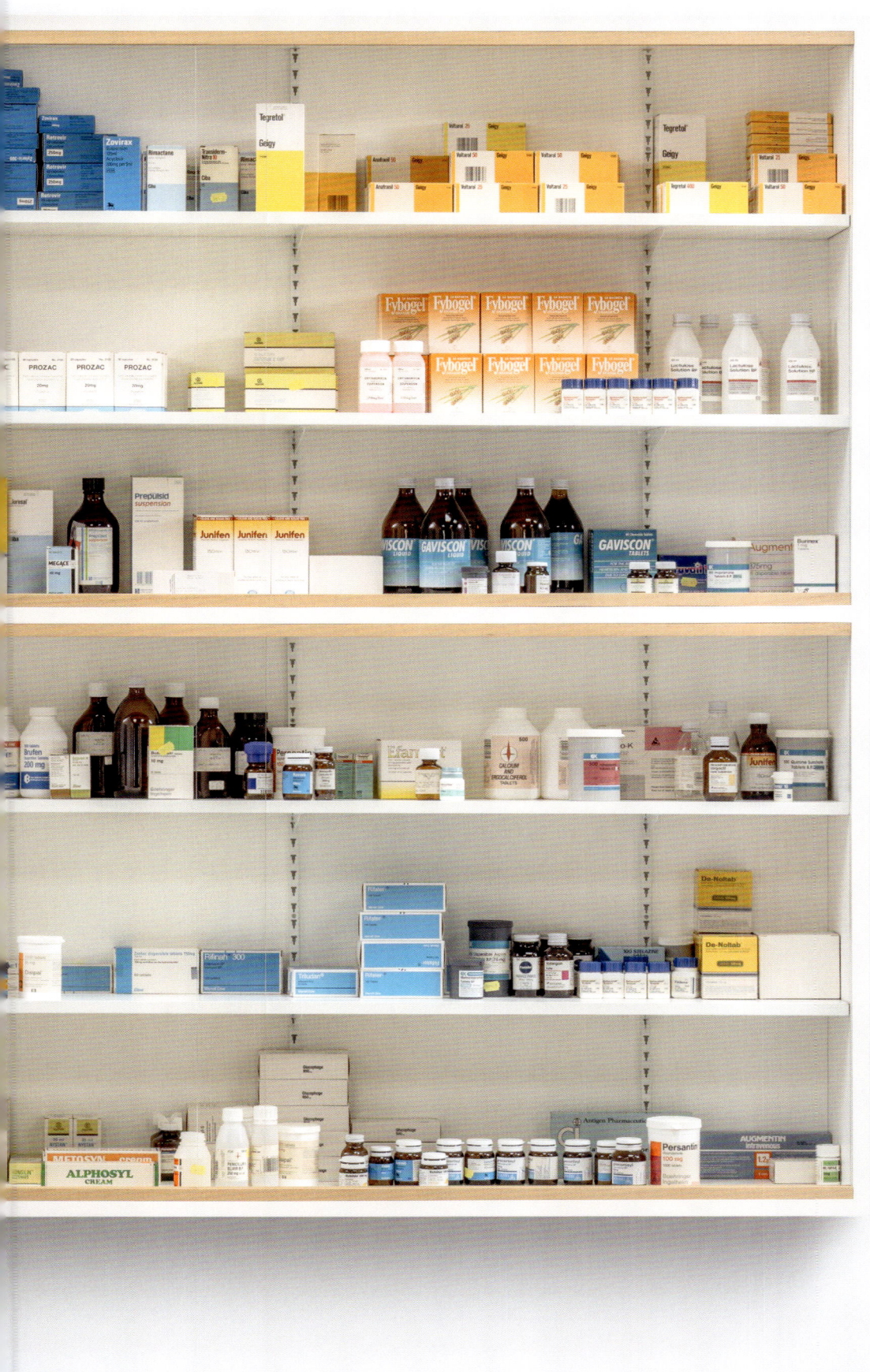

Damien Hirst, *Nothing is a Problem for Me***, 1992. Glass, sprayed MDF, ramin, aluminum, steel and pharmaceutical packaging. 72 × 108 × 12 in. (182.9 × 274.3 × 20.5 cm)**

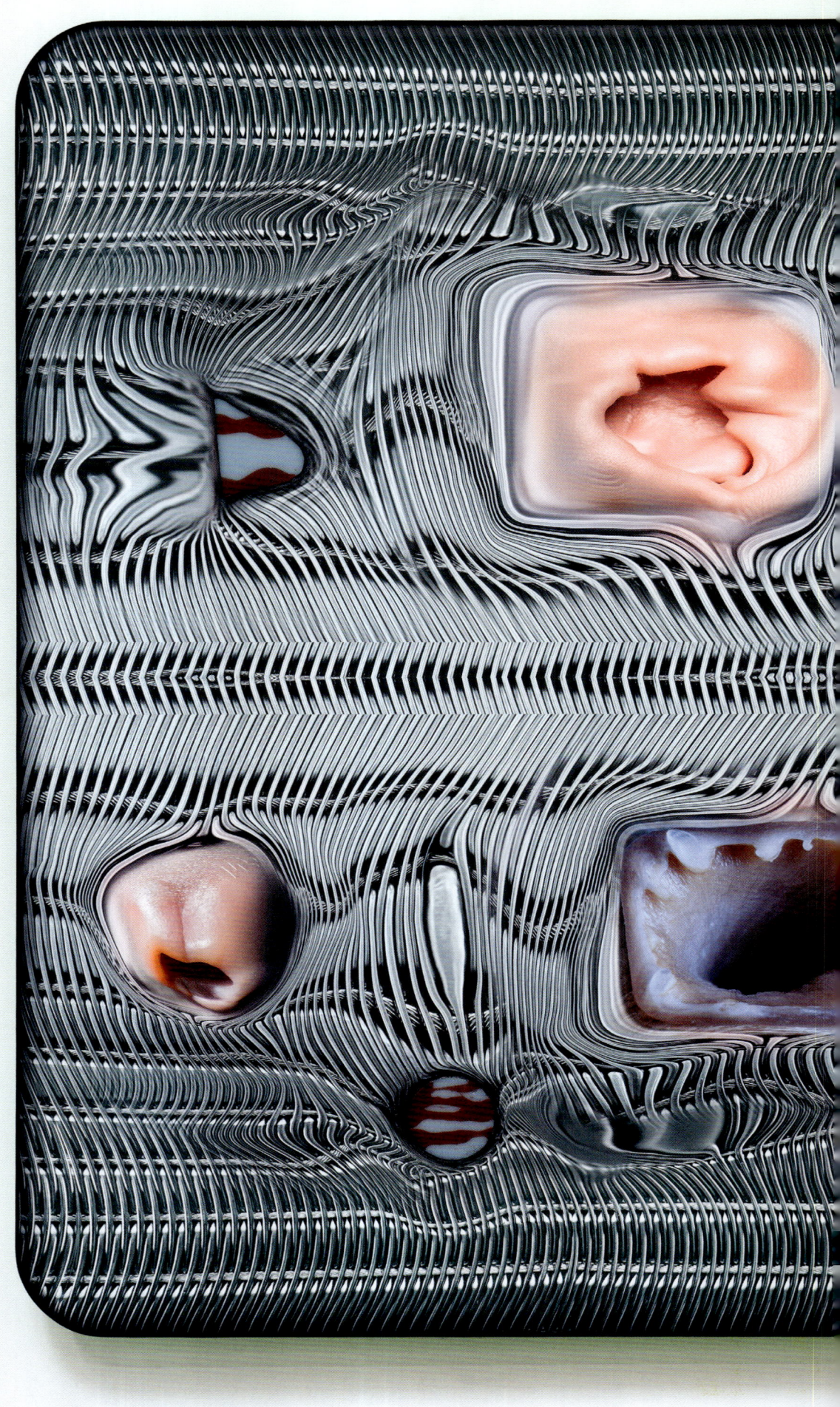

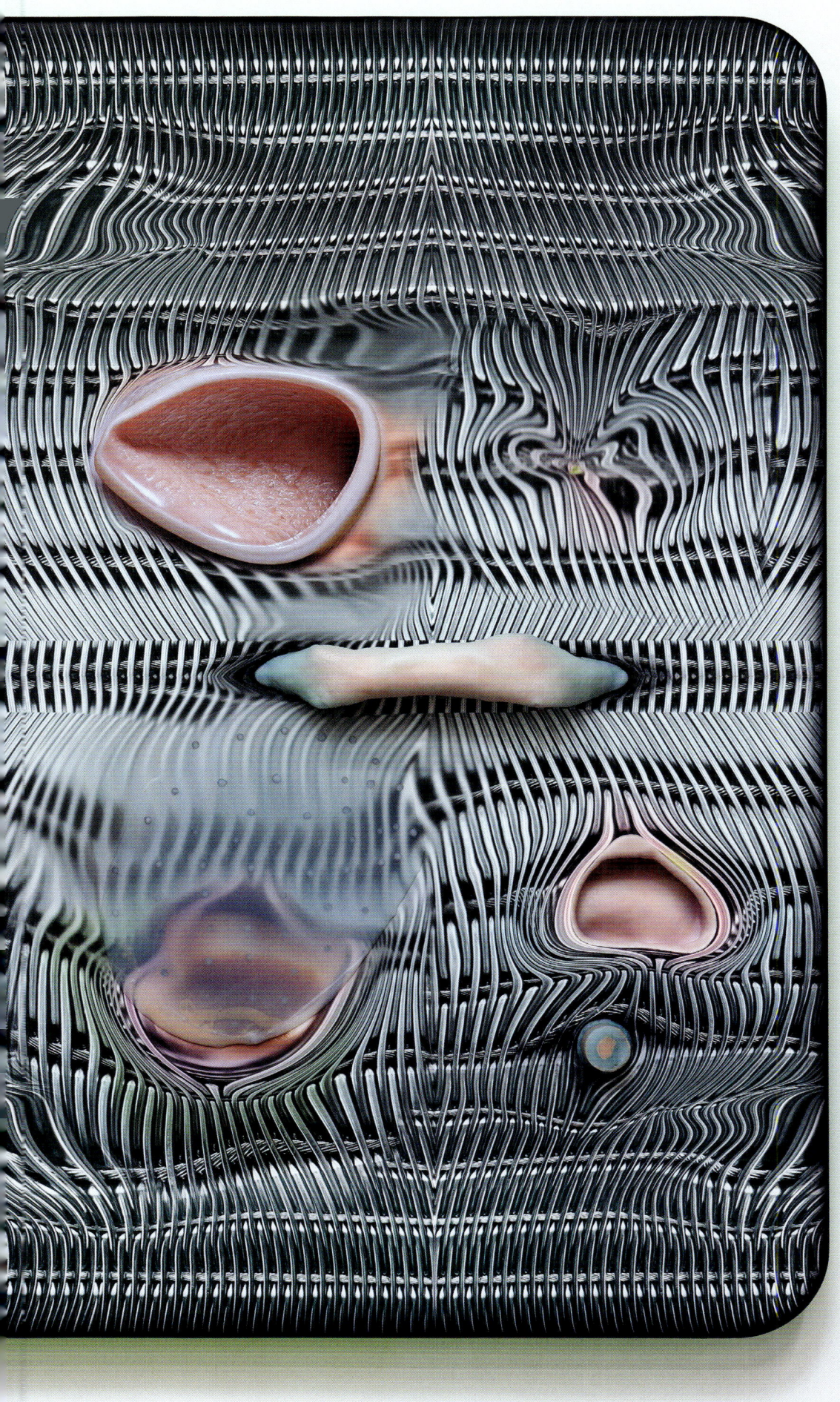

Tishan Hsu, *mammal-screen-green-2*, 2024. UV cured inkjet, silicone, acrylic and stainless steel, ink on wood. 47.5 × 61.5 × 5.5 in. (120.7 × 156.2 × 14 cm)

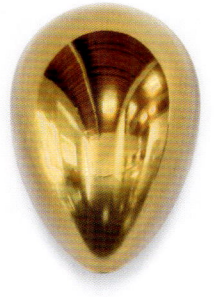

Pierre Huyghe, *Idiom*, **2024. Real-time voice generated by artificial intelligence and golden LED screen masks. 110.25 × 70.88 in. (31 × 19.5 × 19 cm). Set of 1 mask.**
Edition 3 of 15, 2 AP

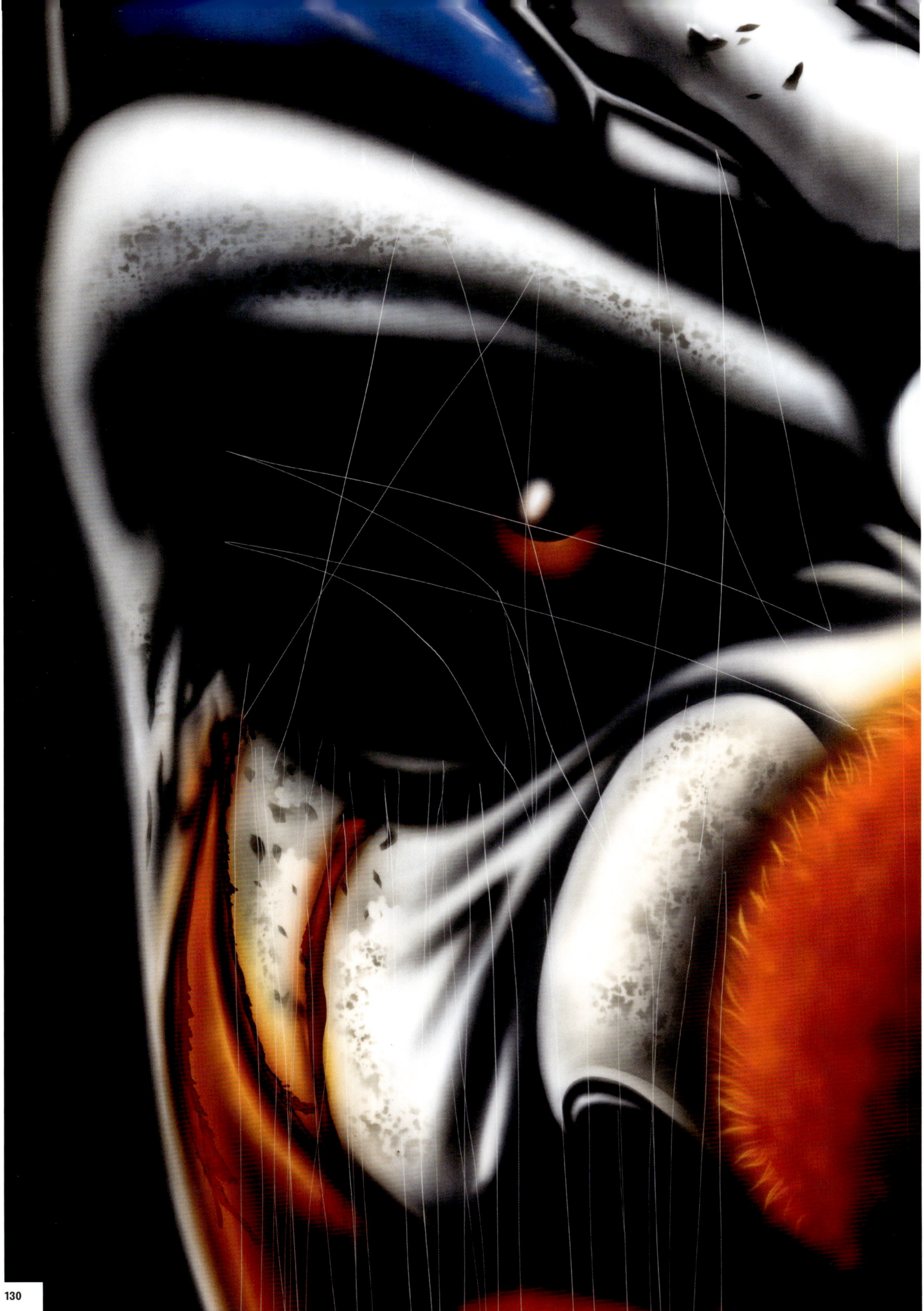

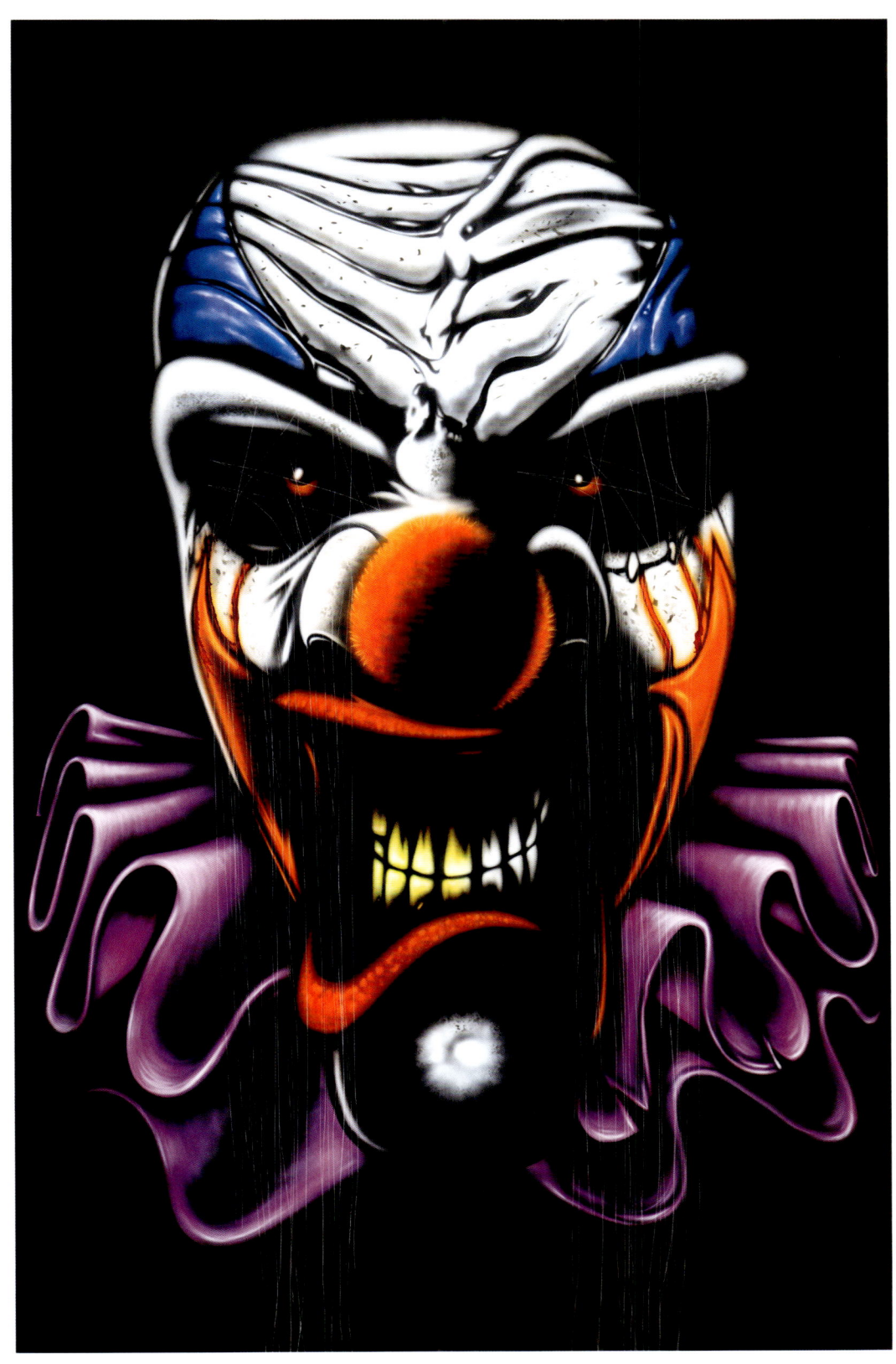

Anne Imhof, *Clown (byzantine)*, 2023. Acrylic on aluminum. 110.25 × 70.88 in. (280 × 180 cm)

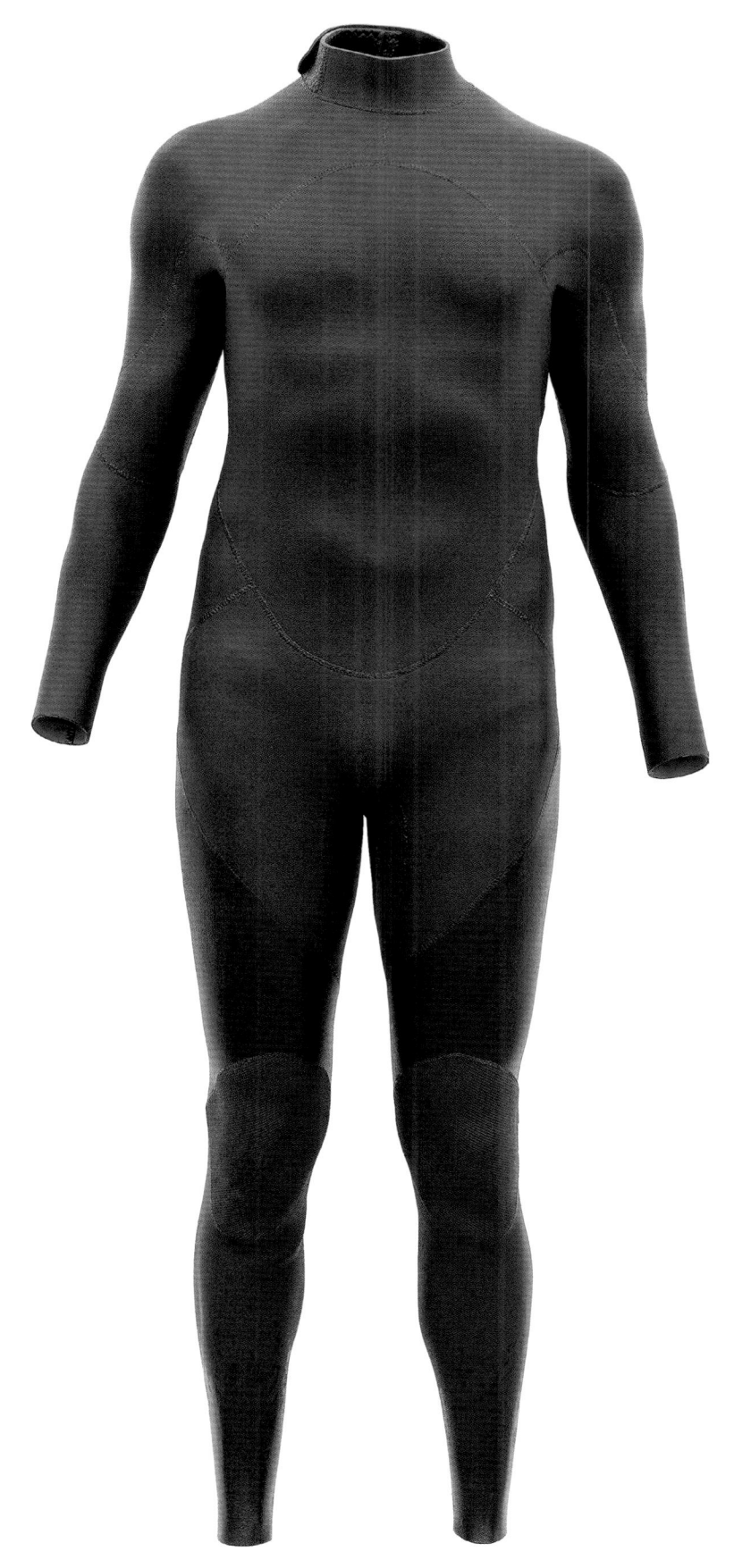

Alex Israel, *Self-Portrait (Wetsuit)*, 2017. Acrylic on aluminum. 55.125 × 24 × 18 in. (140 × 61 × 45.7 cm)

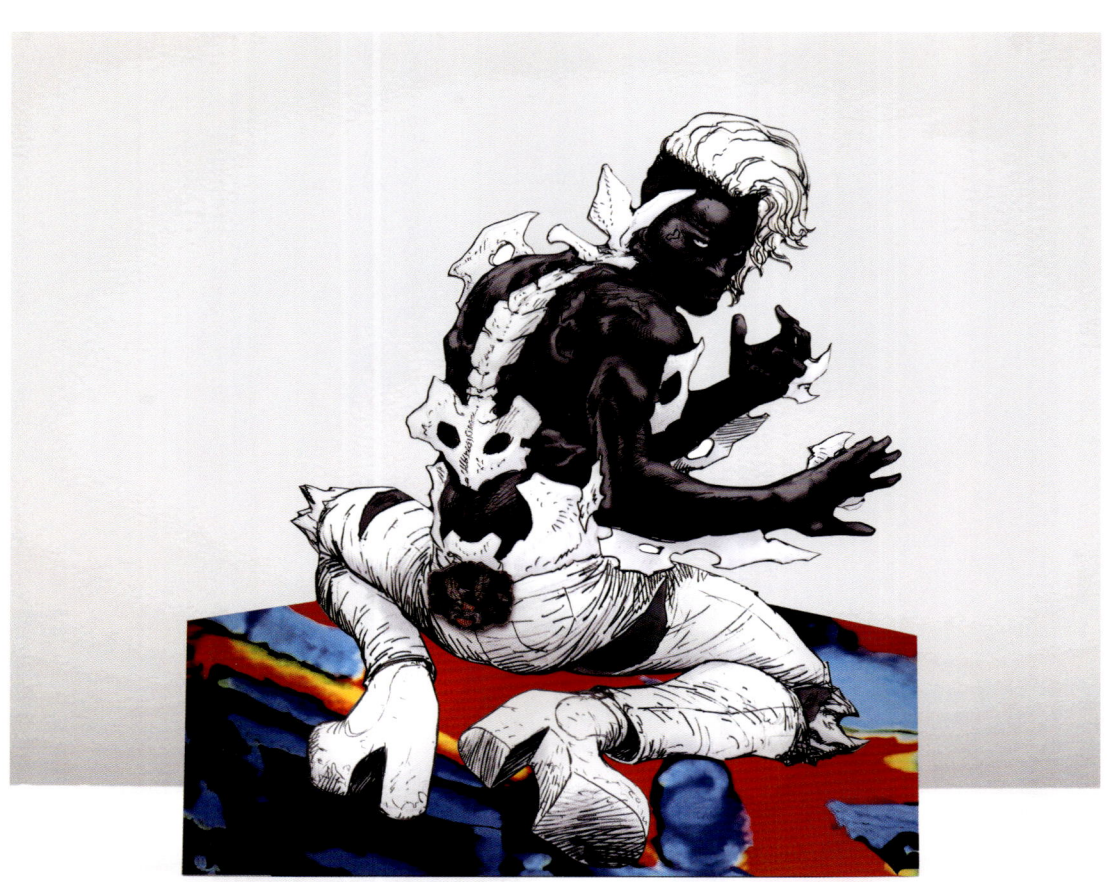

Arthur Jafa, *Don (small)*, 2023. Color print on Dibond and aluminum plate stand. 22 × 20 × 7 inches (55.9 × 50.8 × 17.8 cm). Edition 2 of 20

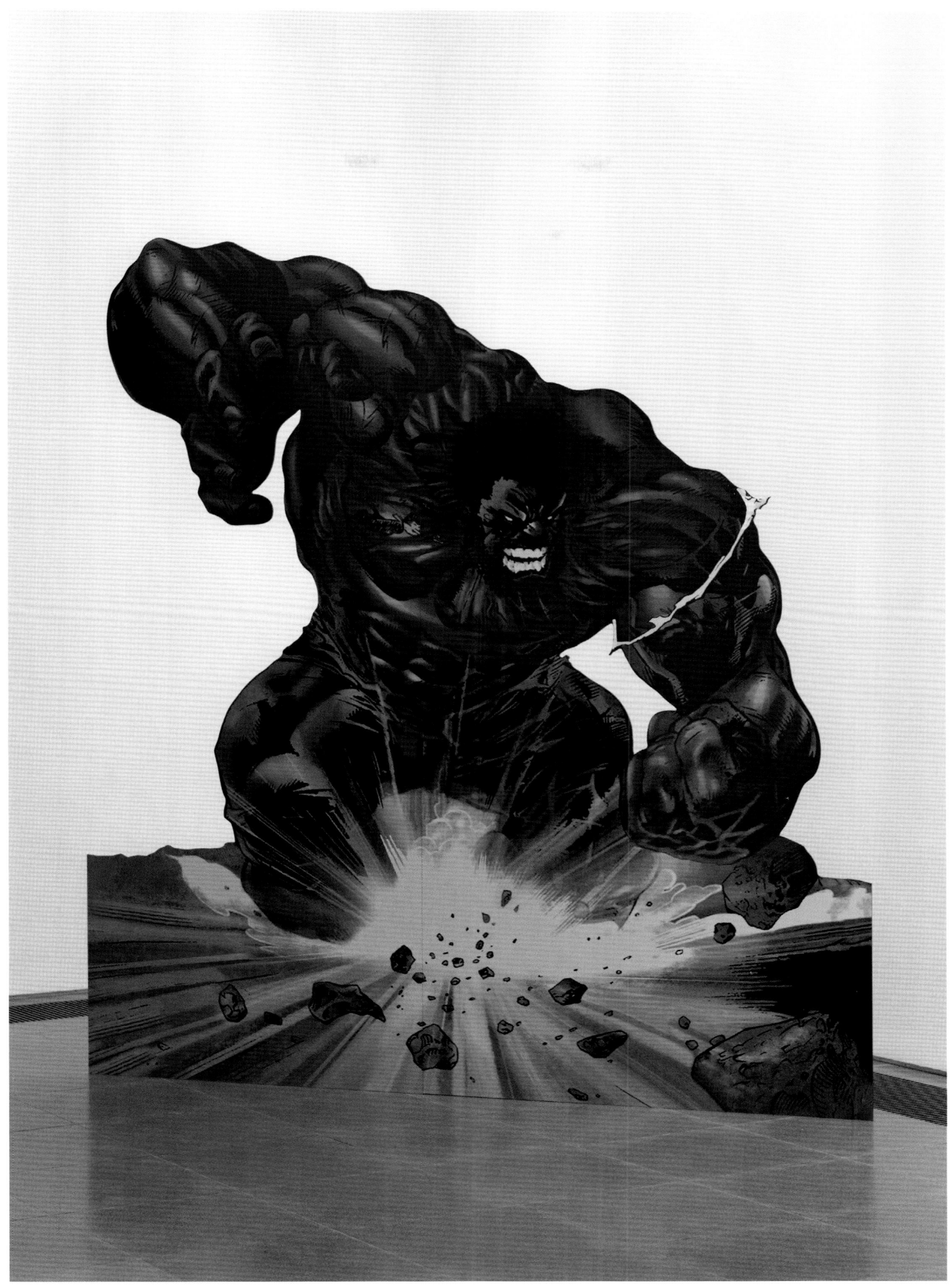

Arthur Jafa, *LeRage*, 2017. Color print on Dibond and aluminum plate stand. 83.88 × 77.25 × 18.25 in. (213 × 196 × 47 cm). Exhibition Copy, Edition of 5, 2 AP

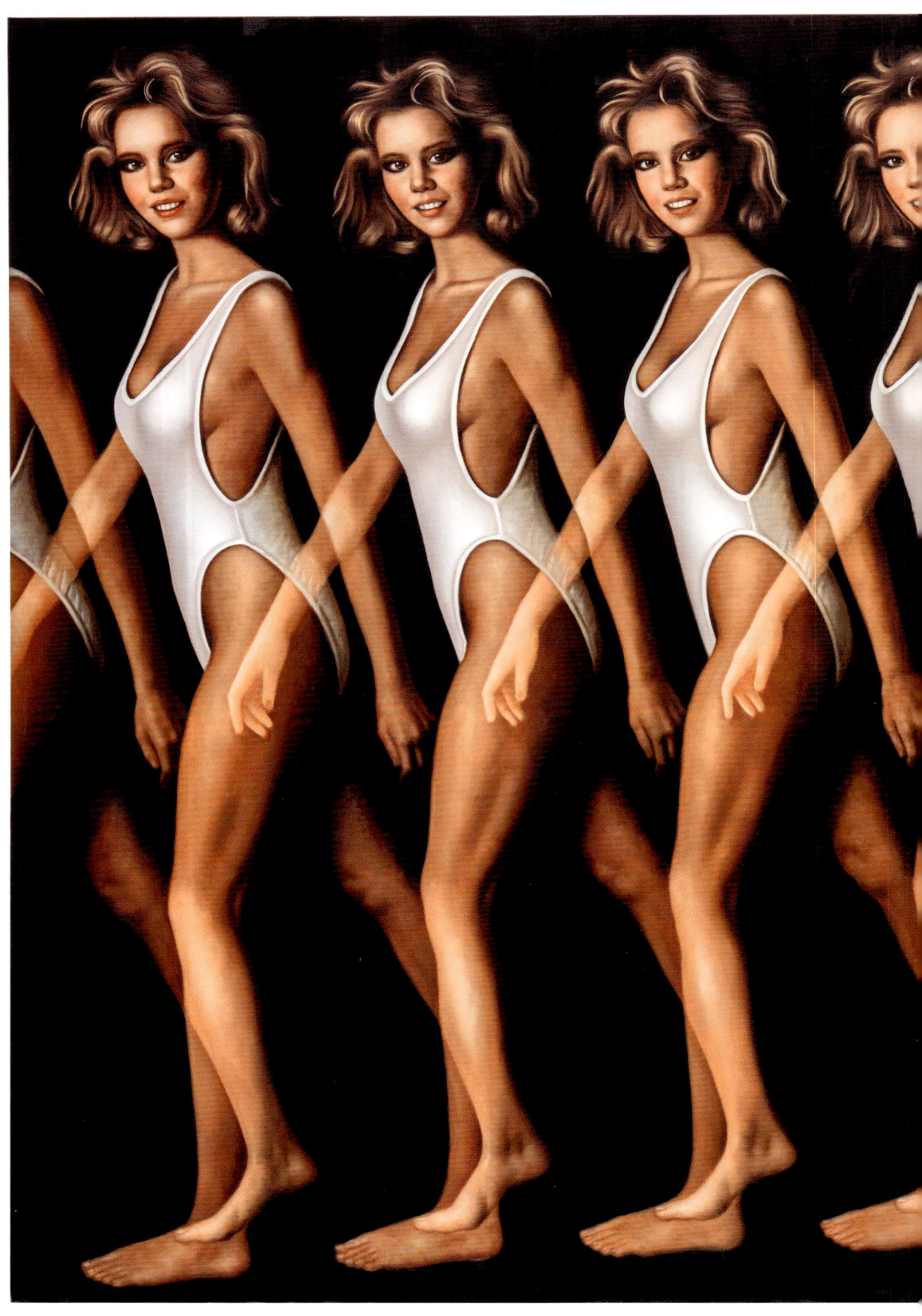

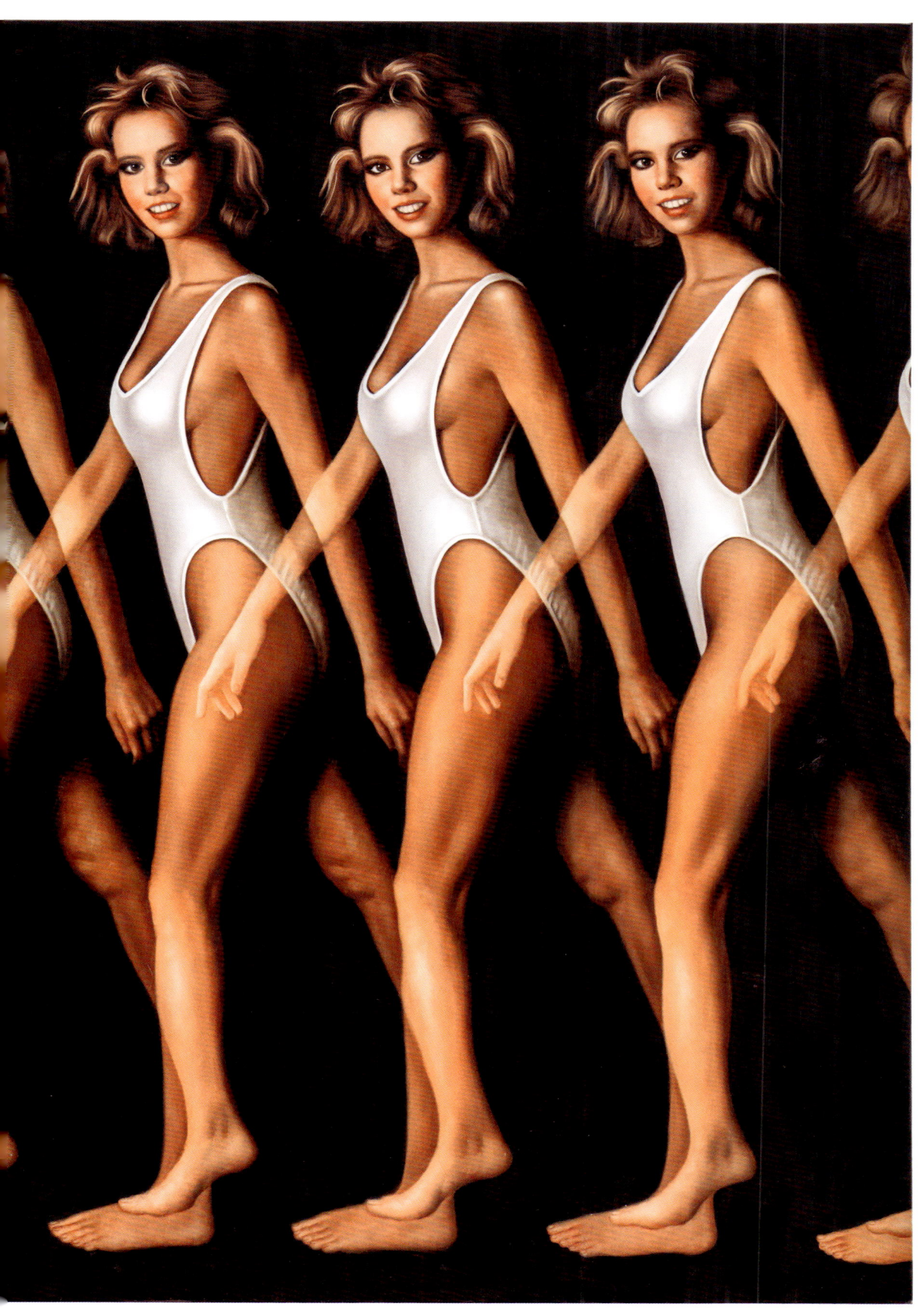

Jamian Juliano-Villani, *Women*, 2024. Oil on canvas. 76 × 111.25 × 1.5 in. (193 × 282.6 × 3.8 cm)

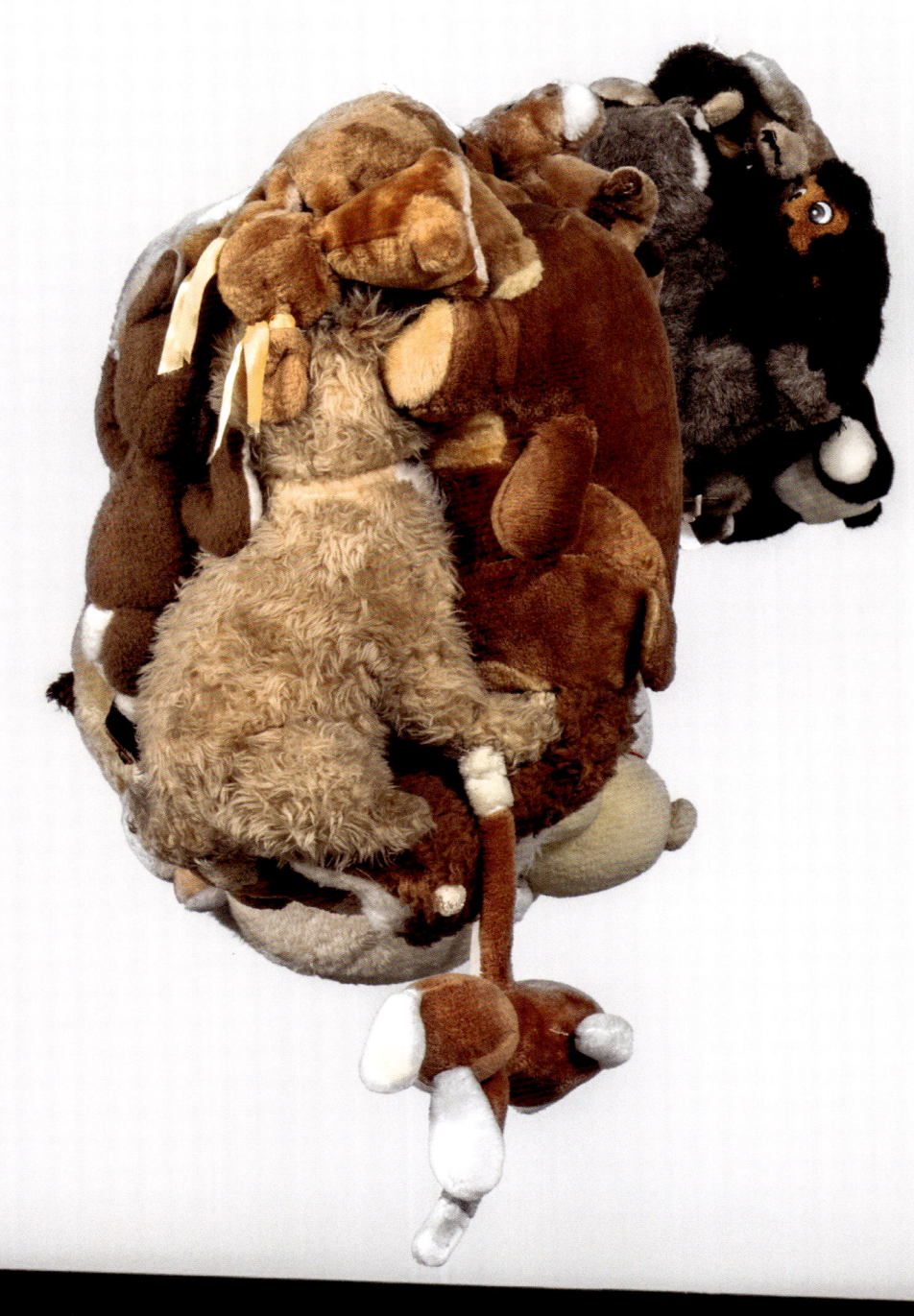

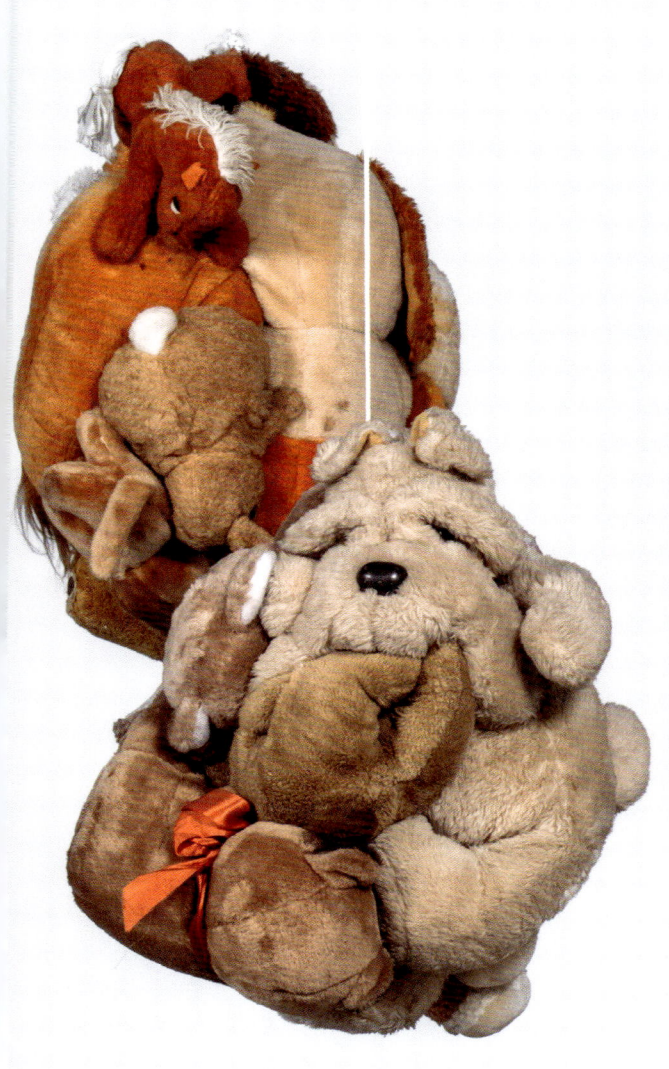
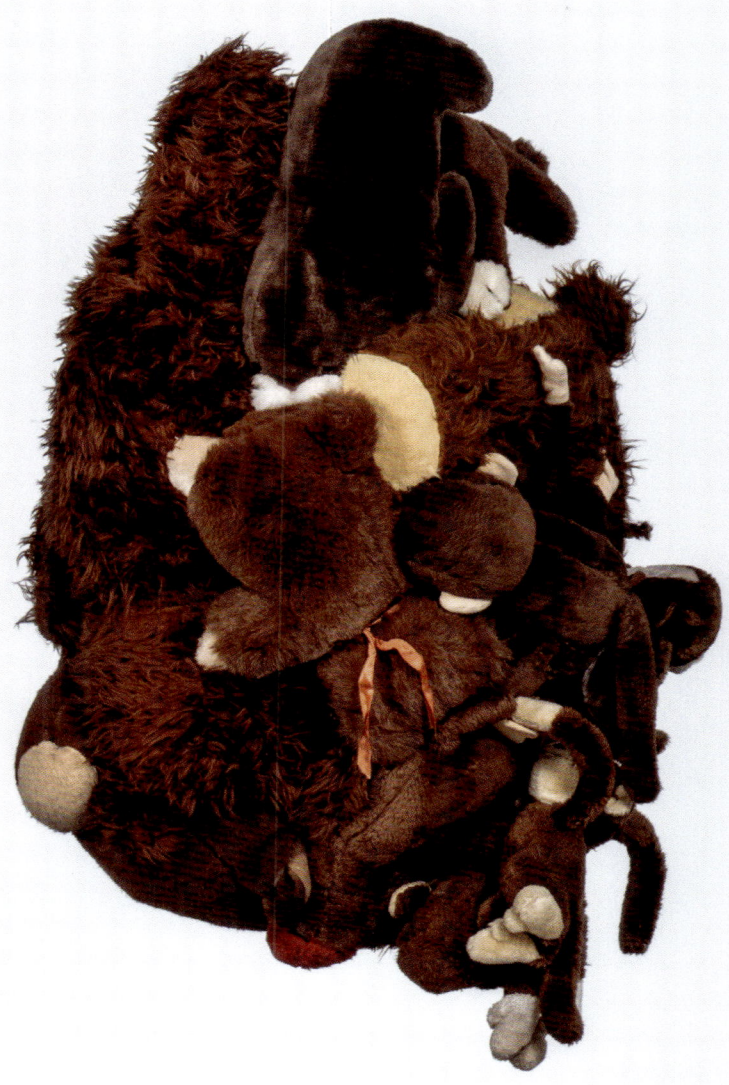

Mike Kelley, *Brown Star*, 1991. Stuffed animals, steel and strings. 101 × 73 in. (256.5 × 185.4 cm), height variable.

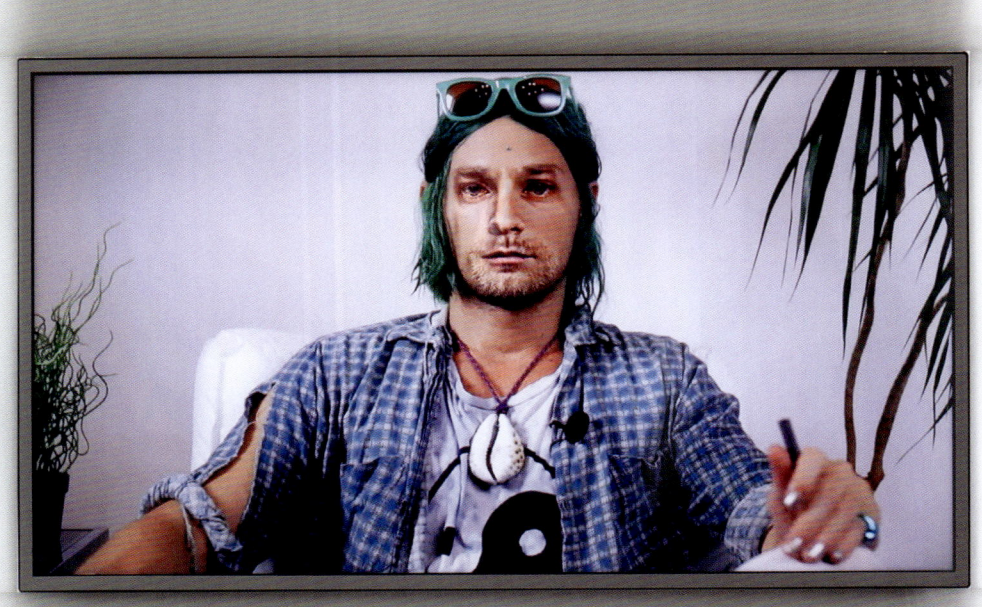

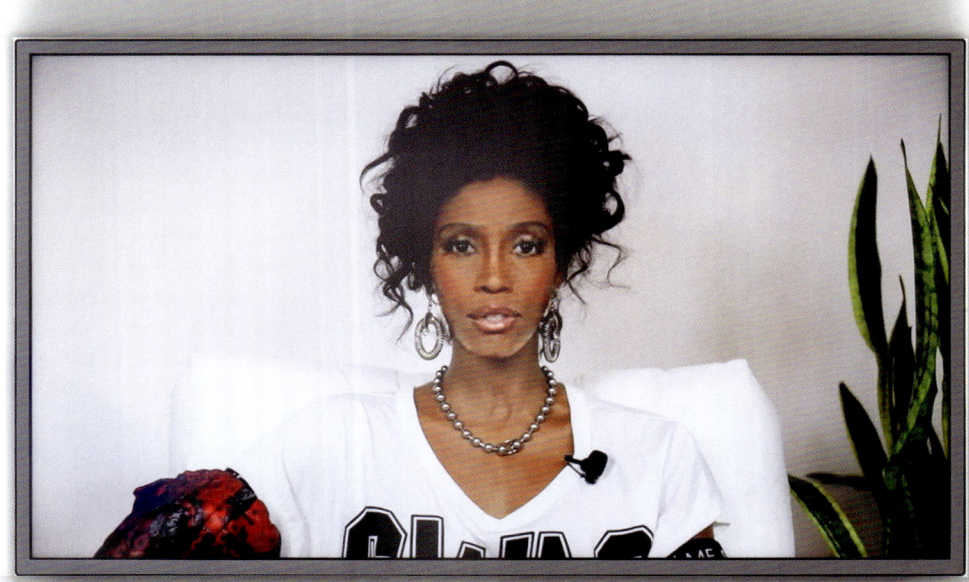

Top: Josh Kline, *Forever 27 (Kurt) / Citi Display Wall 46"*, 2013. HD video, sound, color, 14:39 min. Light-box display: plexiglass, LED lights, MDF, plywood, HD television, media player and SD card. 120 × 47 × 5.75 in. (304.8 × 119.4 × 14.6 cm). Edition 2 of 3, 2 AP

Bottom: Josh Kline, *Forever 48 (Whitney) / Citi Display Wall 46"*, 2013. HD video, sound, color, 16:06 min. Light-box display: plexiglass, LED lights, MDF, plywood, HD television, media player and SD card. 120 × 47 × 5.75 in. (304.8 × 119.4 × 14.6 cm). Edition 2 of 3, 2 AP

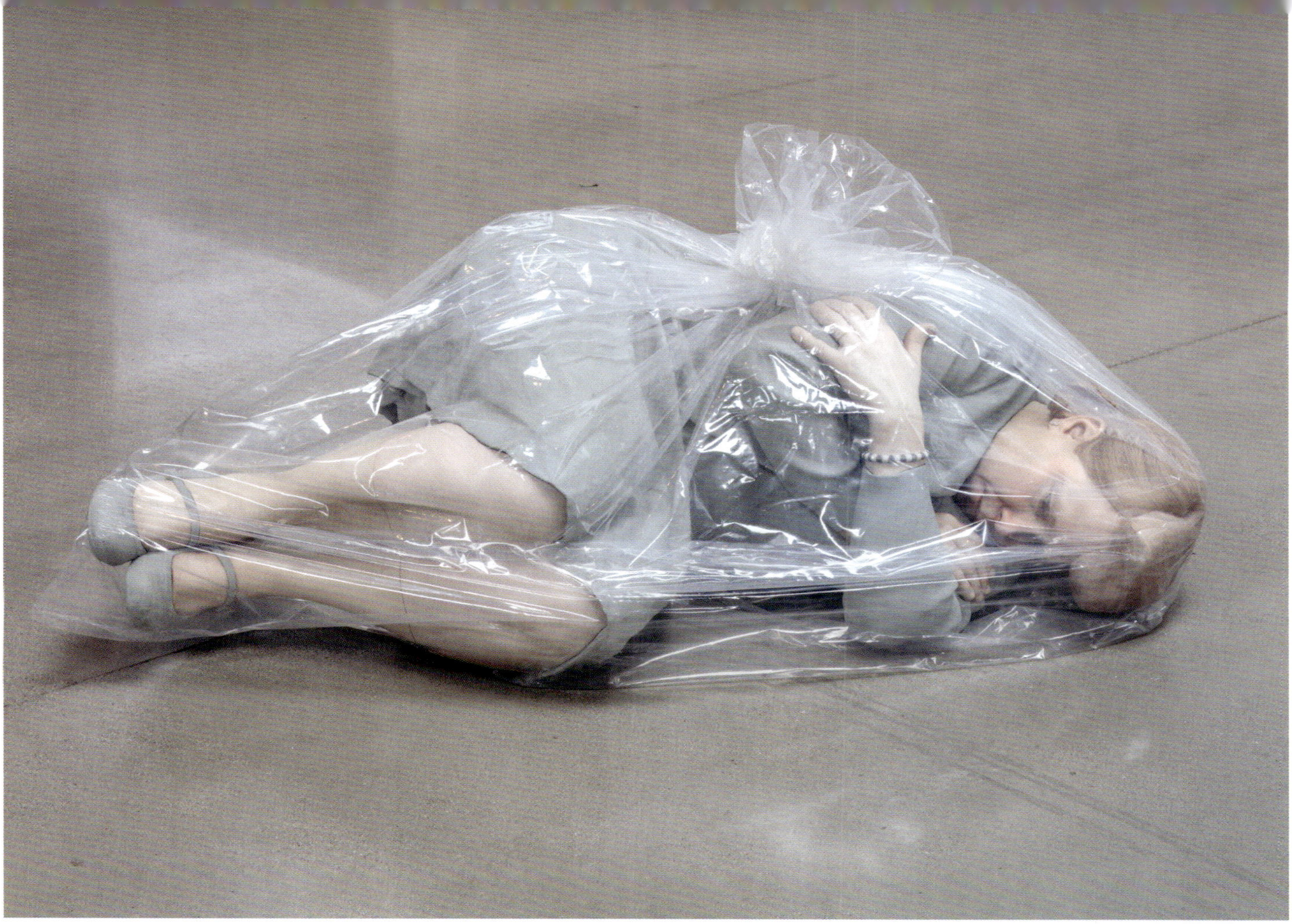

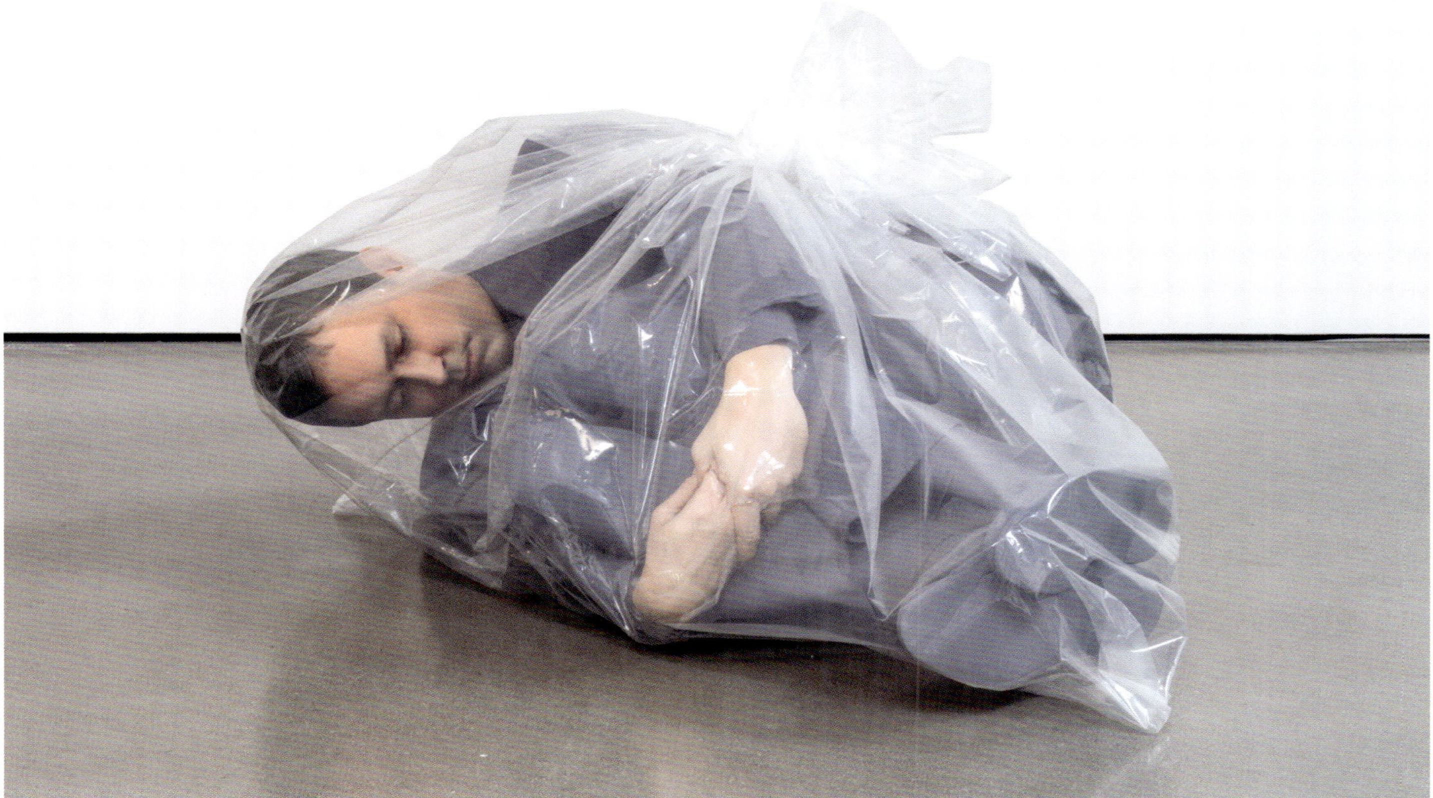

Top: Josh Kline, *MAOI Inhibitors Can't Fix This (Elizabeth / Administrative Assistant)*, 2016. 3D-printed plaster, ink-jet ink, and cyanoacrylate, foam and polyethylene bag. 21 × 28 × 44 in. (58.4 × 71.1 × 99.1 cm). Edition 3 of 3, 2 AP

Bottom: Josh Kline, *Aspirational Foreclosure (Matthew / Mortgage Loan Officer)*, 2016. 3D-printed plaster, ink-jet ink, and cyanoacrylate, foam and polyethylene bag. 21 × 28 × 44 in. (53.3 × 71.1 × 111.8 cm). Edition 3 of 3, 2 AP

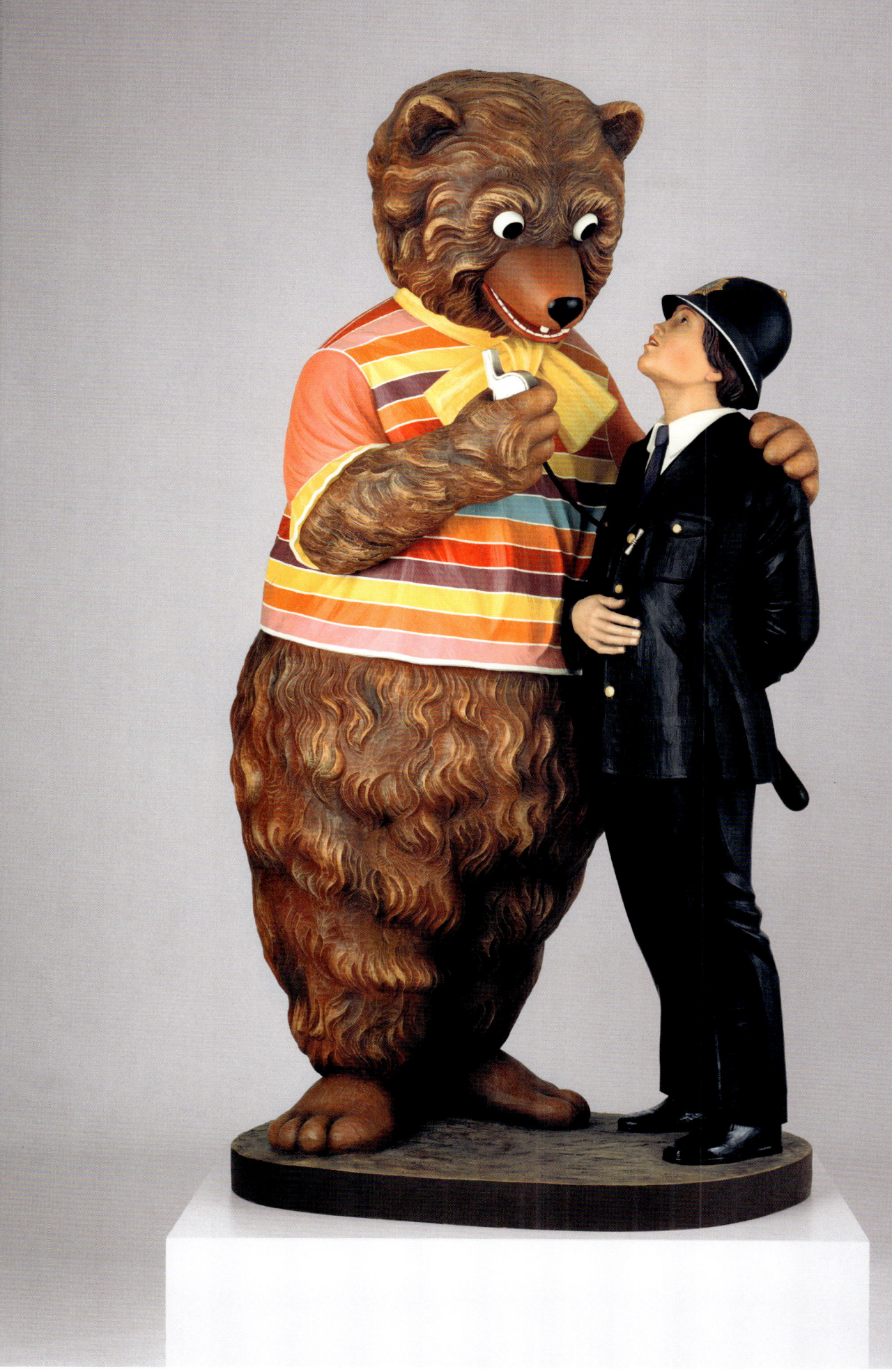

Jeff Koons, *Bear and Policeman*, 1988. Polychromed wood. 85 × 43 × 37 in. (215.9 × 109.2 × 94 cm). Artist Proof from an edition of 3, 1 AP

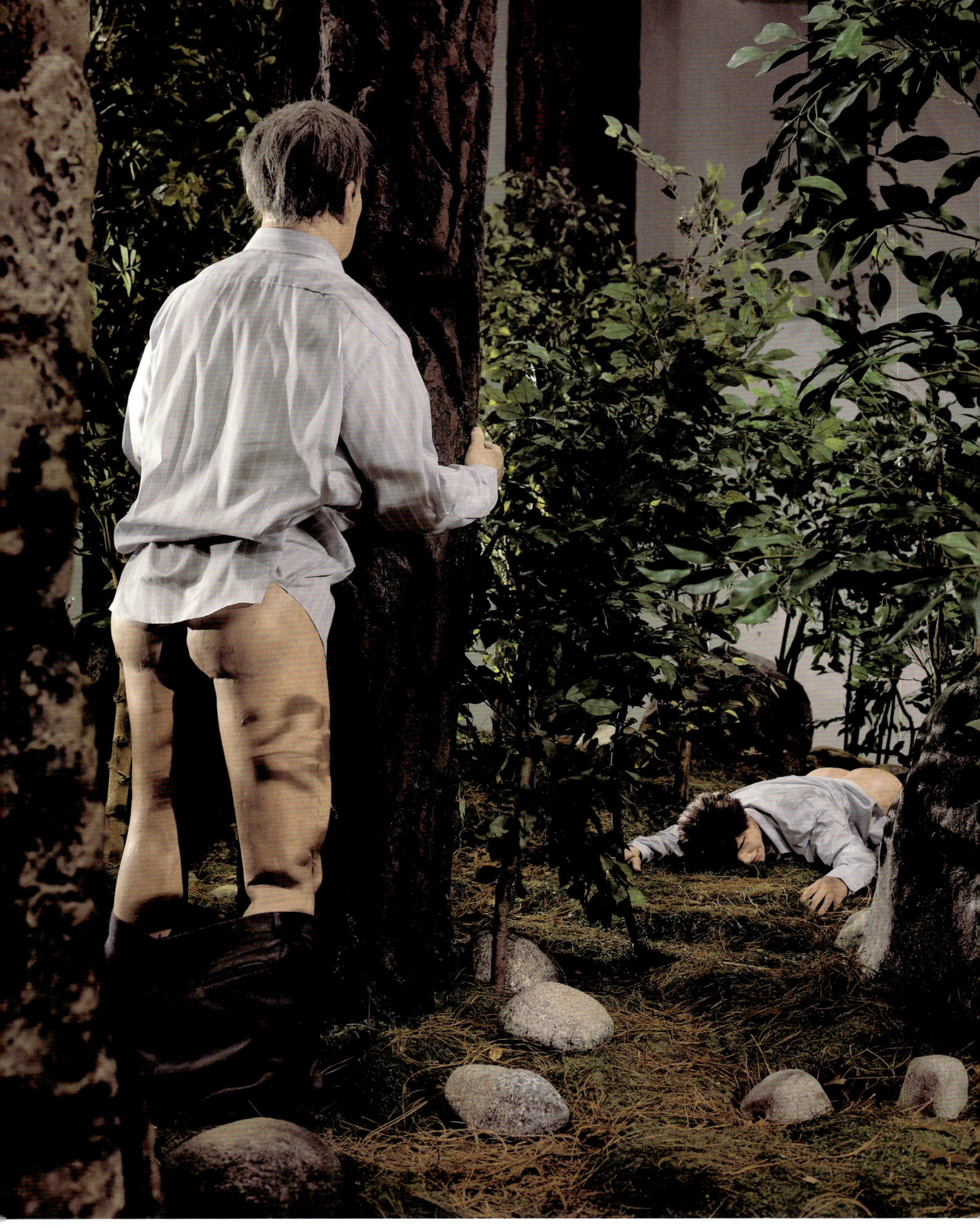

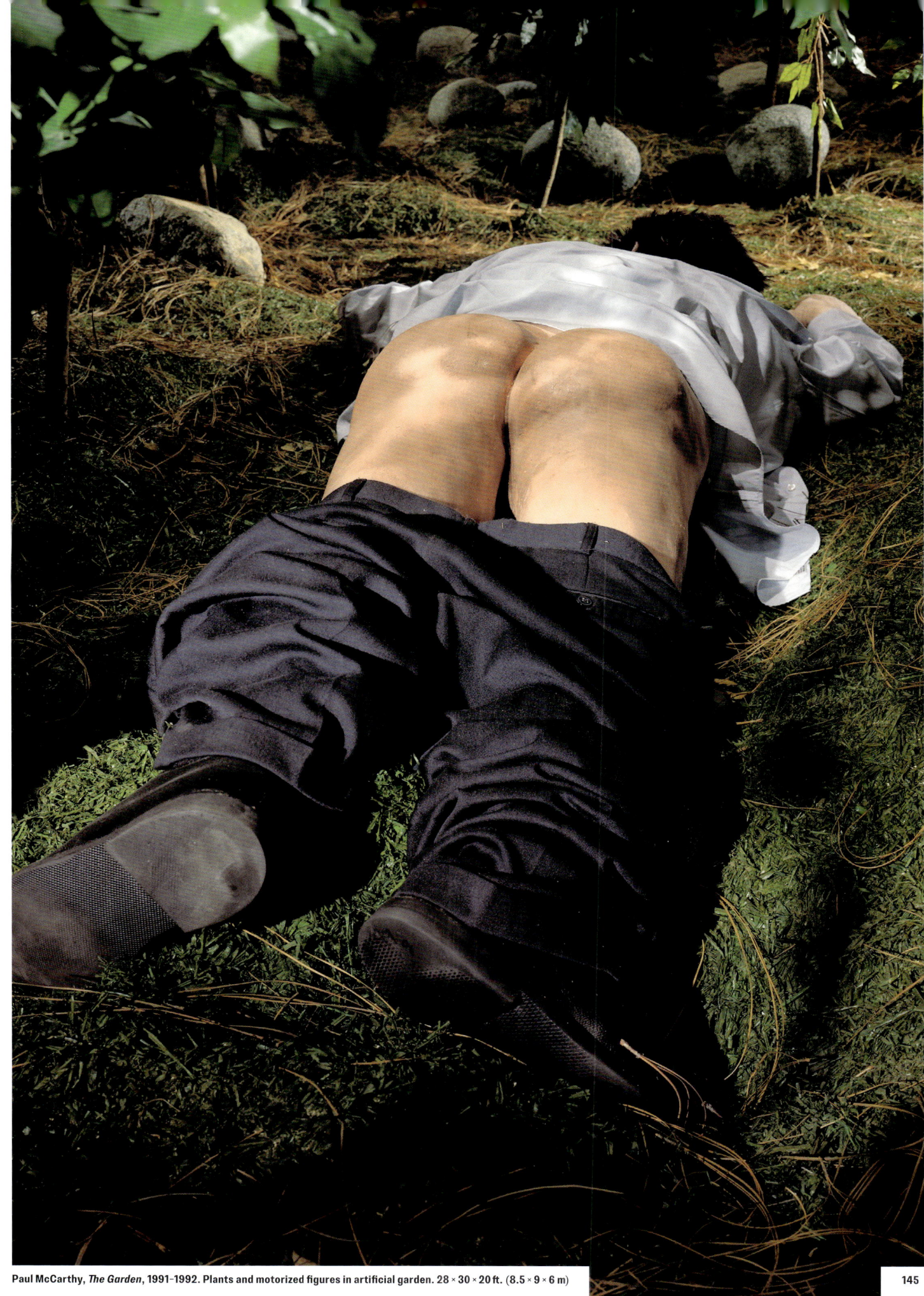

Paul McCarthy, *The Garden*, 1991-1992. Plants and motorized figures in artificial garden. 28 × 30 × 20 ft. (8.5 × 9 × 6 m)

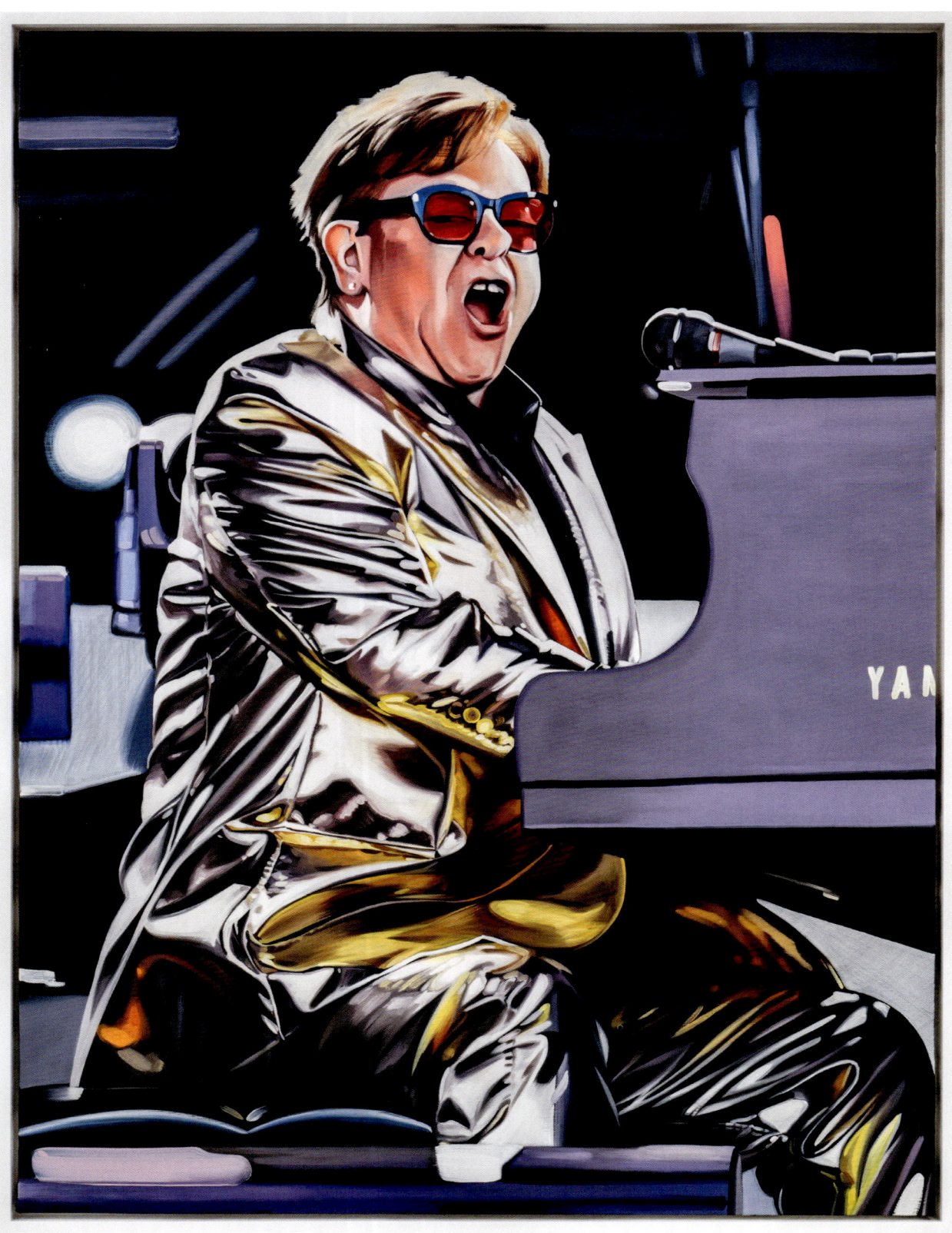

Sam McKinniss, *Elton John*, 2024. Oil on linen. Framed: 45.5 × 34.5 × 2 in. (115.6 × 87.6 × 5 cm)

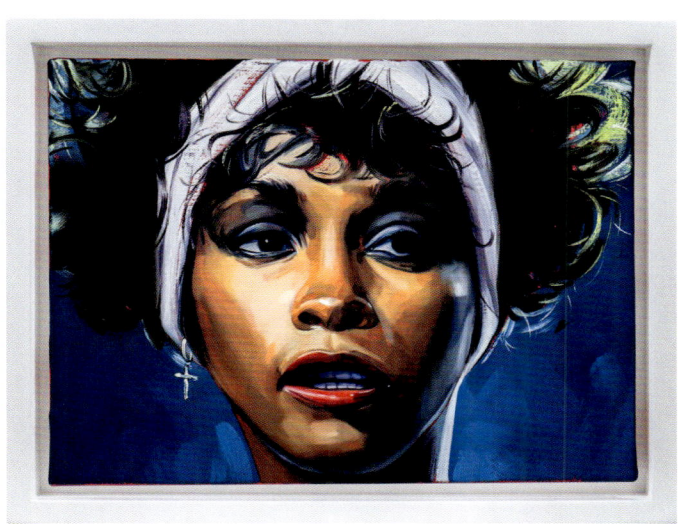

Sam McKinniss, *Star Spangled Banner* *(Whitney)*, **2017. Oil and acrylic on canvas. Framed: 10.5 × 13.75 × 2 in. (26.4 × 35 × 5 cm)**

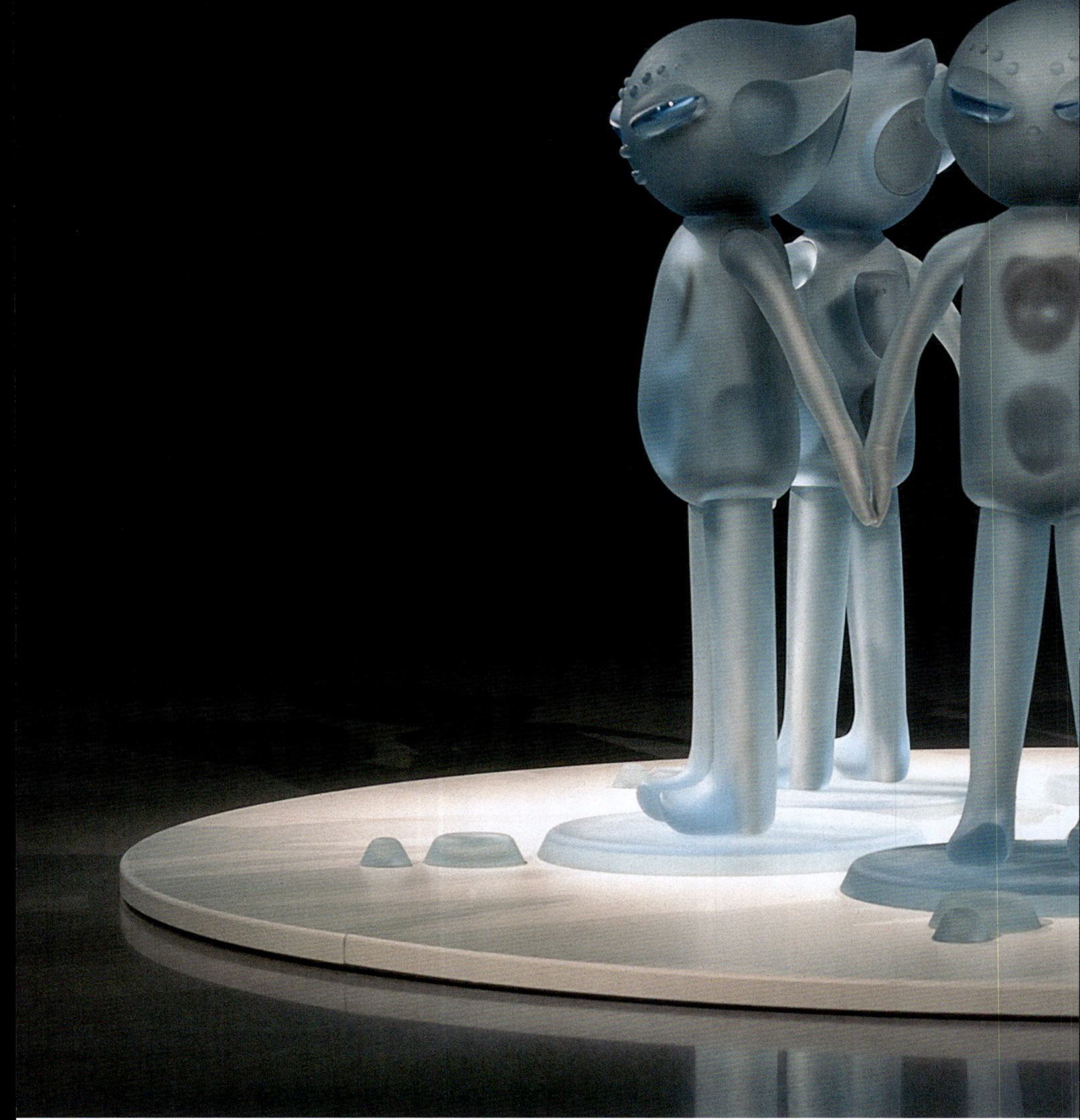

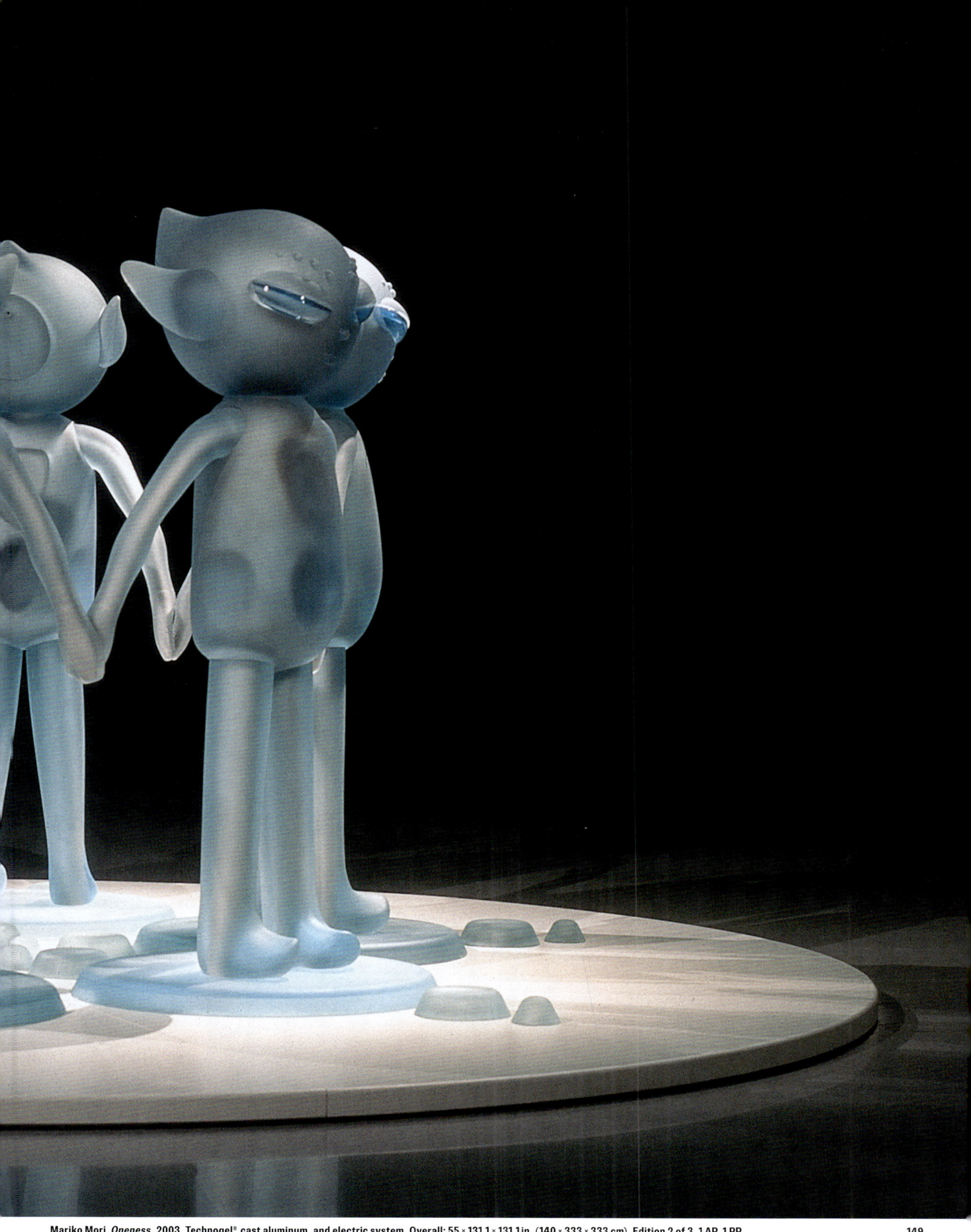

Mariko Mori, *Oneness*, 2003. Technogel®, cast aluminum, and electric system. Overall: 55 × 131.1 × 131.1 in. (140 × 333 × 333 cm). Edition 2 of 3, 1 AP, 1 PP

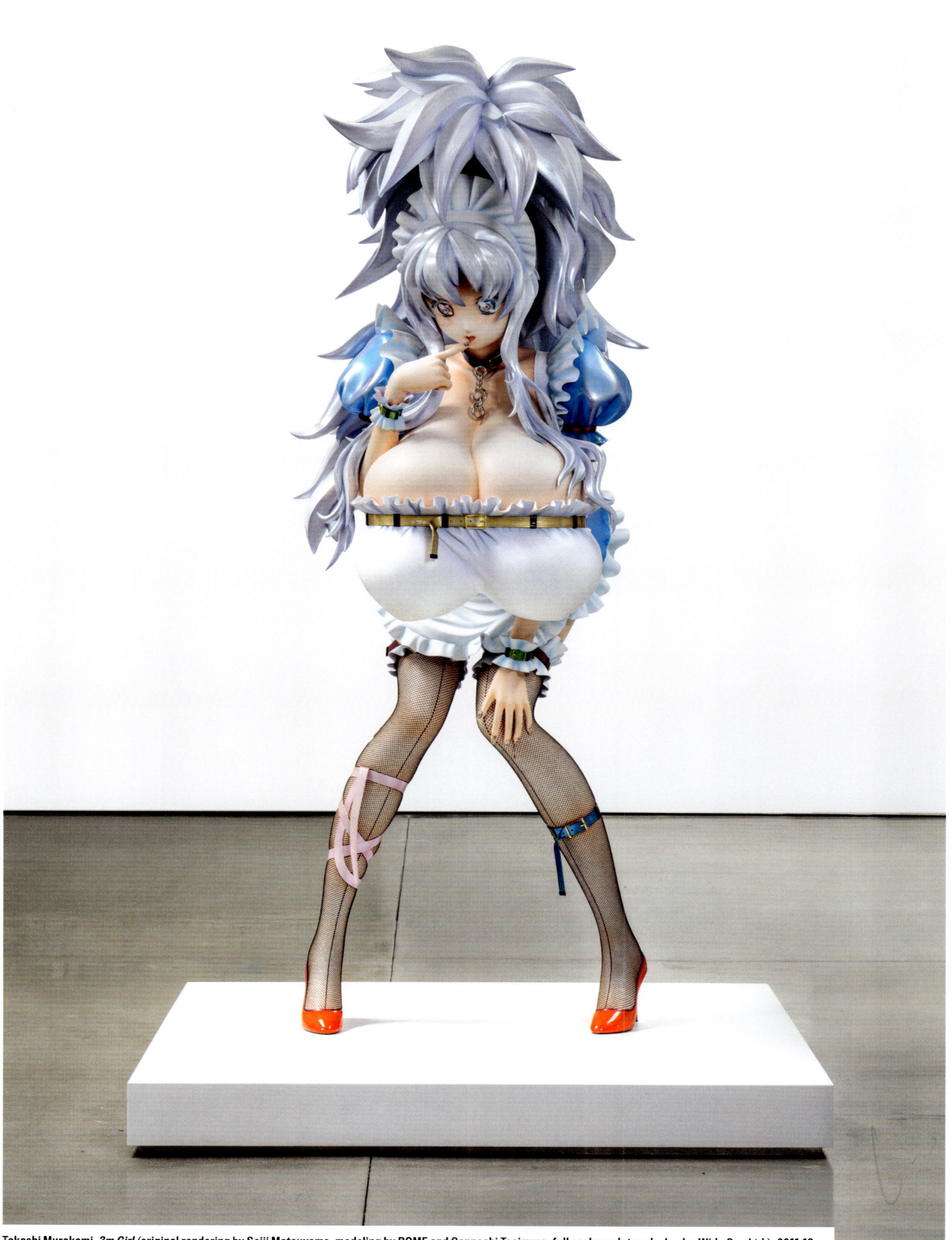

Takashi Murakami, *3m Girl* (original rendering by Seiji Matsuyama, modeling by BOME and Genpachi Toaimura, full scale sculpture by Lucky-Wide Co., Ltd.), 2011-13. Fiberglass, reinforced plastic and steel. 106.31 × 38.18 × 47.19 in. (270 × 97 × 120 cm). Artist Proof 1 from an edition of 3, 2 AP

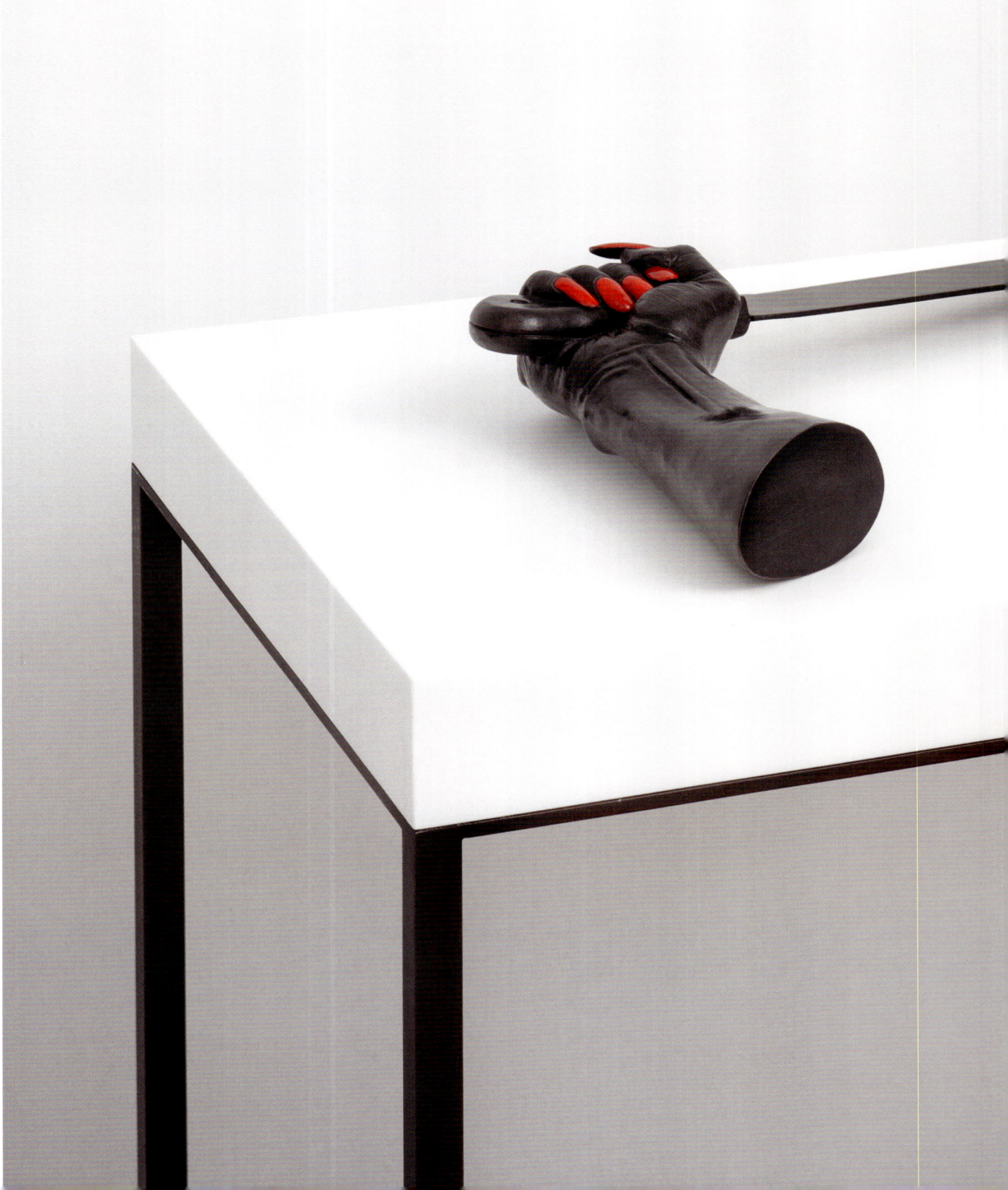

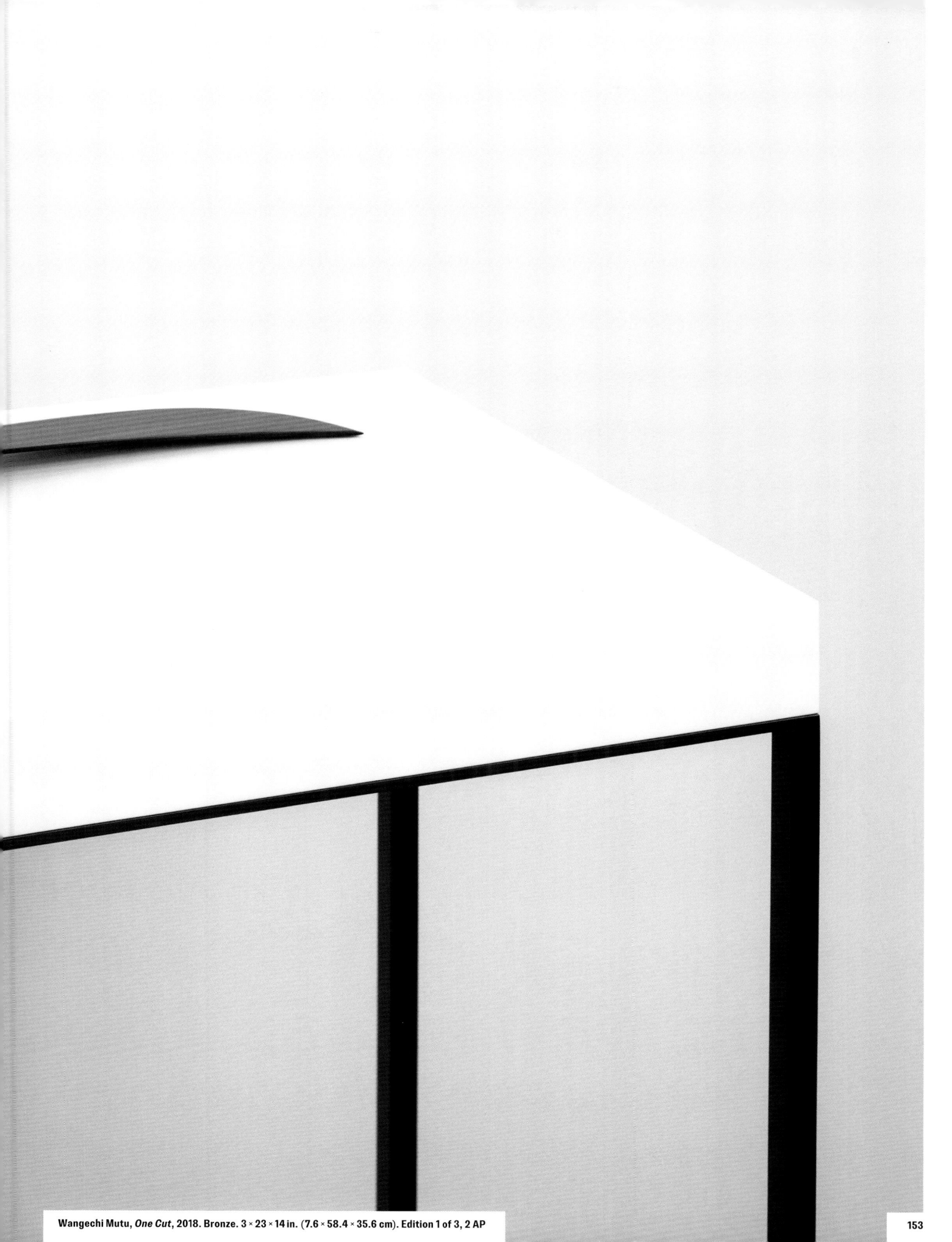

Wangechi Mutu, *One Cut*, 2018. Bronze. 3 × 23 × 14 in. (7.6 × 58.4 × 35.6 cm). Edition 1 of 3, 2 AP

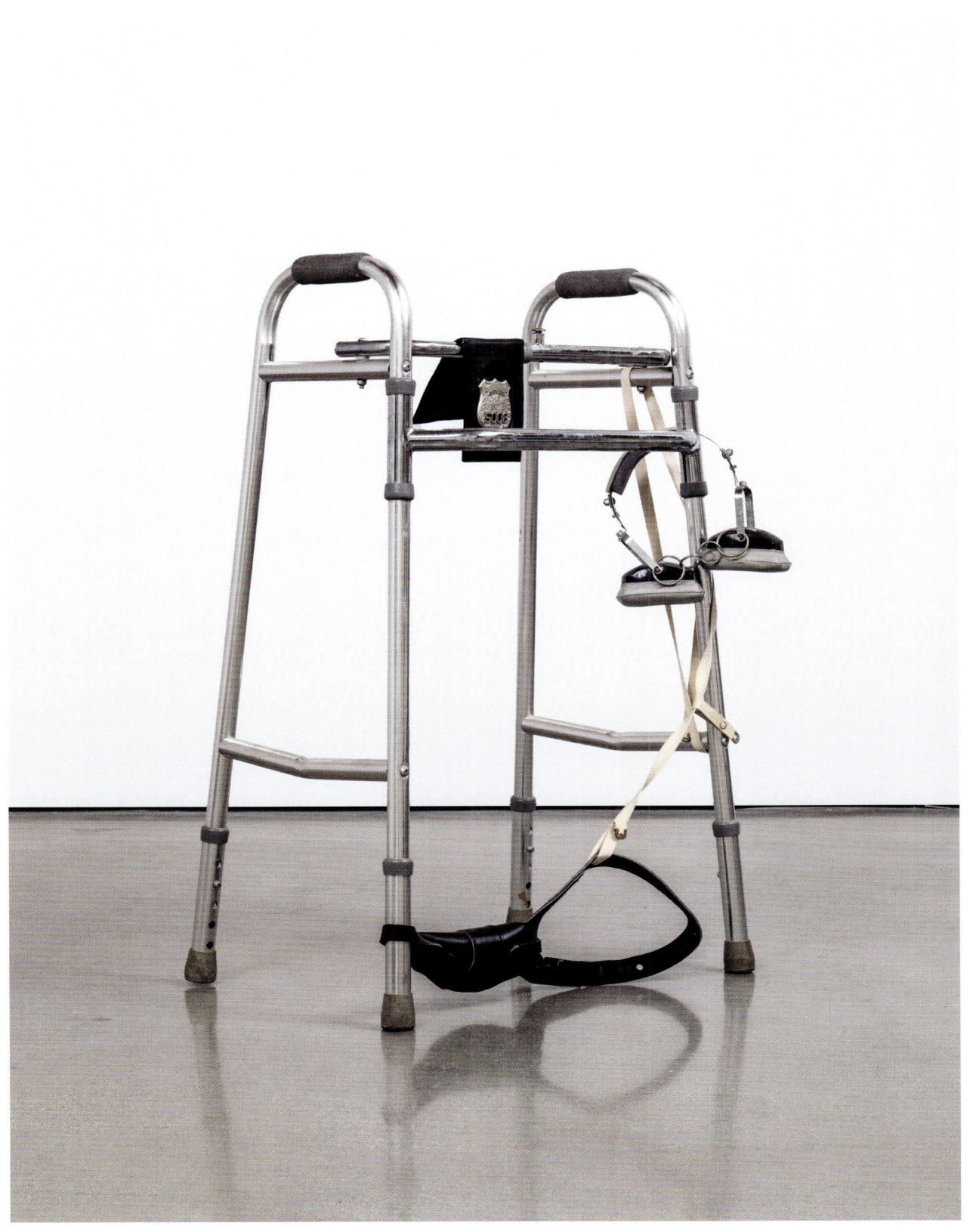

Cady Noland, *Rotten Cop*, **1988. Geriatric walker with holster, police badge and ear protection. 36 × 20 × 16 in. (91.44 × 51 × 40.6 cm)**

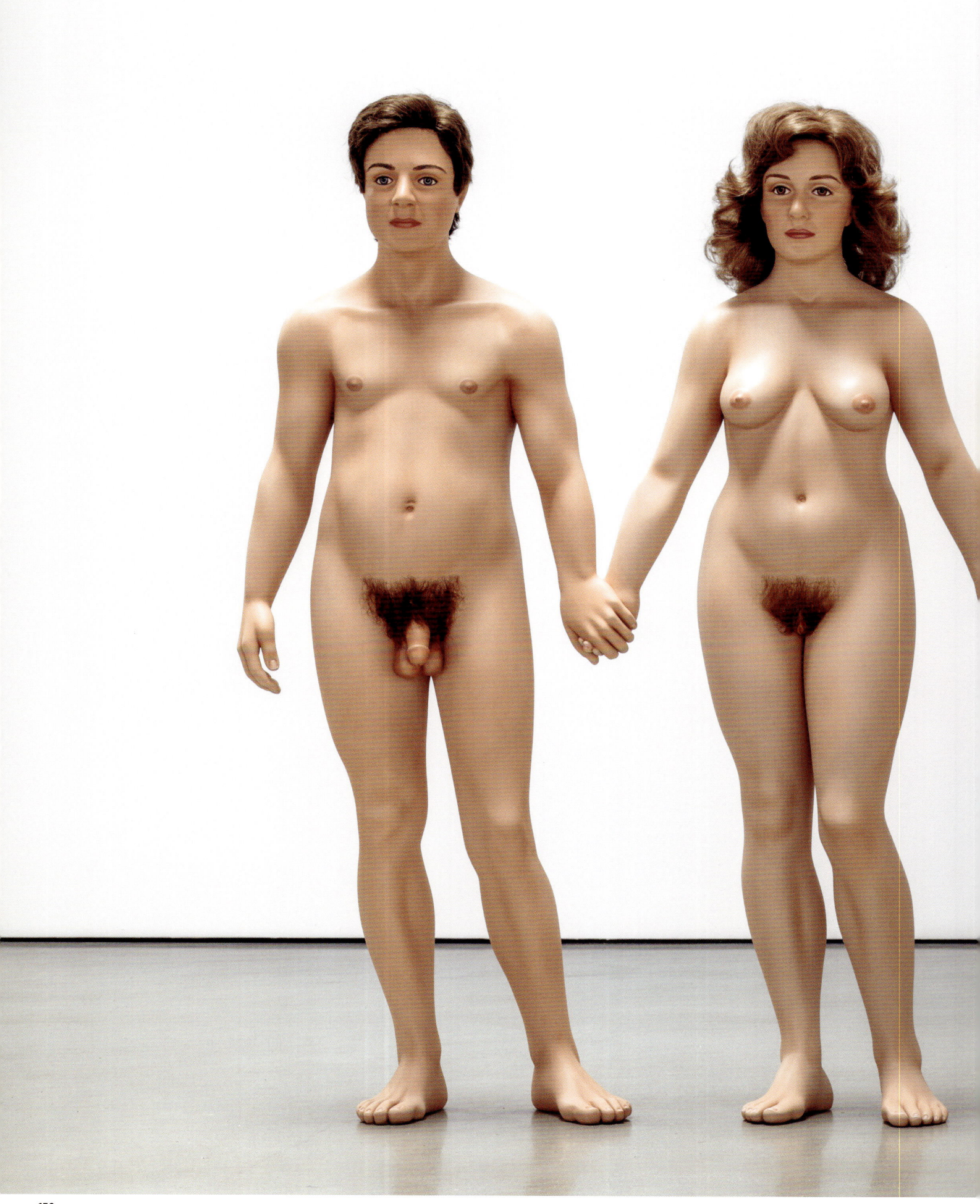

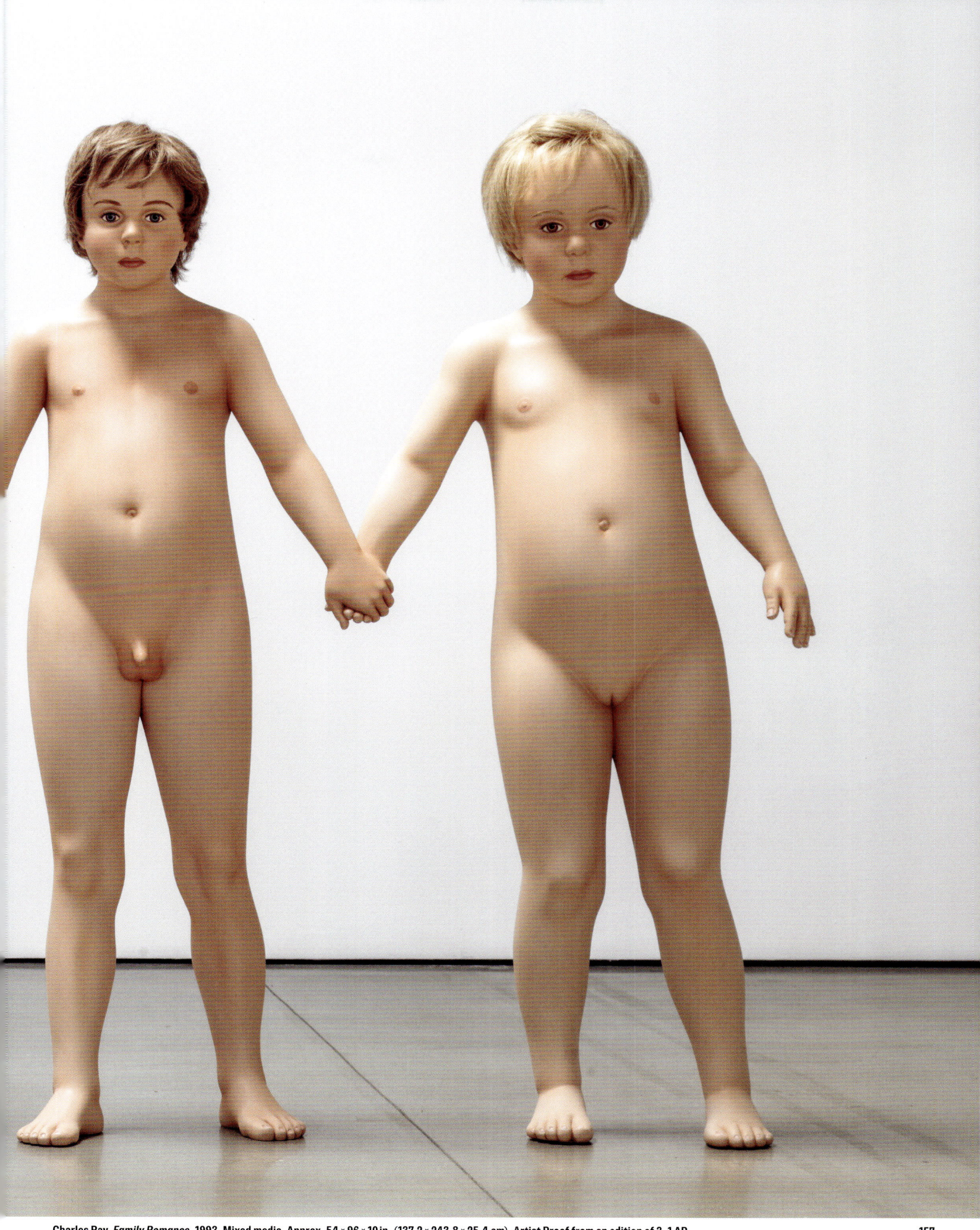

Charles Ray, *Family Romance*, 1993. Mixed media. Approx. 54 × 96 × 10 in. (137.2 × 243.8 × 25.4 cm). Artist Proof from an edition of 3, 1 AP

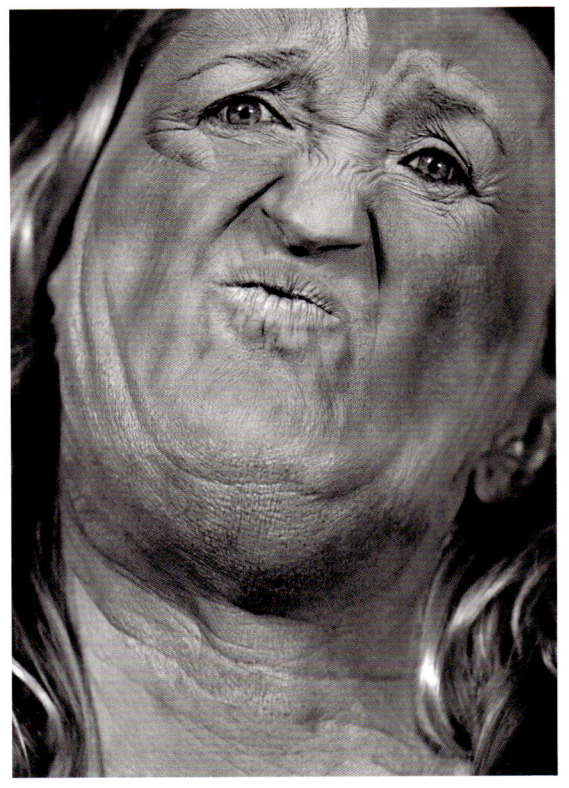

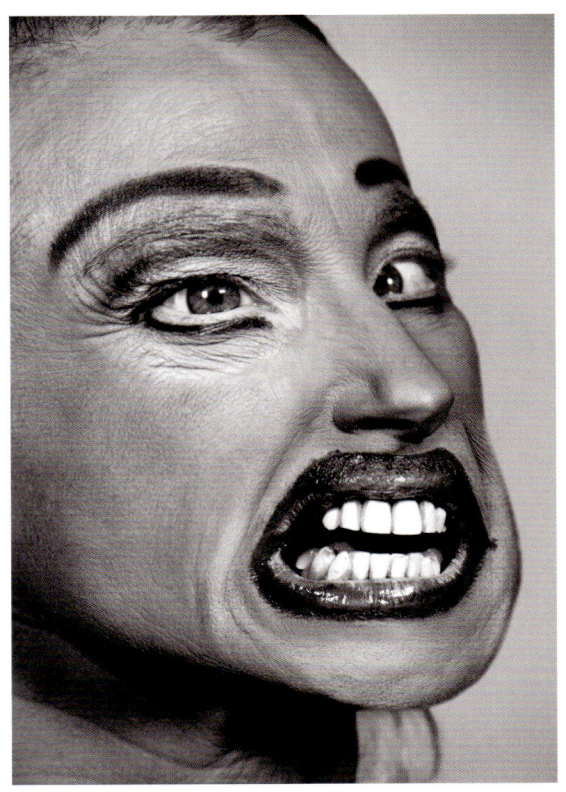

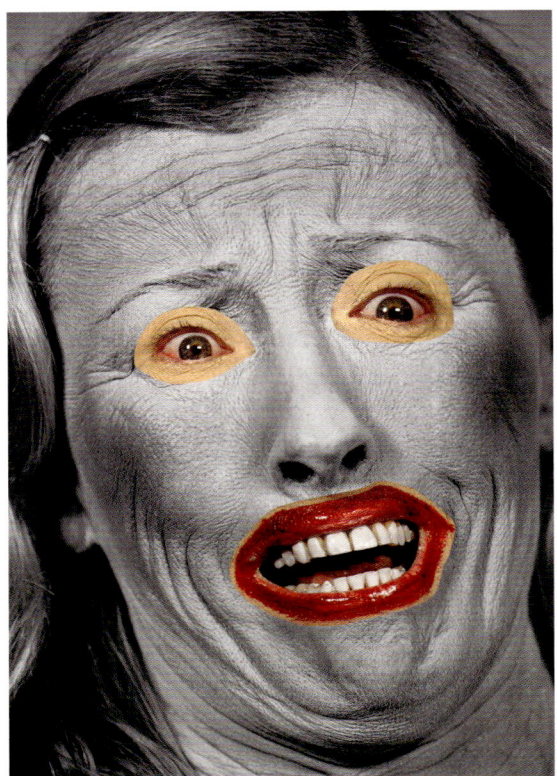

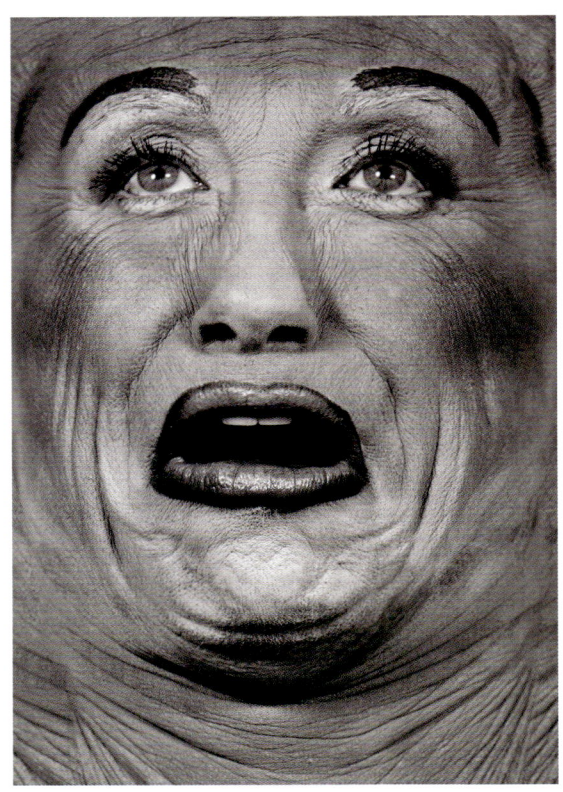

Top left: Cindy Sherman, *Untitled #643*, 2010/2023. Gelatin silver print. Framed: 29.25 × 22.38 × 2 in. (74.3 × 56.8 × 5.1 cm). Edition 1 of 6, 1 AP.

Bottom left: Cindy Sherman, *Untitled #629*, 2010/2023. Gelatin silver print. Framed: 29.13 × 22.5 × 2 in. (74.1 × 57 × 5.1 cm). Edition 1 of 6, 1 AP

Top right: Cindy Sherman, *Untitled #627*, 2010/2023. Gelatin silver print. Framed: Framed: 29.13 × 23.5 × 2 in. (74.1 × 58.9 × 5.1 cm). Edition 1 of 6, 1 AP.

Bottom right: Cindy Sherman, *Untitled #638*, 2010/2023. Gelatin silver print. Framed: 29.25 × 22.38 × 2 in. (74.3 × 56.8 × 5.1 cm). Edition 1 of 6, 1 AP

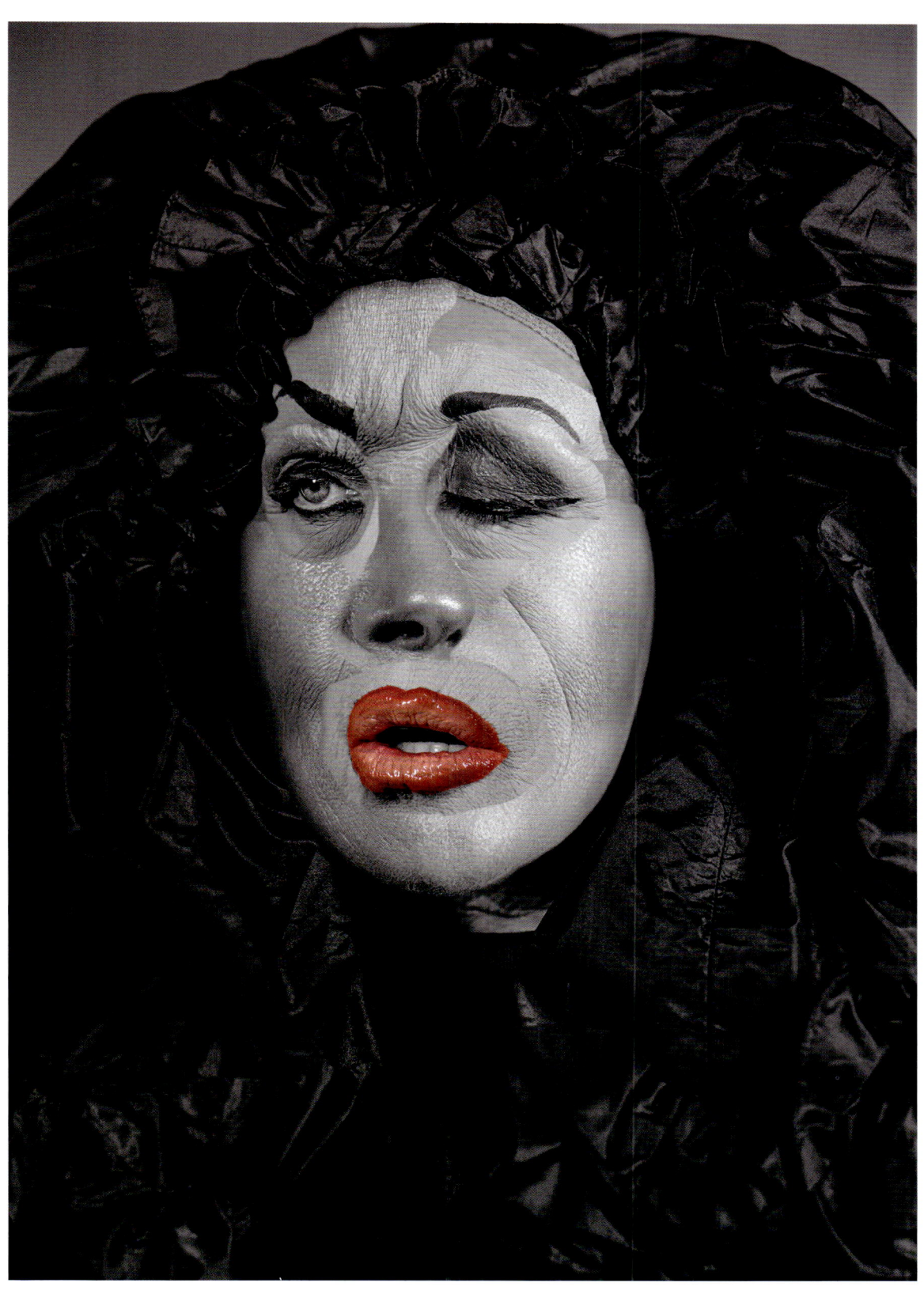

Cindy Sherman, *Untitled #654*, 2023. Gelatin silver print and chromogenic color print. 51.25 × 39.25 × 2 in. (130.2 × 99.7 × 5.1 cm). Edition 1 of 6, 1 AP

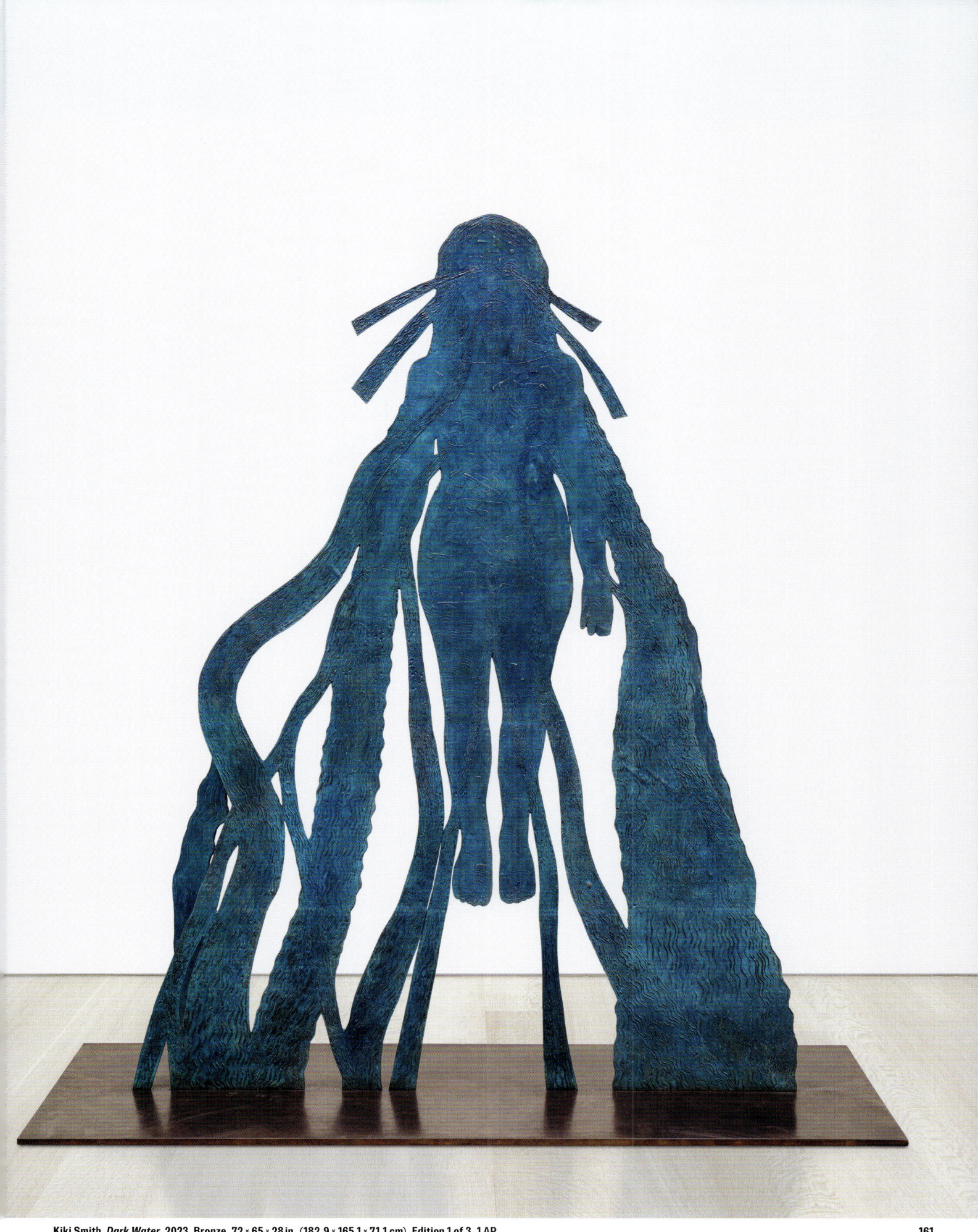

Kiki Smith, *Dark Water,* **2023. Bronze. 72 × 65 × 28 in. (182.9 × 165.1 × 71.1 cm). Edition 1 of 3, 1 AP**

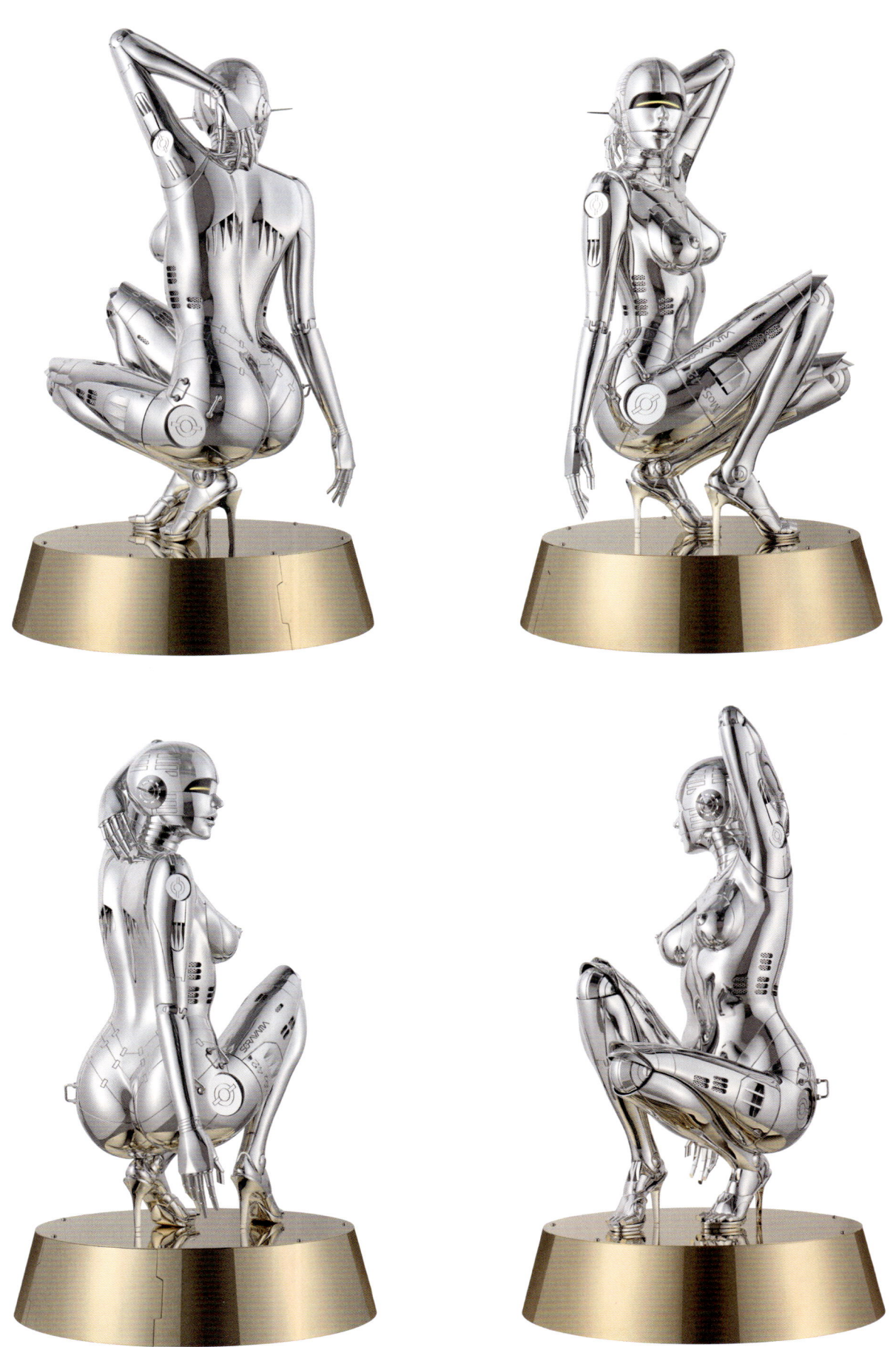

Hajime Sorayama, *Unititled*, 2024. Aluminum, acrylic glass, LED light, copper and steel. 57 × 33 × 33 in. (144.8 × 83.8 × 83.8 cm). Edition 1 of 3, 2 AP

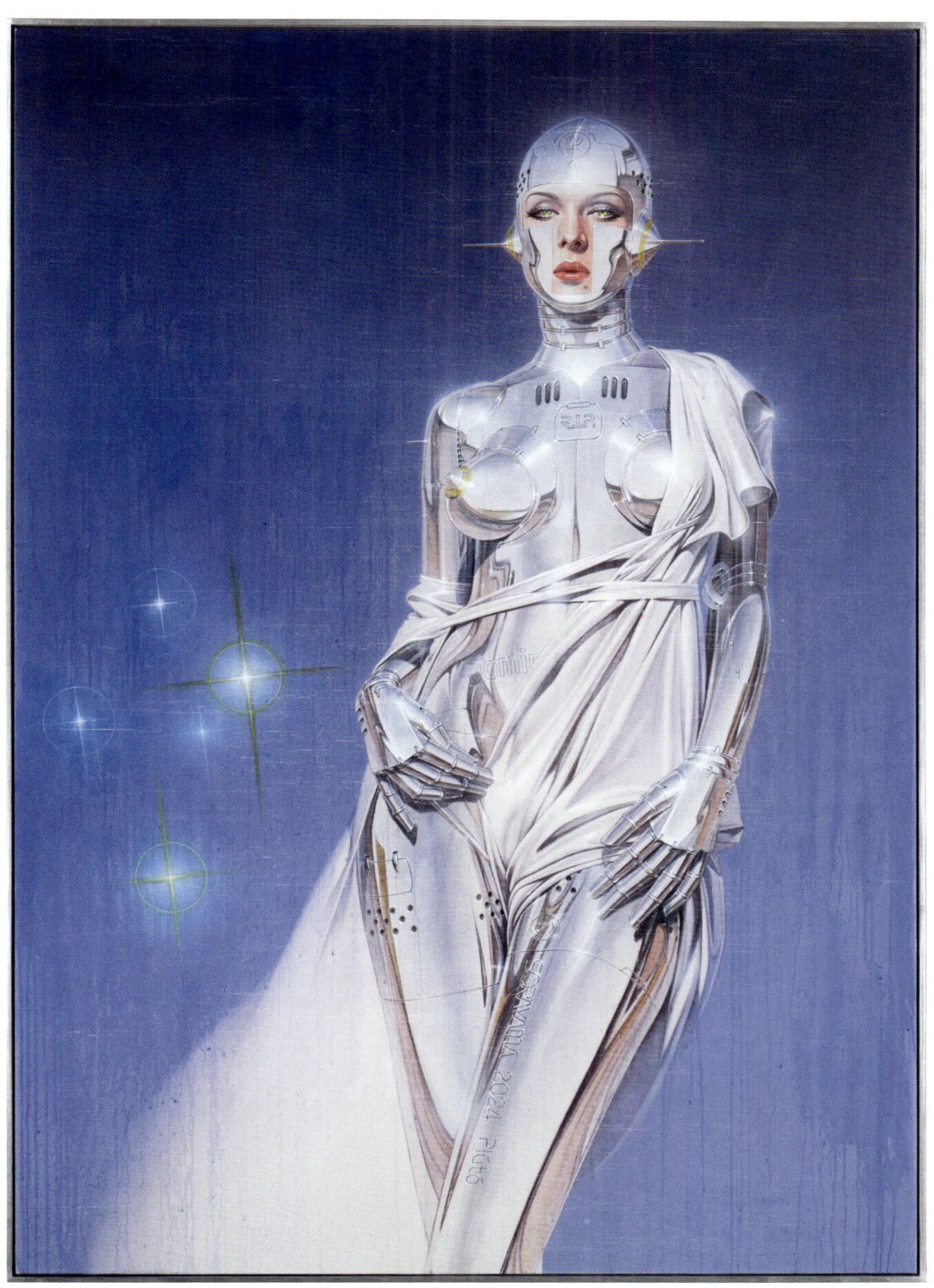

Hajime Sorayama, *Unititled*, **2024. Acrylic and digital print on canvas. Framed: 55.5 × 78.5 × 2.5 in. (141 × 199.4 × 6.4 cm)**

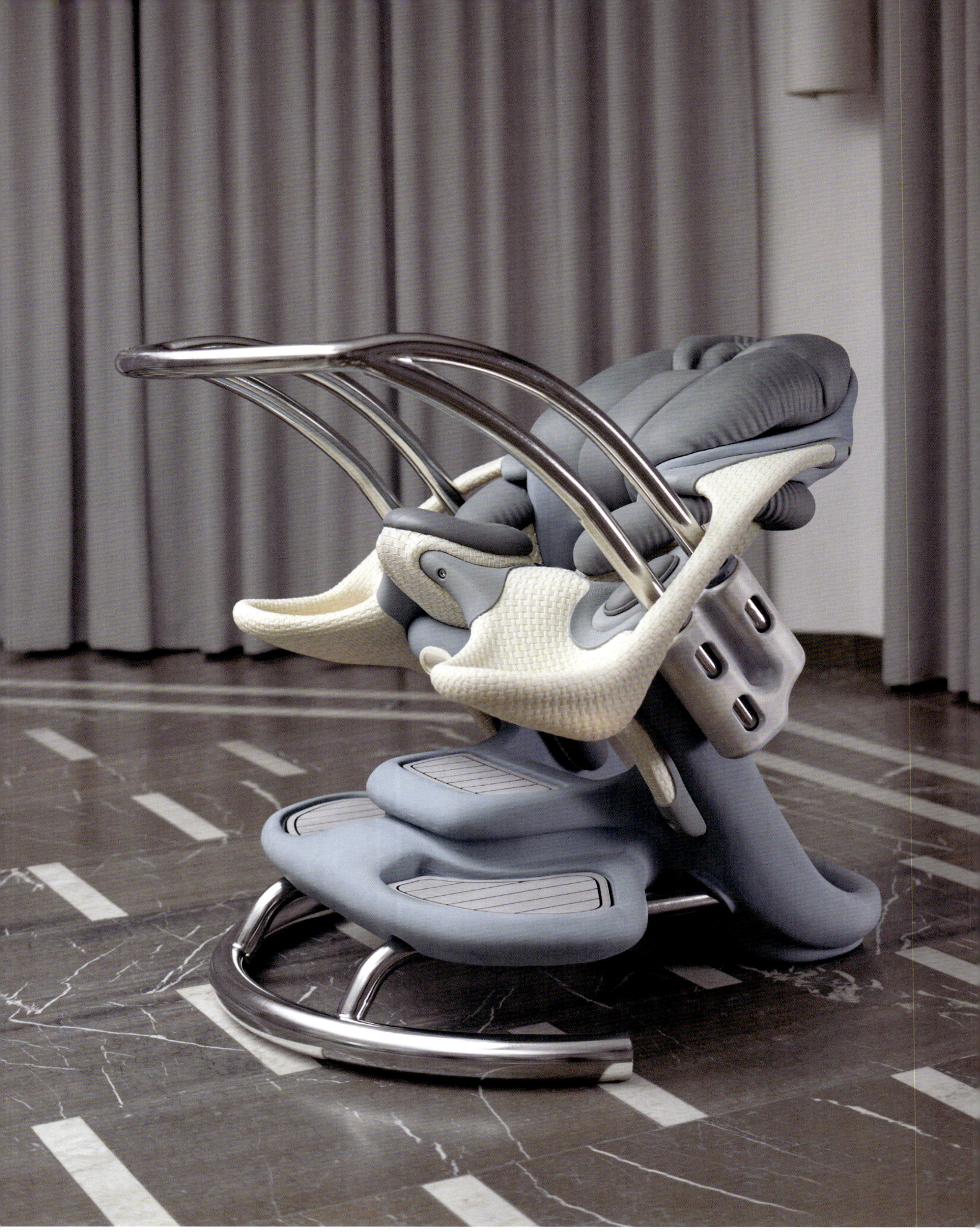

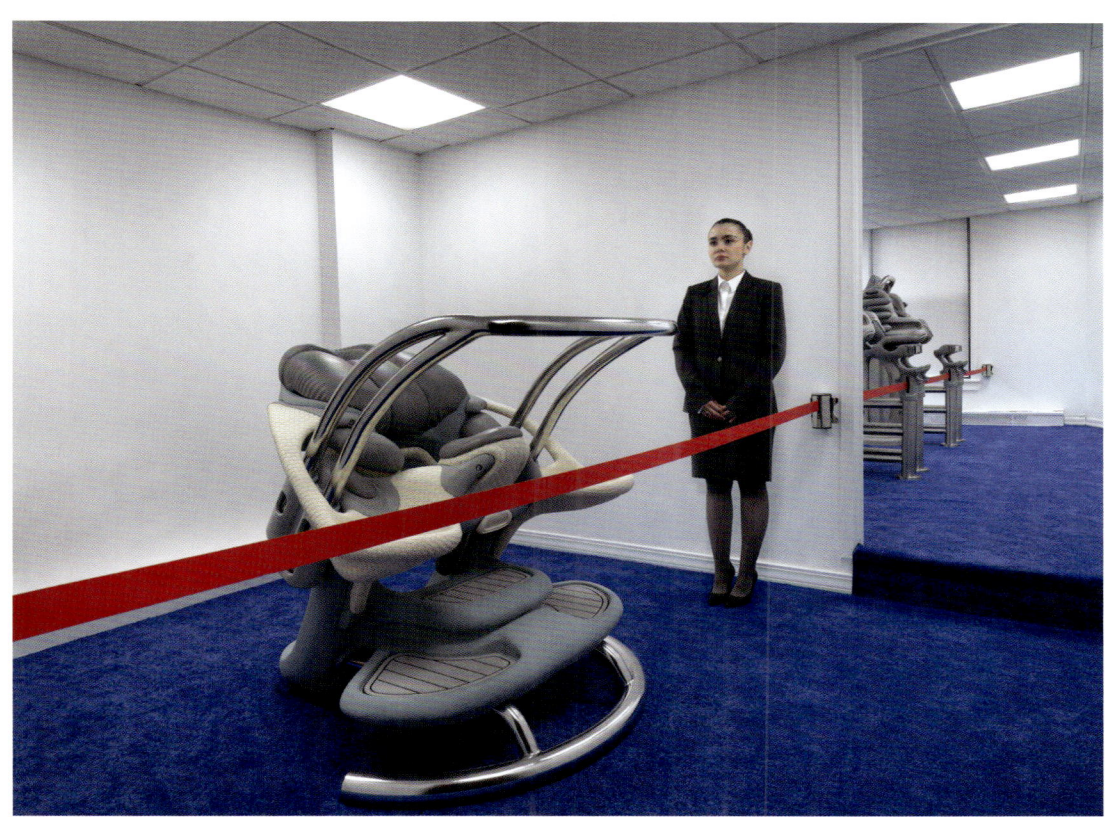

Anna Uddenberg, *T-Top Tummy Tuck*, 2022. Polylactic acid, thermoset polymer resin, electropolished stainless steel, foam boat flooring, leather and chalk paint.
47.25 × 55.25 × 46.75 in. (120 × 141 × 118.5 cm)

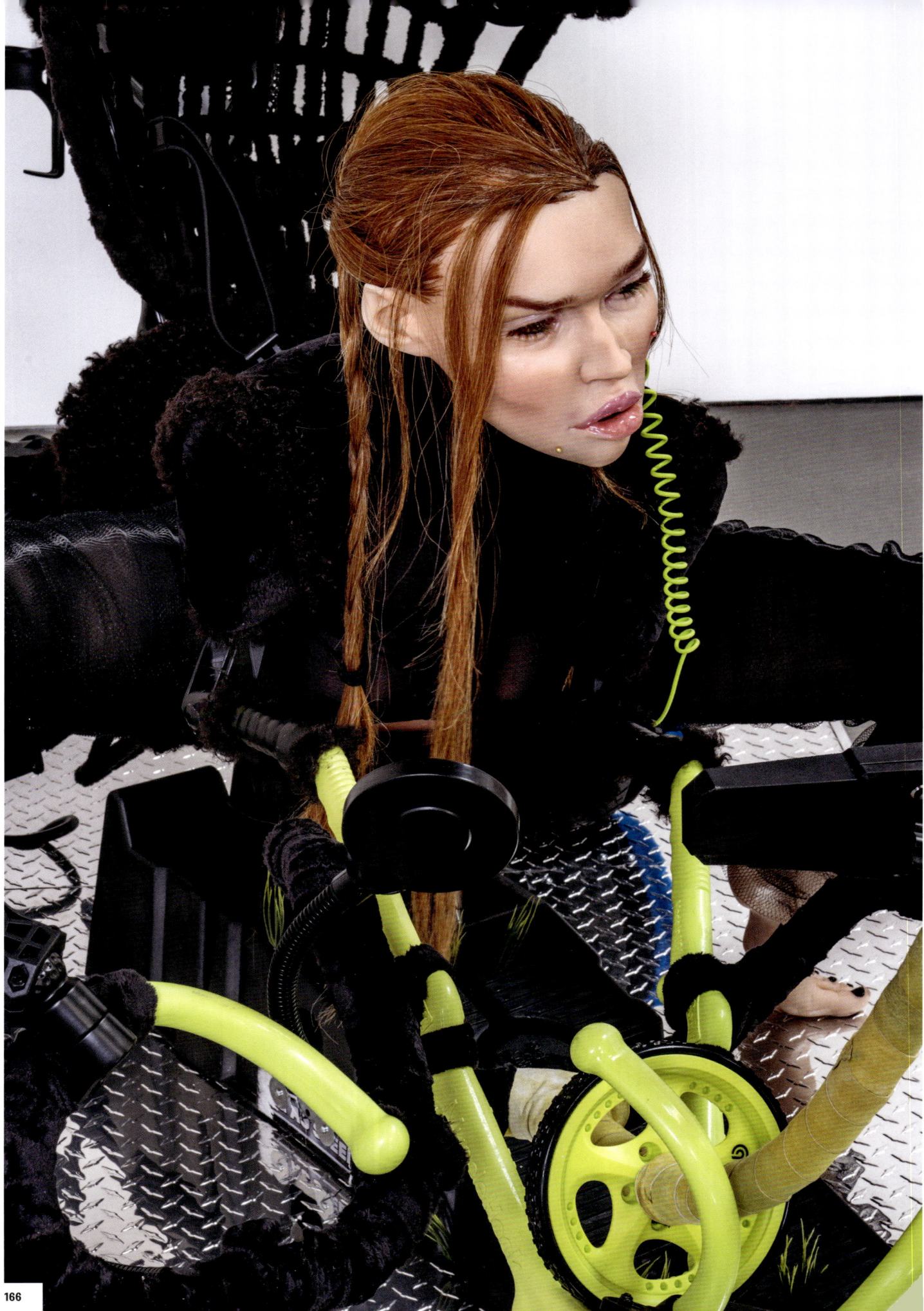

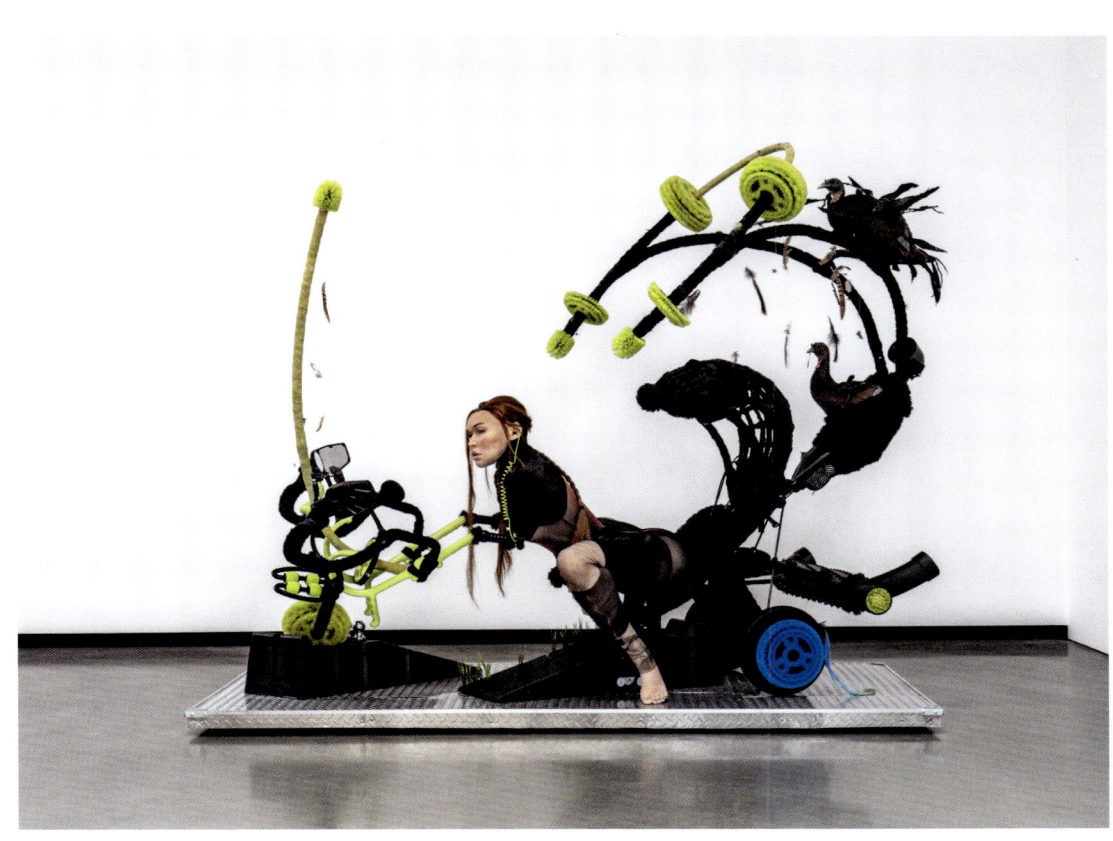

Cajsa von Zeipel, *Pep Talk*, **2024. Silicone and mixed media. 80 × 48 × 84 in. (203.2 × 121.9 × 213.4 cm)**

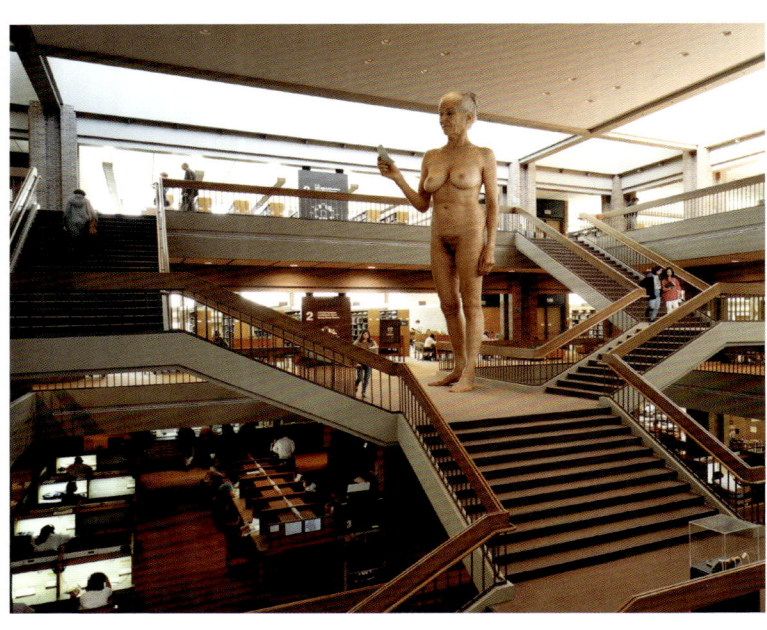

Jeff Wall, *The Giant*, 1992. Transparency in lightbox. 15.5 × 18.9 in. (39 × 48 cm). Artist Proof 1 from an edition of 8, 4 AP

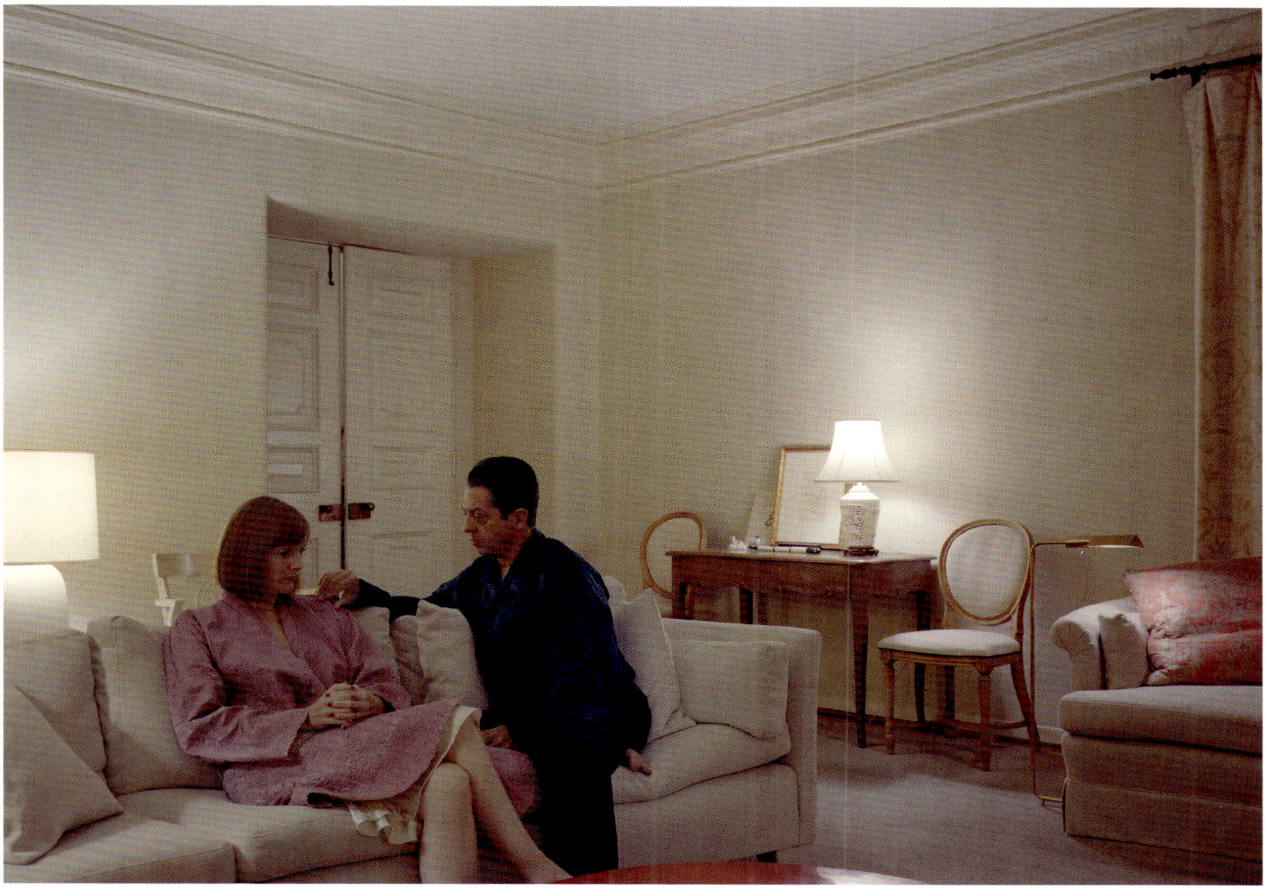

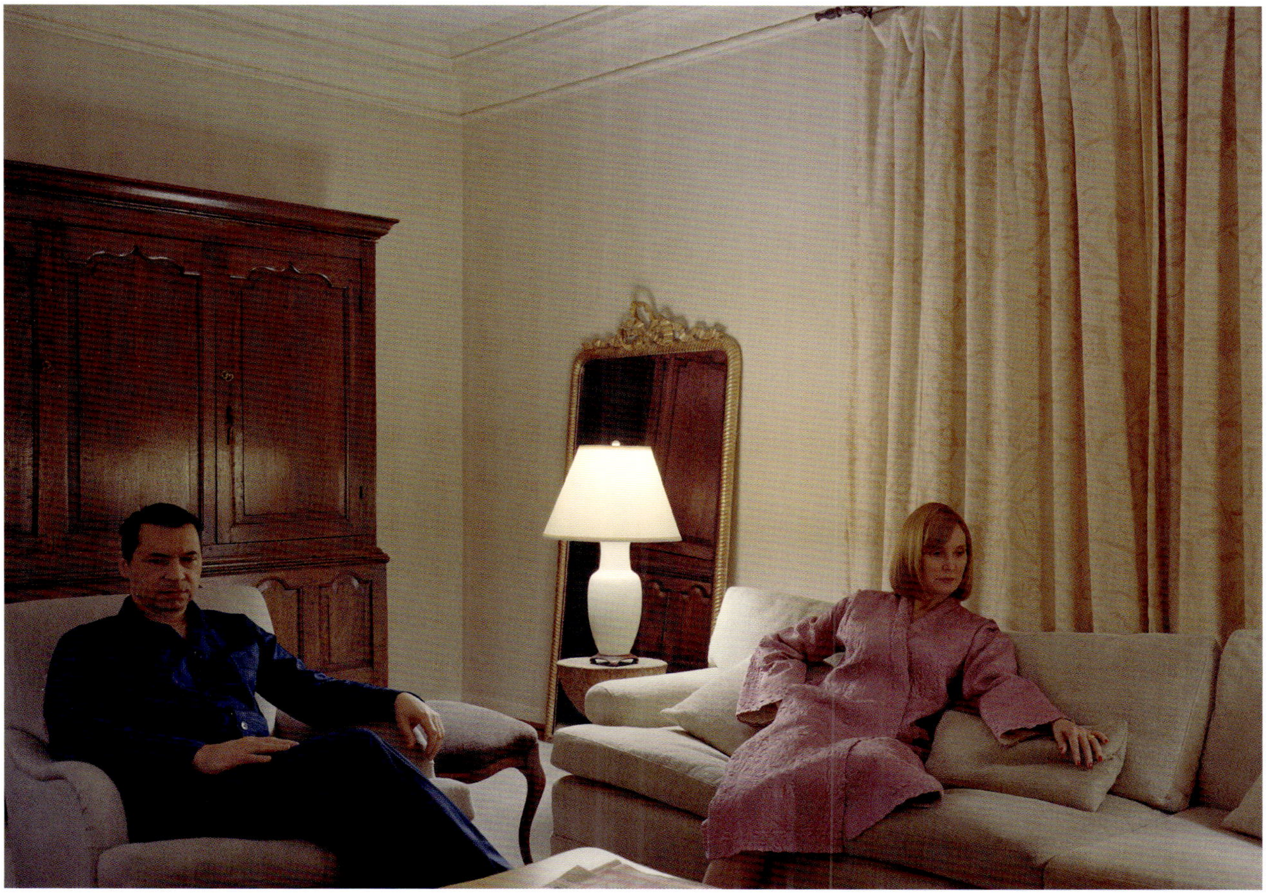

Jeff Wall, *Pair of interiors*, 2018. Two inkjet prints. Each: 59.84 × 81.89 in. (152 × 208 cm). Edition 1 of 3, 1 AP

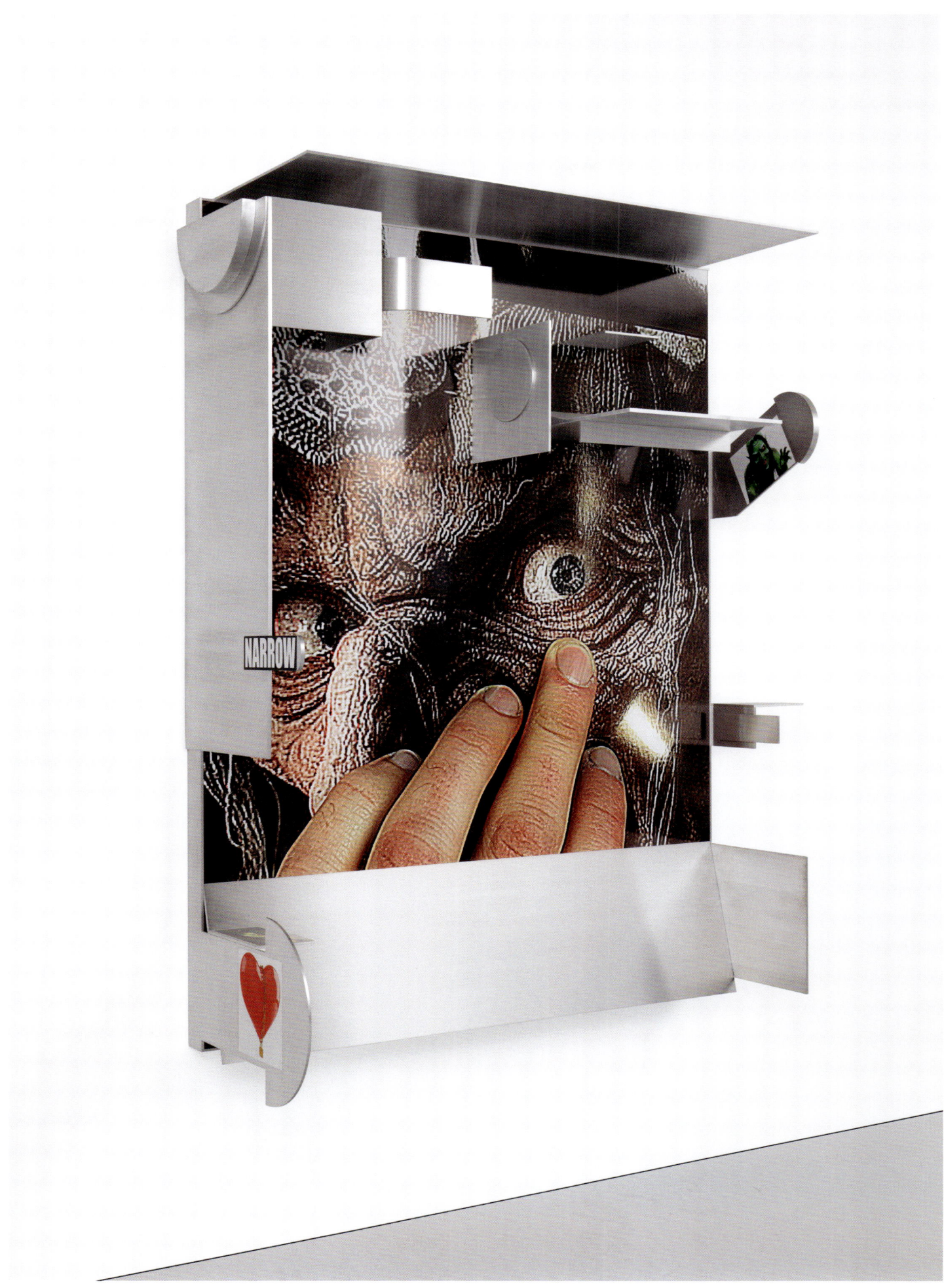

Jordan Wolfson, *Untitled*, 2016. Inkjet print and adhesive media on aluminum. 82.31 × 68.75 × 24.81 in. (209.1 × 174.6 × 63.1 cm)

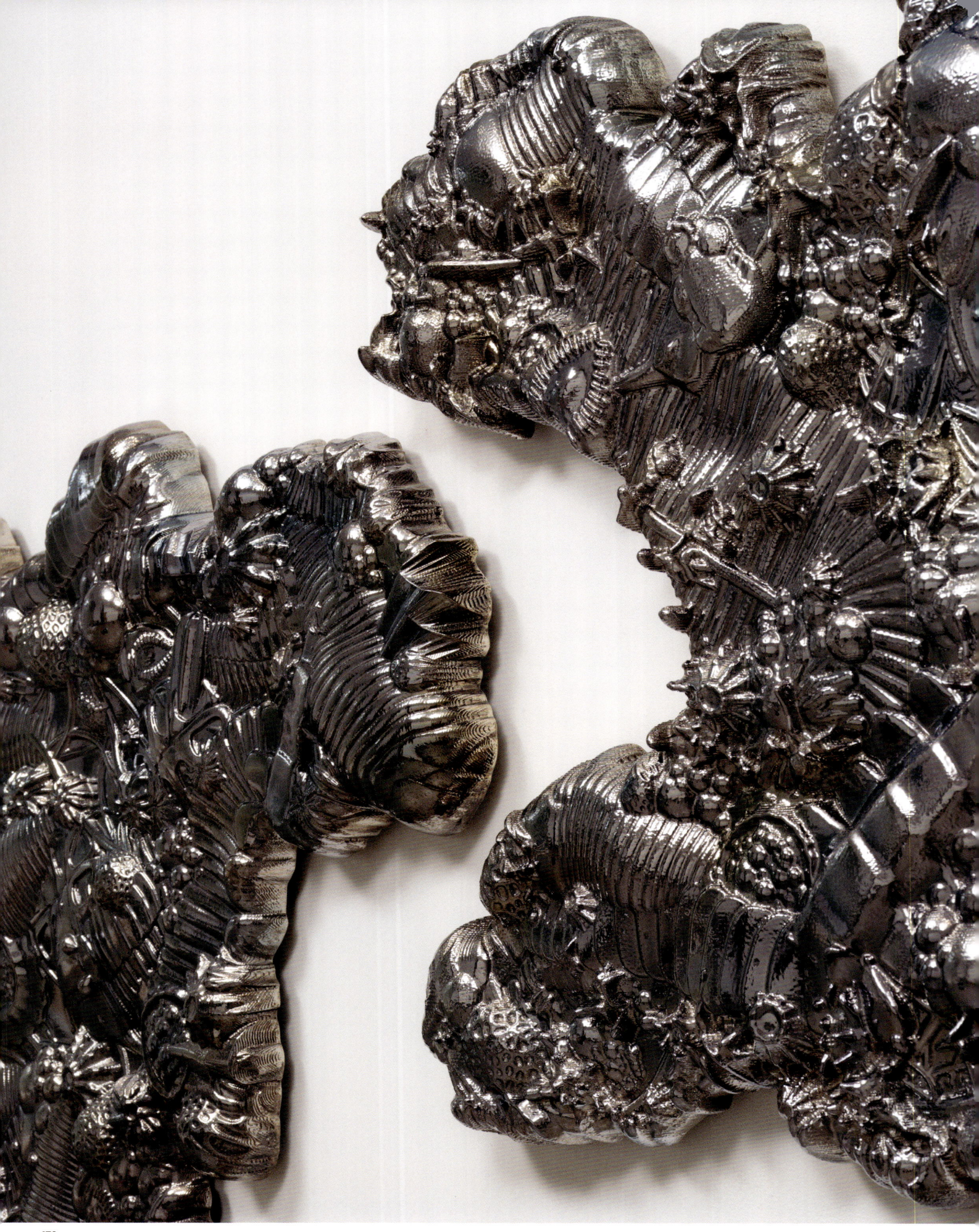

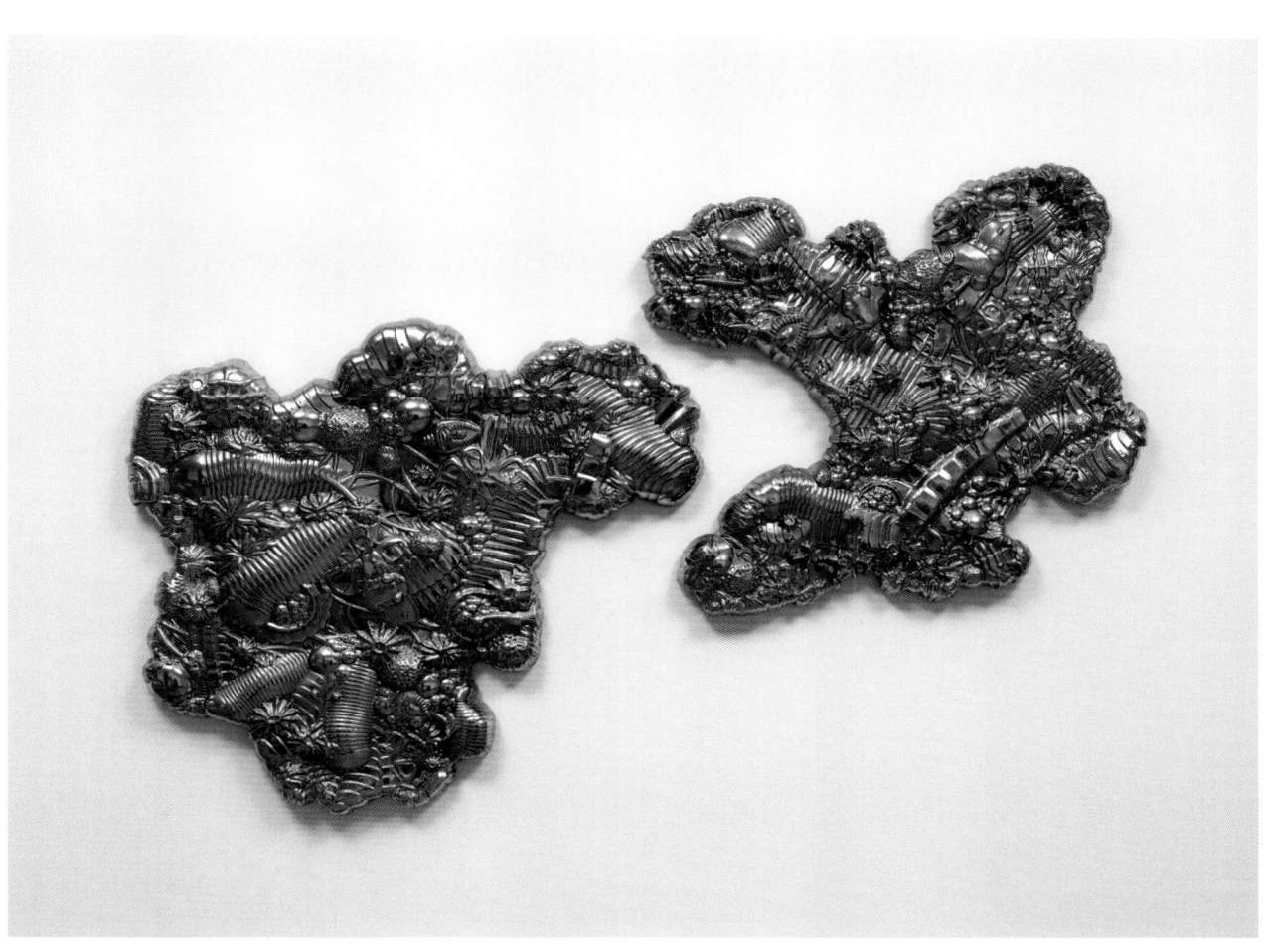

Anicka Yi, *The Sliding World*, 2024. High density foam and chrome. Overall: 110 × 50 inches (279.4 × 127 cm)

Bodies of Work   Philippa Snow

In late 2024, one of the most renowned sex symbols of our era appeared to announce her retirement from conventional romance. WHO NEEDS A BOYFRIEND, screamed a headline on a social media post by the celebrity news site TMZ, over an image of the famous woman with her lips twisted into a smirk, WHEN I'VE GOT A…ROBOT!!! That there was no question mark in evidence did not so much suggest an error of syntax as it did a forceful insistence on the truth of the statement: there would be, as the sex symbol's heroine Elizabeth Taylor had once crowed in a letter to her two-time husband Richard Burton, no more marriages. Across Instagram and X, she posted a shoot with her new lover that looked plausibly pre- or postcoital, the two of them spilling out of a sleek electric sports car that, because it had been made in the same factory as her automated gigolo, could arguably be read as a supersized extension of his body. The pictures—caliginous and grainy, like surveillance footage taken after dark—seemed to be a document of some new form of sex. Here, her thighs in a pair of silken stockings, thrown across a metal lap; there, the shadowed, almost vulval opening of the vehicle's interior being pierced by a stiff, silvery limb, as if that limb were a phallus. Manufacture and nature, orgiastically becoming one, at last! That the sex symbol herself, who had been shaped by many years of both surgical and nonsurgical work, could not be said to be entirely of nature was, of course, part of the point. What we were seeing was not really about pleasure or eroticism at all, but about the production, via procreative means or otherwise, of the future—the refinement of a self beyond flesh, and beyond the usual considerations of biology.

A pornographic novel about technology,[1] the English writer J. G. Ballard called his 1973 masterpiece *Crash.* Did these images of the starlet and the robot not, in a sense, also make up a kind of pornographic novel about technology in and of themselves? Ballard believed that the car, a private-public space on wheels with the potential to facilitate both great personal injury and exhilarating speed, was the defining object of the twentieth century, and that the Hollywood A-lister, with his or her similar ability to serve as a dynamic psychosexual vessel—namely for the anonymous, amorphous desires of their public—followed close behind. One of these symbols often rode inside the other in his work, whether literally or metaphorically, the two of them occasionally smashing together in a bacchanal of violence that, in lieu of breaking each down into its organic or mechanical components, comingled them perversely in a troubling, strangely erotic snapshot of the age itself. In 1970, Ballard mounted an art exhibition at the New Arts Laboratory in London called, simply, *Crashed Cars,* and if attendees had expected something other than the spectacle promised by the title of the show,

1   J. G. Ballard, Introduction for *Crash* (Jonathan Cape, 1973).

they must have found themselves rather disappointed: a Pontiac, an Austin Cambridge A60, and a Mini had been lifted from a scrapyard, with the first in particular being chosen for its easy and symbolic invocation of the midcentury American dream. Metal, glass, and interior leather spilled, gut-like, onto the floor of the space, as if somebody had been performing amateur surgery on the vehicles' chassis. A year later, he clarified in an essay that the cars had been intended to represent "speed, drama and aggression, the worlds of advertising and consumer goods, engineering and mass manufacture, and the shared experience of moving together through an elaborately signalled landscape."[2]

By the early twenty-first century, speaking to the *Guardian* in 2004, Ballard had begun to identify a shift toward a world "that places a greater value on celebrity the less it is accompanied by actual achievement," and in which "celebrity and the media presence of … artists are inextricably linked with their work."[3] No celebrity on earth is better-known for being supposedly famous for no reason than the sex symbol with the robot boyfriend, and no celebrity's physical body is more deeply associated with their media presence and with what might best be described as their work. She has, in a sense, self-actualized beyond the status of a mere star and into the abstracted, bloodless realm of iconography—as an example of contemporary American craftsmanship and engineering, she is arguably every bit as recognizable as a Pontiac, or even an M16. ("Advertising and consumer goods, engineering and mass manufacture.") Not for nothing have both *GQ* and *Interview* run cover shoots that flagrantly juxtaposed her souped-up, half naked body with some version of the Stars and Stripes. The fact that the bottle for her signature perfume is shaped like a headless, limbless version of her torso is in itself a statement, suggesting as it does that we no longer even need to see her face to recognize her. With a body like this, who needs a face, and having built an empire like this—"bigger than US steel,"[4] per *Rolling Stone*—who could possibly say she had no talent?

We have long used the phrase *body of work,* or the Latin *corpus* meaning simply "body," to describe an artist's oeuvre, the phrase suggesting a direct relationship—a mirroring or a fleshy symbiosis, even—between the parts that make up an individual's practice and the parts that make up the individual themselves. In 2004, Ballard also said of Tracey Emin, not entirely unproblematically, that her "beautiful body" was her "one great idea."[5] It is easy enough to see this faintly misogynistic statement as dismissive, and yet doing so effectively relies on the limited assumption that having only one great idea is not enough to make an icon. (A misguided reading, surely, given that many other notable practitioners of art, music, literature, et cetera et cetera, might also be said to rely on variations on, or refractions of, a single idea, too—to say nothing of the fact

2   J. G. Ballard, Untitled essay for *Drive* magazine, 1971.

3   Jeannette Baxter, "Age of Unreason," *Guardian*, June 22, 2004.

4   Rob Sheffield, "The Kardashians: The Ego That Ate America," *Rolling Stone*, September 14, 2014.

5   Baxter, "Age of Unreason."

that many of us have been forced to trade on less.) He suggested that his major issue with Emin's body-based, intimately disclosive work was not her nakedness itself, but the fact that he found her approach to it too "prudish," as if once she had chosen to utilize her physical self as a medium, the only logical continuation of the project would have been to push it to greater extremes—to show us the red-raw inside of her beautiful body, perhaps, or to display it under greater duress. "Meanwhile," he concluded, "too much is made of conceptual art." For all of his own elegant theorizing in writing, he seemed also to believe that art that was purely conceptual, and in no way physical or vital, would fail to press itself sufficiently into the viewer's lizard brain—that lizard brain being the most ancient part of us, and thus, somewhat paradoxically, always the most up-to-the-minute, the most relevant, the most urgent in its pure and vibratory reaction to the world we inhabit.

To fully hold our attention, Ballard might have further hypothesized that Emin's "beautiful body" should be regularly altered into unfamiliarity. "In a TV interview a few years ago, the wife of a famous Beverly Hills plastic surgeon revealed that throughout their marriage her husband had continually re-styled her face and body, pointing a breast here, tucking in a nostril there," he wrote in his experimental novel *The Atrocity Exhibition*, published in the same year that he showed *Crashed Cars*. "She seemed supremely confident of her attractions. But as she said: 'He will never leave me, because he can always change me.'" [6] The famous sex symbol's one great idea is her body, too, and it has continually shifted, just as many celebrities' physical forms seem to permanently flicker between states, between shapes, and between identities. Our gaze will never leave her, because she can always alter herself: new breasts; a new nose; different and more feline eyes; every six months, a newly mounted exhibition of the self. "Shame on me for changing. Shame on you for staying the same," she once captioned an image of herself on social media, only really meaning the last part of the sentence. What would a *Crashed Cars* show for the 2020s look like? In all likelihood, it would not feature cars at all, but bodies—crashed bodies, heavily augmented bodies, customized bodies, bodies built for speed and drama. It would, in other words, feature the bodies of very famous people: bodies which send out their own familiar and elaborate signals across the landscapes of our civilian lives.

The notion of recategorizing the celebrity as a work of art makes particular sense when we consider it in the context of two undeniably seismic changes to our culture that took place between the middle of the aughts and the first half of the 2010s: the normalization of the kind of ultrainvasive hour-by-hour paparazzi coverage championed by the gossip website TMZ, which first went live in 2005, and the launch of Instagram, the ur-visual social media platform, in 2010. Circa roughly 2005–9, it seemed as if we

6   Ballard, *The Atrocity Exhibition* (Jonathan Cape, 1970).

were perpetually being inundated with images of celebrities who had been caught in their unloveliest moments—drunk or drugged, climbing out of limousines in very short skirts with no knickers, furiously shaving their heads and getting into fisticuffs, dropping bags of cocaine on their doorsteps and attending pool parties with legally mandated ankle monitors accessorizing their bikinis, vomiting and crying with their supposedly million-dollar skin studded with angry cystic acne. If all this was sickening to watch, it was infinitely more sickening for the subjects of those paparazzi photos to endure, and the only way for them to win this new version of the game was to become faultless enough, or at least deliberate and cohesive enough in their visual style, that they could not be caught off guard. Coupled with the fact that television and movie cameras had begun to switch to high definition, rendering every pore and wrinkle legible at fifteen feet, it became necessary for the canvas of a famous person's face to be smoothed out, refined from smudged, Monet-like tache into something photorealist in its attention to detail, in order to survive this industry-wide shift. At the same moment, in a development which was either opportune or inopportune depending on your belief about the role of social media in the hastening of the apocalypse, Instagram appeared, providing an outlet for a new brand of self-portraiture as self-mythology, and letting users lie their way into desirability. If it helped make people who were not already famous into famous people, it also permitted those already in the public eye to amplify their images in exactly the way that they preferred.

The acceleration of tabloid culture and the advent of persistent, sometimes frighteningly omniscient fan coverage on social media have meant that the figurative gallery of fame is now open twenty-four hours a day, seven days a week, and it must be said that the lighting is not always flattering. (Sometimes, perhaps, it even resembles the sallowing strip lighting of an art fair, which invariably manages to make even a Gerhard Richter or a Jasper Johns look like a product in a miserable corporate trade show.) There is something self-abnegating about the desire to be a very famous person, requiring a saintlike level of devotion to personal transformation, sometimes extending to mutilation and self-sacrifice. In spite of authenticity supposedly being a quality that is prized in public figures, many of them only manage to perform it through the dissociative splitting of their minds, helping to explain why directors like Ingmar Bergman or David Lynch have used the actress as an archetype in order to make movies about women who have dueling personalities, secret lives. In instances like these, the second self, the public self, might be judged to be an art performance, existing as it does for the pleasure of an audience; if the body has been worked on, made bigger or smaller or less malleable or less creased, it might be seen as a medium in itself, a living sculpture. There is room for the uncanny, too, if the performer's goal is not simple, straightforward immaculacy: lips that are too big, an ass that is too disproportionate to spring from nature, a waist whittled down to nothing. Where questions about whether stars were more evolved than average people once revolved largely around their brilliant genetics—as if they were racehorses, and we were mules—now, after a period of accelerated cultural change across the aughts and the 2010s, it has more than ever to do with design, determination, and bodily craftsmanship; with creating an object, beautiful or otherwise, that reflects and reacts to the times.

"What is being done to me?" the author Rachel Kushner wonders parenthetically in her 2014 essay "Happy Hour," describing the experience of looking at a Jeff Koons work from 1988 that replicates an advertising billboard. "Something, but I can't name it."[7] In placing a liquor ad in the legitimizing setting of a gallery, Koons successfully blows up, and thus makes obvious and unnerving, the glamorously manipulative pull of advertising—a medium which exists to hypnotize us into wanting, to stoke thirst and hunger in both a literal and a metaphorical sense, and to make us feel at once inadequate and eminently fixable, provided we are rich enough and committed enough to dutifully follow its instructions. "If liquor does hold some promise of revelry, of escape, the[se] ads for it are a mediated layer away from that," Kushner writes. "They are corporate fictions that do not ignite privately stored memories from good times, bad times, or any times. Mostly, they ignite memories of *looking at the ads themselves*—in magazines, on roadway billboards, or elsewhere—giving a sense of déjà vu." Here, she puts her finger on the ghostly quality that Koons, by dint of simply recontextualizing the material, makes solid and apparent: a triggering, a sensation of simultaneous familiarity and puzzlement that makes us feel as if our psyche had just missed the middle step of an especially steep staircase. A similar feeling is provoked when we are looking at a very famous person, who hypnotizes us into wanting, who stokes thirst and hunger in a metaphorical sense, who can make us feel at once inadequate and eminently fixable, and whose face alone—familiar in its contours and yet unfamiliar in its distance from us on a personal level—can activate déjà vu, making us believe we are remembering somebody we know when, really, we are merely recalling the many, many other instances in which we have experienced this sensation. When Salvoj Žižek describes the cinema as an art form that does not give us the thing that we desire, but rather teaches us *how* we might desire it,[8] he might have been describing the essential purpose of many great works of art, or of the star in general: a human being who elects to act as an advertisement for themselves, and who in doing so makes, Koonslike, an art form of advertising.

7 Rachel Kushner, *The Hard Crowd: Essays 2000–2020* (Scribner, 2021).

8 Slavoj Žižek, *The Pervert's Guide to Cinema*, dir. Sophia Fiennes, 2006.

"What people read nowadays is advertising," the writer and *Ambit* editor Martin Bax quoted Ballard as observing, "so if you want to have novels that people read, you should publish them as advertisements." [9] People also read celebrity gossip—itself a form of advertising whose internal narratives tend to skew novelistic in the sense that they are full of fiction and depict an often falsified or enhanced version of reality, yes, but also in the sense that they are full of starkly structured morality fables, as well as all the requisite births, marriages, and deaths that make up classic works of literature. Since the novel is inarguably an art form, it makes sense that this selective recounting of the lives of such self-designed individuals might be regarded as one, too. Ballard also said that aside from death itself, the car crash was the most dramatic thing an individual could experience, but it cannot be denied that we experience many things through our observation of famous people in especially dramatic ways, too. What they share with us is a more amplified version of something quotidian and familiar, as if by sizing up they are transforming our regular-sized feelings and milestones into something more symbolic, like one of those educational diagrams in which human body parts are scaled up or scaled down in order of their sensitivity: their bodily transformations are bigger; their marriages are bigger; their divorces are bigger; their homes and their vehicles and their breasts and their pectorals and their bankruptcies are bigger; and so on and so on. Such qualities make the famous person an ideal example of—as Jeffrey Deitch himself wrote in 1992 in the gallery text-cum-manifesto which, along with his original show of the same name, introduced the term *posthuman* into art critical discourse and beyond—an objet d'art that is "descriptive of the 'real' world but [which] cannot, in fact, be called 'realistic' in the conventional sense." [10] Deitch's statement, in fact, neatly reflects an observation made by Virginia Woolf in 1926, in her essay "The Cinema": movie stars, she suggested, are transformed by their appearance on the screen into something "more beautiful" than the audience members looking at them, "in the sense [of being] more real, or real with a different reality from that which we perceive in daily life." [11] Stars are, as *Us Weekly* puts it, *just like us,* but more so; they are *like us* to the nth degree.

"It is becoming routine for people to try to alter their appearance, their behavior, and their consciousness beyond what was once thought possible," Deitch also notes in his 1992 manifesto. "Our current post-modern era can be characterized as a transitional period of the disintegration of self. [12] Perhaps the coming 'post-human' period will be characterized by the reconstruction of self." Or else, to some degree, by the deletion of the self—by a removal of those qualities that make the self *itself* in favor of improving the exterior vehicle of the body. One of those qualities might be a sense of connection to the normal human world. In *The Atrocity Exhibition,* Ballard posited

9   Baxter, "Age of Unreason."

10   Jeff Deitch, ed., *Post Human* (exh. cat.) (Cantz/Deste Foundation for Contemporary Art, 1992).

11   Virginia Woolf, "The Cinema," in *The Nation and Athenaeum*, 1926.

12   Deitch, *Post Human.*

13   Ballard, *The Atrocity Exhibition*.

that post-Warhol, "a single gesture [made by a celebrity], such as uncrossing one's legs" would come to contain "more significance than all the pages in *War and Peace*."[13] What might the single gesture of the sex symbol's photographs with the robot be said to contain, if "single gesture" is not far too reductive a term to describe the simulation of a sex act between a human woman and a machine? Evidently, as previously suggested, they are telling a story about posthuman, post-biological refinement, and a kind of sex beyond sex. More recently, it is also the case that the manufacturer of the android has ascended to a new, unexpected position of political power and has begun to express increasingly terrifyingly right-wing views. The famous sex symbol, in lieu of walking back her attachment to his work, has doubled down, appearing once again with her automaton on the cover of a fashion magazine. Like an artwork, the body of a truly famous person cannot be made or presented in a vacuum—necessarily, it is at least obliquely reflective of its times. It can also, given its status as a frequent subject of both opinion pieces and online debate, be unavoidably charged with political and social significance, and in this respect, it is much like an artwork, as well.

"To understand Homo sapiens' primary wish list," writes Margaret Atwood in the article "Are Humans Necessary?" "go back to mythology. We endowed the gods with the abilities we wished we had ourselves: immortality and eternal youth, flight, resplendent beauty, total power."[14] Abuse of power, as the artist Jenny Holzer once argued, comes as no surprise, and the celebrity—who is, by the reckoning of many cultural critics, something fairly close to a new kind of god when it comes to their position in society—certainly incarnates total power, to say nothing of their seemingly eternal youth, their resplendent beauty, and the flight afforded to them by the use of their climate-throttling jets. An alignment such as this one should by rights have been a reputational car crash for the robot-nuzzling star; if she has so far managed to escape a fall from grace, it is in part due to her sheer prolificity when it comes to making, as Ballard would put it, "gestures" in the media. If a successful celebrity is Koons-like in their embrace of advertising as a form of art, she herself can be said to be Koons-like (or, if you prefer, faintly reminiscent of Tracey Emin's über-prolific wide boy contemporary Damien Hirst) in the volume of her output, rubber-stamping endless images and effigies, and mounting weekly performances of beauty and supersized Realness both on- and off-screen. The last item on Atwood's list of godlike qualities is immortality, a state granted to the very famous by dint of their perpetual documentation, whether by themselves or by others. Particularly documented are those female celebrities whose bodies, whether naturally or via augmentation, approximate those of goddesses in classical sculpture, or in paintings by artists like John Currin. Better yet: those in paintings by the artist Lisa Yuskavage, which depict nude women not merely as they appear in the direct glare of

14   Margaret Atwood, "Are Humans Necessary?" *New York Times,* December 4, 2014.

the male gaze, but in a girlish, high-feminine looking-glass refraction of it. Her subjects are the embodiment of a contemporary female fantasy *of a male fantasy*. "Why have you made this outrageous, hypersexualized white nude female figure the sort of centerpiece of your visual language?" the curator Helen Molesworth asked Yuskavage in an interview in 2023. "Because," Yuskavage answered simply, "that's the history of art." [15]

The hypersexualized white nude female figure is also, to a certain extent, a representative of the history of female celebrity, as well as the history of television, film, and advertising, all of which is to say: the history of Hollywood, and of Los Angeles, and more broadly of America itself. "It's actually so unbelievably not about boobs," James Rondeau, the director of the Art Institute of Chicago, recently said about Yuskavage's work. "It's more like, you've got to have your knockers out—and they've got to be *huge* and *weird*—if I'm going to really talk to you about a landscape of acceptance." [16] The idea of a body that has been expanded outward into such an exaggerated image of sexiness that it has become unsexy, a thing that is genuinely *weird*, is exciting—if not erotically, then certainly conceptually, offering us as it does the possibility of actually seeing a new shape of person. This is an alternative vision of posthuman living from the one where humans begin mating with machines in which we become even fleshier, even more excessive, until this excessiveness feels just as unnatural and perverse as any possible image of automated sex. If any celebrity icon would have made an ideal subject for a Yuskavage painting, it might be said to be Lolo Ferrari, the late actress and singer who was once world-renowned for her cartoonish, impossible-looking 36T breasts— the largest implants, her publicity insisted, in the world. "You wanted to imagine her in a dream world with a big, airy house and white bunny rabbits and pink butterflies," the French journalist Elisabeth Alexandre once said of Ferrari, describing an imagined scene that sounds very much like one, in fact, that might appear in a Yuskavage painting—a coquettish fairy-tale setting for a subject whose voluptuous physicality recalled the bodily trends of contemporary porn. Rumored to have been designed by an engineer who'd helped to create the Boeing 747, the enormity of her bolt-on mammaries was, as Rondeau might put it, *actually so unbelievably not about boobs*, but instead about a startling and dramatic form of personal reinvention. In interviews, she talked often about wanting to be "different"—wanting to escape her very human fears and anxieties about life and its meaning by becoming someone who did not resemble a "real" woman at all. The mystery at the heart of very extreme plastic surgery, as seen from the outside, is its appeal when the final results rarely look natural, and quite often do not look particularly seductive, either. The solution to this mystery is that newness, and not beauty, is the unnamed goal, letting the individual who is being operated on

15 Helen Molesworth, "Lisa Yuskavage's Bodies of Work," *New Yorker*, July 31, 2023.

16 Ibid.

17   Priscilla Frank, "ORLAN Talks Plastic Surgery, Beauty Standards And Giving Her Fat To Madonna," *Huffington Post*, January 29, 2013.

erase not only their past, but their vulnerability, their susceptibility to age and decay, and perhaps a touch of their humanity as well.

When the French artist ORLAN underwent a total of nine elective surgeries in the early 1990s "not to appear younger or better according to the designated pattern, [but] to disrupt the standards of beauty," [17] the modifications that she chose were inspired by art historical depictions of women. Her brow implants were meant to call to mind the *Mona Lisa,* and her chin implant was intended to reform her jawline into something closer to that of the titular historic babe in Botticelli's *Birth of Venus,* albeit with an understanding that such resemblances were impossible in the context of a human body and therefore even an entirely flawless execution of the work would be, in its own way, a failure—a theoretical success that nevertheless would not be especially "pretty" in a conventional sense. How different was this undertaking, in practice if not in spirit, from Ferrari's own tireless work on her body? It was, after all, another example of something like the grand proportions of a large-scale painting—an ideal of womanly beauty just as obvious, if not necessarily as universally accepted, as those dreamed up by Leonardo da Vinci or Botticelli several centuries earlier—being transposed to the medium of flesh, with the result not being aspirational, per se, but striking: outsized enough to serve as commentary on the cultural history of the female form. Even her adoption of the sobriquet "Lolo Ferrari" in place of her birth name, Ève Valois, echoed ORLAN's own brand-conscious rechristening of herself—Lolo being, in Valois's native France, a slang word for breasts, and a Ferrari being a gorgeous European product turned by canny advertising into a worldwide signifier of virility. Her mysterious death in 2000, at thirty-seven—believed to be a suicide—was, in effect, the ultimate bodily

18   Ralf Rugoff, "J.G. Ballard: Dangerous Driving," *Frieze* 34 (May 1997).

car wreck ("a kind of profane mass," [18] as Ballard once said of literal crashes), making her a posthuman martyr. Staying alive, for a person in the public eye who relies on the sale of their image, is its own brand of durational or endurance art, and those figures that succeed often startle us with their huge, mystic-seeming dissimilarity from ourselves. "Beyond our physical touch," Ballard also wrote, "the breasts of these screen actresses incite our imaginations to explore and reshape them. The bodies of these extraordinary women form a kit of spare parts, a set of mental mannequins that resemble Bellmer's obscene dolls. ... The parts are interchangeable, like the operations we imagine performing on these untouchable women, as endlessly variable as the colours silkscreened on to the faces of Warhol's Liz and Marilyn." [19] This observation is, if we are talking about archaic sexism, even harder to defend than his comment about Emin's body, but it also has an undeniable ring of truth about it: the aggressiveness of certain coverage of female celebrities certainly does feel, at times, like a symbolic

19   Ballard, *The Atrocity Exhibition*.

dismemberment, and it is little wonder that the subjects of this coverage choose to change themselves in order to retain a sense of something like artistic control.

Having expanded her body considerably less than a sexual fringe figure like Lolo Ferrari, the famous sex symbol's devotion to surgery has not killed her, but instead made her very, very rich. When she did finally decide to supersize herself in March of 2025, she employed a proxy: a superinflated, Bellmer-esque blow-up doll of herself in a bikini, sixty feet high and prominently positioned in Times Square with the ostensible aim of advertising her lingerie brand. Warhol was no longer alive to canonize her in a silkscreen, and so here, she chose to canonize herself. Like the flickering, hauntingly repeated faces of Monroe and Taylor in his work, this gigantic rubber sculpture served as a metonym for the enormity of her public image: endless, inescapable, and landscape-dominating. It was, like the shoot with her robot lover had been, at once wholly evocative of the basic biological idea of sex and fully sexless, suggestive of a total separation between all that was supposedly erotic about the female body and the filthy act itself. (Even the sculpture's location, in a square that was once dominated by sex shops and sex shows and which now serves as a gleaming shopping shrine, felt like a possible statement about the commodification of women's sexuality.) If it is difficult to admire the sex symbol's politics—or, per the most generous possible reading of her actions, her ability to remain flexibly apolitical in favor of making money—it is easier by far to admire the daunting scope of her creative and conceptual vision. A gigantic inflatable sex doll with huge breasts and no orifices; a perfect-looking woman with a smoothly oiled machine for a husband; a repeating face that alters with each repetition, like a time-lapse photography series of some process from nature. Here are images that describe, for good or ill, the posthuman babe of tomorrow, and their effectiveness as a representative or harbinger of what is to come is both frightening and impressive. Accidentally or otherwise, year by year, the celebrity writes us a new pornographic novel about technology, a pornographic novel about surgery and sex, a pornographic novel about future-womanhood and future-humankind, a pornographic novel, finally, about art itself.

An excerpt of this essay was first published in Philippa Snow, *Trophy Lives: On the Celebrity as an Art Object* (London: MACK, 2024). Reproduced by permission of the author and MACK.

POST HUMAN (2024–25)

Jeffrey Deitch
Los Angeles
September 12, 2024–January 18, 2025

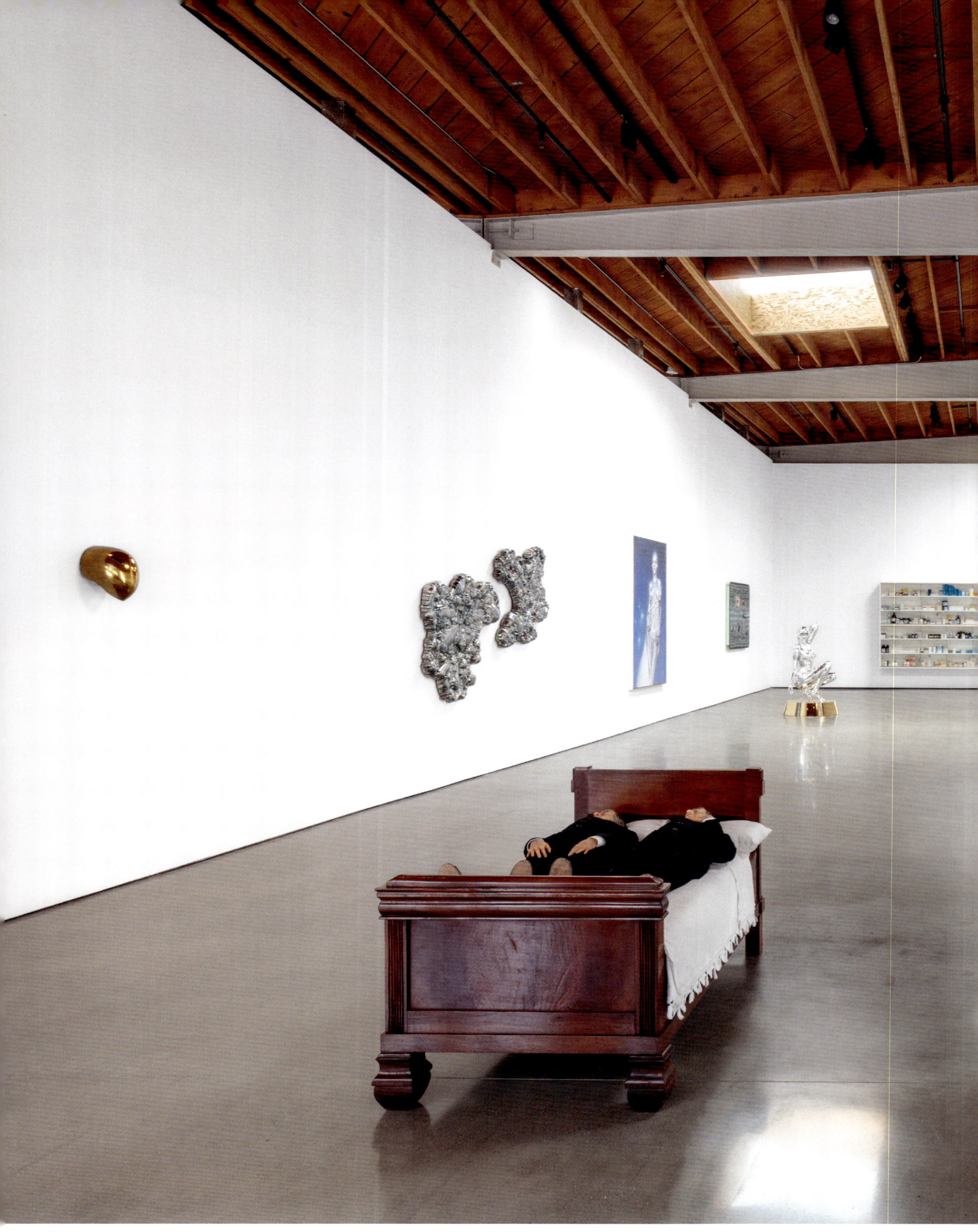

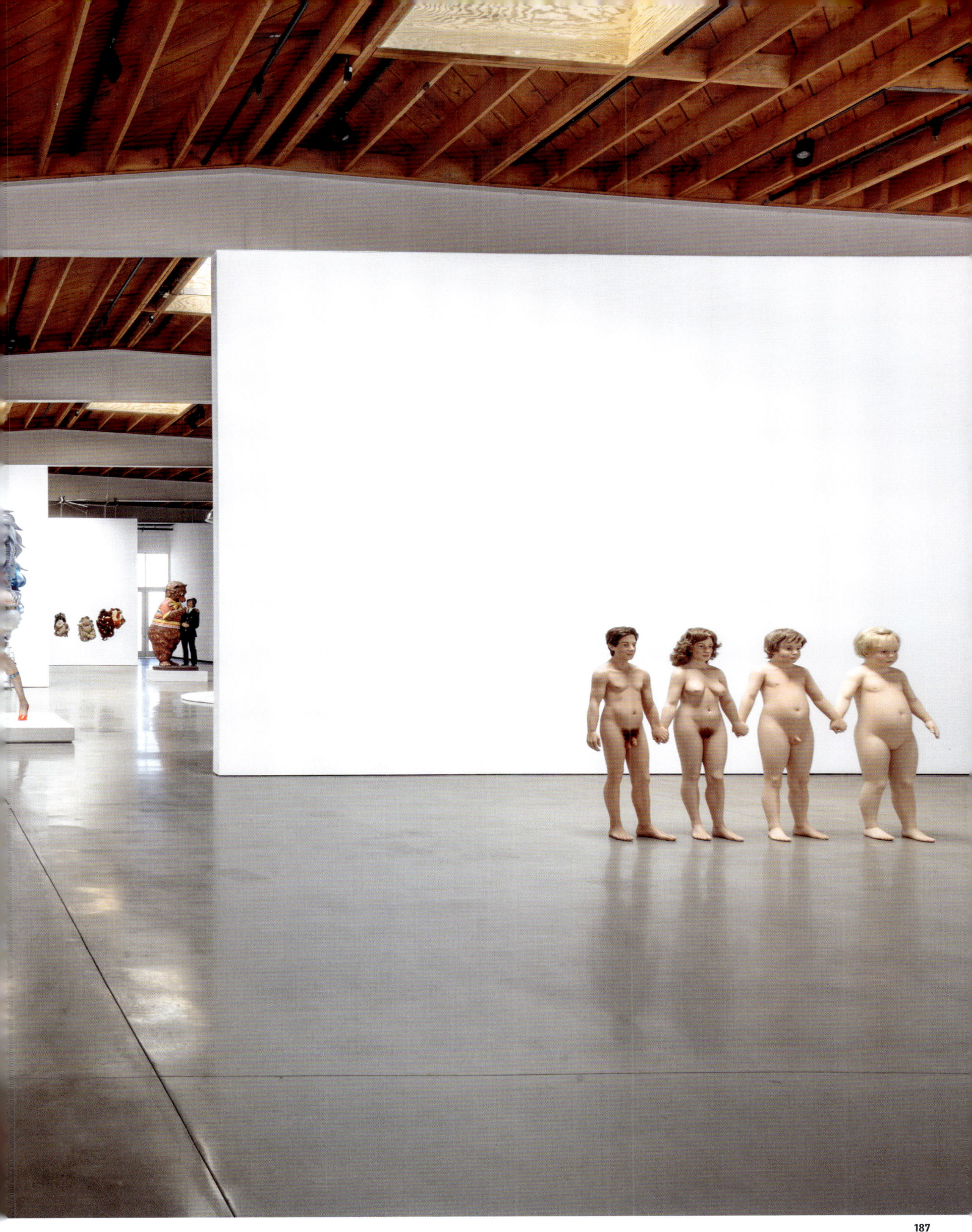

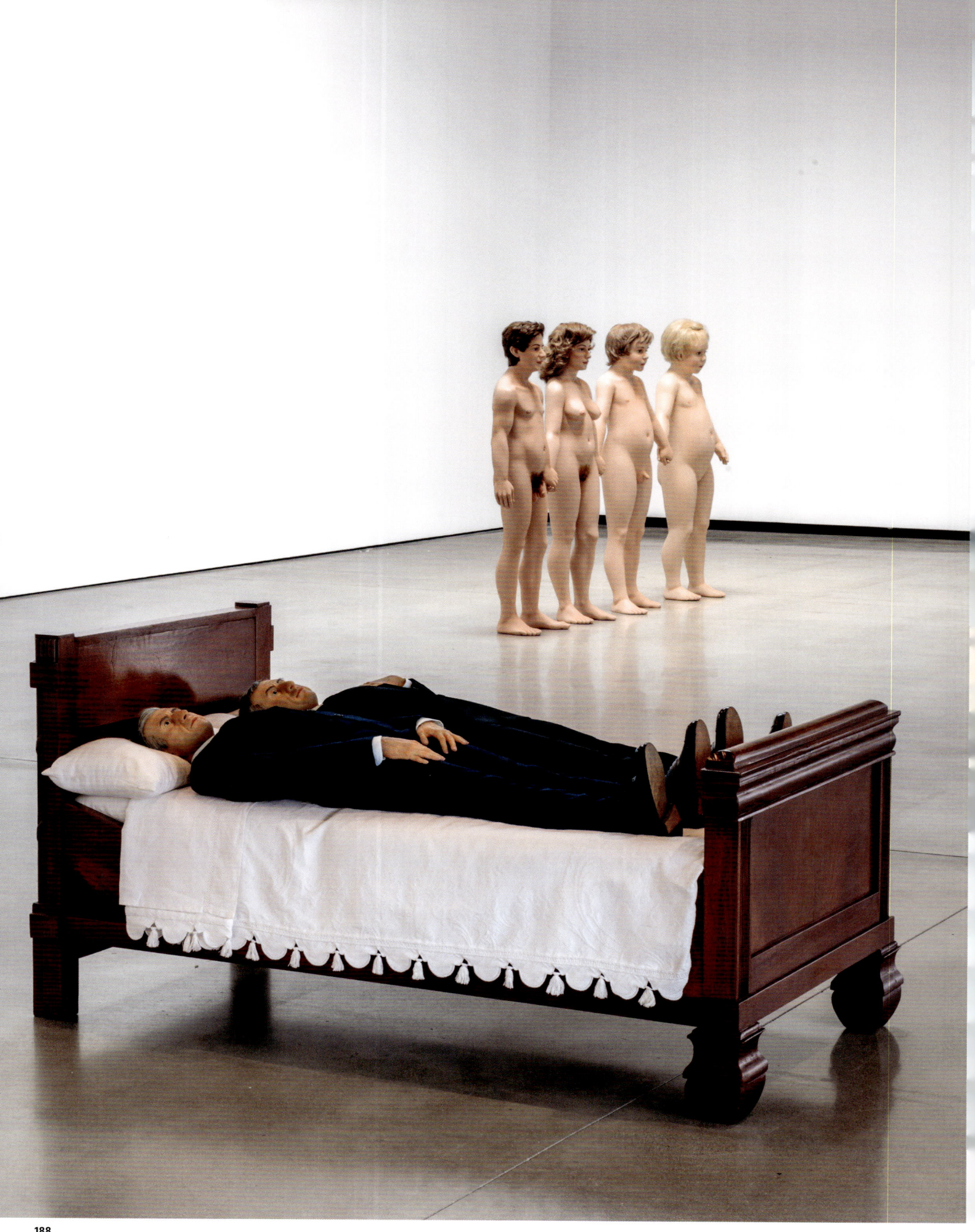

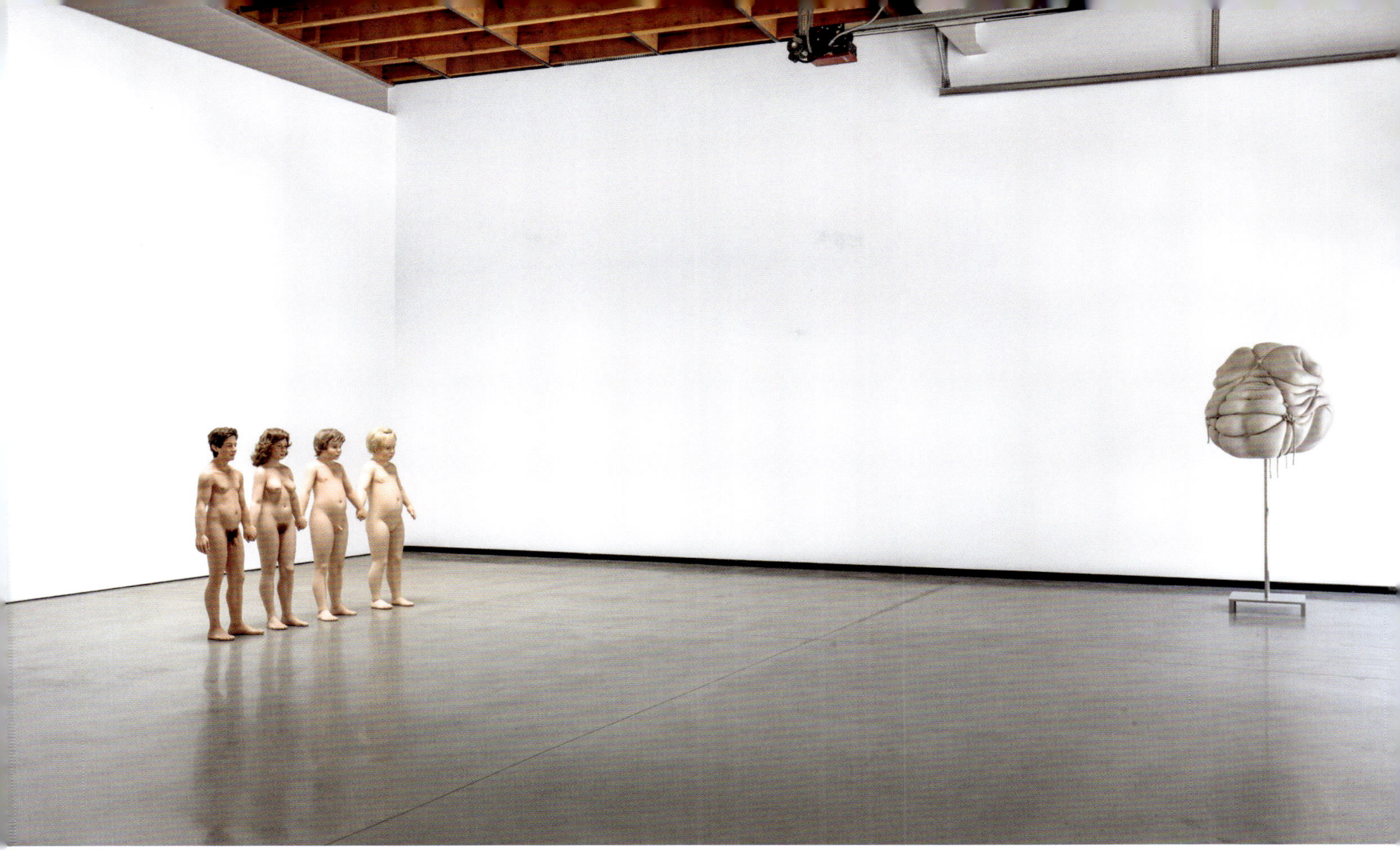

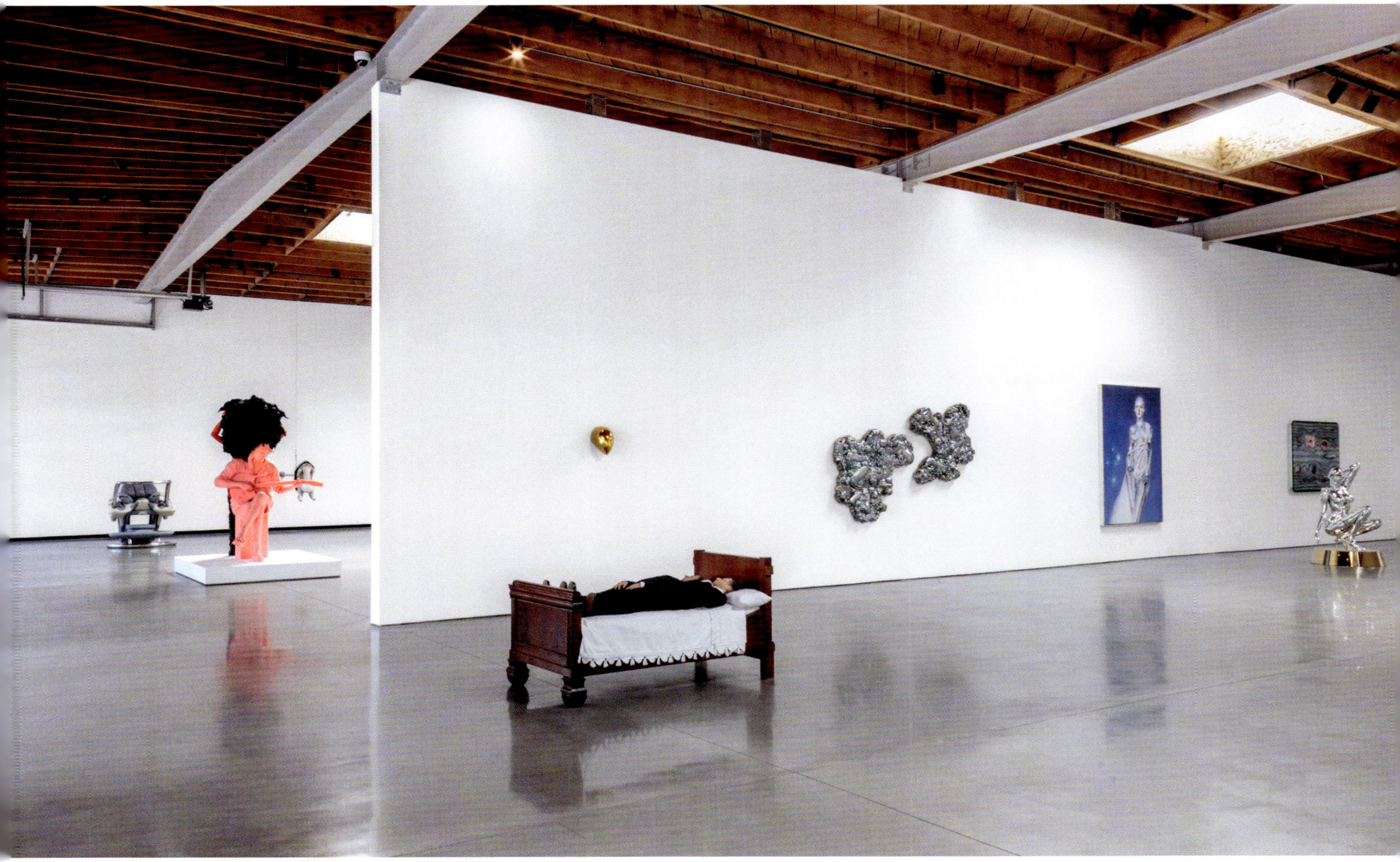

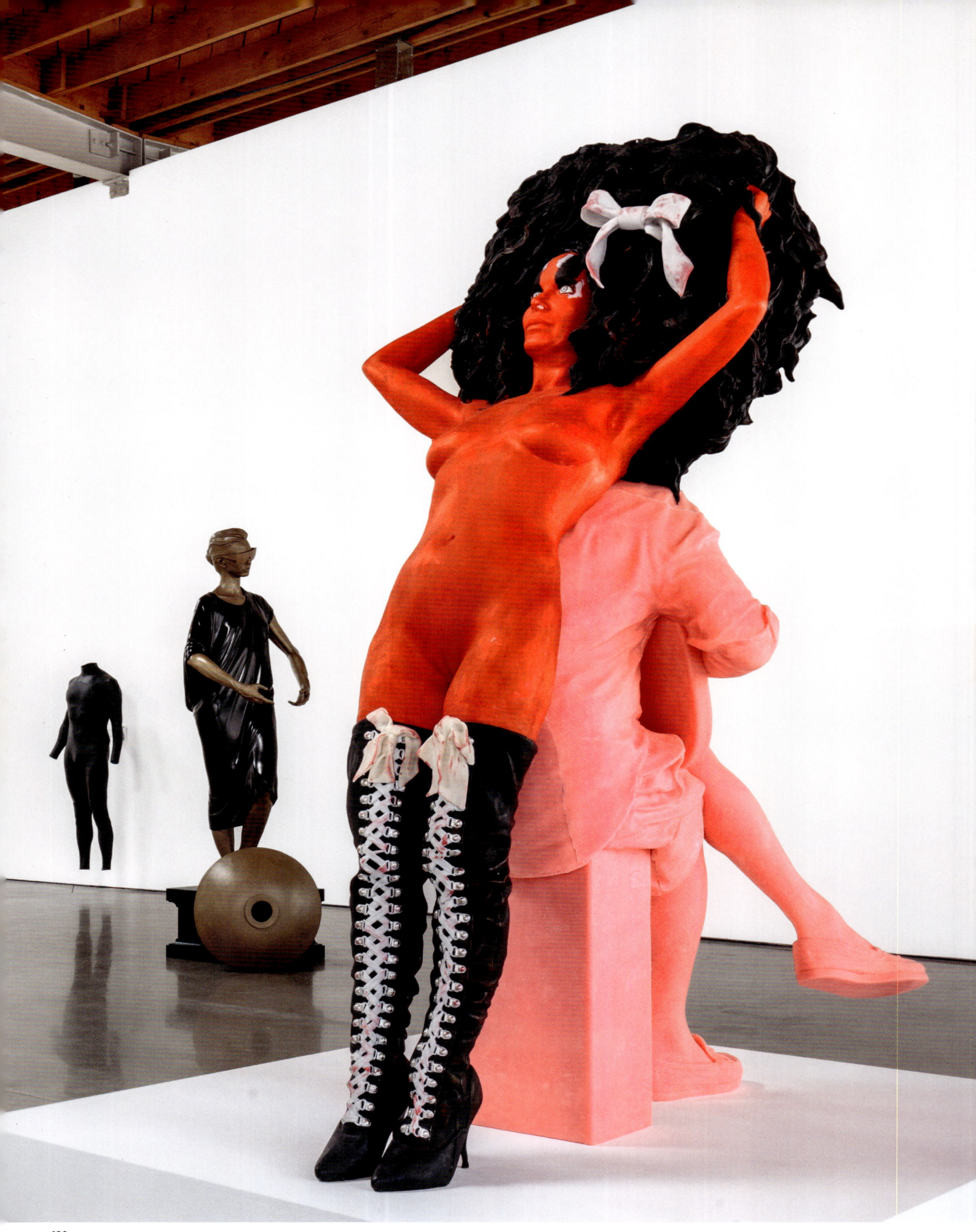

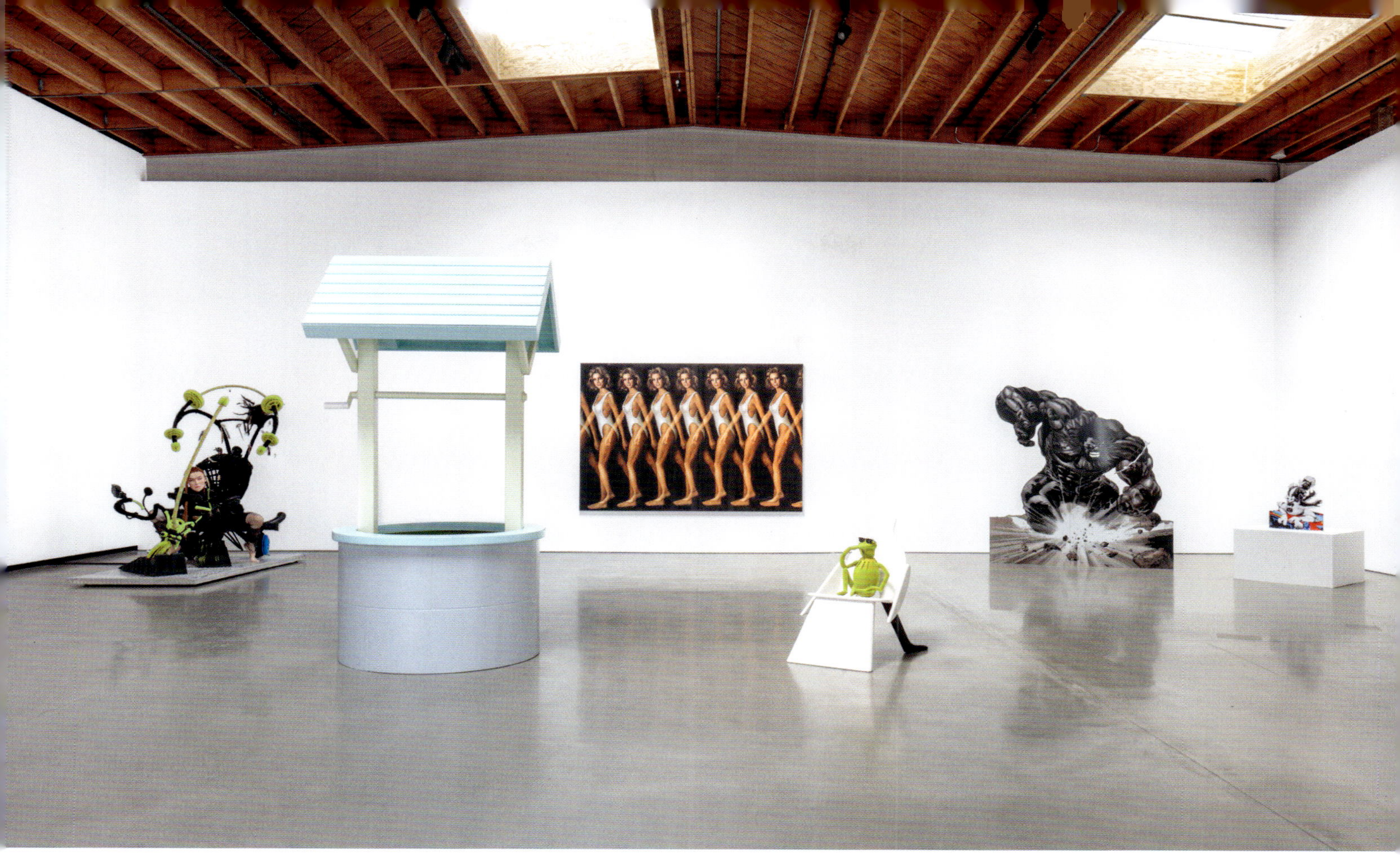

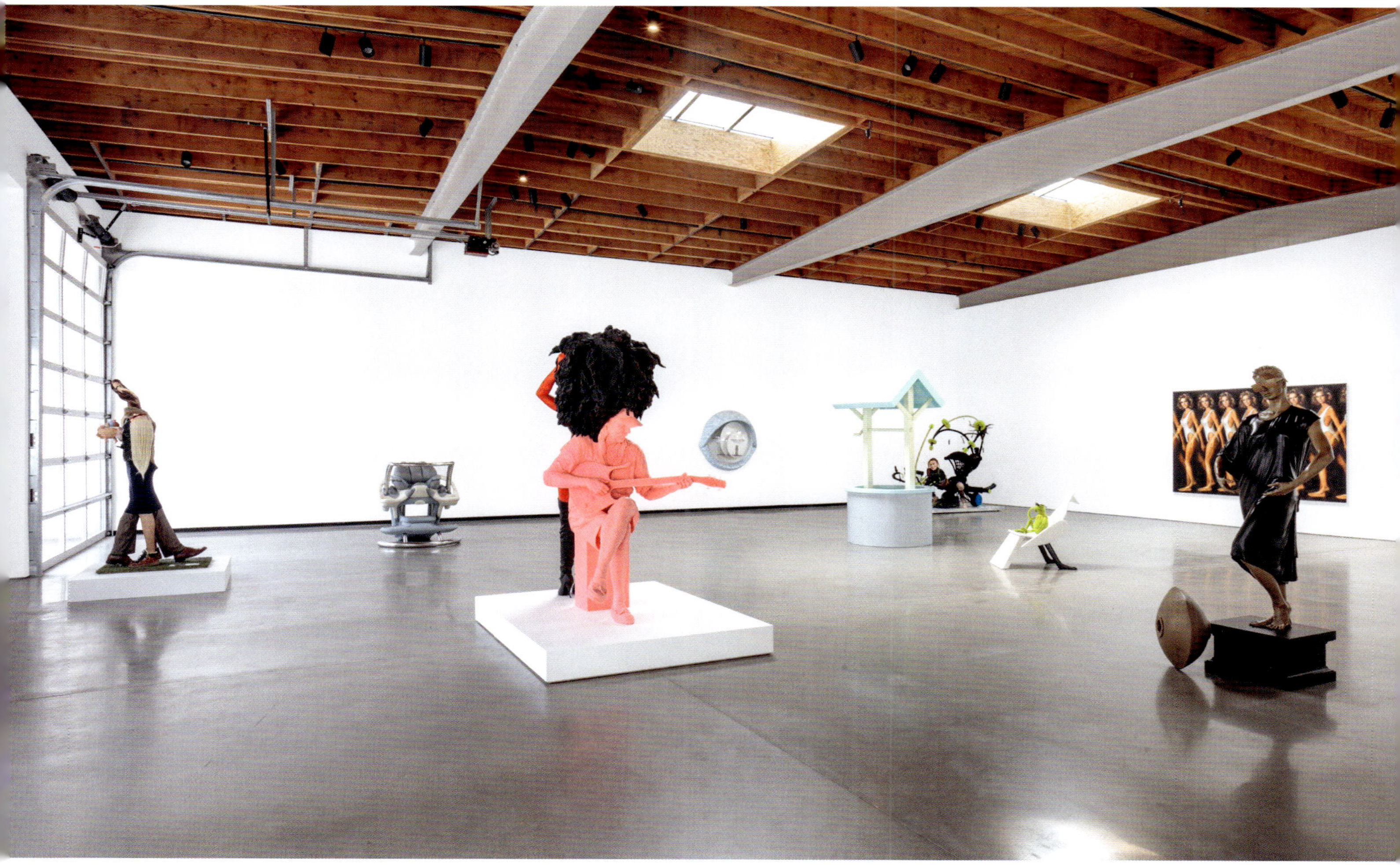

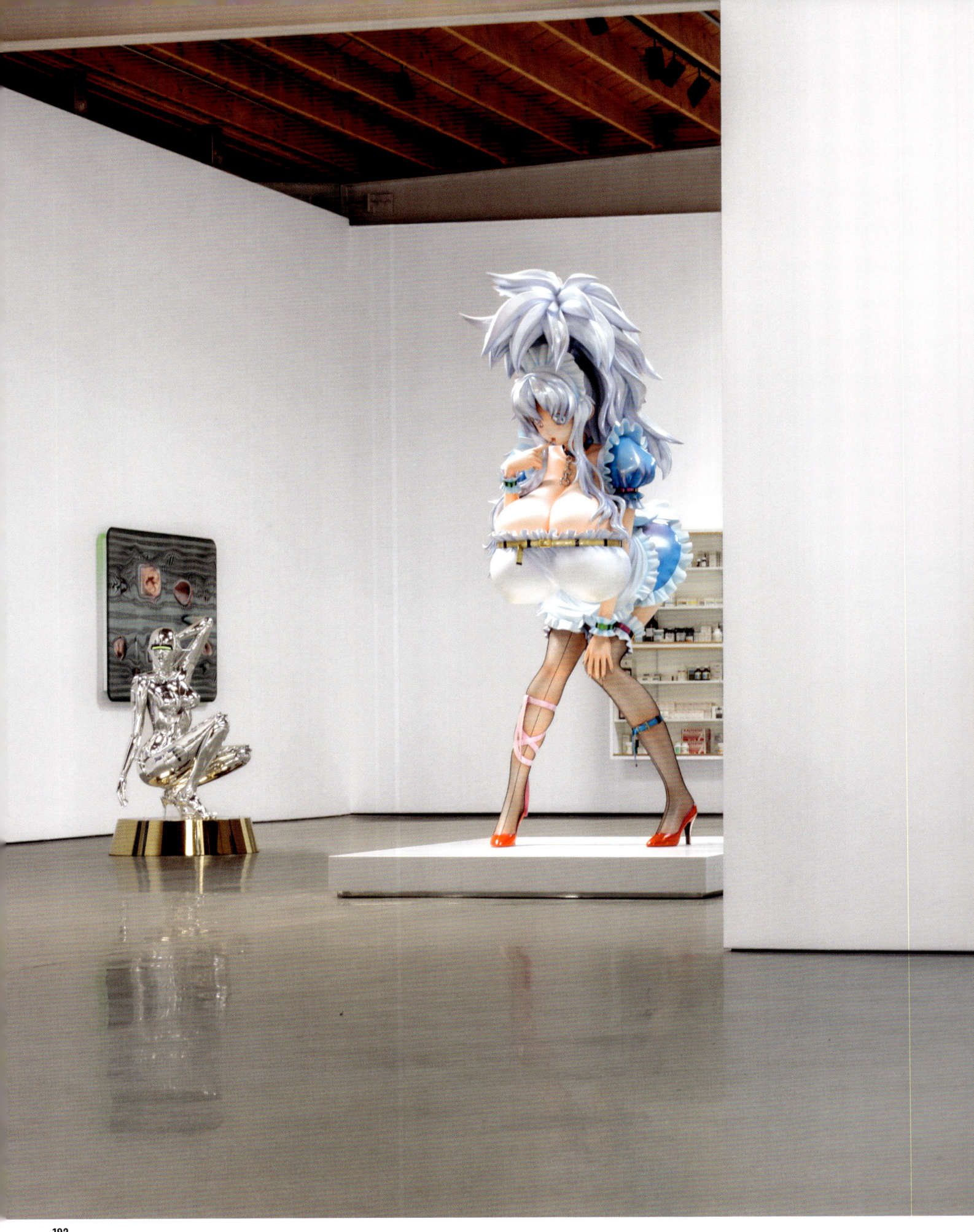

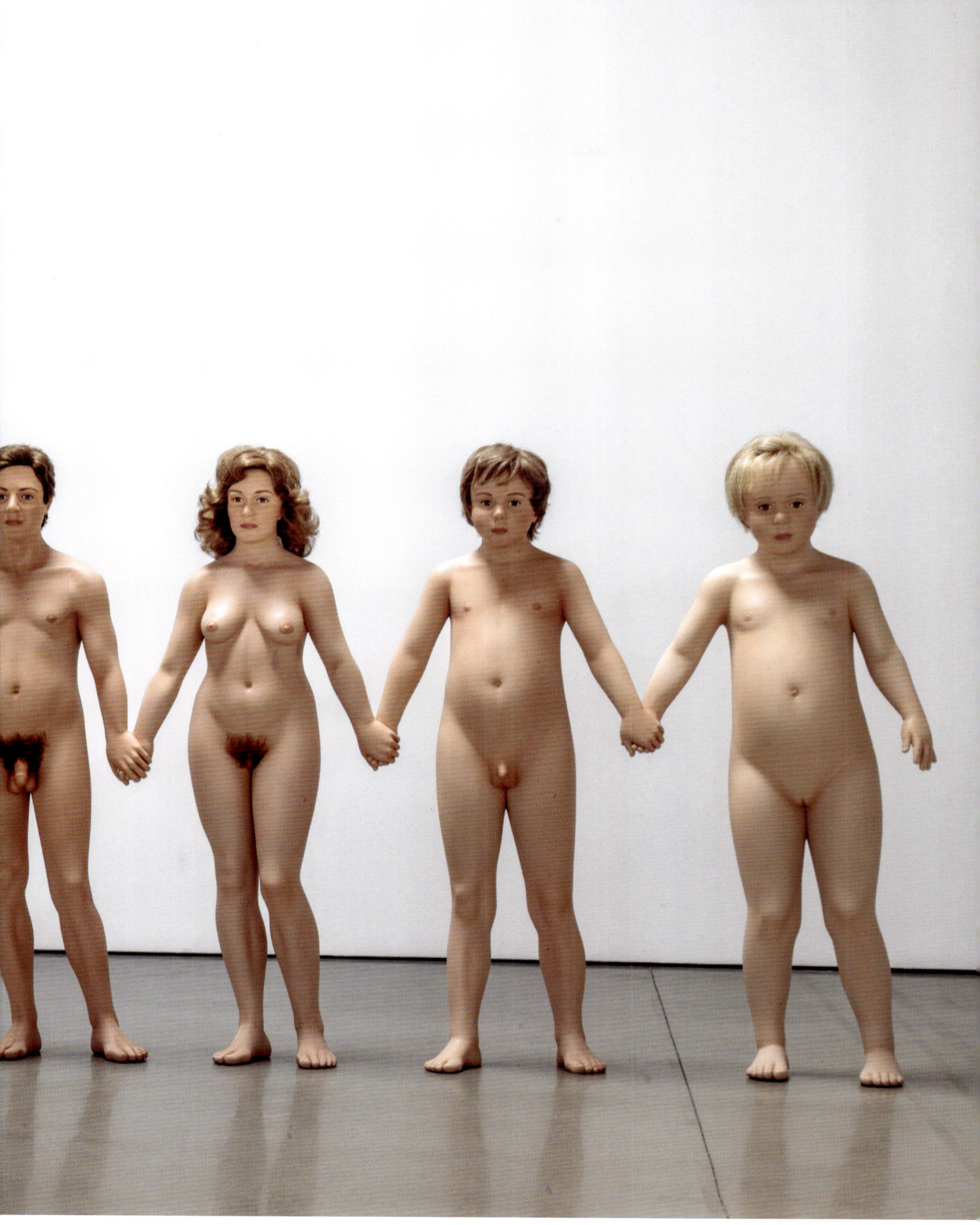

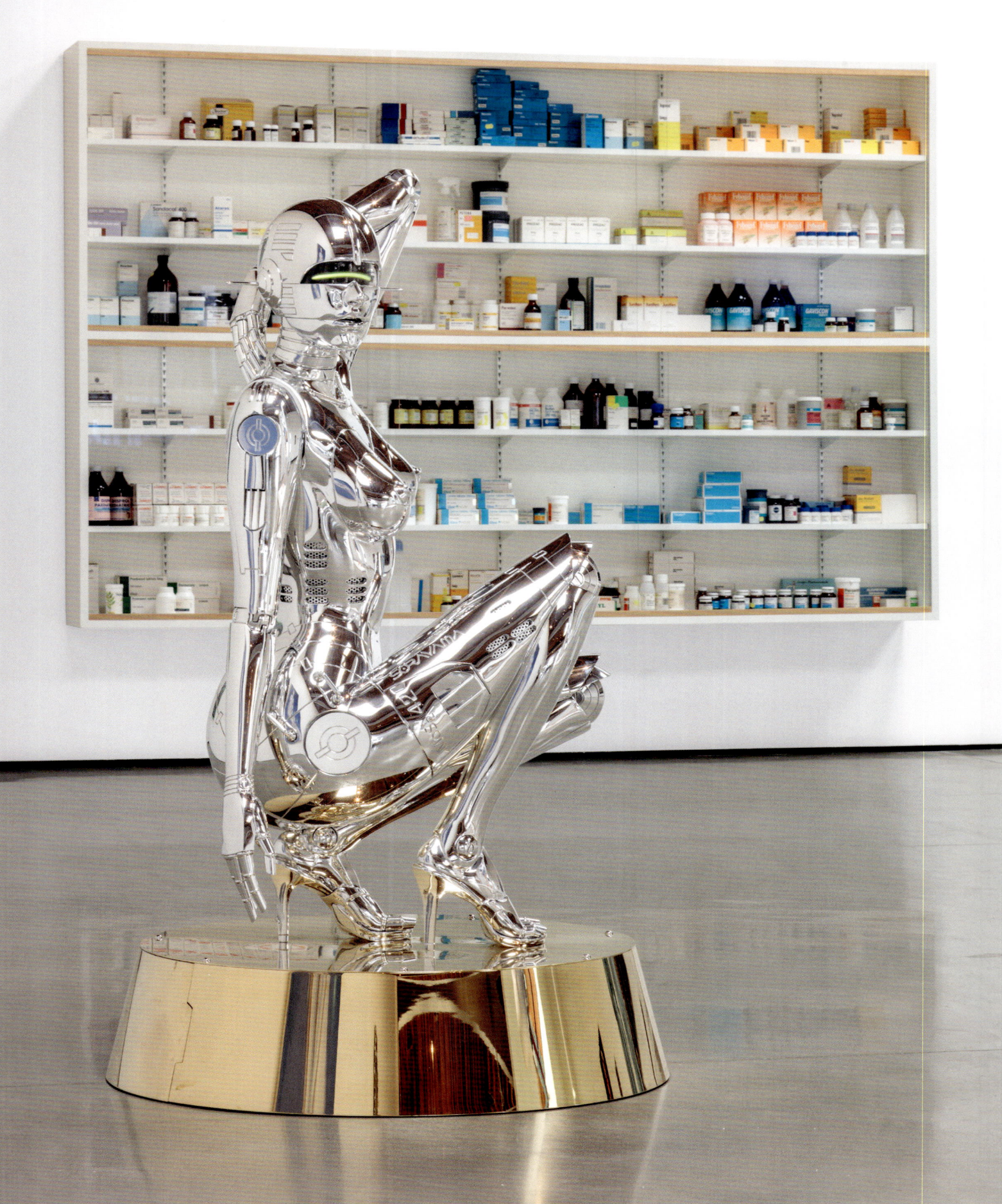

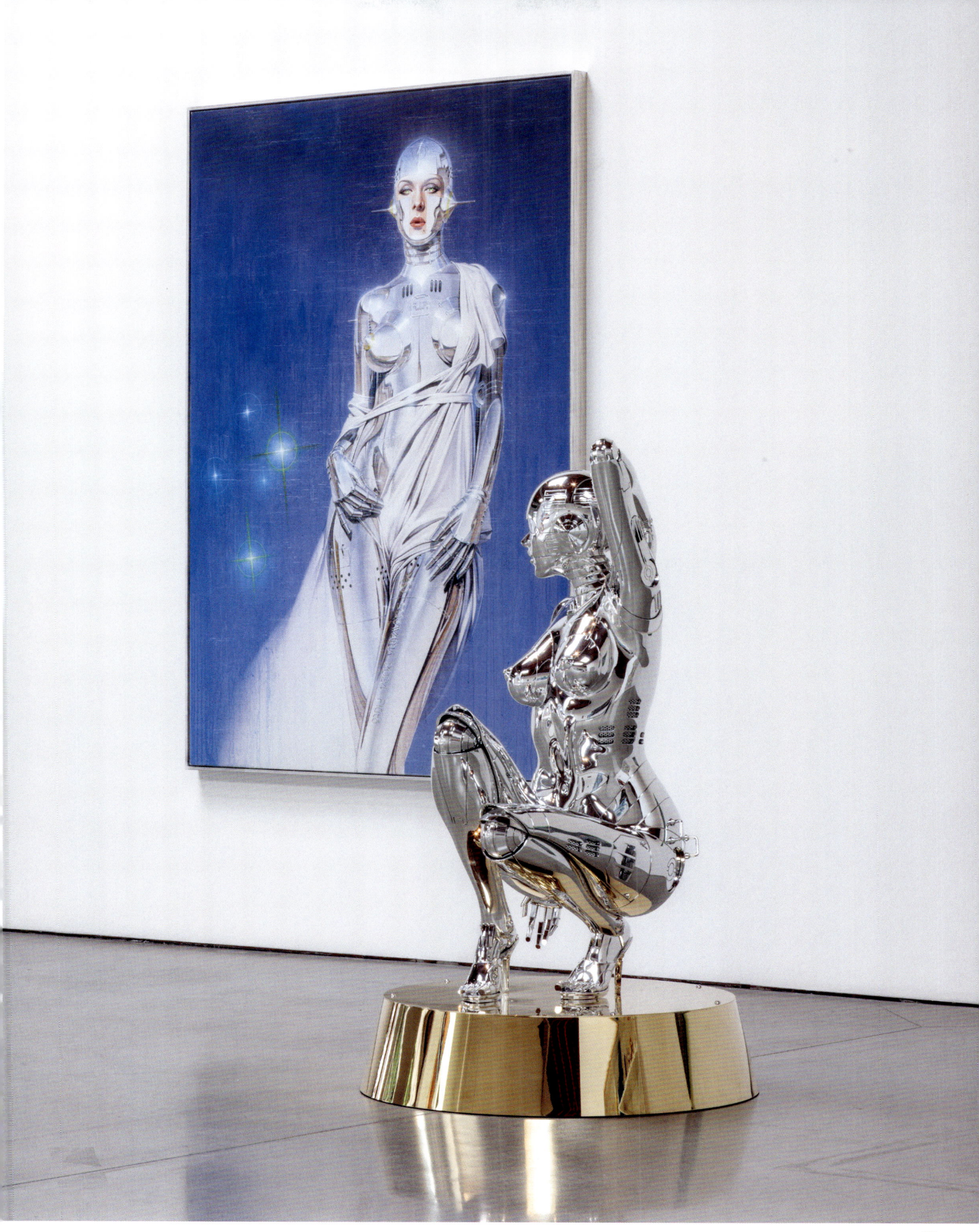

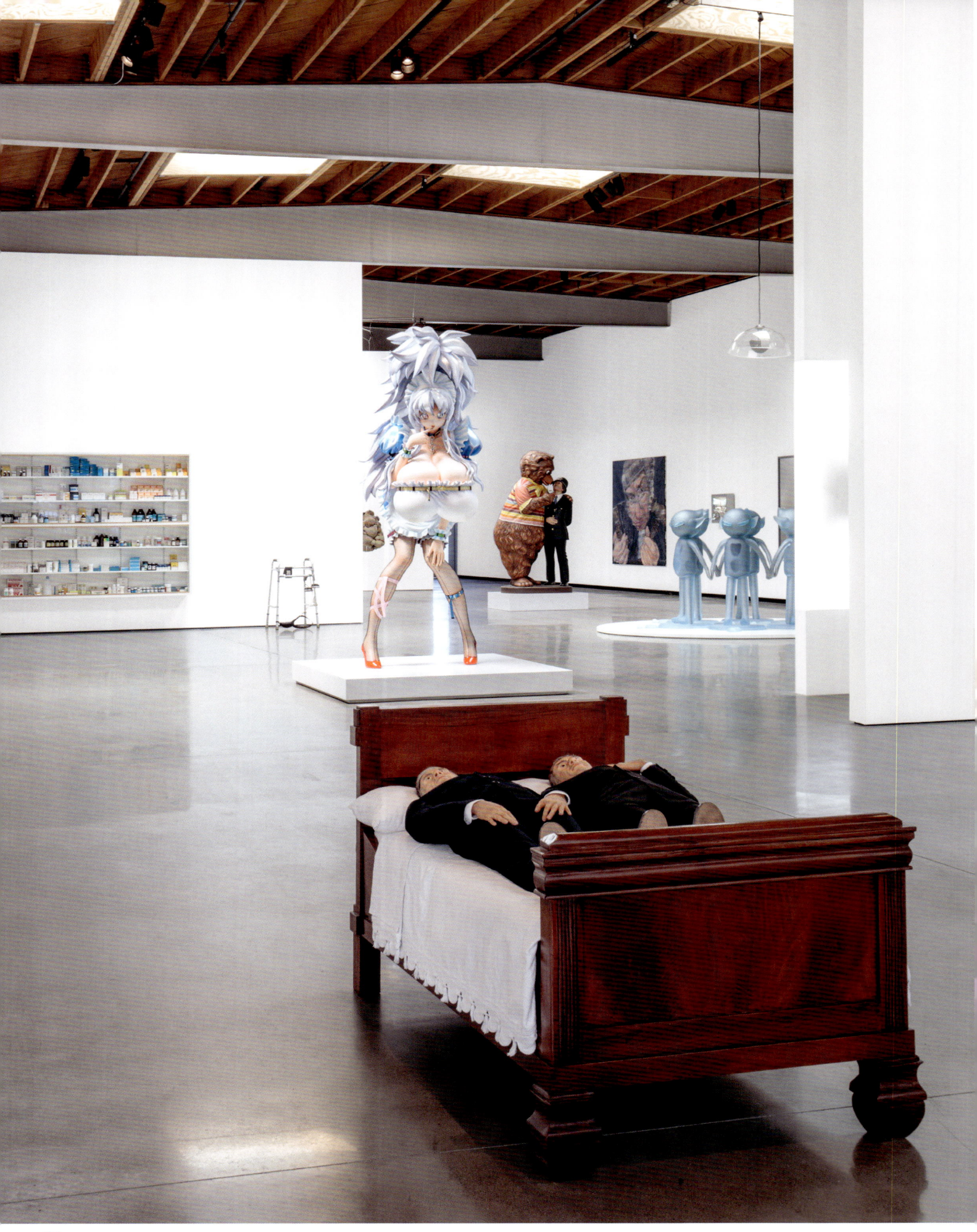

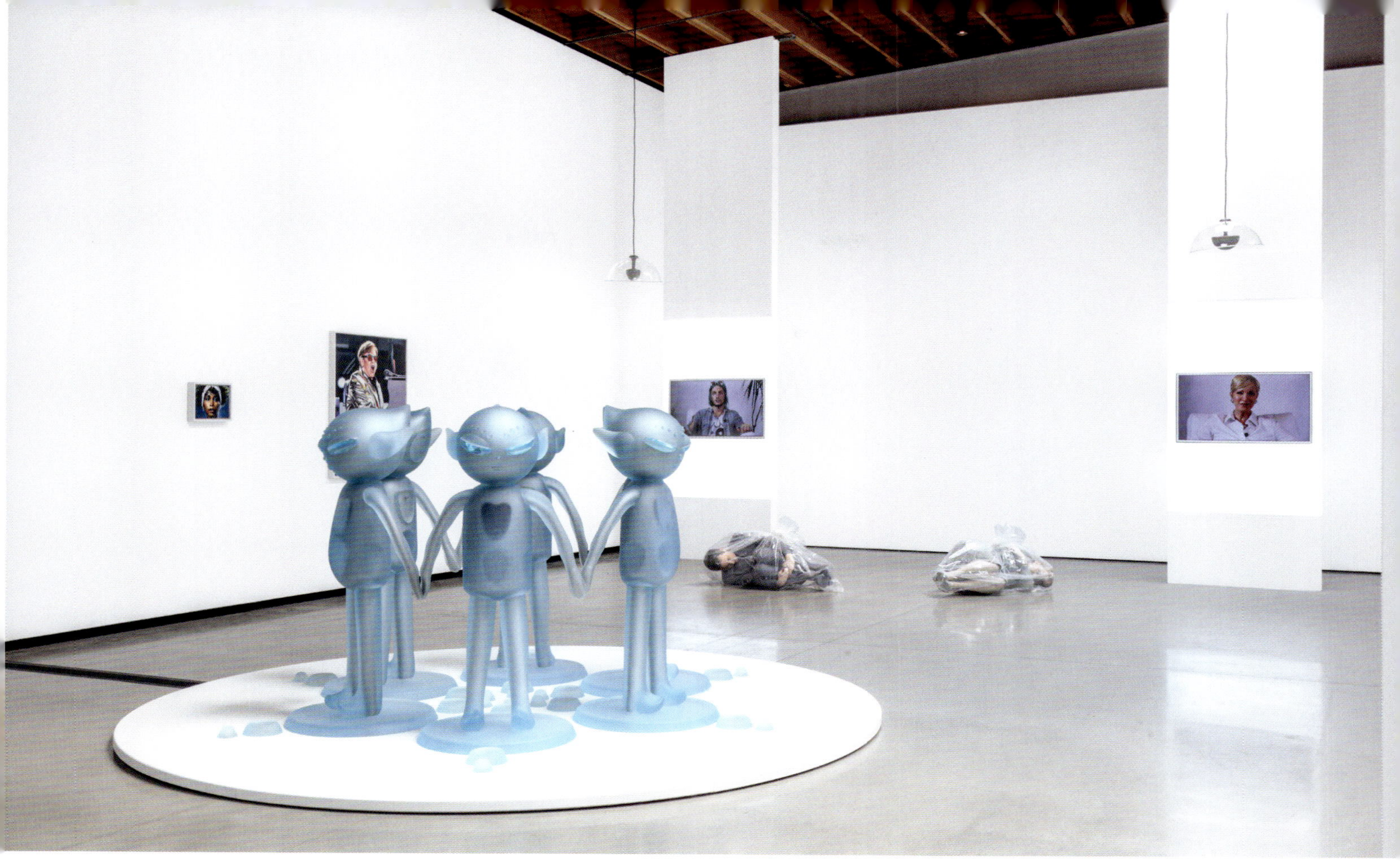

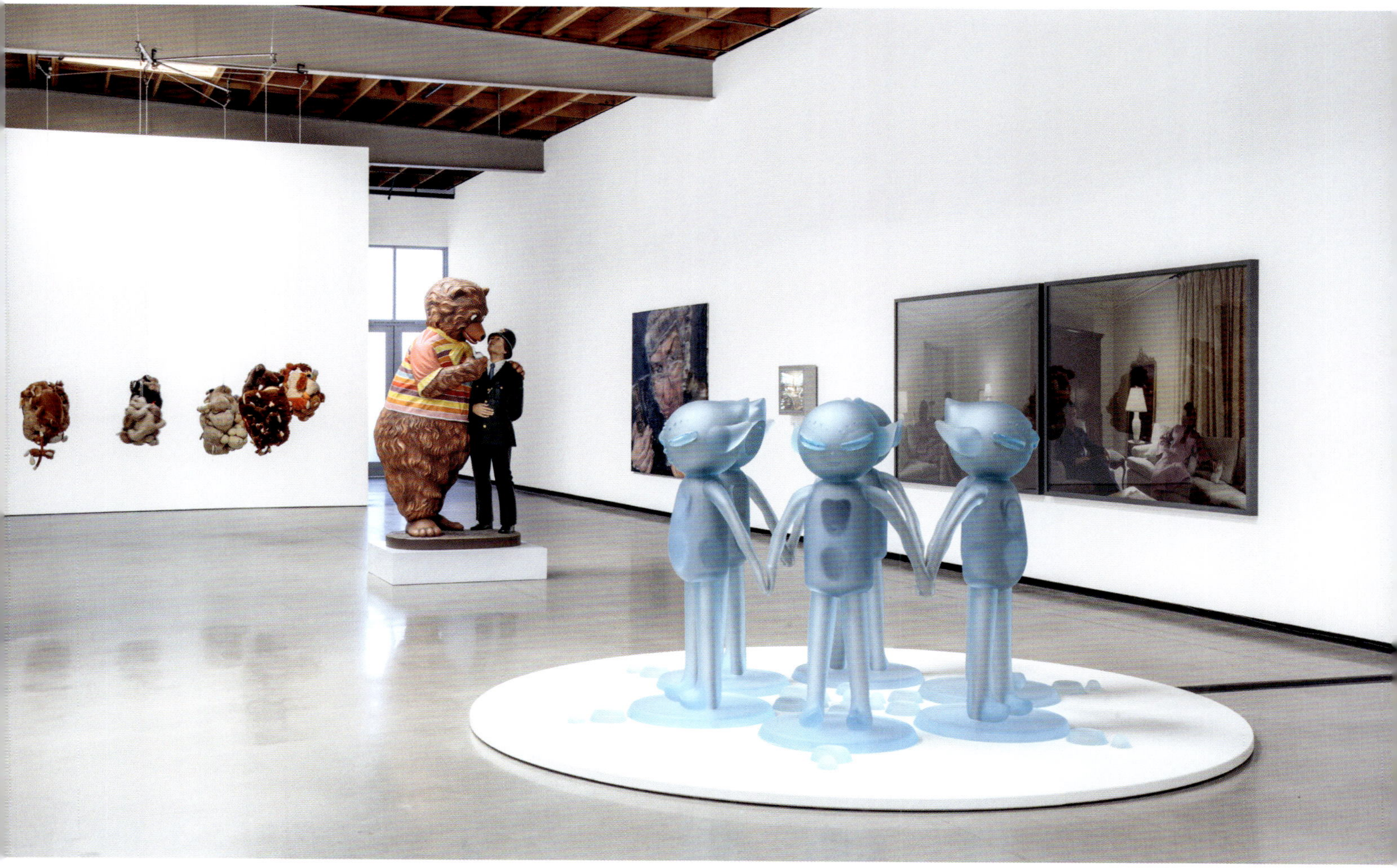

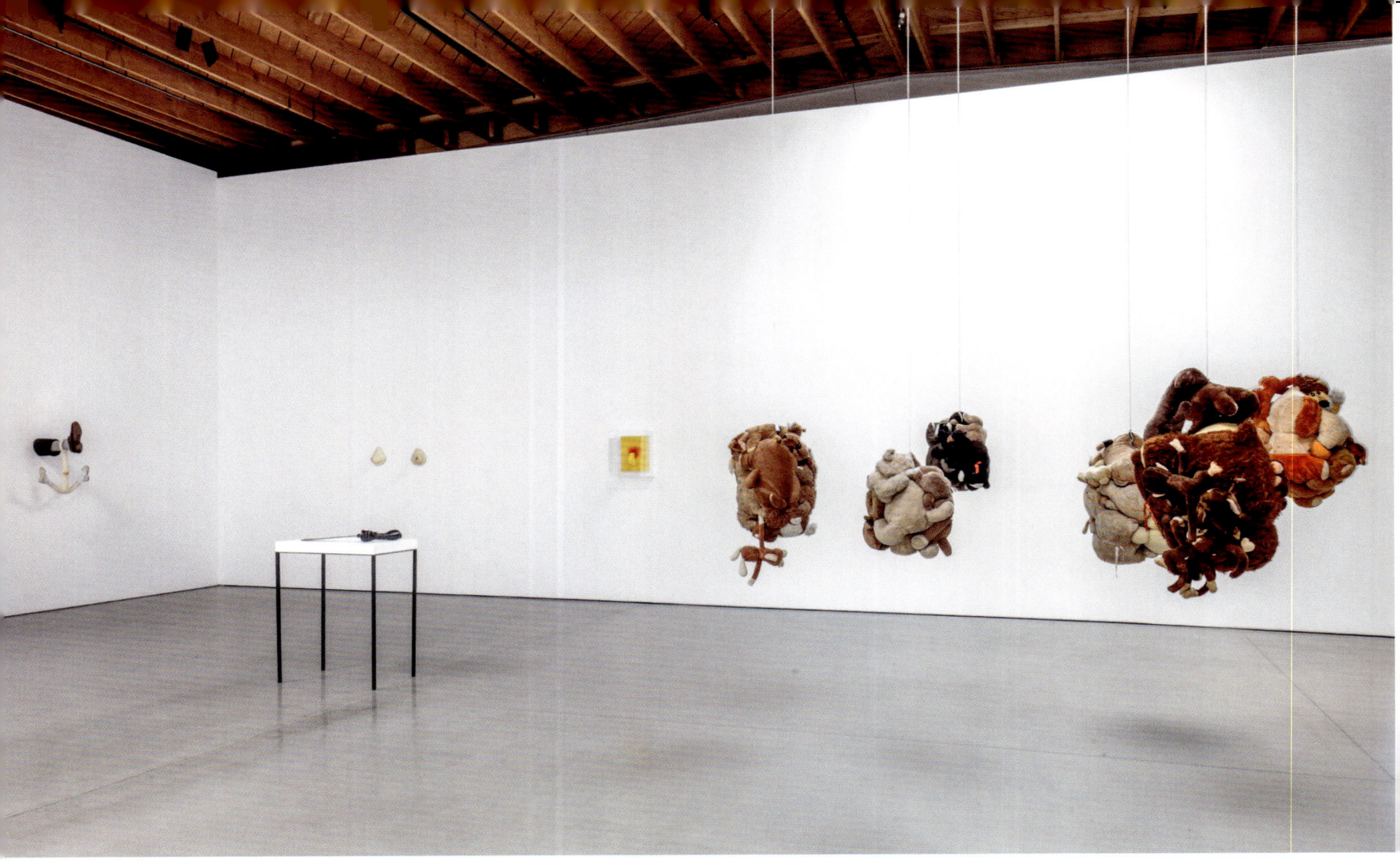

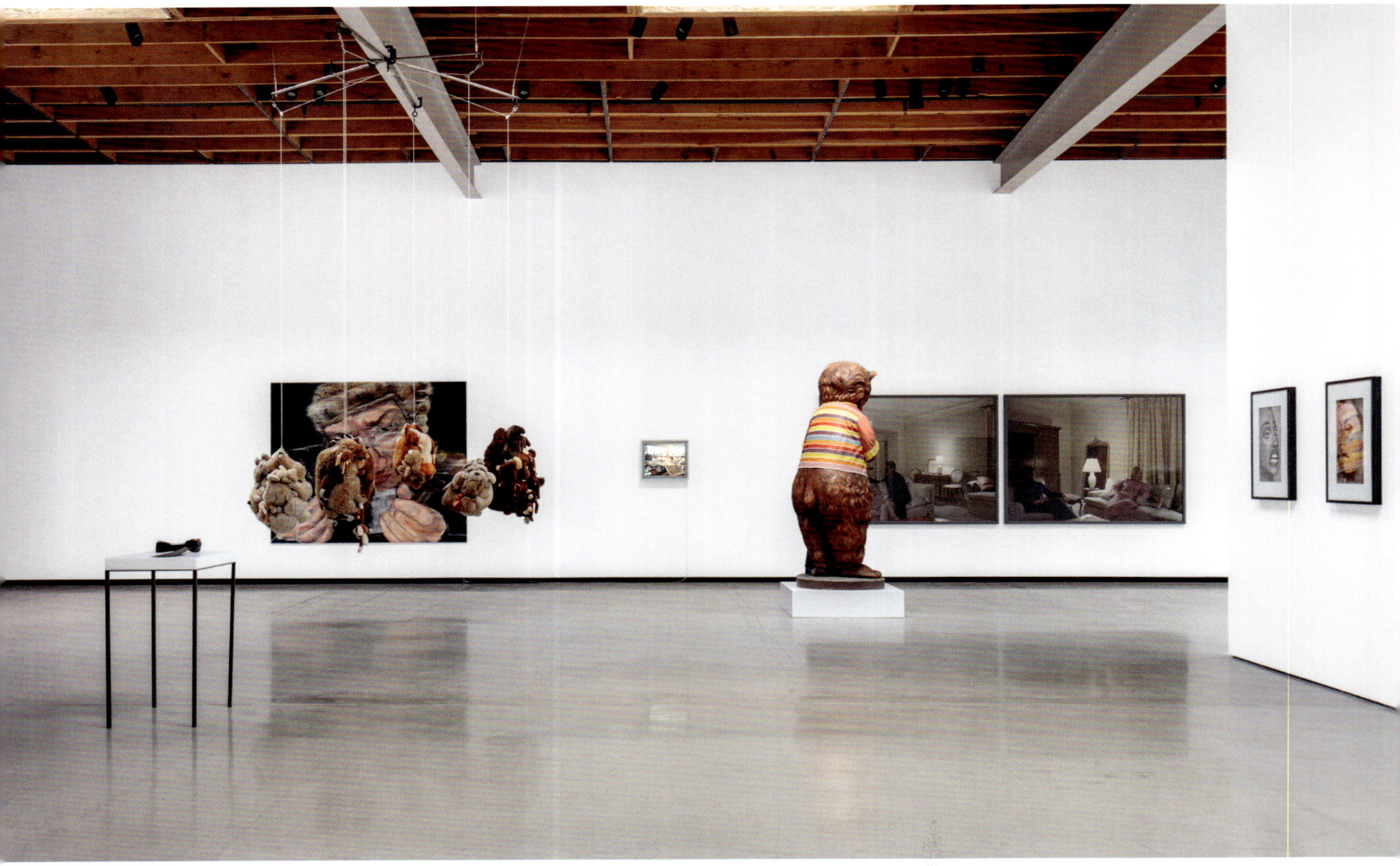

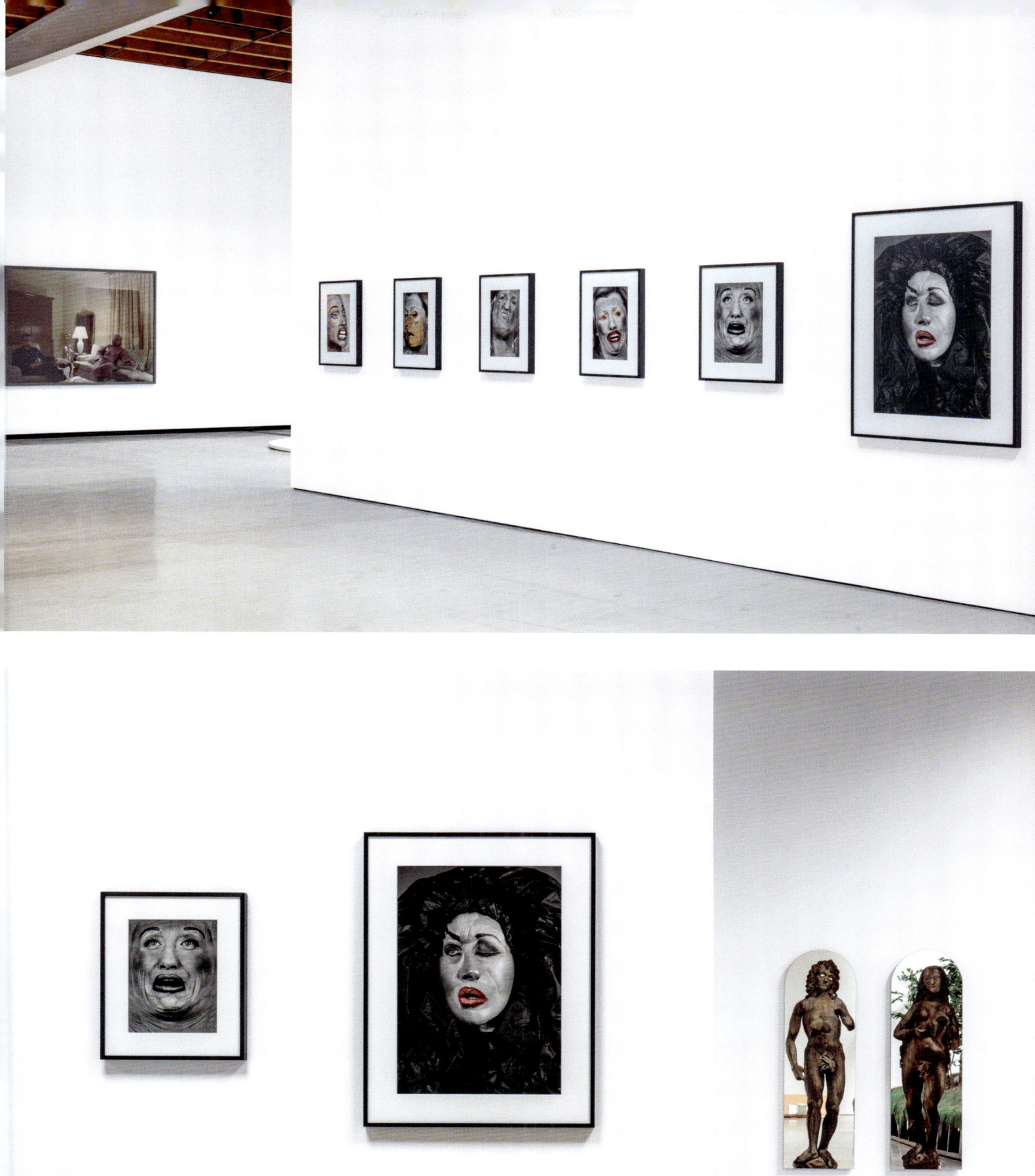

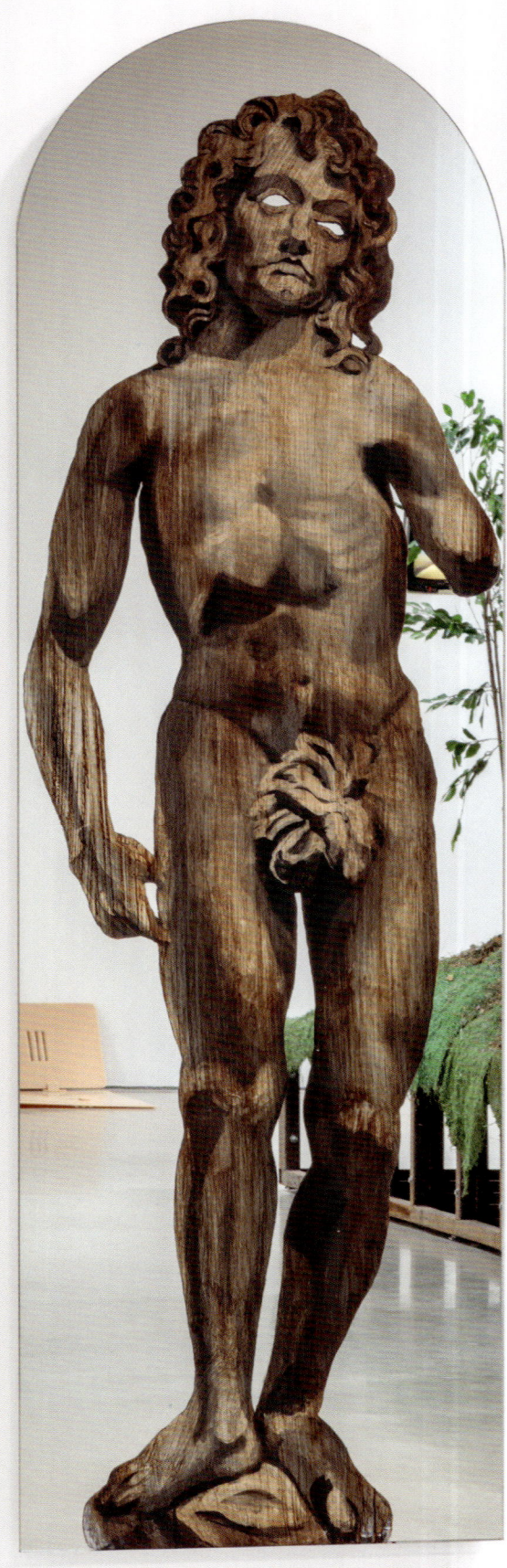
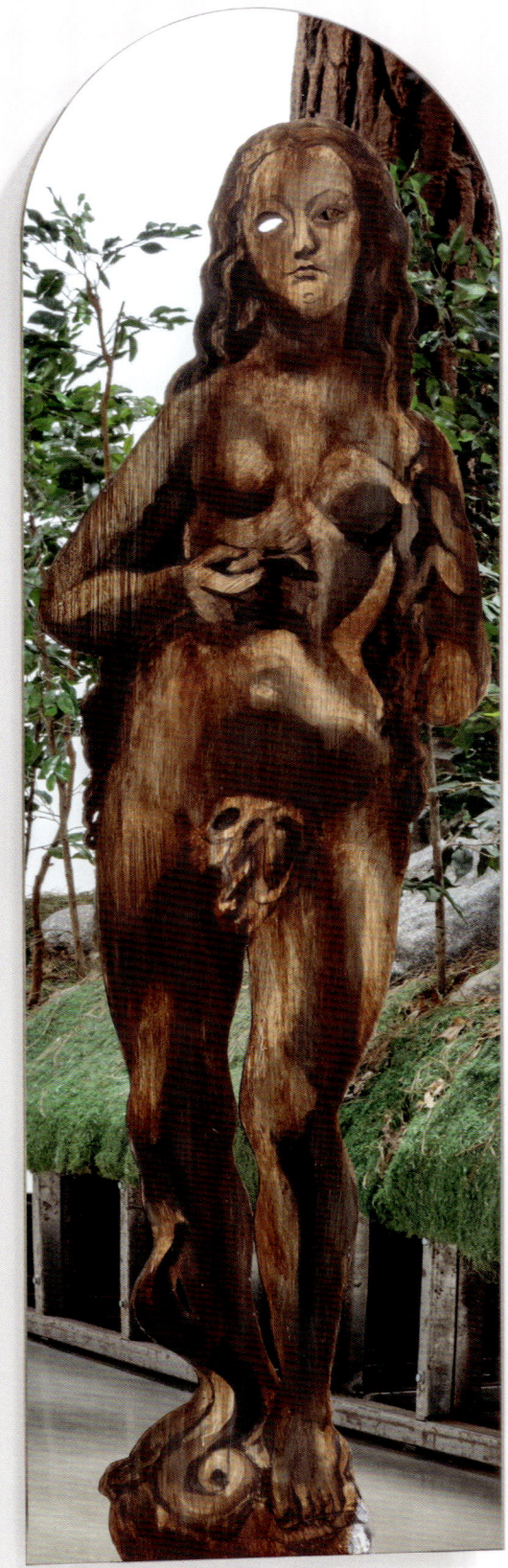

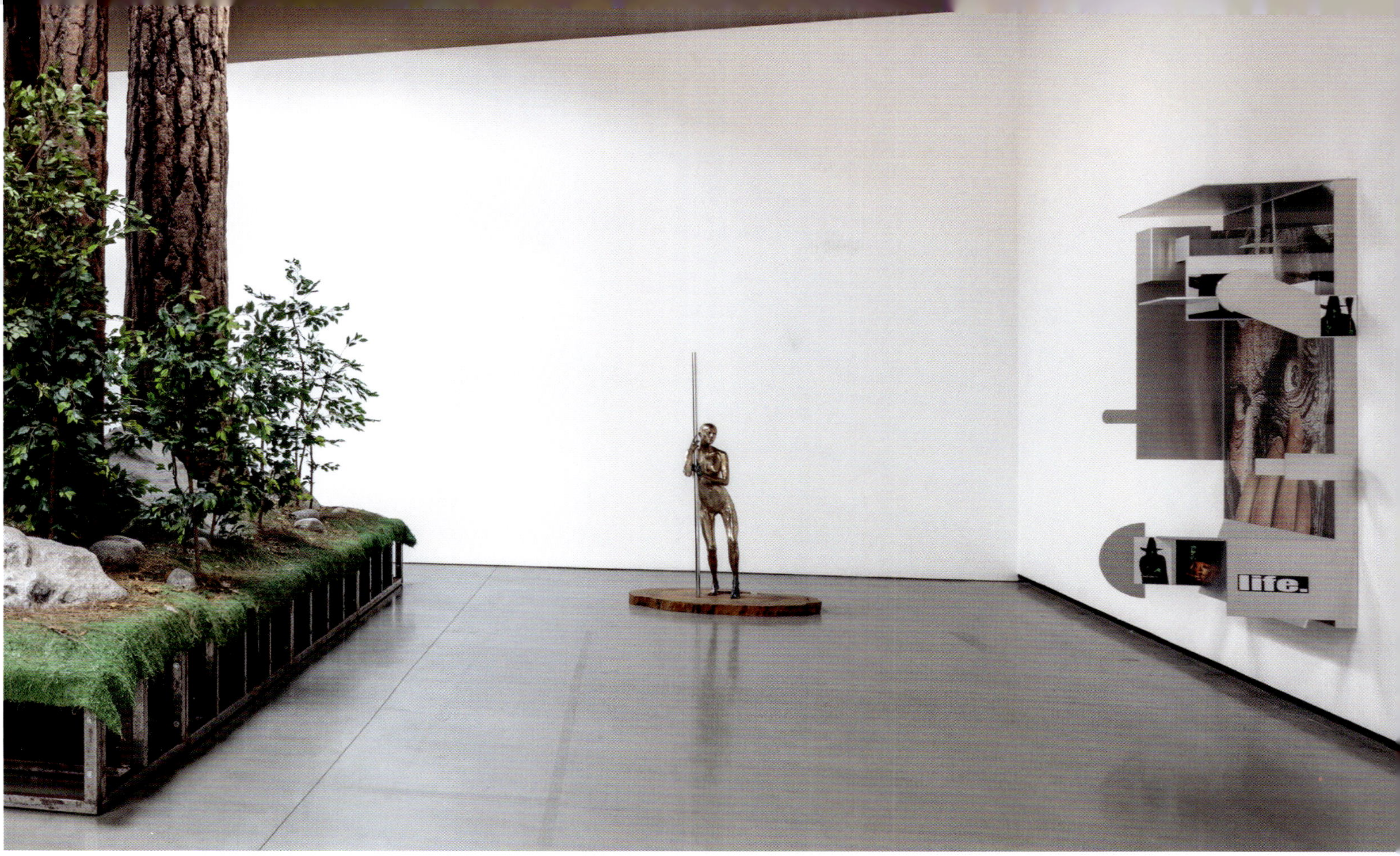
life.

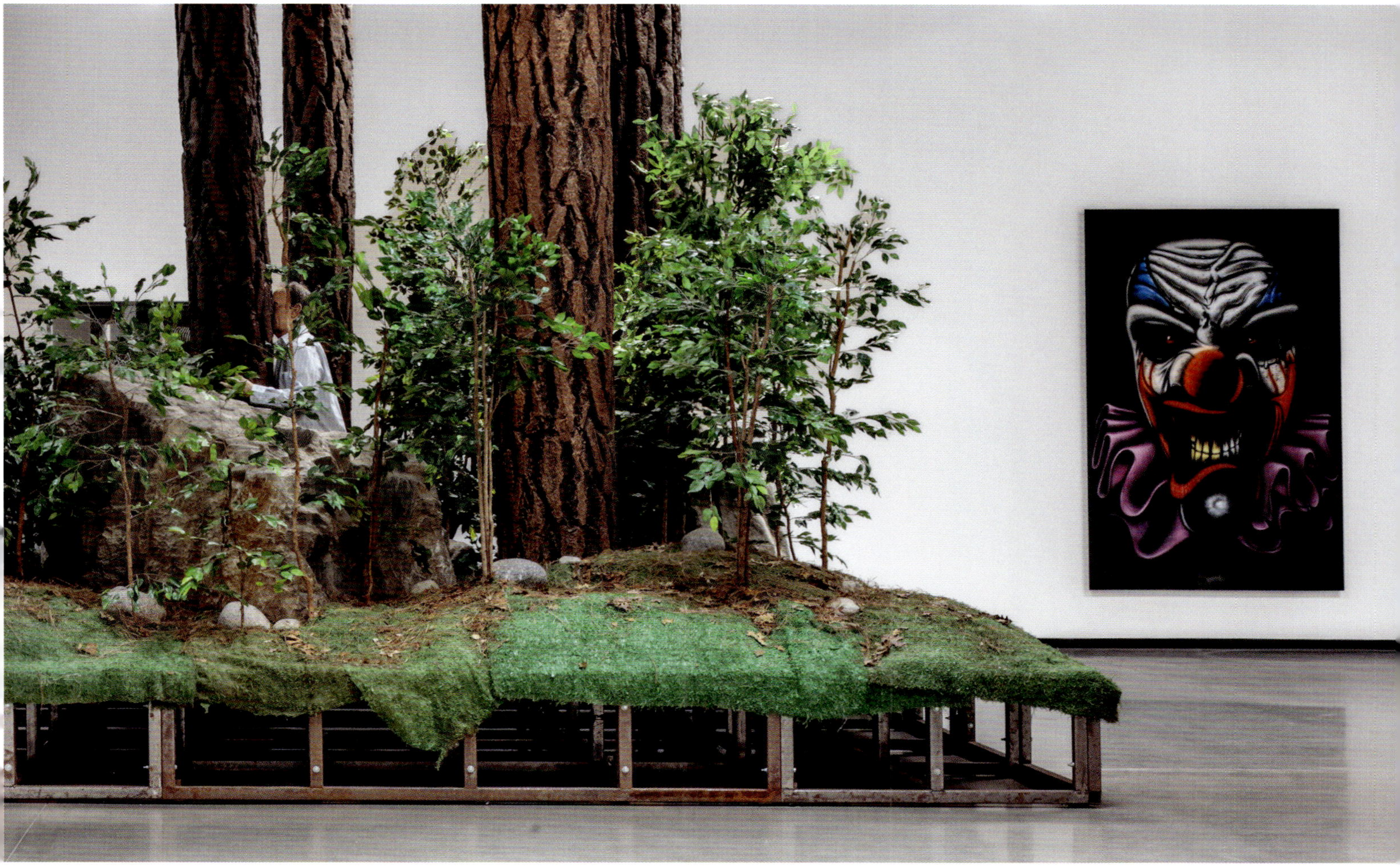

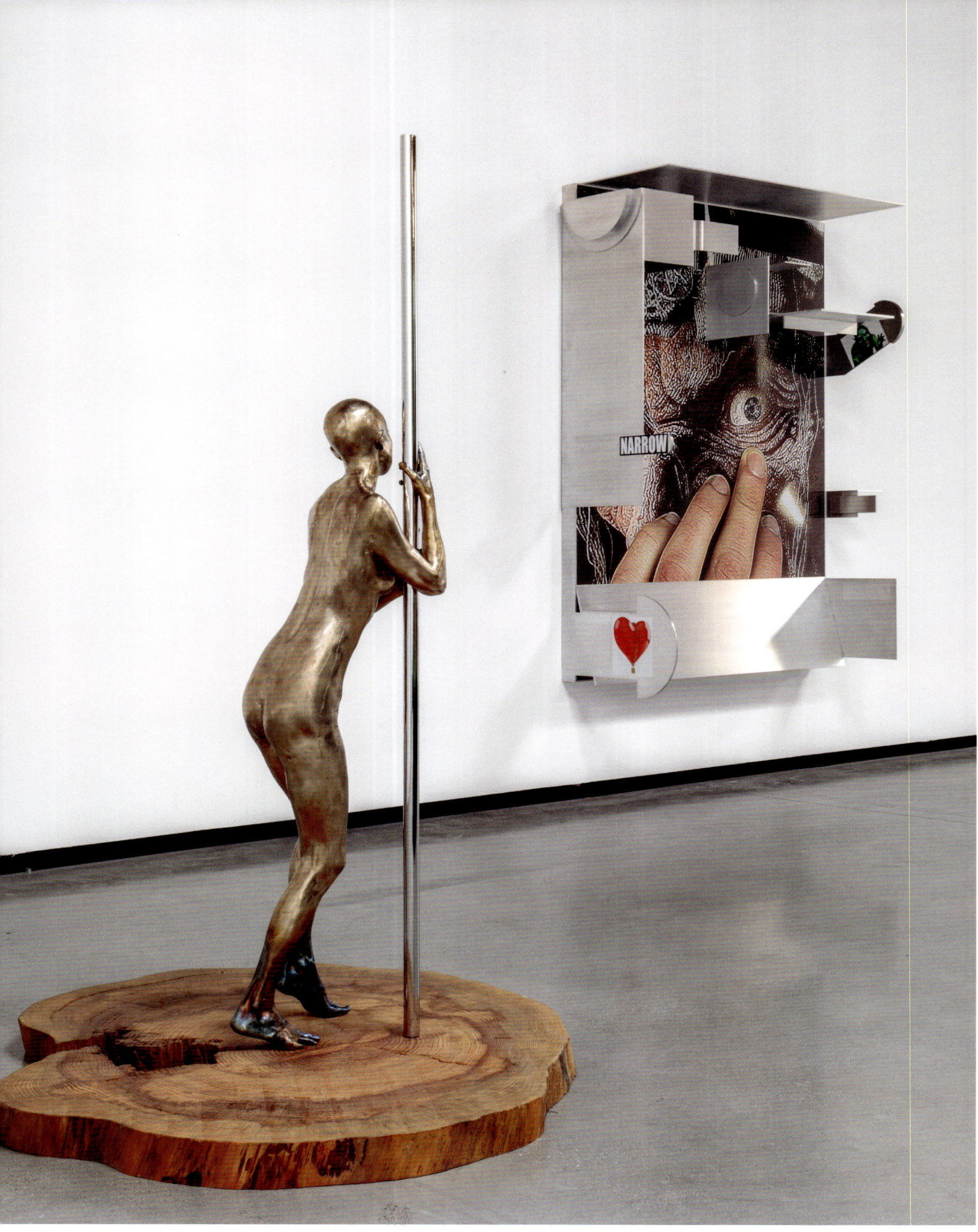

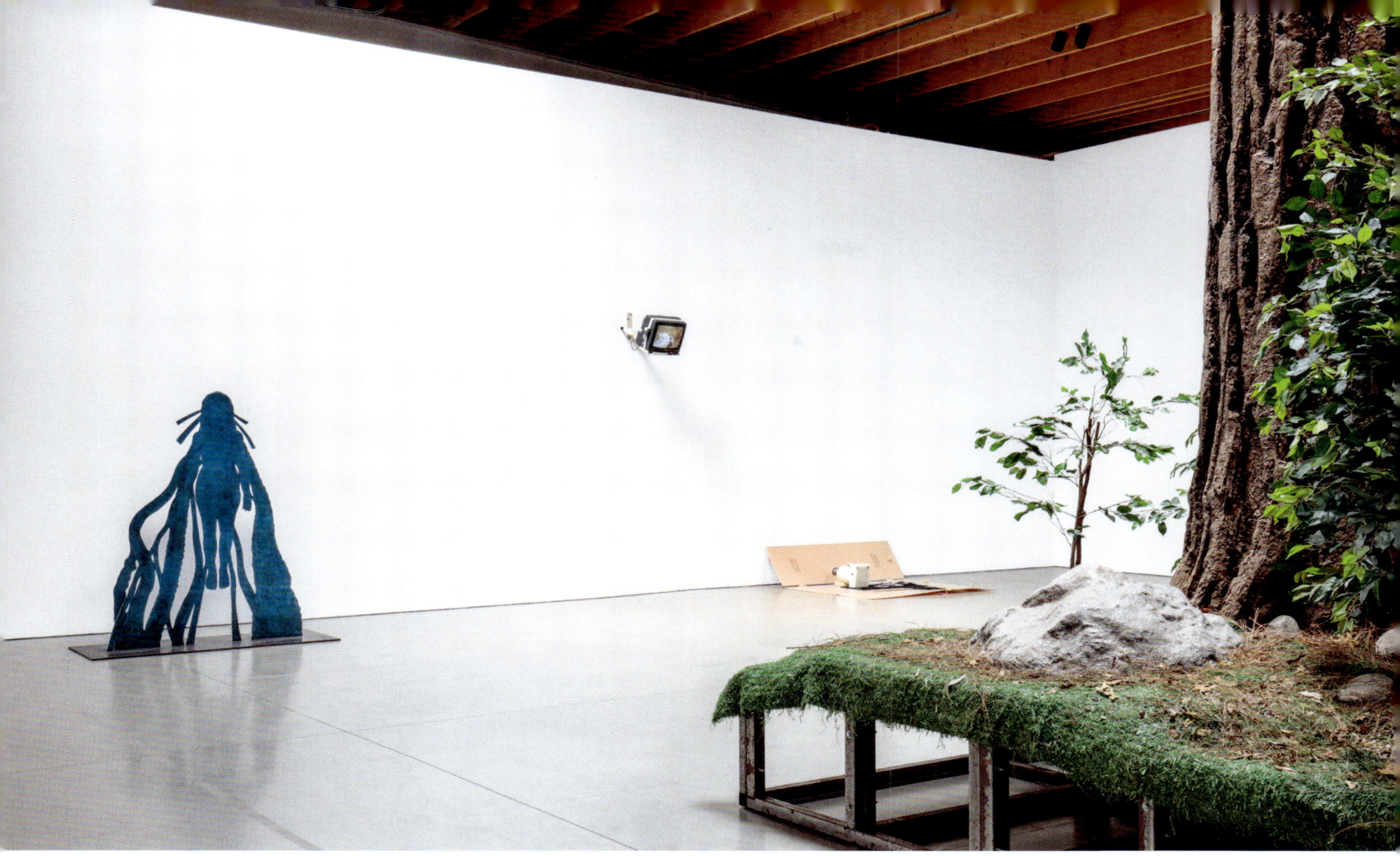

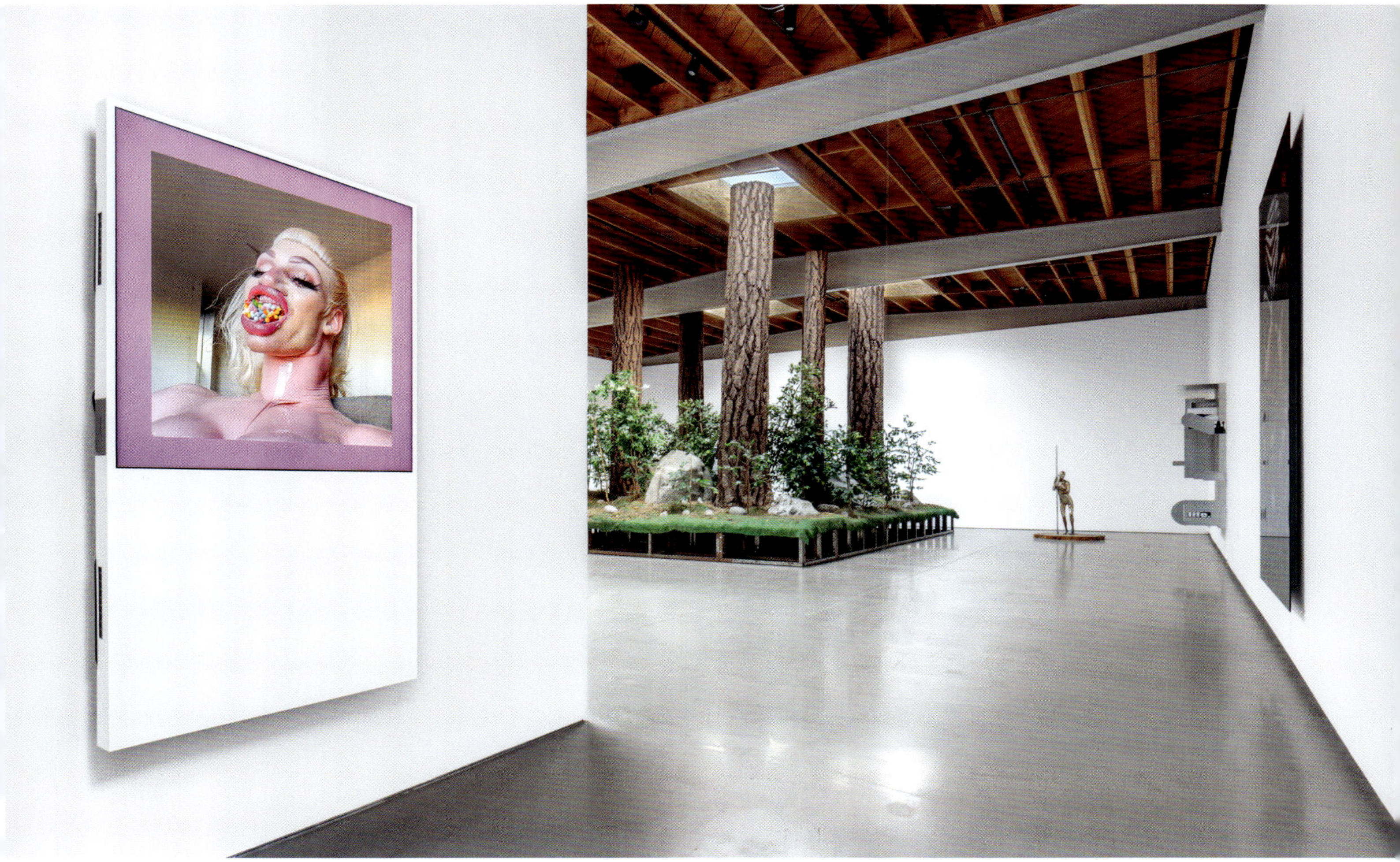

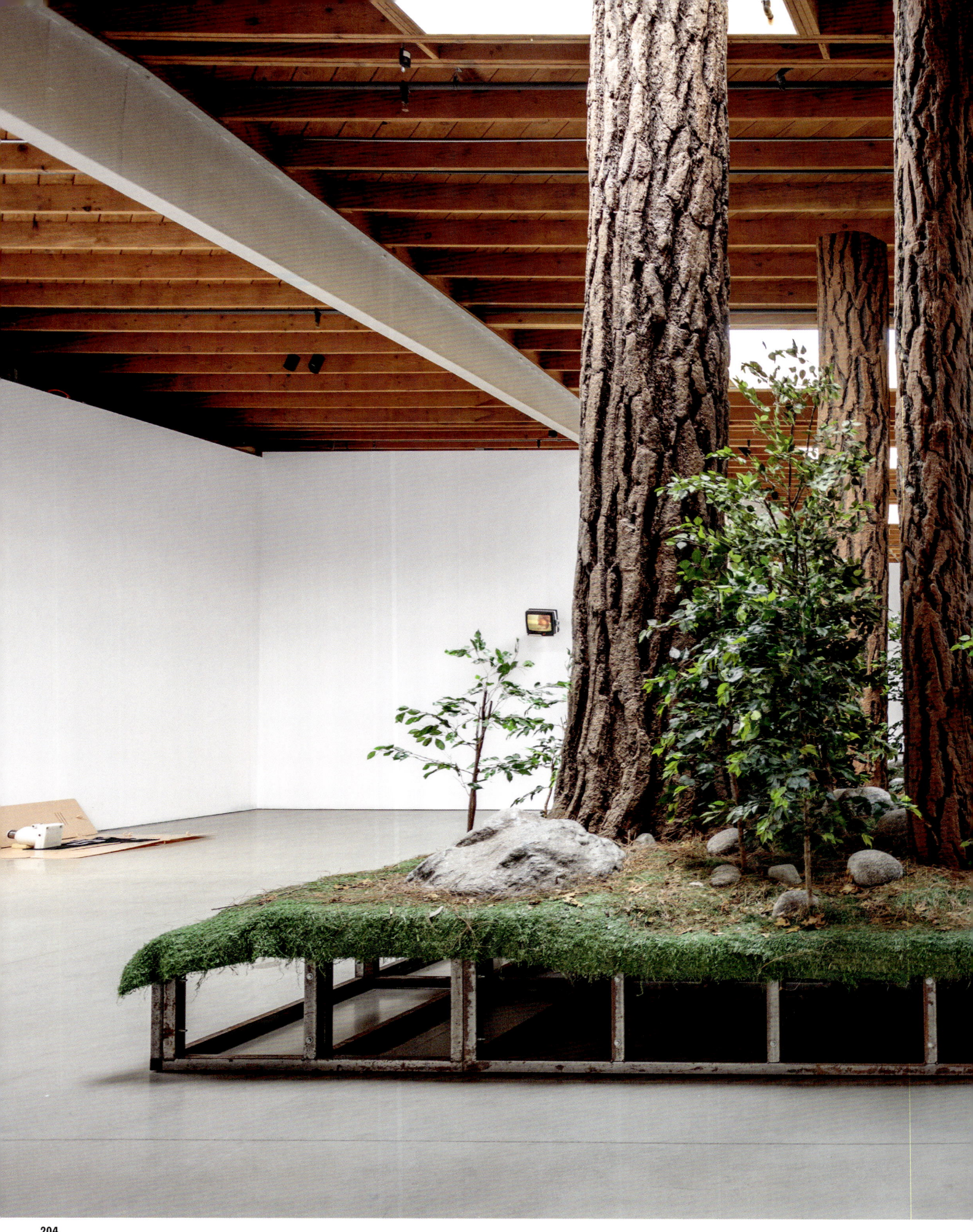

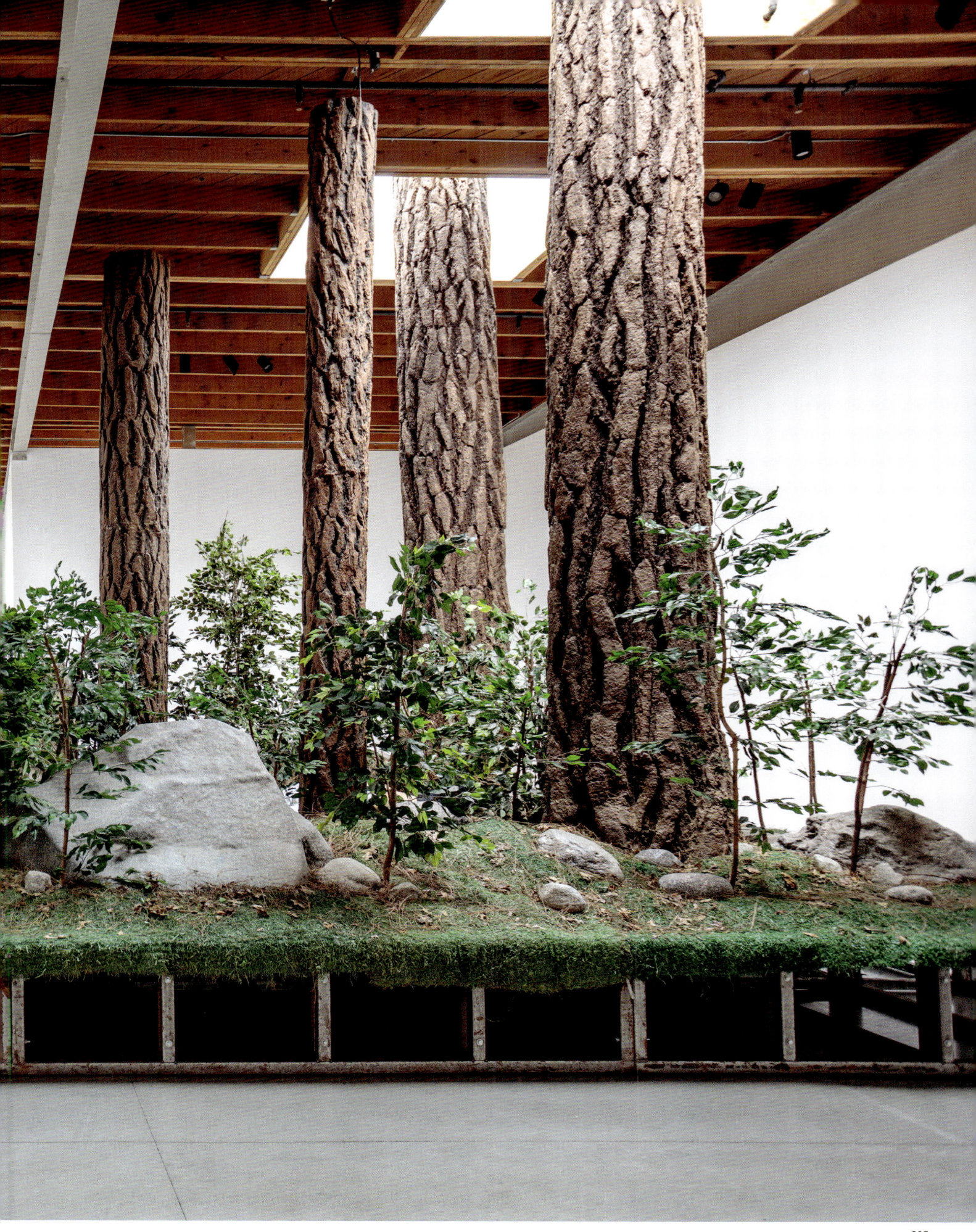

P. 109   Alex Da Corte, *Cool Kermit*, 2024. Photo: Charles White-JW Pictures. Courtesy of Sadie Coles HQ, London. ©Alex Da Corte

P. 111   Olivia Erlanger, *Act V*, 2023. The Stolbun Collection. Photo: Keith Lubow. Courtesy of the artist and Hauser & Wirth. ©Olivia Erlanger

PP. 112–113   Jana Euler, *The Judge*, 2018. Private collection, Los Angeles. Photo: Joshua White-JW Pictures. Courtesy of the artist

P. 115   Rachel Feinstein, *Adam*, 2021; *Eve*, 2021. Courtesy of the artist and Gagosian

PP. 116–117   Urs Fischer, *Kembra & Spencer*, 2021-22. Photos: Ramiro Chaves. Courtesy of the artist. ©Urs Fischer

PP. 118–119   Pippa Garner, *Human Prototype*, 2020. Courtesy of the artist and STARS, Los Angeles

P. 120   Robert Gober, *Untitled*, 2008-9. Private collection. Photo: Charles White-JW Pictures. Courtesy of the artist

P. 121   Robert Gober, *Two Breasts*, 1990. Private collection. Photo: Charles White-JW Pictures. Courtesy of the artist

PP. 122–123   Hugh Hayden, *Happy Meal*, 2024. Photo: Charles White-JW Pictures. Courtesy of the artist and Lisson Gallery

PP. 124–125   Damien Hirst, *Nothing is a Problem for Me*, 1992. Photo: Joshua White-JW Pictures. Courtesy of the artist

PP. 126–127   Tishan Hsu, *mammal-screen-green-2*, 2024. Photos: Stephen Faught Courtesy of Miguel Abreu Gallery, New York. ©2023 Tishan Hsu, Artists Rights Society (ARS), New York

P. 129   Pierre Huyghe, *Idiom*, 2024. Photo: Charles White-JW Pictures. Courtesy of the artist and Marian Goodman

PP. 130–131   Anne Imhof, *Clown (byzantine)*, 2023. Photo: Timo Ohler. Courtesy of the artist and Sprüth Magers. ©Anne Imhof

P. 133   Alex Israel, *Self-Portrait (Wetsuit)*, 2017. Collection of the artist. Photo: Zarko Vijatovic. Courtesy of the artist

P. 134   Arthur Jafa, *Don (small)*, 2023. Courtesy of the artist and Gladstone Gallery

PP. 135   Arthur Jafa, *LeRage*, 2017. Photo: Igano Steed. Courtesy of the artist and Gladstone Gallery

PP. 136–137   Jamian Juliano-Villani, *Women*, 2024. Photo: Joshua White-JW Pictures. Courtesy of the artist and Gagosian

PP. 138–139   Mike Kelley, *Brown Star*, 1991. Private collection. Photo: Joshua White-JW Pictures. ©2024 Mike Kelley Foundation for the Arts. All Rights Reserved/Licensed by VAGA at Artists Rights Society (ARS), NY

P. 140   Top: Josh Kline, *Forever 27 (Kurt)/Citi Display Wall 46"*, 2013. Director/producer: Josh Kline; screenplay: Josh Kline and Domenick Ammirati; casting director: Preston Chaunsumlit; stylist/art direction: Avena Gallagher; director of photography: Alexander Lau; software operator: Merche Blasco; motion graphics: Rodrigo Trombini Pires; cast: Rebecca Bratland as Diane, Bobby Warden as Kurt Cobain; sound recording/sound design: Matthew Patterson Curry; soundtrack: James Ferraro; production coordinator: MacGregor Harp; makeup artist: Juliet Jane; hair design/styling: Nicole Bridgeford; styling assistants: Patric Dicaprio, Paul Daunais; customized open-source software based on experiments by Arturo Castro and Kyle McDonald with real-time face substitution; light-box display original design and fabrication: Lukas Geronimas; light-box display design: Gordon Millsaps; additional assistance: Antoine Catala, Shabd Simon-Alexander, Jesse Greenberg, Karen Archey. Photo: Joerg Lohse. Image courtesy of the artist and 47 Canal, New York. Bottom: Josh Kline, *Forever 48 (Whitney)/Citi Display Wall 46"*, 2013. Director/producer: Josh Kline; screenplay: Josh Kline, Domenick Ammirati; casting director: Preston Chaunsumlit; stylist/art direction: Avena Gallagher; director of photography: Alexander Lau; software operator: Merche Blasco; motion graphics: Rodrigo Trombini Pires; cast: Christina Anderson-McDonald as Whitney Houston, Rebecca Bratland as Diane; sound recording/sound design: Matthew Patterson Curry; soundtrack: James Ferraro; production coordinator: MacGregor Harp; makeup artist: Juliet Jane; hair design/styling: Nicole Bridgeford; styling assistants: Patric Dicaprio, Paul Daunais; customized open-source software based on experiments by Arturo Castro and Kyle McDonald with real-time face substitution; original light-box display design and fabrication: Lukas Geronimas; light-box display design: Gordon Millsaps; additional assistance: Antoine Catala, Shabd Simon-Alexander, Jesse Greenberg, Karen Archey. Photo: Joerg Lohse. Image courtesy of the artist and 47 Canal, New York.

P. 141   Top: Josh Kline, *MAOI Inhibitors Can't Fix This (Elizabeth/Administrative Assistant)*, 2016. Producer: Eliza Ryan; fabrication: Lawrence Pollman; 3D modeling: Direct Dimensions (Ben Frazier); CNC milling: 3Dmass Design and Engineering (Martin G. Gonzalez); 3D printing: NYU LaGuardia Studio (Taylor Absher, Dhemerae Ford, Shelly Smith, Andrew BucklandB; 3D scanning: Direct Dimensions (Peter Kennedy, Greg Chaprnka, Glenn Woodburn); file preparation: Direct Dimensions (Clara Hickman); casting: Kimberly Skyrme

Casting, Betsy Royall Casting; additional assistance: Harry Abramson. Private collection, Los Angeles. Photo: Joshua White-JW Pictures. Courtesy of the artist and 47 Canal, New York. Bottom: Josh Kline, *Aspirational Foreclosure (Matthew/Mortgage Loan Officer)*, 2016. Producer: Eliza Ryan; fabrication: Lawrence Pollman; 3D modeling: Direct Dimensions (Colin Fitzhugh); CNC milling: 3Dmass Design and Engineering (Martin G. Gonzalez); 3D printing: NYU LaGuardia Studio (Taylor Absher, Dhemerae Ford, Shelly Smith, Andrew Buckland); 3D scanning: Direct Dimensions (Peter Kennedy, Greg Chaprnka, Glenn Woodburn); file preparation: Direct Dimensions (Clara Hickman); casting: Kimberly Skyrme Casting, Betsy Royall Casting. Special thanks to Harry Abramson and the Rubell Family. Private collection, Los Angeles. Photo: Joshua White-JW Pictures. Courtesy of the artist and 47 Canal, New York

P. 143   Jeff Koons, *Bear and Policeman*, 1988. Collection of Jeffrey Deitch. Photo: Douglas M. Parker Studios, Los Angeles. ©Jeff Koons

PP. 144–145   Paul McCarthy, *The Garden*, 1991-92. Collection of Jeffrey Deitch. Photo: Fredrik Nilsen. Courtesy of the artist and Hauser & Wirth. ©Paul McCarthy

P. 146   Sam McKinniss, *Elton John*, 2024. Private collection. Photo: Joshua White-JW Pictures. Courtesy of the artist and David Kordansky Gallery

P. 147   Sam McKinniss, *Star Spangled Banner (Whitney)*, 2017. Collection of Jeffrey Deitch. Photo: Joshua White-JW Pictures. Courtesy of the artist

PP. 148–149   Mariko Mori, *Oneness*, 2003. Collection of Jeffrey Deitch. Courtesy of the artist. ©Mariko Mori

P. 151   Takashi Murakami, *3m Girl* (original rendering by Seiji Matsuyama, modeling by BOME and Genpachi Toaimura; full scale sculpture by Lucky-Wide Co., Ltd.), 2011-13. Collection of Maurice and Paul Marciano. Photo: Charles White-JW Pictures. Courtesy of the artist

PP. 152–153   Wangechi Mutu, *One Cut*, 2018. Photo: David Regen. Courtesy of the artist and Gladstone Gallery.

P. 155   Cady Noland, *Rotten Cop*, 1988. Collection of Bill Arning, New York. Photo: Joshua White-JW Pictures. Courtesy of the artist

PP. 156–157   Charles Ray, *Family Romance*, 1993. Collection on Jeffrey Deitch. Photo: Joshua White-JW Pictures. Courtesy of the artist

P. 158   Top left: Cindy Sherman, *Untitled #643*, 2010/2023. ©Cindy Sherman. Courtesy the artist and Hauser & Wirth. Top right: Cindy Sherman, *Untitled #627*, 2010/2023. ©Cindy Sherman. Courtesy the artist and Hauser & Wirth. Bottom left:

Cindy Sherman, *Untitled #629*, 2010/2023. ©Cindy Sherman. Courtesy the artist and Hauser & Wirth. Bottom right: Cindy Sherman, *Untitled #638*, 2010/2023. ©Cindy Sherman. Courtesy the artist and Hauser & Wirth

P. 159   Cindy Sherman, *Untitled #654*, 2023. ©Cindy Sherman. Courtesy the artist and Hauser & Wirth

P. 161   Kiki Smith, *Dark Water*, 2023. Private collection, Los Angeles. Photo: Peter Clough & Robyn Lehr Caspare. Courtesy of Pace Gallery. ©Kiki Smith

P. 162   Hajime Sorayama, *Untitled*, 2024. Courtesy of the artist and NANZUKA. ©Hajime Sorayama

P. 163   Hajime Sorayama, *Untitled*, 2024. Private collection. Courtesy of the artist and NANZUKA. ©Hajime Sorayama

PP. 164–165   Anna Uddenberg, *T-Top Tummy Tuck*, 2022. Right photo: Dario Lasagni. Courtesy of the artist and Meredith Rosen Gallery

PP. 166–167   Cajsa von Zeipel, *Pep Talk*, 2024. Photography by Charles White-JW Pictures. Courtesy of the artist and Company Gallery, New York

P. 168   Jeff Wall, *The Giant*, 1992. Collection of the artist. Courtesy of Gagosian. ©Jeff Wall

P. 169   Jeff Wall, *Pair of interiors*, 2018. Courtesy of Gagosian. ©Jeff Wall

P. 171   Jordan Wolfson, *Untitled*, 2016. Collection of the artist. Photos: Dan Bradica. Courtesy of the artist

PP. 172–173   Anicka Yi, *The Sliding World*, 2024. East West Bank Collection. Photos: Anthony Flores. Courtesy of the artist and Gladstone Gallery

INSTALLATION VIEWS (2024-25)

PP. 186–205   Photos: Josh White and Charles White-JW Pictures. Courtesy of the artists and Jeffrey Deitch, New York and Los Angeles

Monacelli
A Phaidon Company
111 Broadway
New York, NY 10006

Phaidon Press Limited
2 Cooperage Yard
London E15 2QR

Phaidon SARL
55, rue Traversière
75012 Paris

phaidon.com/monacelli

First published 2026
© 2026 The Monacelli Press
and Jeffrey Deitch, Inc.

ISBN 978-1-58093-740-5

Library of Congress Control Number:
2025916081

Editor: Viola Angiolini
Project Management: Sean Newcott
and Carla Sakamoto
Image Researcher: Sabeena Khosla
Production: Michael Vagnetti
Design: Folder Studio

Exhibition (2024–25)
Installation: Jang Park, Nathan Bennett
Assistant: Lilly McClure

Printed in China